Globe Law
and Business

Trust Laws in Cyprus

An International Perspective

Consulting Editor **Paolo Panico**

Consulting editor
Paolo Panico

Managing director
Sian O'Neill

Trust Laws in Cyprus: An International Perspective
is published by

Globe Law and Business Ltd
3 Mylor Close
Horsell
Woking
Surrey GU21 4DD
United Kingdom
Tel: +44 20 3745 4770
www.globelawandbusiness.com

Printed and bound by CPI Group (UK) Ltd, Croydon CR0 4YY, United Kingdom

Trust Laws in Cyprus: An International Perspective

ISBN 9781787428782
EPUB ISBN 9781787428799
Adobe PDF ISBN 9781787428805

Table of contents

Foreword: Perspectives on the Cyprus international trust law journey 5
Peter G Economides
Totalserve Management Limited
Richard FG Pease
Solicitor (England and Wales); Consultant (Geneva, Switzerland)
Stella Kammitsi
Raza Corporate Services Ltd; Chair – STEP Cyprus

Part I

The Cypriot legal system: an overview 13
Eleni Louca
Christodoulos G Vassiliades & Co LLC

Trusts in Cyprus under domestic law 25
Chrysthia Papacleovoulou-Vassiliou
Open University of Cyprus
Evi Papacleovoulou
Law Chambers Nicos Papacleovoulou LLC

***Vakfs*: the Islamic version of trusts** 43
Paolo Panico
Private Trustees SA; Chair – STEP Europe

Charitable trusts and charitable organisations 59
Eleni Drakou
Michael Kyprianou & Co LLC

Part II

The Cyprus International Trusts Law 1992–2012: new dynamics 77
Chrysthia Papacleovoulou-Vassiliou
Open University of Cyprus

Settlor reserved powers trusts 109
Emily Yiolitis
Anemi Trustees Limited

Beneficiaries' right to information 117
Nicky Xenofontos
N Xenofontos LLC

Trustee investment powers and delegation 135
Savvas Georgiou
Christodoulos G Vassiliades & Co LLC

Protectors 145
Emily Yiolitis
Anemi Trustees Limited

Non-charitable purpose trusts 153
Panayiota Kouzoupi
Christodoulos G Vassiliades & Co LLC

The trustee's ability to request directions from the court 165
Constantinos Constantinides
Stefanos Marangos
Christodoulos G Vassiliades & Co LLC

Perpetuity and duration 177
Paolo Panico
Private Trustees SA;
Chair – STEP Europe

Forced heirship: the 'firewall legislation' 183
Stella Kammitsi
Raza Corporate Services Ltd;
Chair – STEP Cyprus

Asset protection trusts 201
Peter G Economides
Totalserve Management Limited

The trustee's liability to third parties and mistake 209
Nicky Xenofontos
N Xenofontos LLC

The main ingredients of an international trust law – some proposals for reform 221
Paolo Panico
Private Trustees SA;
Chair – STEP Europe
Nicky Xenofontos
N Xenofontos LLC

Analysis of Cyprus case law involving Cyprus international trusts 237
Chrysthia Papacleovoulou-Vassiliou
Open University of Cyprus

Part III

Taxation 257
George Economides
E & G Economides LLC

Trusts and ultimate beneficial ownership registers in Cyprus 265
Eleni Drakou
Michael Kyprianou & Co LLC

Appendix 277

About the authors 279

About Globe Law and Business 285

Foreword: Perspectives on the Cyprus international trust law journey

Peter G Economides
Totalserve Management Limited

A trust is a relationship that has evolved over centuries of practice, whereby one party – known as the 'settlor' – transfers to another party – the 'trustee' – the legal title to assets to hold on behalf of and for the benefit of a third party – the 'beneficiary'. Trusts are managed in accordance with the terms under which they are created, which are usually contained in a trust deed.

The concept of a trust was developed in the 12th century by Crusaders. On leaving England to embark on the Crusades, a wealthy landowner would convey the ownership of his lands to a trusted party to manage those lands in his absence and receive feudal dues, on the understanding that, on his return, ownership would revert to him. On their return, the Crusaders' claim to their property was not recognised under English common law, and they found themselves bereft of the lands that they once had claim to. The Crusaders petitioned the King to right this injustice, who would refer the case to his Lord Chancellor. The Lord Chancellor opined that it was unconscionable that the person left in charge of the property would fail to deliver the land back to the returning owner and so recognised the claim of the Crusaders. From this recognition, by the Court of Chancery, the concept of what we now know as 'trusts' evolved. Trusts today are established for a variety of purposes including investing, estate planning, protection of children and vulnerable adults, charitable giving and asset protection.

Cyprus, being a former British colony, derives its trust law from English common law and equity, which were applied in Cyprus during the British administration of the island. Cyprus enacted its own statute, the Trustee Law (Cap 193) 1955 before its independence, reproducing, to a large extent, the provisions of the English Trustee Act 1925. The same principles of equity that apply to English trusts are likewise applied by the Cyprus courts to Cyprus trusts and the same duty of loyalty developed as an equitable doctrine to support the Crusaders' claim applies to trustees holding property under modern Cyprus trusts. As the trust evolved from an understanding to temporarily hold property *in absentia* to a complex asset-management mechanism, the role of the trustee and the incumbent fiduciary duties also became more complex. At the core, however, remains the trustee's fiduciary pledge to place the beneficiaries' interests ahead of its own and the basic principles that were derived from case law thereafter, such as that the trustees must be diligent and use reasonable care and must not commingle funds.

Today, trusts can be set up in Cyprus either as local trusts under the Trustee Law 1955 or as Cyprus international trusts under the provisions of the Cyprus International Trusts Law (69/1992) as amended by the International Trusts (Amending) Law of 2012. The complex history of Cyprus is also reflected in its trust laws and constitution, which also makes provision for the Islamic *vakf* as trustee of religious properties in the Turkish Cypriot community.

The trust today has assumed a central role in the transfer of intergenerational wealth and is now a common feature in most estate planning. The crusading knights of the 12th century could never have imagined that their historic understanding to receive feudal dues *in absentia* would result in the litigious and complex industry that trusts comprise today. *Trust Laws in Cyprus* gathers, for the first time, both the historical and modern facets of trusts in Cyprus, and provides valuable insight as to the workings of the trustees, the pitfalls to avoid and the case law to consider. Most importantly, it reminds us that despite the trimmings offered by legislation in Cyprus and abroad, it is wise to remain cautious about ultra-modernising a trust arrangement, whether by a settlor keeping too many powers or a trustee divesting itself of too many duties, because, at its core, the trust has changed very little since the Crusades. It remains a relationship, created at the bequest of a settlor by passing legal title to trustees, to hold and manage loyally, for the benefit of the beneficiaries.

Trusts in Cyprus have actually picked up following the enactment of the Cyprus International Trusts Law, thus creating a new business for professionals in the country. It will be interesting to see the future of trusts under the current and forthcoming stringent regulations.

Richard FG Pease
Solicitor (England and Wales); Consultant (Geneva, Switzerland)

My first visit to Cyprus was in 1975, and during the following decade I developed lasting contacts with many Cypriot lawyers and accountants.

At that time, Cyprus was well established as a centre for shipping and as a base for international business companies, particularly those engaged in commerce in the Middle East. However, the island had not sought to develop its fiduciary services sector, unlike other offshore centres that were actively promoting themselves as modern trust jurisdictions.

The Cayman Islands was an early pioneer (1965) in a move to update its trust law, and more comprehensive trust legislation was later introduced by Jersey (1984) and Guernsey (1989). Other jurisdictions in the Caribbean would soon to follow this trend.

In 1989, one of my Cypriot correspondents introduced me to the senior management of the Central Bank of Cyprus (CBC) and at an initial meeting with the governor and the head of supervision it was suggested that Cyprus could broaden its appeal as an international finance centre by introducing an updated trust law for use by non-resident settlors and beneficiaries.

Cyprus had the great advantage of its heritage in an existing law of trusts (Cap 193, 1955), which was closely modelled on the United Kingdom's Trustee Act 1925. Following independence in 1960, the English legal system was largely preserved, including the principles of common law and equity.

At the outset of the project, it seemed clear to me that while the new legislation would introduce the concept of international trusts for use by non-residents of Cyprus it would supplement, but not replace, the existing law. The CBC made it clear that the new international trust would only be available to settlors who were not permanent residents of Cyprus and that no Cypriot resident could be a beneficiary of such a trust. However, the appointment of a least one resident trustee would be a statutory requirement.

The provisions of the draft law would include the following:

- validity of the trust;
- protection against creditors;
- 100-year duration;
- a broad definition of charitable trusts and purpose trusts; and
- power to change the applicable law.

None of the above provisions would be considered particularly novel now, but in the 1990s they represented a modern, if modest, update of more traditional trust law.

The draft law was finalised in 1990 and submitted to the necessary legislative procedure, being finally approved by the House of Representatives and enacted in 1992. Since that date, it has been gratifying to witness the development of international trust business in Cyprus, aided greatly by the skill of the local professional community and the support of the Cypriot courts. Clearly, the development of trust law in the international centres has proceeded apace since 1992, and the additions and amendments to the law on international trusts in 2012 have been timely and serve to further enhance the attraction of Cyprus as a major and highly respected trust centre.

Stella Kammitsi
Raza Corporate Services Ltd; Chair – STEP Cyprus

This year STEP celebrates 30 years, which coincides with the 30-year anniversary of the Cyprus International Trusts Law 1992. Cyprus began its trusts journey in 1955 with the enactment of its first trust law, Cap 193, which was one of the first laws adopted by Cyprus following its independence from the British Crown and which was modelled on the United Kingdom's Trustee Act 1925. Being a common law jurisdiction and an ex-British colony, the Cyprus legal framework governing trusts developed a combination of the English law principles of Equity and the statutory law.

Much has happened since then and this small island in the Mediterranean has, despite its political hurdles, become an international business centre, which in 2003 led to the establishment of STEP Cyprus by its honorary member Peter Economides. Over the years that followed, STEP Cyprus has evolved into one of the largest branches of STEP when compared to population size – and this should not be surprising.

Trust Laws in Cyprus has been inspired, coordinated and made a reality by Paolo Panico, chair of STEP Europe, whose interest in Cyprus trusts is astonishing. This is the first book ever written on the Cyprus International Trusts Law and its related laws and regulations.

I would like to express my heartfelt thanks to Paolo for making this publication happen and for the dedicated work, assistance and guidance that he has provided to all of us who have contributed to *Trust Laws in Cyprus*. My sincere thanks also go to all our esteemed professionals that have written the separate chapters of this book. I hope the knowledge that is shared in this publication will assist practising professionals, as well as students and future practitioners.

The timing of producing this book appears to have been ideal, not only marking the 30-year landmark since the enactment of the Cyprus International Trusts Law, but also at a time when the world around us is changing rapidly and global political and economic events are overturning what we had once considered never-changing legal environments.

During the past few years, the terms 'unprecedented' and 'unpredictable' events have been given new meaning in our lives and in those of our clients. The challenges that we witnessed during 2020–2021 could not have been anticipated: a world pandemic that led to international lockdowns, followed by a war in Europe that resulted in the emergence of a series of EU sanctions – some of them affecting trusts. At the same time there have been fundamental changes to the concepts of privacy and confidentiality, with the introduction of the ultimate beneficial owner (UBO) registries, demanding duties of disclosure and exchange of information, increased and complex reporting requirements, new tax transparency requirements – the list grows longer by the year. Acronyms of regulations have become part of our working vocabulary, such as AML/CFT, DACs, UBOs, CRS and FATCA.

All this has concurred with the globalisation trend of the past two decades. It has led to an astonishing increase of highly mobile clients with globally dispersed family members and assets, which have proven to be a heavy burden on practitioners both in terms of costs and of time for compliance.

The constant changes in geopolitical events cause deep concern and anxiety for our clients, especially those who struggle with the administration of assets in different jurisdictions, divorce disputes and inheritance issues over these assets, including forced heirship claims, enforcement and recognition of foreign judgments, asset protection and sanctions. These are just a few of the endless concerns for which our clients rely on us to advise them and for which we are sought out to address and understand their needs. Inevitably, they trigger the need for all of us – the practitioners in our industry – to share our knowledge and expertise in order to maintain the highest professional standards, entailing the engagement of combined professional minds from different jurisdictions seeking the best available 'common sense' advice and approach in terms of legislation and regulation that can match the needs of each client individually. There is no perfect scenario of advice, but there can be a best scenario under each set of circumstances.

As the world is changing so too is the professional industry in Cyprus, allowing the island to remain an attractive jurisdiction in the international world. Over the past decade it has developed a strong but flexible regulatory environment on trusts and its emphasis has shifted to the quality of supervision and proper engagement with the business sector. In 2012 the Fiduciaries Law Regulating Companies Providing Administrative Services and Related Matters was enacted to ensure that local practitioners abide by professional standards and are properly regulated in offering their fiduciary services, including those for trusts.

We are happy to say that Cyprus continues to amend and develop its legislative framework to keep pace with changes in the international business environment, while remaining a location of choice for international wealthy clients. Winston Churchill once said: "To improve is to change; and to be perfect is to change more often." While John F Kennedy stated: "Change is the law of life. And those who look only to the past or present are certain to miss the future."

As Cyprus international trusts are widely chosen by international clients in their succession and wealth planning, we hope that *Trust Laws in Cyprus* will provide assistance to their advisers. Its various topics attempt to address the major concerns in the trust industry and to share knowledge and information among practitioners. Each chapter is a standout on its own, and I am confident that you will find information here that would not have been easily accessible in any other edition.

I trust you will enjoy the variety and subject matter of the contributions in this book. Enjoy reading!

The Cypriot legal system: an overview

Eleni Louca
Christodoulos G Vassiliades & Co LLC

1. The Cypriot legal system as a mixed legal system

The peculiarities of the Cypriot legal system are a result of it having been shaped over the long and intricate history of the island. It is thus illustrative of the multiple influences that it has been exposed to over the last centuries. The result of this exposure was the formation of a mixed legal system, a hybrid of common law and continental tradition that is worthy of analysis.

1.1 The road to a mixed legal system

The strategic location of the island of Cyprus has always been a source of enviable benefits. And, undoubtedly, of a great deal of misfortunes. Initially settled by Mycenaean Greeks, in the course of its history the island has been occupied by Assyrians, Egyptians, Persians, Romans, Lusignans and Venetians before coming under Ottoman rule. The ancient Greek law and the Roman-Byzantine[1] law applied by the former inhabitants and occupiers of the island were succeeded by Ottoman laws that originated from Muslim law and featured the characteristics of European legal models.[2]

The necessity of having the support of the British during the Congress of Berlin 1878, led to the 'bleeding' Ottoman Empire entering the Cyprus Convention for the lease of the island to the British Empire,[3] thus bringing the island, whose inhabitants were of Greek and Muslim origin, under British rule. It was only natural for such a surrender of administration to pave the way for the gradual introduction of common law as the law of the land. In the first decades of the British administration Ottoman laws were applied by British judges using their homeland's procedural law. These were officially replaced by British Law in 1935,[4] following the annexation of the island by United Kingdom in 1914 amidst the outbreak of World War I, and its proclamation as a Crown colony in 1925 on the basis of the Treaty of Lausanne 1923.

Ottoman laws may have been replaced by British law, however, the diversity

1 Nikitas E Hatzimihail, "Cyprus as a Mixed Legal System", *Journal of Civil Law Studies* (2013) 6(1), 38, 43.
2 Elina N Moustaira, *Comparative Law University Courses* (in Greek) (Ant N Sakkoulas Publishers, 2004), p76.
3 Hatzimihail (n 1), 44.
4 Moustaira (n 2), p77.

of the sources of law was preserved. Certain Ottoman laws remained in force while the jurisdiction of Muslim and Orthodox Church courts was recognised for matters of personal status of the members of the respective communities. New laws were also introduced by the British, taking from, among other things, the codification of contract law in another of their colonies, India. Aside from the Indian – and Hindu religious – law elements, sections of the Italian civil code as well as of the Greek estate law influenced the island's legal order.[5]

Cyprus' internal affairs were conducted through a minimal and flexible structure of institutions comprising the governor, the Legislative Council along with municipal councils, the king's advocate and a two-tier judicial system of district courts and the Supreme Court, with the possibility to appeal to the Judicial Committee of the Privy Council.[6]

At the time, the Greek community of the island counted for four-fifths of its population, with the Muslim community the remaining one-fifth. The members of the Legislative Council were British, Greek and Muslim and the decision-making procedure was structured in a way that allowed the British to impose their will and essentially rule by decree. The Muslim members of the Legislative Council, inspired by Kemalism, eventually required their administrative autonomy.[7] While the unquenched thirst of the Greek community (the island's ethnic majority) for unification (*Enosis*) with Greece led to the 1931 Cyprus revolt, also known as the 'October Events'. The Legislative Council and the municipal councils were suspended as a result of the October Events and a period of autocratic rule commenced under the governance of Richmond Palmer.

In 1950 the Church of Cyprus – leading the Orthodox Greek community of the island on both a spiritual and secular level – organised an unofficial referendum. Voting took place in churches and was not secret – an astonishing 97% of Greek Cypriots voted in favour of *Enosis*.[8] The result of the referendum was ignored by the British, but it was not long until the end of the colonial era in Cyprus began.

The political struggle against British rule transformed into military action, with the ultimate goal to achieve the *Enosis* with Greece. The National Organisation of Cypriot Fighters (*Ethniki Organosi Kiprion Agoniston* (EOKA)) started an armed resistance campaign under the leadership of Georgios Grivas (with *nom de guerre Digenis* – inspired by the famous ideal Byzantine hero), with Grigoris Afxentiou as second in command. In spite of the disapproval of the Archbishop of Cyprus at the time, and later of first President of the Republic,

5 *Ibid*, p77.

6 Hatzimihail (n 1), 46.

7 Alexios Alecou, "Safeguarding Through Stability: British Constitutional Proposals in Post-War Cyprus", *Journal of Human Rights in the Commonwealth* (2016) 2(1), 50.

8 Roderick Beaton, *Greece: Biography of a Modern Nation* (Patakis Publishers, 2020), p399.

Makarios III, EOKA led a fight that involved not only acts of sabotage, but also shootings, bombings, ambushes, raids, demonstrations and increased public disorder.

The divide-and-conquer practices applied by the British during their rule of the island included the promotion of the representation of the Turkish Cypriots, beyond demographic proportion, to the courts, the police and other bodies of the colonial administration and even the Bar. This disproportionate allocation of powers, and especially powers of a repressive nature such as policing, sparked ethnic rivalries among the island's inhabitants.[9] The assassination of a Turkish Cypriot senior officer of the secret services of the police led to a reaction by the Turkish Resistance Organisation and the ultimate transformation of the liberation struggle of the Greek Cypriots against the British into a tripartite conflict in 1958. The desire of the Turkish Cypriots for division (*Taksim*) of the island into Turkish and Greek portions, as opposed to the desire of the Greek Cypriots for union with Greece, was now bolstered.[10]

The idea of Cyprus becoming an independent state, instead of proceeding with *Enosis* or *Taksim*, with the United Kingdom putting an end to its rule but maintaining sovereign military bases on the island, materialised through the Zurich and London Agreements signed in February 1959. The governments of Greece and Turkey negotiated the terms of the agreements between them, and after some modifications proposed by the United Kingdom, the leaders of the Greek and Turkish communities of Cyprus, Archbishop Makarios III and Dr Fazil Kucuk respectively, were asked to sign them without having been allowed to take part in the negotiations or exercise any discretion. The Republic of Cyprus officially became an independent state on 16 August 1960 under the guarantees of the United Kingdom, Greece and Turkey.

This essentially imposed[11] settlement generated the 1960 constitution, a lengthy, uncommonly detailed and complex instrument setting out the citizens' basic rights and the fundamental rules of operation of the newly established Republic.[12] The constitution was given to the people of Cyprus – they were never asked to ratify it. The constitution's main and simultaneously unique features include the establishment of bi-communalism, in that the citizens of the Republic of Cyprus are grouped into two communities, the Greek Cypriot community and the Turkish Cypriot community, which remain separate and participate as two distinct bodies in the government and administrative functions of the state. The counterbalancing mechanisms adopted throughout the constitution to ensure that both communities

9 Hatzimihail (n 1), 47.

10 Beaton (n 8), pp408–409.

11 Polyvios G Polyviou, *Cyprus: A Study in the Theory Structure and Method of the Legal System of the Republic of Cyprus* (Chryssafinis & Polyviou, 2015), p8.

12 *Ibid*, p10.

unanimously decide on matters that are critical to the operation of the state is another noteworthy feature.[13] The checks and balances between the Greek Cypriot president elected by the Greek Cypriot community and the Turkish Cypriot vice-president elected by the Turkish Cypriot community made Article 1 of the constitution (which provides that the regime of the state is presidential) sound incongruous. The 80:20 ratio of the two communities' members was not reflected in the 70:30 ratio that Article 62 of the constitution provides for regarding their representation in the House of Representatives. Interestingly, Article 62 also provides that the proportion of representatives "shall be independent of any statistical data". The disproportionality continued to play out in the 70:30 ratio regarding the recruitments in the public sector, the 70:30 ratio in the security forces and the 60:40 ratio in the army. The atypical magnitude of the core of the constitution, comprising articles that cannot be amended, alongside the alterability of the rest of the bylaws voted for by at least two-thirds of all the Greek Cypriot and two-thirds of all the Turkish Cypriot members of the House of Representatives, added to the rigidness of the instrument.

The Treaty of Guarantee, one of the three treaties that resulted from the Zurich-London negotiations, was signed between Cyprus, Greece, Turkey and the United Kingdom and gained constitutional force based on one of the unalterable articles of the constitution, Article 181. Aside from prohibiting any of the *Enosis* or *Taksim*, the treaty gave the three guarantor powers, which were Greece, Turkey and the United Kingdom, the right to jointly or solely intervene, even with a military operation, where the constitutional arrangements were not respected.[14] The sovereignty of the state of the Republic of Cyprus was undermined from its very inception.

The inflexibly bi-communalist state of things, the conspicuous avoidance of any reference to the people of Cyprus as a whole,[15] combined with the members of the two communities (as the constitution wanted them) spread out across the island brought the first dark clouds over the Republic. The mistrust and unaccommodating stance of the Turkish Cypriot community became evident and was countered by the frustration of the Greek Cypriot community for the disproportionate protection given to the former. Archbishop Makarios III had been extremely sceptical about signing the Zurich-London treaties and had at the time expressed his deep concern about their provisions. These provisions had, after all, resulted from negotiations that neither the Greek Cypriot nor Turkish Cypriot community had been given the opportunity to participate in. In 1963,

13 *Ibid*, pp16–18.

14 *Ibid*, pp10–11.

15 Christis T Lottidis, *The Constitution of the Republic of Cyprus, its Complexity and the Unsuccessful Attempt for its Amendment in 1963* (in Greek) (Sakkoulas Publications, 2009), p20, www.sakkoulas.gr/el/editions/ch-lottidis-to-syntagma-tis-kypriakis-dimokratias-i-polyplokotita-tou-kai-i-anepitychis-prospatheia-anatheorisis-tou-to-1963-2009/.

having experienced its harmful dysfunctionality, President Makarios returned to the matter with a 13-point proposal for the amendment of the constitution addressed to Vice President Dr Kucuk. In brief, the proposals included:

- the abolition of the right to veto the president and vice president;
- the Turkish vice president should act as deputy to the president in case of absence of the latter;
- the Turkish vice president of the House of Representatives should act as deputy to the president in case of absence of the latter;
- the Greek president and the Turkish vice president of the House of Representatives should be elected by vote of all members of the House, not by the members of the respective community;
- the obliteration of the constitutional provisions of separate majorities;
- the establishment of unified municipalities;
- the unification of the system of administration of justice;
- the abolition of the division of the security forces into police and *gendarmerie*;
- the determination by ordinary law instead of the constitution of the number of the members of the security forces;
- the alteration of the ratio of the participation of the members of the communities in the public service commission and the security forces to 80:20;
- the reduction of the number of members of the public service commission from 10 to five;
- the adoption of decisions of the public service commission by simple majority; and
- the abolition of the Greek communal chamber.

Makarios noted in the preamble of his 13-point proposal that the intention of the authors of the Zurich-London agreements was for the interests of the Turkish Cypriots to be safeguarded, but not to the detriment of the smooth functioning of the state.[16] Makarios' proposals were not welcomed by the Turkish government. They reiterated that the constitution should not be amended in any way. The Turkish Cypriots then, through Vice President Dr Kucuk, accused the Greek Cypriots of seeking to overthrow the constitution in an attempt to violate the rights warranted to the Turkish Cypriots. Following a period of intercommunal violence, the United Nations, acceded by the Republic on the declaration of its independence, sent a sizeable peacekeeping force to the island (which is stationed in Cyprus to this day),[17] while the Turkish Cypriots

16 Glafcos Clerides, *My Testimony* (in Greek), (Alithia Publishing Co Ltd, 1989), Volume 1, pp191–207.

17 Polyvios G Polyviou, *The Case of Ibrahim: the Doctrine of Necessity and the Republic of Cyprus* (Chryssafinis & Polyviou, 2015), p31.

withdrew from their government posts, including the Council of Ministers and the House of Representatives, leaving the state crippled and unable to function. The attorney general, opining by order of the president, held that the various organs of the state needed to continue functioning to preserve their operation. And so long as meetings of the various organs were quorate, they continued performing their assigned duties.

Something groundbreaking, posing as a distinctive feature for the Cypriot legal system, came out of the hardship in which the state had become hostage. The doctrine of necessity, traditionally associated with criminal law, is the basis on which the constitution continues to exist to this day, while maintaining its (no longer possible to apply) bi-communal character. The doctrine of necessity came into operation in 1964 through *The Attorney General of the Republic v Mustafa Ibrahim,*[18] renowned for its legal and political dimensions. The foreign presidents of the Supreme Constitutional Court and the High Court, both established on the basis of the constitution, had resigned, rendering the administration of justice non-functional. The establishment of a new court unifying the jurisdictions of the Supreme Constitutional Court and the High Court under one forum called the Supreme Court, in accordance with the Administration of Justice (Miscellaneous Provisions) Law 33/1964 enacted by the House of Representatives without the participation of the Turkish Cypriot members that had resigned, was challenged as unconstitutional. The Supreme Court heard an appeal for *Ibrahim* that challenged the lawfulness of the Administration of Justice (Miscellaneous Provisions) Law 1964 and thus its very own jurisdiction. The Supreme Court itself was to deliberate on whether its creation and operation was lawful. It was held that the letter of the constitution, which neither the people of Cyprus nor the two communities' representatives had been given the chance to negotiate, should not be an impediment to the administration of justice. The creation of the Supreme Court may have not been in accordance with the provisions of the constitution, but the anomalous situation in Cyprus made it compelling for the constitution to be read subject to the doctrine of necessity.[19] Following *Ibrahim*, the doctrine of necessity was used to address not only the issue of the legality of laws enacted by the House of Representatives, but also of various administrative acts as well as the issue of the operation of government organs and other bodies that were supposed to be bi-communal, and other matters with human-rights aspects. History took its tragic course and following Turkey's deplorable invasion into Cyprus in 1974 and its subsequent occupation of 37% of its land, the anomalous situation became the distressing *status quo*. Even though it was initially thought to be temporary it has resulted

18 (1964) CLR 195.
19 Polyviou (n 17), pp168–179.

in the doctrine of necessity reinventing the state, the government and the constitution, respectful of the limitations governing its use.[20]

On 1 May 2004, after years of discussions in the interior and negotiations with its international counterparties,[21] Cyprus became a full member of the European Union and thereafter amended its constitution in order for the *acquis communautaire* (the European Union's body of law) to supersede domestic law. Cyprus had already become a party to the European Convention on Human Rights and Fundamental Freedoms and the Council of Europe soon after its declaration of independence and the decisions of the European Court of Human Rights have since been observed where applicable.[22]

1.2 A fascinating legal marble

The laws that were already in force when the constitution came into effect found their way into the legal order of the newly established Republic through one of the constitution's transitional provisions, Article 188. Article 188 stipulated that the entire body of those laws would remain in force until amended, or would be applicable with any modifications necessary for them to be in compliance with the provisions of the constitution.

Various laws enacted before the declaration of independence remain in effect, as they may have been amended from time to time, up to this day, since they are also compatible with the constitution. The Trustee Law (Cap 193), which was based on the English Trustee Act 1925 and governs trusteeship in Cyprus, was enacted as Law 46 in 1955 and is a prime example of such survival.[23] As in other codes or chapters enacted before independence for regulating other areas of law and surviving up to this day, here too was stated that in the event of a vacuum, common law and the principles of equity would become applicable. Further, most areas of private law, criminal law and procedural law, also having been codified before independence, were influenced by and follow common law.

Even though nowhere in the constitution is reference made to common law, the principle of *stare decisis* and the principles of equity as being applicable in the internal legal order of the Republic of Cyprus, the Courts of Justice Law 14/1960, enacted shortly after independence, established in Article 29 a hierarchy of the sources of law that was inclusive of those. Following the constitution and the laws enacted thereunder, Cyprus courts are bound by the laws existing on independence as per Article 188 of the constitution, common law and the doctrines of equity so long as no relevant legislation is enacted under the constitution or already applicable pursuant to Article 188 and, finally,

---

20 *Ibid*, p115.
21 Hatzimihail (n 1), 80.
22 Polyviou (n 11), p124.
23 Hatzimihail (n 1), 77.

the acts of the Parliament of the United Kingdom that were applicable immediately prior to independence, unless other provisions are enacted pursuant to the constitution.[24]

The maintenance after independence of the applicability of the pre-existing laws and common law and equity, always subject to anything contrary provided in the constitution, seemed like a safe harbour, a safeguard of the smooth transition to an independent state of affairs and a guarantor of the continuity of the existing legal relationships. The lawyers and judges at the time, most of whom were educated and qualified in England, would thus not come across a profoundly reformed system and would continue their work with little inconvenience and obstruction.

This persistence on the use, under certain conditions, of common law and the doctrines of equity in the internal legal order of Cyprus was thought likely to prejudice the retraction of the Cypriot legal system from common law authorities. The Cypriot legal system reinforced its position as a mixed system nevertheless.[25]

This is evidenced by another addition to the Cypriot legal system being of Greek and therefore continental origin. Cypriot family law was influenced heavily by Greek family law, following the modernisation of Greece during the 1980s. The Cypriot law was reformed based this modernisation alongside the establishment of family courts that would overturn the previous personal law administration regime. Adoption and protection of adult matters, however, are still handled based on English law.[26] England, lacking an evolved legal framework concerning matters of public law, and especially of an administrative nature, also led Cyprus seeking relevant guidance from other jurisdictions. The academic works of major figures of the Greek public law scene, as well as the case law produced by the Greek Council of State, are responsible for the formation of the Cypriot administrative law.[27] The Cypriot case law produced as a result, was codified under the General Principles of Administrative Law 158 (I)/1999.

When it comes to the other branch of public law – constitutional law – the Supreme Court has, from the beginning of its operation, pronounced that it would be turning to US Supreme Court case law for any guidance necessary.[28] The sources of inspiration resorted to for forming the Cypriot legal order do not stop there. The Cyprus International Trusts Law 69(I)/1992 was influenced by the common law jurisdictions of the Caribbean.[29]

Statutory law, even though generally coexisting with case law, is the main

24 Polyviou (n 11), pp263–264.
25 Moustaira (n 2), p78.
26 Hatzimihail (n 1), 80.
27 *Ibid*, 92.
28 Polyviou (n 11), p262.
29 Hatzimihail (n 1), 79.

source of law in Cyprus. In contrast with – even mixed – common law jurisdictions, Cypriot law is codified largely with Cypriot judges interpreting and being bound by statutory law.[30]

Since 2006 all directives, regulations and other binding acts of legislative nature issued by the European Union, the European Communities or their institutions supersede the provisions of the constitution and the provisions of the latter must be interpreted in accordance with the former. This was the result of the addition of Article 1A to the constitution, an obligation undertaken by Cyprus further to its accession to the European Union. International treaties' provisions also supersede domestic law as long as they are also applied by the respective counterparties, as per Article 169(3) of the constitution.

Other factors also contributed to the formation of the Cypriot legal system, this "colorful plurilegal mosaic".[31] The increasing number of lawyers and judges studying (continental) law in Greece post-independence in conjunction with the influences from the Greek legal system as aforementioned, assisted for terms, concepts and authorities forming part of the Greek legal culture to infiltrate the Cypriot legal system.[32] The use of the teleological method of interpretation, the reading in accordance with the spirit of the law, instead of the grammatical method of interpretation in strict adherence to the word of the law, depicts such importation from the Greek legal culture. Of course, teleological interpretation is used mostly in areas of law with continental origins or framework, while the grammatical interpretation is normally used for statutes stemming from common law.

Cyprus is not only at the crossroads of many civilisations, it is also at the crossroads of many legal cultures. The colonial era left an indelible mark on its legal system. Even today, Cyprus is considered a common law jurisdiction. In reality, a mixed legal system has arisen out of the geopolitical and social history of the island. Cyprus is home to a legal system where common law and equity, continental law, *acquis communautaire* and the US constitutional tradition are all prominent actors in the same judicial scene.

2. The structure of the judicial system and latest developments

The administration of justice in Cyprus is served by a two-tier system operating independently based on the principle of separation of powers featured in the constitution. The doctrine of necessity has been the cornerstone of the operation of the judicial system despite the retention of the initial wording of the constitution even when circumstances ceased allowing this.

After almost 60 years from the first reform of the judiciary, which took place

30 *Ibid*, 70.
31 Symeon S Symeonides, "The Mixed Legal System of the Republic of Cyprus", *Tulane Law Review* 78 (2003), 441.
32 Hatzimihail (n 1), 84.

for the sake of the smooth administration of justice in the Republic, another significant reform is now taking place, ultimately, for the same reason.

2.1 The judiciary up to 2022

Cypriot courts are divided into two tiers. Starting from the bottom tier, we have the special jurisdiction courts, namely the family courts, the industrial dispute courts and the rent-control courts hearing civil law matters, the assize court hearing criminal law matters and the military court having jurisdiction over matters of military personnel. Any matters that do not fall within the jurisdiction of the specialised courts are heard by general jurisdiction courts – the district courts. District courts also have jurisdiction for matters of criminal law punishable with imprisonment not exceeding five years.

The Supreme Court is at the top of the structure and has the role of second-instance court, hearing civil and criminal law cases from the lower-tier courts. The Supreme Court has exclusive jurisdiction over administrative law matters and is the only court that can issue the prerogative writs of *habeas corpus*, *mandamus*, *certiorari*, *quo warranto* and prohibition. Admiralty cases can also be brought before it both on first and second instance. Finally, the Supreme Court hears electoral and constitutional law cases.

2.2 Judicial reform

The year 2022 represents yet another historic year for the judicial system of the Republic of Cyprus. Almost six decades after the merger of the Supreme Constitutional Court into the Supreme Court, the realisation that the accumulation of competences and responsibilities, as well as jurisdiction over a wide range of cases, were beyond its means and incompatible with the guidelines of the Venice Commission, has led to the need for reform. It had become more than evident in recent years that the judicial system formed after 1964 hampered the swift administration of justice and prejudiced the application of the constitutional principle of the rule of law. The constitution, the Courts of Justice Law 14/1960 and the Administration of Justice (Miscellaneous Provisions) Law 33/1964 were all amended in order for the Supreme Constitutional Court to come back to existence, an appellate court to be established for providing the possibility of hearings at third instance for certain cases. The doctrine of necessity was once again invoked for securing the validity of the amendments since the special circumstances justifying its use are still present.[33] Another two courts of special jurisdiction, the Commercial Court and the Admiralty Court, were created as part of the wider reform.[34] In response to the needs of the times, an electronic platform for filing court documents has

33 Recitals of Law for the Seventeenth Amendment of the Constitution 101(I) 2022.
34 Law for the Amendment of the Courts of Justice Laws from 1960 until 2022 146(I) 2022.

also come into operation. The long-anticipated reform is expected to considerably reduce the workload of the Supreme Court and the district courts, leading to a faster, more efficient and fairer system of administration of justice.

3. The legal profession in Cyprus

3.1 Advocates in Cyprus

On completion of 12 months' legal training and having successfully passed the Legal Council exams, the holders of recognised law degrees can register with their local bar association and the Cyprus Bar Association and thereafter practise in Cyprus. The licence to practise is renewed annually on payment of the applicable fee and a contribution to the Lawyers' Pension Fund.

Even though Cyprus has adopted the unitary concept of the practice of the legal profession originating from common law, legal professionals are not distinguished to barristers and solicitors. The Advocates Law (Cap 2), the law regulating the legal profession in Cyprus, is one of the colonial laws remaining in effect until today.[35]

3.2 The attorney general

The attorney general, supported by the assistant attorney general, is an independent official acting as the legal adviser to the president, the Council of Ministers and the ministers. In other words, the attorney general is the legal adviser of the state. The attorney general is the head of the Law Office of the Republic, an independent body of legal professionals that do not need to be members of the Bar Association and that assist the attorney general with the provision of legal support and legal representation to the state. Taking into account the principle of independence, the attorney general is also, surprisingly, the leader of the Bar.[36]

---

35 Hatzimihail (n 1), 55.

36 Christos Clerides, *The Legal Profession in Cyprus, Regulatory Framework and Practice of the Profession* (in Greek) (Nomiki Bibliothiki, 2017), p47.

Trusts in Cyprus under domestic law

Chrysthia Papacleovoulou-Vassiliou
Open University of Cyprus
Evi Papacleovoulou
Law Chambers Nicos Papacleovoulou LLC

1. Introduction

The use of trusts is well-established under Cyprus law and their recognition is linked directly to the fact that the Cypriot legal system is a common law system. The doctrine of equity,[1] case law as it applied in England and Wales before 1960,[2] and the case law of the Supreme Court of Cyprus are also sources of law governing domestic trusts.[3] This is particularly important for the purposes of interpretation or guidance, as no express provision under Cyprus law exists. Cyprus' concept of trusts has been influenced by the development of trusts in England, as well as international practice.

This chapter describes trusts in Cyprus under domestic law. The main legal instruments that relate to the setting up of trusts under domestic law are the Trustee Law 1955 (Cap 193), which mirrors the United Kingdom's Trustee Act 1925, and the International Trusts Law 69(I) 1992 as amended in 2012, which governs Cyprus international trusts (CITs).[4]

2. Definitions and terminology

In the Greek use of the word 'trusts', two distinct terms are often used in case

---

1 Section 29(1)(c) of the Courts of Justice Law 14/1960. Civil and criminal courts were instructed to adhere to the common law and doctrine of equity, "save in so far as other provision has been or shall be made by any law and so long as not inconsistent with the constitution". See, Andreas Neocleous & Co, *Introduction to Cyprus Law* (Yorkhill Law Publishing, 2000), p852. In *National Bank of Greece v Masonou* ((1980) 1 CLR 195 (ca)), it was held that equity intervenes to stop the abuse of a legal right and to ameliorate the rigidity of contract law, and that equity would be applied where the strict application of contractual rights would manifest in injustice. In *Iranian Tanker v Pastella* ((1987) 1 CLR 120), the court affirmed that equity applies as part of national law by virtue of Section 29(1)(c) of Law 14/60. In *Limmare Shipping v Boustani* ((1981) 1 CLR 386) the court upheld the doctrine of promissory estoppel.

2 In 1960 Cyprus became an independent republic. Section 29(1)(c) of the Courts of Justice Law 14/1960 identifies the sources of Cyprus law.

3 According to established case law, where there is no express or specific legal provision for a particular matter, the Supreme Court has held that reliance may be placed on common law or the doctrine of equity as it is applied in England. *Solomos Stylianou v The Police* ((1962) CLR 152); *A Mouzouris v Xylofagou Plantations Ltd* ((1977) 1 CLR 287), at p300. *Constantinou v Democritos Publishers Ltd* ((1996) 1 AAD 206), Andreas Neocleous & Co, *Introduction to Cyprus Law* (Yorkhill Law Publishing, 2000), p852. It is also well established that English case law and the case law of the Privy Council and other commonwealth jurisdictions have persuasive weight and are considered by Cyprus courts.

4 See the chapter "The Cyprus International Trusts Law 1992–2012: new dynamics" by Chrysthia Papacleovoulou-Vassiliou.

law and legislative provisions: 'εμπιστευμα' or 'καταπίστευμα'. Both terms denote the same meaning and are considered accurate translations of the English term 'trust'.[5]

What is a trust under domestic law? Ostensibly, except where the specific type of trust[6] is expressly defined, the term 'trust' is not conclusively defined by legislative provisions. The Cyprus International Trusts Law 69(I)/1992 as amended, defines 'trust' as having the meaning assigned to the term by the Trustee Law (Cap 193). This does not offer sufficient guidance, considering that the definition in Section 3 of the Trustee Law (Cap 193) is even more general. Section 3 defines 'trust' as follows:

> *'Trust' does not include the duties of a mortgage lender but with this exception the terms 'trust and 'trustee' extend to silent/implied and constructive trusts,*[7] *and in cases where the trustee has an interest in the trust property, and in the duties that relate to the office of a personal representative, and trustee includes a personal representative.*

Therefore, principles of equity and the case law of England and Cyprus are useful.

According to Section 2 of the Hague Convention on the Law Applicable to Trusts and on their Recognition, a trust is defined as follows:

> *For the purposes of this Convention, the term 'trust' refers to the legal relationships created –* inter vivos *or on death – by a person, the settlor, when assets have been placed under the control of a trustee for the benefit of a beneficiary or for a specified purpose. A trust has the following characteristics:*
>
> *a) the assets constitute a separate fund and are not a part of the trustee's own estate;*
>
> *b) title to the trust assets stands in the name of the trustee or in the name of another person on behalf of the trustee;*
>
> *c) the trustee has the power and the duty, in respect of which he is accountable, to manage, employ or dispose of the assets in accordance with the terms of the trust and the special duties imposed upon him by law.*
>
> *The reservation by the settlor of certain rights and powers, and the fact that the trustee may himself have rights as a beneficiary, are not necessarily inconsistent with the existence of a trust.*[8]

The above definition provides a general, although not an all-encompassing

---

5 The term 'εμπιστευμα' is used in the Trustees Law (Cap 193), the Law Ratifying the Hague Convention on Trusts, as well as in numerous cases. The term 'καταπίστευμα' is found in considerable case law including *Pentavkas v Pentavkas* ((1991) 1 AAD 547), *Stylianou v Stylianou* (9214/29.10.99 (1999) 1 AAD 1833), *Protopapa v Protopapa* (10836/13, (2002) 1 AAD 1329), Article 2 of the Acquisition of Immovable Property (Aliens) Law (Cap 109), and Article 2 of the International Trusts Law 69(I) 1992 as amended in 2012, where it is expressly stipulated that the term 'εμπιστευμα' includes 'καταπίστευμα'. See the analysis in Christos Clerides, *The Cyprus Law of Equity* (Nomiki Bibliothiki, 2021), pp133–134.

6 For example, CITs, charitable trusts and purpose trusts.

7 However, silent or implied trusts, as well as constructive trusts, are not defined under Cap 193.

8 The Hague Convention on the Law Applicable to Trusts and on their Recognition (1985), www.hcch.net/en/instruments/conventions/full-text/?cid=59.

definition. For example, 'trusts for a specified purpose' (eg, charitable trusts) do not have beneficiaries so that their interest can be enforced. In *Westdeutsche Landesbank Girozentrale v Islington London Borough Council*,[9] the basic principles that relate to trusts have been determined as follows:

The Relevant Principles of Trust Law

(i) Equity operates on the conscience of the owner of the legal interest. In the case of a trust, the conscience of the legal owner requires him to carry out the purposes for which the property was vested in him (express or implied trust) or which the law imposes on him by reason of his unconscionable conduct (constructive trust).

(ii) Since the equitable jurisdiction to enforce trusts depends upon the conscience of the holder of the legal interest being affected, he cannot be a trustee of the property if and so long as he is ignorant of the facts alleged to affect his conscience, i.e. until he is aware that he is intended to hold the property for the benefit of others in the case of an express or implied trust, or, in the case of a constructive trust, of the factors which are alleged to affect his conscience.

(iii) In order to establish a trust there must be identifiable trust property. The only apparent exception to this rule is a constructive trust imposed on a person who dishonestly assists in a breach of trust who may come under fiduciary duties even if he does not receive identifiable trust property.

(iv) Once a trust is established, as from the date of its establishment the beneficiary has, in equity, a proprietary interest in the trust property, which proprietary interest will be enforceable in equity against any subsequent holder of the property (whether the original property or substituted property into which it can be traced) other than a purchaser for value of the legal interest without notice.

Some definitions are provided in Section 2 of the Cyprus International Trusts Law. A 'beneficiary' is defined as a legal or natural person, including a person not yet born at the time of the creation of the trust, or a person who is part of a class of people entitled to a right or interest in property that is subject to the trust. An 'enforcer' is defined as a person or persons whose duty is to enforce an international trust, with the exception of trusts for charitable purposes. A 'protector' is defined as a person other than the trustee to whom powers of any nature are conferred by the trust instrument creating or evidencing the trust, including the power to advise a trustee as to the exercise of the trustee's powers or as to the trustee's right in respect of a consent or veto and includes the power to appoint or remove a trustee. 'Trustee' means a legal or natural person who holds or has had trust property transferred to them or is deemed to hold or have had trust property transferred to them, or is expected to have trust property delivered or transferred to them to be held by them:

9 [1996] AC 669, p705, per Lord Browne-Wilkinson.

- for the benefit of a beneficiary irrespective of whether the trustee is also beneficiary of the trust; and
- for any purpose which is not for the exclusive benefit of the trustee.

'Trust property' means property that is held on trust at the relevant time. Ostensibly, these definitions are applicable to CITs or charitable trusts under Section 7. Although discretionary trusts are not expressly defined, an 'object of discretionary trust' is defined as a legal person or individual who forms part of a class of persons to whom a distribution may be made in accordance with a discretionary trust or on the basis of the discretionary power of the trustee or of the holder of the power. These definitions apply to CITs.

Cap 193 does not provide for definitions for the settlor, the trustee or the beneficiary. Section 2(2) of Cap 193, provides that the powers of trustees under the Trustees Law (Cap 193) are in addition to the powers vested by the trust settlement, if one exists, but that such powers are exercised to the extent that they are not contrary to the express powers in the trust settlement. Therefore, the principles of equity and case law apply with regard to definitions of domestic trusts other than CITs.

Simply put, the settlor is the person who creates the trust; they are the owner of the initial property placed under trust who vests the property into the trust property. The trustee may be a natural or legal person who agrees to hold the legal interest of the trust property or trust assets for, and for the benefit of, the beneficiaries under the trust. Therefore, the trustee holds legal title or legal interest of the trust property or trust assets for the beneficiary who has the beneficial interest or equitable title to the trust assets. Except in cases of bare trusts, the beneficiary usually has no say in the management of the trust property or the termination of the trust. The protector, who is not compulsory, but who if appointed is the person that has the power to restrict key powers of the trustee, such as the power to add beneficiaries to the trust. The enforcer (who could also be the protector) is the person or persons whose duty it is to enforce an international trust for a non-charitable purpose in accordance with the Cyprus International Trusts Law. A trust may be created by the owner of property on their death, by a testamentary disposition of the property into the trust accompanied by a letter of wishes; however, it is more appropriate and common that the trust is created during the lifetime of the owner of the property by a trust instrument or deed or settlement. A trust created through a testamentary disposition would not avoid inheritance laws or taxes where applicable, whereas a disposition of the trust property during the settlor's lifetime avoids such issues.

3. The three certainties and the law against perpetuities

The settlor must be of full age and have legal capacity[10] and the trust ought to meet the classic test of the 'three certainties', as established in *Knight v Knight*, which provide that in order to be valid a private express trust must demonstrate the three certainties – only then will a court recognise the trust as binding in equity, and so enforce its terms to provide for a beneficiary;[11] namely, certainty of intention,[12] subject matter[13] and objects.[14]

3.1 Certainty of intention

Certainty of intention is evidence of express intention of the settlor to create the trust. This is usually evidenced by the trust instrument. The test in determining whether the intention exists is based on the words used and the behaviour of the parties, indicating that there is a distinct and clear intention that the property is to be held on trust for the benefit of a third party.[15] Care

---

10 For example, under Section 11 of the Contract Law (Cap 149), a person has capacity to enter into a contract if they are of sound mind and over 18 years of age.

11 *Knight v Knight* ((1840) 3 Beav 148), also *Wright v Atkyns* ((1823) Turn & R 143), per Lord Eldon at p157: "In order to determine whether the trust is a trust this court will interfere with, it is a matter of observation, first that the words must be imperative, secondly, that the subject matter must be certain and, thirdly, that the object must be as certain as the subject." The three certainties apply to Cyprus trusts, see Christos Clerides, *The Cyprus Law of Equity* (Nomiki Bibliothiki, 2021), p138.

12 Certainty of intention was examined in more modern declarations of trust in *Paul v Constance* ([1977] 1 WLR 527), per Scarman LJ at p532: "when one bears in mind the unsophisticated character of the deceased and his relationship with the plaintiff during the last years of his life, Mr Wilson submits that the words that he did use on more than one occasion, 'this money is as much yours as mine', convey clearly a present declaration that the existing fund was as much the plaintiff's as his own. The judge accepted that conclusion. I think that he was well justified in doing so and, indeed, I think that he was right to do so." Also in *Hunter v Moss* ([1994] 3 All ER 452), and *Gold v Hill* ([1999] 1 FLR 54). See the analysis in R Clements and A Abass, *Equity and Trusts, Texts, Cases, and Materials*, 4th edn (Oxford, 2015), pp95–98.

13 Clearly describing the trust property, see *Palmer Simmonds* ((1854) 2 Drew 221), where the testatrix left the "bulk of my said residuary estate to Thomas Harrison to hold on trust for various people", the meaning of the residue was clear but the meaning of the world 'bulk' was not, so the trust was not established; *Boyce v Boyce* ((1849) 16 Sim 476), where a fixed trust set up by a will that consisted of two houses for two beneficiaries, Maria and Charlotte. Maria was to choose which house she wanted, and Charlotte was to have the other. Maria died before the testator and therefore did not make her selection. The trust failed because the beneficial shares were uncertain. *Re Golay's Will Trusts* ([1965] 1 WLR 969), the will directed the executors to "let Tossy ... Mrs F. Bridgewater ... enjoy one of my flats during her lifetime and to receive a reasonable income from the other properties". The executors could choose which flat Mrs Bridgewater could use and the phrase 'reasonable income' did not cause the trust to fail for uncertainty; *Re Lehman Brothers International (Europe) (in Administration)*, also known as *Pearson v Lehman Brothers Finance SA* ([2011] EWCA Civ 1544), per Lloyd LJ at para 70: "its duties as such trustee were more limited than those of an ordinary trustee, because it did not have to keep the holding segregated, and could not only mix it with other assets, with different beneficial ownership, but could deal with it, on a short term basis, for its own benefit or that of others than LBF. However, its trusteeship was constituted at once, and difficulties in accounting as a result of what happened later do not subvert the proposition that the securities were held on trust from the time of their first acquisition." Also, *Lehman Bros International (Europe) (a company) (in admin)* ([2012] 3 All ER 1), per Lord Clarke at p59: "there is no doubt that money in a mixed fund may be held on trust, and that a trust of money can be created without an obligation to keep it in a separate account". See the analysis in R Clements and A Abass, *Equity and Trusts, Texts, Cases, and Materials*, 4th edn (Oxford, 2015), pp98–101.

14 *Re Gulbekian* ([1970] AC 508), per Lord Upjohn at p521: "a mere or bare power of appointment ... among a class is valid if you can with certainty say whether any given individual is or is not a member of the class; you do not have to be able to ascertain every member of the class"; at p524: "But I should add this: if the class is sufficiently defined by the donor the fact that it may be difficult to ascertain the whereabouts or continued existence of some of its members at the relevant time matters not." *Re Manisty's Settlement* ([1974] Ch 17); *McPhail v Doulton* ([1971] AC 424); *Re Baden (no 2)* ([1973] Ch 9). See R Clements and A Abass, *Equity and Trusts, Texts, Cases, and Materials*, 4th edn (Oxford, 2015), pp98–112.

15 (a) *Re Kayford* ([1975] 1 All ER 604), Megarry J held that: "it is well settled that a trust can be created without using the word 'trust' or 'confidence' or the like; the question is whether in substance a sufficient intention to create a trust has been manifested." (b) *Twinsectra Ltd v Yardley* ([2002] 2 AC 164),

must be taken with word choices since precatory words (ie, words of mere hope and desire; eg, 'in the hope that' or 'I would like that') may be insufficient to create a trust.[16] An exception to the rule that equity cannot perfect an imperfect trust is the Privy Council decision in *T Choithram International SA v Pagarani*.[17]

3.2 Certainty of subject matter

Certainty of subject matter means that the trust assets must be readily identifiable otherwise the trust is void for uncertainty. The trust assets may consist of, for example, money, shares or other movable or immovable property. In the case of intangible assets such as a trust of a specific number of shares, the trust will not be void for uncertainty merely because it refers to an unspecified number of shares in a company, but not to the specific shares; shares of the same class are indistinguishable from each other and it is therefore unnecessary for the particular shares to be identified or segregated.[18]

3.3 Certainty of objects

Certainty of objects means that the identity of the beneficiaries of the trust must be ascertained or ascertainable at the time of setting up the trust.[19] The beneficiaries may be a specified class of beneficiary that is an ascertainable group of people.[20] It is therefore unnecessary for each and every potential beneficiary to be identified by the trustee.

Lord Millett said (Section 71): "A settlor must, of course, possess the necessary intention to create a trust, but his subjective intentions are irrelevant. If he enters into arrangements which have the effect of creating a trust, it is not necessary that he should appreciate that they do so; it is sufficient that he intends to enter into them."

16 *Re Adams and the Kensington Vestry* ((1884) 27 Ch D 394). The testator's estate was devised by will to the absolute use of his widow "in full confidence that she will do what is right as to the disposal thereof between my children". These were merely words of aspiration and did not impose a legal obligation.

17 In *T Choithram International SA v Pagarani* ([2000] UKPC 46), Lord Browne-Wilkinson considered that most important question was this: on the basis that Mr Pagarani intended to make an immediate absolute gift "to the Foundation", but had not vested the gifted property in all the trustees of the foundation, are the trusts of the foundation trust deed enforceable against the deposits and the shares, or was it (as the first-instance judge and the Court of Appeal had held) a case where there has been an imperfect gift that cannot be enforced against Mr Pagarani's estate whatever his intentions might have been? A perfected gift could be made in only one of two ways: (a) by a transfer of the gifted asset to the donee, accompanied by an intention in the donor to make a gift; or (b) by the donor declaring themself to be a trustee of the gifted property for the donee. In this case, Mr Pagarani used words of gift to the foundation (not words declaring himself a trustee) – unless he transferred the shares and deposits so as to vest title in all the trustees, he had not done all that he could to effect the gift; so under the law as it had been previously understood, the gift would have failed. Further, it would not be possible to treat Mr Pagarani's words of gift as a declaration of trust, because there is no reference to trusts. Therefore, if the case does not fall within either of the possible methods by which a complete gift can be made, then the gift should have failed.

18 (a) In *Hunter v Moss* ([1993] 1 WLR 452), it was held that the test should be whether, immediately after the declaration of trust, the court could, if asked, make an order for the execution of the trust, which it could do only if the subject matter of the trust is identified with sufficient certainty. (b) Re *Lehman Brothers International (Europe) (in Administration)* ([2010] EWHC 2914 (Ch)) mentions *Hunter v Moss*.

19 In *Double Happiness Trust, Re* (also known as *Grant Thornton Stonehage Ltd v Ward*) ([2003] WTLR 367) it was held that for a trust to be valid there had to be certainty as to the subject matter, the beneficiaries and the beneficial interests. While the subject matter of the settlement could be ascertained, there was some difficulty in respect of certainty as far as the beneficiaries were concerned. Accordingly, the settlement had to be declared void for lack of certainty.

In other words, by the deed, instrument or settlement purporting to create a trust, the settlor must demonstrate an intention to create a trust, the trust fund must be specified with reasonable certainty and the beneficiaries must be ascertainable.

Trusts may not exist indefinitely. The general rule is that trusts may continue to exist for the lifetime of a life in being plus 21 years, or where that the life in being is not a natural person, merely for 21 years. CITs established under the Cyprus International Trusts Law are exempt from this rule. Under the amended law, there is no limit on the period over which an international trust may continue to be valid and enforceable.[21] According to Vassiliades, excluding express terms of the trust to the contrary, no concession, distribution, payment, holding or disposal of the income or capital of the trust to another trust is invalidated merely by reason that the recipient trust continues to be valid and enforceable after the date on which the first trust ceased to exist.[22] Even under Cap 193, the perpetuity rules do not apply in the case of charitable or purpose trusts that may continue indefinitely.

4. Classification of trusts under domestic law

The classification of trusts under domestic law follows the English and other common law jurisdictions:

- Private trusts:
  - must be expressly created by the settlor;
  - can be created by deed, in writing, through a will and, with some exceptions, orally;
  - must see the settlor's intention made absolutely clear;
  - must satisfy three certainties; and
  - must see that the beneficiaries have enforcement powers in respect of the trust.[23]

  The beneficiaries are people.[24] There is usually a trust deed, trust settlement or trust instrument in writing.

- Express private trusts – express private trusts are created intentionally.[25] In a similar manner to private trusts, express private trusts must:
  - be expressly created by the settlor;
  - be created by deed, in writing or through a will;

20 *Re Baden's Deed Trust* (also known as *McPhail v Doulton*) ([1971] AC 424). The test to be applied in ascertaining the validity of a trust is whether it can be said with certainty that a given individual is or is not a member of the designated class.

21 See further the "Perpetuity and duration" chapter by Paolo Panico.

22 Christodoulos G Vassiliades & Co LLC, *Cyprus: International Trusts 2014*, www.vasslaw.com/wp-content/uploads/2015/01/Cyprus-international-trusts_EN_2014.pdf.

23 *Ibid.*

24 R Clements and A Abass, *Equity and Trusts, Texts, Cases, and Materials*, 4th edn (Oxford, 2015), p66.

25 *Ibid*, p67.

- demonstrate that the settlor's intention is absolutely clear; and
- satisfy the three certainties.[26]

Express private trusts may relate to shares, immovable property or wills – for the latter two, the satisfaction of specific formalities is necessary. Usually, there is a trust deed, trust settlement or trust instrument in writing.

- Declarations of trusts – under Section 112 of the Companies Law (Cap 113), "No notice of any trust, expressed, implied or constructive, shall be entered on the register, or be receivable by the registrar, in the case of companies registered in the Republic". Therefore, where the settlor intends for shares to be held on trust, such shares may be entered as part of the trust property of a deed or instrument of trust. In Cyprus it is often the case that shares held by nominee shareholders are vested under declarations of trusts. Nominee shareholding services are offered by fiduciary service providers for a fee, to hold the shares as shareholders on behalf of the ultimate beneficial owner (UBO). The nominee shareholder appears as the shareholder in the registry of the company and the company's registrar. Declarations of trust are arrangements, usually accompanied by an instrument of transfer of shares[27] so that the UBO retains control as to when to transfer the shares and to whom.[28] Bare trusts[29] fall under the types of arrangement referred to as 'declarations of trust' and are recognised under domestic law.
- Fixed trusts – are trusts where the share or interest of the beneficiaries in the trust property is specified by the settlor.[30]
- Discretionary trusts – are trusts where the trustees may, at their discretion, determine what share or interest of the trust property should go to each member of a class of beneficiary.[31] The powers of trustees are discretionary. These discretionary powers are expressly stipulated in the trust settlement or instrument. Discretionary trusts are typically used where the settlor intends for the trustees to have maximum or discretionary control over who will benefit and when. They can be created during lifetime or upon death. The beneficiaries may not have an automatic entitlement to the trust income or capital until the trustees exercise their discretion to determine who will benefit, and when and

---

26 Christodoulos G Vassiliades & Co LLC, *Cyprus: International Trusts 2014*, www.vasslaw.com/wp-content/uploads/2015/01/Cyprus-international-trusts_EN_2014.pdf.

27 Usually a blank and undated instrument of transfer of shares.

28 To be exercised, for example, where the relationship between the fiduciary service provider and the UBO breaks down.

29 In *Saunders v Vautier* ((1841) 4 Beav 115), it was held that Vautier could have the whole fund now as he had "an absolute indefeasible interest in the legacy".

30 Christodoulos G Vassiliades & Co LLC, *Cyprus: International Trusts 2014*, www.vasslaw.com/wp-content/uploads/2015/01/Cyprus-international-trusts_EN_2014.pdf.

31 *Ibid.* See *Annabel's (Berkeley Square) Ltd v Revenue and Customs Commissioners* ([2009] 4 All ER 55).

what the beneficiaries will receive.[32] This arrangement gives trustees flexibility, control and discretion over the exercise of their powers, which may include the management of the trust property or trust assets, the power to name, add or remove beneficiaries.[33]

- Charitable trusts – there is no express legal definition of what constitutes a charity. Usually, a trust that is set up for the relief of poverty, the advancement of education or religion, or any other purpose that is beneficial to the community or a public purpose, is regarded as a charitable trust.[34] An international charitable trust may be established under the Cyprus International Trusts Law.
- Implied trusts – are trusts that arise from the implied intention of the settlor.[35] Clerides suggests that implied trusts are essentially express trusts that are determined where terminology or wording implies the intention for their creation.[36]
- Resulting trusts – a resulting trust arises from the implied, rather than the expressed, intention of the settlor. This intention can be inferred by the way that the settlor acts or behaves. The trust has not deliberately been created and so it is not an express trust. The trust arises by operation of law or a court decision, and in different situations. Meggary J in *Re Vandervell's Trust (No 2)*[37] identified two main categories of resulting trust:
    - automatic resulting trusts; and
    - presumed resulting truss.[38]

  The distinction between the two categories is important. In the first category, the matter is one of intention, with the rebuttable presumption of a resulting trust applying if the intention is not made manifest.[39] An automatic resulting trust arises when the trust fails for some reason and the property returns to the settlor. It does not depend on any intention on the part of the original settlor. Such as in the case of Mr Vandervell, who was trying to rid himself of his shares to minimise his tax burden, but the court decided that he had not done so, therefore the shares "resulted back to him".[40] A presumed resulting trust depends on the

---

32 CITs are usually discretionary trusts to avoid challenges to the validity of the trust by tax authorities or other creditors. Cyprus courts will uphold the interests of the beneficiaries. See the chapter "Analysis of Cyprus case law involving Cyprus international trusts" by Chrysthia Papacleovoulou-Vassiliou.

33 See the chapter "Analysis of Cyprus case law involving Cyprus international trusts" by Chrysthia Papacleovoulou-Vassiliou, where trustees duties include the duty to provide information to beneficiaries but not a duty to explain the reasons for exercising their discretion.

34 Christodoulos G Vassiliades & Co LLC, *Cyprus: International Trusts 2014*, www.vasslaw.com/wp-content/uploads/2015/01/Cyprus-international-trusts_EN_2014.pdf.

35 *Ibid*. Vassiliades considers that an implied trust is either a resulting trust or a constructive trust. The latter two may constitute distinct categories of trust.

36 Christos Clerides, *The Cyprus Law of Equity*, (Nomiki Bibliothiki, 2021), pp139–156.

37 [1974] Ch 269.

38 R Clements and A Abass, *Equity and Trusts, Texts, Cases, and Materials*, 4th edn (Oxford, 2015), pp70–72.

39 *Ibid*, p70.

40 *Ibid*, p71.

presumed intention of the settlor, who is the original owner or holder of the property; namely, what the settlor would have intended had they thought about it. If A pays for property and puts it legally into B's name, it is presumed that A intended to keep it because A paid for it and B holds the property on resulting trust for A. If A and B both contribute to purchase the property, where A pays €30,000 and B pays €60,000 and the property is legally in their joint names, they hold it on resulting trust at one-third share for A and two-third shares for B. If A transfers property to B and receives nothing in return, unless there is evidence that A intended it to be a gift for B, it is presumed that B who holds the legal interest of the property, holds it on resulting trust for A, who has the equitable interest.[41] If, however, there is evidence that a gift was intended there will be no resulting trust and property will belong to B. According to Section 25 (1)(a) of the Contract Law (Cap 149), a contract without consideration is void unless it is in writing and is signed by the party that bears the burden of proof and it is entered by reason of the natural love and affection between the parties who have a close family relation between them. Therefore, consideration is not necessary for donations to family members. The transfer of immovable property by way of donation, does not in itself create a trust.[42] Both types of resulting trust ultimately depend on the intention of the settlor or the donor and give effect to the common intention of the parties. If the trust property could not be used for the trust, the settlor would want it back, therefore the property results back to the settlor.[43] According to Lord Browne-Wilkinson in *Westdeutsche Landesbank Girozentrale v Islington London Borough Council*, "a resulting trust is not imposed by law against the intentions of the trustee (as is a constructive trust) but gives effect to his presumed intention".[44]

- Quistclose-type trusts – are trusts created where a creditor has lent money to a debtor for a particular purpose. If the debtor uses the money for any other purpose, then it is held on trust for the creditor. Any inappropriately spent money can then be traced and returned to the creditor.[45] In *Junport International Limited v FBME Bank Limited*, the court

---

41 See *Prest v Petrodel Ltd* ([2013] 3 WLR 1) at 3.3. According to the maxim of equity, equity will not assist a volunteer.

42 *Charalambos Damianos Ioannou v Ioannou Ioannou Georgiou*, Civil Appeal 9549 ((1998) 1 AAD 589).

43 R Clements and A Abass, *Equity and Trusts, Texts, Cases, and Materials*, 4th edn (Oxford, 2015), pp70–72.

44 *Westdeutsche Landesbank Girozentrale v Islington London Borough Council* ([1996] AC 669) at p708.

45 *Barclays Bank Ltd v Quistclose Investments Ltd* (1970); *Bellis v Challinor* ([2015] EWCA Civ 59) at pp56–57, per Briggs LJ:

> *Quistclose-type trusts are a species of resulting trust which arise where property (usually money) is transferred on terms which do not leave it at the free disposal of the transferee. That restriction upon its use is usually created by an arrangement that the money should be used exclusively for a stated purpose or purposes. There must be an intention to create a trust on the part of the transferor. This is an objective question. It means that the transferor must have intended to enter into arrangements which, viewed objectively, have the effect in law of creating a trust.*

Cyprus recognises Quistclose trusts.

dismissed the application because it was filed by way of an originating summons application instead of a civil action.[46] *Per curiam*, Judge Panayiotou commented on the facts of the case that a Quistclose trust could not be found because the main characteristic of such a trust is that it should have a particular purpose for the payment of moneys. In the case of bank deposits, where the bank uses the deposits for the general purposes of its activities, no Quistclose trust can be established.

- Constructive trusts – are imposed by law independently of what anyone intended. These are imposed by the court in a variety of situations, usually when someone has wrongly acquired the property of another (eg, by the breaking of a promise or knowingly taking someone else's property). Courts concentrate on obtaining a result that they consider "just and fair".[47] An example of a constructive trust would be where A gives money to B to hold for C. If B then gives the money to D and D knows that B was holding the money for C, then D will be construed as also holding the money on trust for C. These are trusts that arise from the implied intention of the settlor and will be either resulting trusts or constructive trusts. In *Hanbury and Martin: Modern Equity*,[48] a constructive trust is defined as:

  one which arises by operation of law, and not by reason of the intention of the parties, express or implied. 'English law provides no clear and all-embracing definition of a constructive trust. Its boundaries have been left perhaps deliberately vague, so as not to restrict the court by technicalities in deciding what the justice of a particular case may demand'. It has been 'a ready means of developing our property law in modern times'. The principle is that where a person who holds property in circumstances in which in equity and good conscience it should be held or enjoyed by another, he will be compelled to hold the property in trust for that other.

4.1 Constructive and resulting trusts recognised over immovable property

Section 4 of the Immovable Property Law (Cap 224), which excludes common law and principles of equity as a legal basis of obtaining rights over immovable property, is subject to exceptions. In *Odysseos v Pieris Estates*,[49] it was held that

---

46 *Junport International Limited v FBME Bank Limited*, Originating Summons application 454/16, 28 July 2017. In *Re the application of Junport International Limited and others*, civil application 115/2017, 15 September 2017, the Supreme Court upheld the decision, considering that the scope of an originating summons application is indeed limited to interpretation, and where there are complex matters, a writ of summons, a civil action is the appropriate judicial procedure. A similar approach was taken in *Re the application of Junport International Limited and others* (civil application 321/2017, 2 April 2018). See the chapter "Analysis of Cyprus case law involving Cyprus international trusts" by Chrysthia Papacleovoulou-Vassiliou.

47 R Clements and A Abass, *Equity and Trusts, Texts, Cases, and Materials*, 4th edn (Oxford University Press, 2015), p72.

48 J Martin and H Hanbury, *Hanbury and Martin: Modern Equity*, 14th edn (Sweet & Maxwell, 1996), pp291–292.

49 *Odysseos v Pieris Estates* ((1982) 1 CLR), p557 and p570.

rights over immovable property may be created not only by express trusts, but also by any form of trust, including resulting and constructive trusts:

Section 4 of Cap. 224 aims to limit the application of the English common law and doctrines of equity for the acquisition of immovable property rights outside the system of registration created by the Cyprus Immovable Property Law. Trusts, however, that form the principal device of equity for the acquisition of property rights outside a system of registration, are expressly excluded from the ambit of s.4. The exclusion is not limited to express trusts, but trusts generally, including constructive, as well as resulting trusts. A contract for the sale of land gives rise to a constructive or resulting trust. (See, Lysaght v Edwards [1875–76] 2 Ch.D. 499). The interest of the purchaser is assignable in equity (see Halsbury's Laws of England, Vol.4, paras. 994-998). Further, the concept of a constructive trust is an ever expanding concept, designed to keep the hands of the Court free, to meet the demands of justice and good conscious. The subject is discussed in Snell's Principles of Èquity, 27th ed. at p. 185. At times, it has been used as a remedy to prevent unjust enrichment.

The existence of a constructive trust cannot, in Cyprus, create an estate in land, unless there is compliance with the provisions of the Sale of Land (Specific Performance) Law, Cap. 232, as amended by Laws 50/70 and 96/72; and there was none in this case. Consequently, a contract for the sale of land cannot be enforced either by the purchaser or an assignee in the absence of strict compliance with the provisions of Cap. 232.

The Supreme Court has acknowledged equitable estoppel as part of the law of Cyprus. (See, inter alia, Hadji Yiannis v The Attorney-General *(1970) 1 C.L.R. 32, and* Papadopoulos v National Bank of Greece *(1979) 1 C.L.R. 10). More recently, in the case of* Stylianou & Others v Papacleovoulou and Another *– Civil Appeal No. 6163, delivered on 24.9.82, – it pronounced proprietary estoppel is applicable in Cyprus, by virtue of the provisions of s.29(c) of the Courts of Justice Law – 14/60. However, in that case, the relationship between the person asserting property rights and the registered owners, was not that of purchaser and vendor. The registered owners were bare trustees, having done, years ago, all in their power to divest ownership of the property and pass it on to the person from whom the plaintiffs had acquired the land. That they did not accomplish their intention, was due to a mistake that was liable to be rectified. Thereafter, they reinforced by their conduct the belief in the plaintiff that he had no property whatever in the land in question. In those circumstances, the Court found that the plaintiff could assert proprietary estoppel and formally divest the original owners of their property in land.*

Moreover, in *Miltiadous v Miltiadous*,[50] it was decided that:

Equitable interests, arising from a trust relationship, are susceptible to precise

50 *Miltiadous v Miltiadous* ((1982) 1 CLR 797), p800.

definition, and in appropriate circumstances may become the subject of registration. The trial Court correctly observed that s.4 of the Immovable Property (Tenure, Registration and Valuation) Law, Cap. 224 expressly exempts trusts from the network of the law, a proposition recently affirmed by the Supreme Court in Odysseos v A. Pieris Estates Ltd. and Another.

In *Christoforou v Christoforou,*[51] it was held that Article 65IE of Cap 224 does not exclude the principles of equity in relation to resulting or constructive trusts.

Courts will enforce constructive trusts in relation to immovable property in Cyprus. In *Pantelis Charalambides v Georgiou Andrea Constantinou*[52] there was a tenancy agreement between the owner and a tenant over the immovable property. Before the tenancy expired, a new owner acquired the property by public auction, having notice of the tenancy. The Supreme Court held that a contractual tenancy of immovable property grants rights to the tenant against the new owner who acquires ownership before the termination of the tenancy, even where the new owner was not party to the tenancy agreement. The rights of the tenant emanate from the tenancy agreement and the new owners are obliged to respect and meet the tenancy obligations as trustees, including the obligation to allow the tenant peaceful possession of the property for the duration of the tenancy agreement.

In *Christos Clerides v Herodotus Stavrides*, the Supreme Court considered that the representations made by the deceased to his cohabitee partner that the apartment would be hers, constituted clear testimony of the common intention that the apartment belonged to her. The court found that the cohabitee partner spent her afternoon hours carrying out the tasks and work of the deceased, which affirmed common intention. A constructive trust was thus created in favour of the cohabitee partner.[53]

4.2 Constructive trusts and proprietary assets of spouses

Holding immovable property under trust does not exclude the jurisdiction of the Family Tribunal under Cyprus law.[54] According to Sections 2 and 14 on the Regulation of Property Relations of Spouses Law (232(I)/1991), the Family Tribunal has exclusive jurisdiction to adjudicate proprietary disputes between spouses.[55] Therefore, the Family Tribunal has jurisdiction to hear claims from spouses for contribution under Section 14(1) where the immovable property is under trust, even where the property is held in favour of the spouse by a third

51 *Christoforou v Christoforou*, Civil Appeal 8559 ((1998) 1 AAD 1551).

52 *Pantelis Charalambides v Georgiou Andrea Constantinou* ((1996) AAD 709).

53 *Christos Clerides v Herodotus Stavrides*, Civil Appeal 8918 and 9064 ((1997) 1 AAD 1348).

54 Christos Clerides, *The Cyprus Law of Equity*, (Nomiki Bibliothiki, 2021), p160. See also *Kourou v Konou*, Civil Appeal 325/2009, 10 October 2014.

55 See *Re Manolis Yiangou* ((1991) 1 AAD 703); *Logginou v Logginou* ((2000) 1 AAD 1347); *Philippou v Philippou* ((2003) 1 AAD 1343); *Michael v Yiangou* ((2001) 1 AAD 1643).

party (who may be a natural or legal person) under trust, and the trustee is included as a necessary party in such an application.[56] In fact, most cases involving resulting or constructive trusts relate to proprietary disputes between divorcing spouses.

4.3 Constructive trusts and power of attorney

It is often the case to appoint a person to act as a power of attorney to execute transactions on behalf of a principal. In general, the granting of a power of attorney does not create a trust relationship. If there is a breach of the terms of the power of attorney, then the principal may challenge this under agency, contract law or tort. The court may only determine that a trust is created under the principles of equity where there are reasons that extend beyond the contractual determination of the rights and obligations of the parties.[57]

Exceptionally, where the power of attorney is used beyond its authorised purpose – for example, where a wife grants a power of attorney to her husband to withdraw money from her bank account to cover her medical bills, and the husband withdraws the balance in the account, the husband will then be deemed to hold the funds under a constructive trust for her estate and is liable to return funds to the administrators of her estate. The persons who received the funds from the husband were aware of the circumstances and are therefore also obliged to return the moneys.[58]

Other categories of trust that are recognised under English law may also be recognised under domestic law, such as secret trusts and bare trusts.

5. Trusts created according to legislative provisions

Here we consider express private trusts according to legislative provisions, as well as trusts that satisfy express formalities required under legislative provisions, such as will trusts, CITs and trusts over immovable property. Trusts created during the lifetime of the settlor are usually (though not necessarily) in writing. In relation to the following types of trust, formalities ought to be satisfied. Where a fiduciary provider is providing fiduciary services, the requirements of the law must be met.[59] Moreover, there are registration and reporting requirements for trusts established in Cyprus.[60]

---

56 *Prest v Petrodel Ltd* ([2013] 3 WLR 1); *Perikleous v Englezou* ((2011) 1 AAD 1015). Christos Clerides, *The Cyprus Law of Equity*, (Nomiki Bibliothiki, 2021), pp160–161.

57 Christos Clerides, *The Cyprus Law of Equity*, (Nomiki Bibliothiki, 2021), pp157–158; see also *Omex Enter Ltd v Elia*, Civil Action 469/12, 20 September 2019.

58 *Constantinides v Tsirides*, Civil Appeal 386/2006 ((2006) 1 AAD 1435).

59 See the section 5.12 in the chapter "The Cyprus International Trusts Law 1992–2012: new dynamics" by Chrysthia Papacleovoulou-Vassiliou.

60 See below section 5.5 and 6.1 and the "Trusts and ultimate beneficial ownership registers in Cyprus" chapter by Eleni Drakou.

5.1 Will trust

A will trust may be created by way of testamentary disposition prior to the death of the testator. In accordance with Section 23 of the Wills and Succession Law (Cap 195), no will is valid unless it is in writing and it is executed by:

- the signature at the bottom of the page by the testator or a person that acts for the testator in their presence and under their instructions;
- the signature is signed or recognised by the testator in the presence of two or more witnesses present at the same time;
- the testators confirm and co-sign the will testament in each other's presence, with no other formality is required; and
- if the will testament consists of more than one piece of paper, then each sheet must be initialled or signed by or on behalf of the testator and the witnesses.

5.2 Charitable trusts

Cyprus international charitable trusts may be created under Section 7 of the Cyprus International Trusts Law, where the trust has as its main purpose the achievement of one or more of the following:

- the relief of poverty;
- the advancement of education;
- the advancement of religion; and
- other purposes beneficial to the public in general.

An international trust established for one or more of these objects or purposes will be deemed to be charitable notwithstanding:

- that the object or purposes may not be of a public nature or for the benefit of the public, but may benefit a section of the public, or that it may benefit particularly one or more persons or objects or persons within a class of persons;
- that the international trust is liable to be modified or terminated, whether by the exercise of a power of appointment or the disposition of assets;
- that the trustee has the power to defer the distribution of the benefits to any charity of the trust for a period not exceeding the period of the trust; or
- that the international trust is or is considered to be in the category of discretionary trusts.

The rule against perpetuities will not render void or voidable such a charitable international trust.

5.3 Cyprus international trusts[61]

A CIT may be described as a trust created by a non-resident settlor for the benefit of non-resident beneficiaries. A trust can still qualify as an international trust for the purposes of law even if the settlor, trustee or beneficiaries are corporate entities or partnerships. To establish a CIT, all the following criteria[62] must be met:

- The settlor must not be a resident of Cyprus in the year preceding the year of the creation of the international trust.
- No beneficiary, other than a charity, is a resident of Cyprus in the year preceding the year of the creation of the international trust.
- There must be at least one trustee resident in Cyprus at all times.

The Income Tax Laws 2002 to 2016 assign the meaning to the term 'resident of the republic'. The settlor, trustee or any one or more of the beneficiaries may be a partnership or a company.

Effectively, a CIT that was established during or after the entry into force of the Cyprus International Trusts Law 2012 has no limit on the period over which an international trust may continue to be valid and enforceable. Accordingly, the 2012 law abolishes all restrictions on the duration of trusts. Moreover, excluding express terms of the trust to the contrary, no concession, distribution, payment, holding or disposal of the income or capital of the trust to another trust is invalidated merely by reason that the other trust continues to be valid and enforceable after the date on which the first trust ceased to exist.

5.4 Local trusts

A trust that fails to meet the criteria for the establishment of a CIT will be deemed a local trust governed under the Trustees Law (Cap 193) and the principles of equity. The Cyprus trust is a local trust whereby the settlor, the trustees and the beneficiaries are Cypriot and the trust property may include immovable property in Cyprus. The Cyprus local trust is governed by the Trustees Law (Cap 193) enacted in 1955 and based on the English Trustees Act 1925 and by the doctrines of equity and case law as it was applied in England before the independence of Cyprus in 1960.

Local trusts can be classified as:

- a discretionary trust;
- a fixed trust;
- a combination of a fixed trust and a discretionary trust; and
- a declaration of trust.

---

61 See section 4.1 in chapter "The Cyprus International Trusts Law 1992–2012: new dynamics" by Chrysthia Papacleovoulou-Vassiliou.

62 Section 2 of the Cyprus International Trusts Law.

5.5 Trust over immovable property in Cyprus

According to Section 4 of the Immovable Property Law (Cap 224), common law and equity are expressly excluded as a legal basis for the acquisition of rights in immovable property.[63] Trusts are exempt from this exclusion of the principles of equity under Section 4. Under Section 65IE of Cap 224, it is implied that Section 4 does not include a trust.[64] Section 65IE(1) provides that no trust that relates to immovable property is valid unless it is created by trust deed signed by the person entitled to this or by a will. The trust deed or will is submitted to the registry of trusts of the lands registry office that has competence. Express trusts that satisfy the formalities of Section 65IE are valid and binding in relation to immovable property and may be enforced for the purposes of the trust or for specific performance purposes.[65]

It is not necessary to use technical terms to create an express trust, although to be registrable this must be evidenced in writing. It is sufficient that the settlor indicates with reasonable certainty:

- the intention to create the trust;
- the property that is subject matter of the trust;
- the persons (natural or legal) that are intended to be beneficiaries; and
- the purpose of the trusts so that the trust can be operative.

Whether an intention to create the trust exists sufficiently is a matter of interpretation in each case and may be induced from the content.[66] Section 65IE requires a trust deed and its deposit to the competent lands registry, that is the district lands registry where the immovable property is situated. Section 65IE leaves no room for interpretation, there must be a deed that expressly states that this deed intends to create a trust.[67]

6. Public registries and stamping requirements

6.1 Trust registry

Pursuant to Article 61C(4)(a) of the Prevention and Suppression of Money Laundering Terrorist Financing Law (188(I)/2007), the Cyprus Securities and Exchange Commission establishes and maintains a Beneficial Ownership Register of Express Trusts and Similar Legal Arrangements, in which information regarding express trusts, similar legal arrangements and their beneficial owners is submitted and the Trusts Beneficial Owners Registry is kept. The registration, disclosure, management, keeping and updating of information on beneficial

---

63 *Cyprus Cinema & Theatre Co Ltd v Christodoulos Karmiotis* ((1967) 1 CLR 42), *Aspasia Millington-Ward v Chloi Roubina* ((1970) 1 CLR 88).

64 As amended by Law 2(I)/78.

65 *Pantelis Charalambides v Georgiou Andrea Constantinou* ((1996) AAD 709).

66 See Christos Clerides, *The Cyprus Law of Equity*, (Nomiki Bibliothiki, 2021), p140.

67 *Eliades v Papakyriakou*, Civil Appeal 220/2012, 27 November 2018.

owners of express trusts and similar legal arrangements, and access to this registry, is carried out.[68]

6.2 Stamping requirement

Under the Cyprus Stamp Duty Law, as amended by Law 173(I)/2012 and effective as of 1 March 2013, stamp duty is payable on any document that concerns any property situated in Cyprus or matters or things to be executed or done in Cyprus, irrespective of the place of execution of the document. CITs are subject to a fixed stamp duty of €430. Where the deed establishing the trust (other than a CIT) declares no value, it is deemed to be a deed with no specific fixed value, and the stamp duty is €34.17. Where the deed establishing the trust (other than a CIT) specifies the value of the trust property, then the stamp duty is assessed on the basis of this value.[69] The stamp duty is payable within 30 days of the date of the deed. Stamping is possible after 30 days from the date of the deed, subject to the payment of a penalty. The fine is calculated based on the time that elapsed up to the date of stamping.[70] For a testamentary will or will trust, the stamp duty is €18.

---

68 See the "Trusts and ultimate beneficial ownership registers in Cyprus" chapter by Eleni Drakou.

69 The stamp duty is payable based on the value on the deed. For deeds with a value of €1 up to €5,000, no stamp duty is payable. Where the value on the deed is between €5,000 up to €170,000, the stamp duty payable is €1.50 for every €1,000. Where the value on the deed is over €170,000, the stamp duty payable is €2 for every €1,000 up to €20,000.

70 Non-stamping of the trust deed does not render the trust deed invalid. If a trust deed is challenged or sought to be enforced in court, then the stamp duty must be paid. This is subject to the general rule that deeds that are subject to stamp duty cannot be accepted as admissible evidence in court – except for criminal proceedings – unless such deeds are duly stamped (Section 36). In such a case, the deed must be stamped and the amount of the stamp duty, penalty and interest be paid.

Vakfs: the Islamic version of trusts

Paolo Panico
Private Trustees SA; Chair – STEP Europe

The Evcaf and Vakfs Law (Cap 337) was enacted in Cyprus on 22 October 1955 to regulate the creation and administration of *vakfs*, also known as *wakfs*, *waqfs* or closer to the original Arabic plural word *awqaf* (or *evcaf*). *Vakfs* are Islamic legal arrangements that can serve some of the functions for which trusts have developed and are used in the common law tradition.

An analysis of the Cypriot Evcaf and Vakfs Law will benefit from a comparison with another similar legislative experience in the British Empire, the Mussalman Wakf Validating Act 1913 of India. The word *vakf* will be used in this chapter to refer to the legal institution under Cypriot law and *wakf* for the general Islamic legal arrangement, particularly the one regulated under Indian law.

It is suggested that *wakfs* may stand at the origin of the development of trusts in Medieval England and that the incorporation of Merton College in Oxford in 1274 may have been influenced by the Islamic experience of Koranic schools (*madrassas*), which were usually organised in properties held on *wakf*.[1]

The Evcaf and Vakfs Law was enacted expressly with a view to dealing with matters that were relevant for the Turkish Cypriot community, to the extent that most mosques traditionally consisted of properties held in *vakf*. On this basis, and in light of the current political situation in Cyprus, this topic may trigger some understandable political frictions. Further, some aspects of the administration of *vakfs* under the Evcaf and Vakfs Law are problematic, if not impossible, as a consequence of the institutional changes that followed the Turkish military invasion of the northern part of the island in 1974.

Nevertheless, an analysis of the Evcaf and Vakfs Law, and more generally of the institution of the *vakf*, may provide some useful insights into the possibility of creating a *vakf* in the form of an international trust governed by the Cyprus International Trusts Law (Law 69(I)/1992), as amended in 2012 (Law 20(I)/2012). At a time when some of the traditional markets for the Cypriot professional and financial sectors appear likely to shrink, a new offer in the

1 M Gaudiosi, "The influence of the Islamic law of *Waqf* on the development of the Trust in England: the case of Merton College", *University of Pennsylvania Law Review* 136 (1987–1988), 1231–1261.

form of a *shari'a* compliant version of trust could be a useful addition to the international attractiveness of the island. The existence of a legal framework dating back to the British Empire on *vakfs* and a flexible, state-of-the-art trust law allowing to structure them in the form of international trusts could be a successful combination permitting Cyprus to aspire to become a fiduciary centre for Islamic finance.

1. *Wakfs* under Islamic law and the Indian Mussalman Wakf Validating Act 1913

The word *wakf* comes from an Arabic root meaning 'detention' or 'making a thing stop and stand still'. It relates therefore to the holding of property for specified purposes. A valid *wakf* must always include a charitable purpose and this is the case for the *wakfs* that have traditionally been created as endowments to fund and maintain mosques, schools, hospitals and charitable institutions for the benefit of the poor. Nonetheless, a *wakf* can also be created for the benefit of subsequent generations of a specified family – provided, however, that a default charitable purpose is expressly specified.

In other words, an Islamic *wakf* can be described as an equivalent arrangement to a trust for the benefit of the settlor's family across generations with a mandatory charitable purpose that must be furthered either immediately or on default after the extinction of the settlor's family. In this context 'charitable' must be construed in compliance with the principles of Islamic law.

The validity of private purpose *wakfs* appears to be confirmed by the following quotation from the Prophet Muhammad: "A pious offering to one's family, to provide against their getting into want, is more pious than giving alms to beggars. The most excellent of sadaka (charity) was that which a man bestowed upon his family."[2]

This principle was expressly quoted by Lord Hobhouse in the Privy Council decision *Abu Fata Mahomed Ishak v Russomoy Dhur Chowdhry*.[3] The Judicial Committee of the Privy Council, the highest court of the British Empire, heard a number of appeals relating to *wakfs* from all the Muslim populated colonies and territories of the Empire, the majority originating from India.[4] It is fascinating to review such judgments and to witness how a board of British judges attempted to apply Islamic law with a view to securing uniformity of treatment of the relevant matters across the Empire.

The judgment in *Abu Fata* is relevant because the *wakf* in question was in

---

2 Quoted in M Stibbard, D Russel QC and B Bromley, "Understanding the *waqf* in the world of the trust", *Trusts and Trustees* 8, 18 (2012), 785 at 786-787.

3 (1894) Law Rep 22 Ind Ap 76 (PC).

4 A review of all the Privy Council judgments from India on *wakfs* between the mdi-19th and the mid-20th century is made by Muhammad Zubair Abbasi, "The Judicial Committee of the Privy Council and the Muslim Endowments (Awqaf)", Contemporary Primary Sources, Court Cases, 1437/13, June 2016, https://beta.shariasource.com/documents/1918.

fact a family settlement in perpetuity where the charitable purposes would come into play, if at all, only after the death of the last family member and the consequent extinction of the family. The Privy Council held that such a perpetual family settlement was void, as it would have been the case had it been an English law family trust intended to last in perpetuity.[5] The judgment caused considerable dissatisfaction in the Muslim community in India, to the point that the Mussalman Wakf Validating Act 1913 was enacted with a view to providing statutory grounds to the prevailing practice of family *wakfs*. It may be useful to read the relevant sections of the Indian act by way of comparison to the corresponding piece of legislation introduced 40 years later in Cyprus.

Section 2 defines the notion of '*wakf*':

In this Act, unless there is anything repugnant, in the subject or context –

(1) 'Wakf' *means the permanent dedication by a person professing the Mussalman faith, of any property, for any purpose recognised by the Mussalman law as religious, pious or charitable.*

(2) 'Hanafi Mussalman' *means a follower of the Mussalman faith who conforms to the tenets and doctrine of the Hanafi School of Mussalman law.*

The Hanafi school was founded by Abu Hanifa (699–767 AD) and is one of the four main Sunni schools of Islamic law. Since the Moghul emperors of India were followers of the Hanafi school, it remains the most common school of Islamic law in India.

Section 3 of the Mussalman Wakf Validating Act 1913 deals expressly with the purposes of a valid *wakf*:

It shall be lawful for any person professing the Mussalman faith to create a wakf *which in all other respects is in accordance with the provisions of Mussalman law, for the following among other purposes:*

(a) for the maintenance and support wholly or partially of his family, children, or descendants, and

(b) where the person creating the wakf *is a Hanafi Mussalman, also for his own maintenance and support during his life-time, or of the payment of his debts out of the rents and profits of the property dedicated:*

Provided that, *the ultimate benefit is, in such cases, expressly or impliedly reserved for the poor or for any other purpose recognised by the Mussalman law as a religious, pious or charitable purpose of a permanent character.*

Finally, Section 4 of the same act clarifies that a *wakf* will not fail for remoteness of its charitable purpose:

No such wakf *shall be deemed to be invalid, merely because the benefit reserved for the poor or other religious, pious or charitable purpose of a permanent nature is postponed until after the extinction of the family, children or descendants of the person creating the* wakf.

5 On the rule against perpetuities, see the "Perpetuity and duration" chapter by Paolo Panico.

This piece of legislation thus established that a *wakf* can be validly created as a family settlement with a charitable purpose as its ultimate benefit in default. The 1913 act was not retroactive and as a result it applied only to *wakfs* created after its entry into force on 7 March 1913. The Mussalman Wakf Validating Act 1930 was then enacted on 25 July 1930 to extend the validity of these provisions to all the *wakfs* created before 7 March 1913.

To appreciate the other requirements for a valid *wakf* it is now useful to review the five essentials of a *wakf* according to the Hanafi school of Islamic law:[6]

- permanent dedication of property;
- the *wakif* must be competent;
- the *wakif* must be the owner of the property;
- the object must be religious; and
- it must be unconditional.

It will have been noted that the Indian 1913 act expressly mentions a "charitable purpose of a permanent character". A *wakf* must be a permanent dedication of property that lasts in perpetuity. As a result, a condition that in case of mismanagement the *wakf* must be terminated and its property divided among the heirs of the settlor – or *wakif* – makes the *wakf* invalid.[7] For the same reason, a *wakf* for a set, limited duration is also invalid.[8] As a result, the person creating the *wakf*, known as the *wakif*, cannot reserve power to revoke the *wakf* unless the *wakf* is created by will. In such case, the testator can always revoke their will during their lifetime, irrespective of the provisions relating to the creation of a *wakf*.[9]

One of the reasons for the permanent duration and irrevocability of *wakfs* is that the ownership of the *wakf* property is not vested in the *wakf* administrator or *mutawalli* (*Mutevelli* in the Cypriot Evcaf and Vakfs Law). Unlike the trustee of a trust, the *mutawalli* of a *wakf* is not the owner of the *wakf* property, only its manager. Presently, when a *wakf* is created and comes into being, the *wakf* property vests in Allah the Almighty. This explains why a *wakf* must be irrevocable and perpetual, unlike an English law trust that may be revoked if the settlor reserves the relevant power and must comply with the rule against perpetuities. Another consequence of this doctrine is that in principle the *mutawalli* cannot sell, mortgage or lease the *wakf* property unless they are expressly empowered to do so under the terms of the *wakf*.

On the creation of a *wakf*, the dedicated property vests in the Almighty and ceases to belong to the person who created the *wakf*. Consequently, another

6 NH Jhabvala, *Principles of Muhammadan Law*, 23rd edn (Jamnadas, 2002).
7 *Habib Ashraff v Syed* ((1933) 144 IC 654).
8 *Mst Peeran v Hafiz Mohammed* (AIR 1966 All 201).
9 *Muhammad Ashan v Umardaraz* ((1906) ILR 28 All 633).

requirement for the creation of a valid *wakf* is that the person creating it, the *wakif*, is a competent individual and the owner of the property that is dedicated to the *wakf*. The mere negotiation to purchase a property does not make a person its owner and as a result a *wakf* of that property is invalid.[10]

Similarly, if a condition is imposed on the dedication of property to a *wakf*, the *wakf* is invalid from the outset. It is the case of a *wakf* where some property was originally settled for the benefit of the *wakif* and her children with a view to transferring it to the children on their reaching a certain age and to some religious purposes if the *wakif* were to die without children. The *wakf* was invalid because the religious purpose was contingent on the *wakif* dying without children.[11]

Under the Hanafi legal school, the creation of a *wakf* is a unilateral declaration that is valid without the participation or acceptance of the *mutawalli* or *wakf* administrator. A mere declaration of endowment by the owner of the property is sufficient to create a valid *wakf*.[12] If the *wakif* remains in possession of the dedicated property they do so as trustee for the *wakf*. The creation of a *wakf* by a unilateral declaration by the *wakif* is thus equivalent to the creation of a trust by a unilateral declaration by the settlor.[13] A registration requirement pursuant to the Indian Registration Act 1908 applies only if the *wakf* includes immovable property.

The ultimate object of a *wakf* must be charitable, pious or religious according to Islamic law. The non-exhaustive list of valid objects for a *wakf* includes:[14]

- mosques and provision for imams to conduct worship therein;
- colleges and provision for professors to teach in colleges;
- aqueducts, bridges and caravanserais;
- distribution of alms to poor persons and assistance to the poor to enable them to perform the pilgrimage to Mecca;
- repairs of *imambaras* (apartments in private houses set apart for the performance of Muslim ceremonies);
- celebrating the death anniversary of the *wakif* and of members of their family;
- burning lamps in a mosque;
- reading the Koran in public places as well as in private houses;
- performance of annual *fateha* (recital of prayers for the welfare of the

10 *Masih-ud-din v Ballabh Das* ((1913) ILR 35 All 68).

11 *Pathukutti v Avathalakutti* ((1883) ILR 13 Mad 66).

12 *Mohammad Yasin v Rahmat Illahi* (AIR 1947 All 201).

13 The *Shia* school on the other hand considers the *wakf* as a bilateral contract and requires that the dedicated property must be delivered to the *mutawalli*. For the Shia Muslims an *inter vivos wakf* cannot come into being until the *mutawlli* comes in possession of the dedicated property.

14 M Hidayatullah and A Hidayatullan, Mulla's *Principles of Mahomedan Law*, 19th edn (LexisNexis Butterworths, 2004).

souls of deceased people accompanied with the distribution of alms to the poor) for the *wakif* and their family;
- construction of free boarding houses for the pilgrims to Mecca;
- payment of money to the poor and to fakirs; and
- constructing a school, college, mosque or hospital.

As it was mentioned earlier, these objects must be specified in the creation of a *wakf*, but they need not be pursued immediately. A *wakf* may be valid even though such purposes are just its default objects, which may start to be furthered after the extinction of the *wakif*'s family.

The office of *mutawalli* may be initially undertaken by the *wakif*, who reserves the right to appoint successor *mutawalli*s and to lay down the rules governing the line of succession. Women may be appointed *mutawalli* if the role does not involve the performance of spiritual duties that are forbidden to women under Islamic law.[15] In case of a vacancy, if the *wakif* or their executor does not appoint a new *mutawalli*, the power to make the appointment vests with the court.

2. *Vakfs* under the Cypriot Evcaf and Vakfs Law

The principles laid down under Indian law reflect the prevailing Islamic practice in relation to *wakfs*, particularly in accordance with the Hanafi school. The same principles, with some slight variations, can be recognised in the Cypriot Evcaf and Vakfs Law.

The definition of a '*vakf*' is provided in the following terms under Section 2 of the Law: "'*vakf*' means the permanent dedication by a person professing the moslem faith of any property in order that the use of, or the income accruing from such property may be devoted to any charitable purpose."

The instrument creating the *vakf* is known as *vakfieh*.

2.1 Requirement to create a valid *vakf*

Similar to the Indian law, any competent persons professing the Muslim faith may dedicate some property they own to a *vakf*. Section 5 of the law provides that: "Any person of the moslem faith competent to contract may dedicate any property, which he may dispose, as a *vakf*." Section 6(2) further requires that: "No property may be dedicated as *vakf* unless the dedicator at the time of the dedication is the owner thereof."

Stricter formal requirements were introduced under the Cypriot law than under the Hanafi school of Islamic law that is followed in India. Section 8 provides that:

No dedication shall be valid unless –

---

15 *Hussainbi v Khairuddin* (AIR (1939) Bom 487).

(a) if made inter vivos

(i) its declaration is made in writing in any appropriate words showing an intention to make a dedication by way of a vakf;

(ii) the written declaration of vakf *is signed by the dedicator in the presence of at least two witnesses, competent to contract, and where the dedicator is illiterate in the presence of two such witnesses and a certifying officer subscribing the same as witnesses and certifying the signature as certifying officer;*

(iii) is registered as in Section 9 provided;

(b) if made by will the provisions of Section 10 are complied with.

A Cypriot *vakf* is therefore a unilateral declaration in the same way as under the Hanafi school. However, a valid Cypriot *vakf* must be created in writing and the declaration of *vakf* must be registered according to Section 9: "(1) The dedicator or his duly authorised agent shall present the *vakfieh* to a Judge within the jurisdiction of whom he resides or the subject of the *vakf* is situated."

The word 'judge' is defined under Section 2 as "a judge of a Turkish Family Court" and as a result this provision is currently not workable. One could envisage to register a declaration of *vakf* with a district court or perhaps more aptly to use the provisions of the Cyprus International Trusts Law to achieve the same features of a valid *vakf* in the form of an international trust, as is further discussed in section 3 of this chapter.

2.2 Objects of a *vakf*: family and charitable

Section 6 specifies the objects of a valid *vakf*:

(1) Subject to the provisions of subsection (2), the object of dedication shall be charitable.

(2) No dedication shall be made for an object which –

(a) is unlawful or prohibited by Islam;

(b) is of a limited duration;

(c) if at the time of the dedication it appears that it will fail;

(d) is subject to a contingency;

(e) consists of the repair or upkeep of a private tomb except that of a saint;

(f) is not defined with certainty.

The notion of 'charity' is defined in Section 2 in terms of: "any purpose for the relief of poverty, the advancement of education, the advancement of religion or any other purpose beneficial to the moslem Turkish community."

Apart from the express reference to the Turkish Cypriot community, which is unlikely to be operational for the time being, it will be apparent that the first three items correspond to the first three 'heads of charity' specified by Lord Macnaghten in *The Commissioner for Special Purposes of the Income Tax v Pemsel*.[16]

16 [1891] AC 531.

This definition of 'charity' is consistent with a *hadith* by the Prophet Muhammad, who was recorded saying: "When a man dies, all his acts come to an end, but three: recurring charity (*sadaka gariya*) or knowledge (by which people benefit), or a pious offspring who prays for him."[17]

However, Section 12 confirms that life interests and limited estates can be created under a *vakf* in the same way as under the Indian Mussalman *Wakf* Validating Act 1913:

> *Subject to the ultimate benefit being, expressly or impliedly, reserved for any charitable purpose, provisions may be validly made in a declaration of* vakf –
>
> *(a) for the benefit of a succession of persons, during their lives, or during specified periods and notwithstanding that at the time of the declaration of* vakf *or the making of vakfieh the said persons are not in being;*
>
> *(b) for the maintenance and support wholly or partially of the family, children, or descendants of the dedicator or the maintenance of the dedicator himself during his lifetime or fir the payment of his debts out of the rents and profits of the subject of the* vakf.

A *vakf* for the benefit of the dedicator's family across subsequent generations is therefore valid provided that its ultimate purpose is charitable in compliance with Islamic law.

Part III of the law, which includes sections relating to the interpretation of a declaration of *vakf* (*vakfieh*), provides some further clarifications to this effect. Section 15 explains that:

> *Where the* vakfieh *refers to one or two generations of the descendants of a specified person as being entitled to the benefit of the* vakf, *the benefit shall be confined to the said generations. But where three generations or more are referred to, the benefit shall be for the descendants in perpetuity, so long as they exist.*

Section 19 introduces a presumption that concurrent beneficiaries will be entitled to equal shares of benefit under the *vakf*, unless a different intention is expressly specified:

> *(1) Where several objects or beneficiaries are referred to in a* vakfieh, *they take the benefit of the* vakf *concurrently or simultaneously and in equal shares, unless there is anything to show an intention that they should benefit in a different proportion or in succession to one another.*

Section 20 provides for the default charitable purpose of a *vakf* once a family of beneficiaries is extinct:

> *(1) In the absence of anything showing a contrary intention the interest of a beneficiary shall lapse on his death and shall accrue to the benefit of the poor or other ultimate charitable object of the vakf.*
>
> *(2) Where it is provided, either expressly or impliedly, in a* vakfieh *that the*

17 Quoted in M Stibbard, D Russel, QC and B Bromley, "Understanding the *waqf* in the world of the trust" (2012) 18 *Trusts and Trustees* 8, 785.

descendants of the beneficiaries thereunder shall succeed to the respective interests of the said beneficiaries, and there is nothing to show a contrary intention, the said descendants shall succeed per stirpes and not per capita, and males and females shall take equal shares.

The last provision is a significant departure from the traditional Sunni succession rule, where female heirs usually take half the share of the male heirs.

Section 27 provides for the case where a *vakf* is created for different objects, some of which are possible and lawful under an Islamic perspective, while some are not. A general approach is to save the *vakf* to the extent possible, in relation to its lawful and possible purposes, so that only the unlawful or impossible ones will fail:

(1) Where some of the objects for which a vakf *is purported to be made fails or cannot be given effect to, the validity of the other objects of the* vakf *is not thereby affected, except as provided in this section.*

(2) Where a vakf *is created for mixed purposes, some of which are unlawful ort prohibited by Islam (hereinafter referred to as 'unlawful purpose'), effect shall be given to those purposes which are lawful and, so much of the property as is dedicated for the unlawful purpose shall revert to the dedicator or his personal representatives:*

Provided that where the property so dedicated is immovable property which cannot be divided such property shall be sold by public auction and the proceeds of the sale shall be divided proportionately between the vakf *and the dedicator or his personal representatives.*

(3) When in construing the terms of a vakfieh *the beneficiaries or its object are found to be not in existence, the benefit of the* vakf *property shall be given to the poor, provided that if at any time thereafter, the said beneficiaries or the object come into existence, such beneficiaries or object shall be entitled to the said benefit.*

2.3 Main features of a *vakf*

Part IV of the law defines the main features of a *vakf*, which are in line with the main tenets of Islamic law.

Section 22 provides that a *vakf* must last in perpetuity:

A dedication by way of vakf shall be in perpetuity:

Provided that in cases where a vakf *is not expressed or does not purport to be limited in point of duration it shall be presumed to be made in perpetuity, and effect shall be given to it accordingly.*

Section 23 introduces a general principle that *vakf* property is inalienable:

On the registration of a vakfieh *under Section 9, the subject of the* vakf *cannot thereafter, subject to the provisions of this Law, be alienated or transferred either by the dedicator or the Mutevelli nor may their heirs take it by way of inheritance.*

This principle is consistent with the doctrine that the *vakf* property ceases to belong to the dedicator but does not vest in the *Mutevelli*. As we have seen in section 1 of this chapter, the *vakf* property is deemed to belong to Allah the Almighty. However, some exceptions may be introduced to the general principle of inalienability under the terms of the instrument creating the *vakf* according to Section 25:

(1) A vakfieh *may validly empower the dedicator to exchange any land forming the subject of the* vakf *for other land, or to sell the land and to purchase other land of equivalent value in exchange therefor:*

Provided that the dedicator may not validly exchange or sell the vakf *land except in strict accordance with the terms of the* vakfieh.

(2) The land taken in exchange or purchased as in subsection (1) provided, shall become subject of the vakf *and shall be registered in accordance with the provisions of Section 9.*

In other words, if the terms of the *vakf* so provide, the *vakf* property may be sold or exchanged and the proceeds of sale or the property received in exchange will be subject to same *vakf* and undergo the required registration formalities. In this respect, the *vakf* property has the same nature of a trust fund, where the composing elements may change but the dedication of the overall fund continues to apply.

An unauthorised attempt to alienate *vakf* property is set out under Section 24: "Where the subject of a *vakf* is unlawfully alienated any person interested in the object of the *vakf* may apply to the Court to have the alienation set aside and effect given to the *vakf*."

The word 'court' in this context is defined according to Section 2 as the 'Supreme Court'.

2.4 The *Mutevelli*, their powers and duties

Part VI of the law regulates the office of *Mutevelli*, the equivalent of a trustee under a *vakf*.

The rules concerning the appointment of a *Mutevelli* and the succession to their office are specified by the dedicator in the instrument creating the *vakf*. Section 28 provides that:

The dedicator may provide in the vakfieh *for the appointment of a person or persons to act as the manager ort administrator of the* vakf, *in this Law referred to as 'the* Mutevelli*', and of a successor or successors to such* Mutevelli, *and may specify the conditions on which, the manner in which, the period for which, and the person by whom, the* Mutevelli *and his successors may be appointed.*

Provided that where a Mutevelli *is resident outside the Colony the High Council shall be the* Mutevelli *for all intents and purposes.*

The High Council is the High Council of *Evcaf* established under the law, which would make this last provision unworkable at present. However, to the extent that the *Mutevelli* is resident in Cyprus, no issue will arise in this respect.

The dedicator may reserve the right to remove the *Mutevelli*, but in the absence of an express provision in this respect the appointment is irrevocable. Section 30(2) provides that: "A *Mutevelli* once appointed cannot be removed by the dedicator unless there is a specific provision thereof in the *vakfieh*."

The following persons may be appointed as *Mutevelli* under Section 29(3), provided that they are of sound mind and not incapacitated:

(a) any person appointed by the dedicator to be a Mutevelli*;*

(b) the descendants of any person appointed by the dedicator to be a Mutevelli*;*

(c) the dedicator himself

(d) the children or descendants of the dedicator of the vakf*;*

(e) any other person who is a moslem:

Provided that in cases where the *Mutevelli* has to perform religious or spiritual functions which cannot be performed by a female, a female shall not be appointed.

Section 29(3)(a) appears to allow the appointment of a non-Muslim *Mutevelli*. The dedicator of a *vakf* must be "a person professing the moslem faith" according to the definition under Section 2 but the *Mutevelli* must not necessarily be a Muslim and the office may also vest in a woman provided that it does not involve religious functions or services that are reserved for men under Islam.

Although the legal ownership of the trust property does not vest in the *Mutevelli*, unlike in the case of a trustee, the powers associated with the two offices are quite similar. Under Section 29(2): "A *Mutevelli* shall have the power to do all acts which are reasonable and proper for the protection of the *vakf* property and for the management or administration of the *vakf* property."

Similar to a trustee, a *Mutevelli* shall have a duty to diligently manage the *vakf* property and to account for it. Section 38 specifies these duties:

It shall be the duty of every Mutevelli *of a* vakf –

(a) to administer vakf *properties diligently and in a business-like way;*

(b) to prepare once every year and not later than the first day of March, a true statement of accounts of the vakf *property in respect of the preceding year supported with vouchers or receipts and submit the same to the High Council, through the Director, for consideration by the High Council.*

The reference to the High Council is a consequence of the ultimate charitable nature of a *vakf*. This provision is not applicable at present but the principle remains that a *Mutevelli* has a duty to account for their stewardship of the *vakf* property in a similar way to a trustee.

The prohibition from the alienation of the *vakf* property, established under Section 23, is confirmed in relation to the *Mutevelli*'s powers under Section 34:

(1) The Mutevelli *shall not sell or mortgage the* vakf *property in the absence of any provision in the declaration of vakf authorising him to do so:*

Provided that the Court may order the sale of vakf *land if satisfied that it has become unfit for the objects of the* vakf.

> *(2) Any* Mutevelli *acting without such authority shall be deemed to be guilty of a breach of trust for which he may be removed by an order of the Court.*

It is significant that the phrase used in Section 34(2) is 'breach of trust', which impliedly confirms the very close nature of a *vakf* and a trust.

Section 33 introduces a further restriction on the *Mutevelli*'s ability to borrow from the *vakf* property that is intended to avoid any conflicts of interest:

> *In the absence of any express provision to that effect in the* vakfieh, *the* Mutevelli *as such shall not borrow any money for any purpose whatsoever save by an order of the Court given on consideration of the case and upon the recommendation of the High Council:*
>
> *Provided that he may borrow such sums as the Judge may authorise him to do for the payment of Government taxes.*

This rule appears to reflect a prohibition against self-dealing that applies equally to trustees.

Similar to a trustee, who may be authorised to withdraw a remuneration out of the trust fund, a *Mutevelli* may be authorised to receive a remuneration under Section 31(2) and (3):

> *(2) The* Mutevelli *may lawfully take from the income of the* vakf *such remuneration as the dedicator or the Judge may have authorised him to receive.*
>
> *(3) The remuneration of a* Mutevelli *shall not exceed one-tenth of the income of the* vakf *where the* Mutevelli *has no beneficial interest in the subject of the* vakf*: Provided that the Judge may, upon a review of the funds and surplus available, increase the said remuneration as he may think fit.*

As per the workability of these provisions in practice, it must be remembered that the word 'judge' is defined in Section 2 as "a judge of a Turkish Family Court".

3. *Vakfs* in the form of Cypriot international trusts

The Evcaf and Vakfs Law provides a comprehensive regulation of the Islamic legal arrangement known as *vakf*. Its provisions rely on the extensive experience of the Privy Council in judging appellate cases from all over the British Empire. To this effect, it provides a detailed guidance to the creation and functioning of a *vakf*.

However, the law was essentially intended for the Turkish Cypriot community and many of its references to the Turkish Family Court and the High Council of *Evcaf* are not applicable in practice.

This legislative experience may be the starting point to create a *vakf* in the form of a Cypriot international trust under the Cyprus International Trusts Law 1992, as amended 2012. The rest of this section attempts to demonstrate that an international trust can be organised in such a way as to reflect all the salient features of a *vakf*, thus potentially opening a new market for 'Islamic trusts' under Cyprus law.

As we have seen, the dedicator of a *vakf* (ie, the person dedicating property under the terms of a *vakf*) must be "a person professing the moslem faith". This is not contrary to the requirement under Section 2 of the Cyprus International Trusts Law that the settlor is not a resident of Cyprus during the calendar year immediately preceding the creation of the trust. Very few Muslims have lived in the free part of the island since the Turkish military occupation of 1974, but a number of Muslims from the Middle East may consider Cyprus as an appealing jurisdiction to create a *shari'a* compliant trust, irrespective of whether they intend to transfer their residence to the islands after that.

At least one of the trustees of an international trust must be resident in Cyprus for the whole duration of the trust. This is not inconsistent with the definition of a *Mutevelli* under Section 29(3) of the Evcaf and Vakfs Law. As we have seen in the preceding section of this chapter, the office of *Mutevelli* may even be held by a non-Muslim. The dedicator might consider appointing themself or another trusted person as co-trustee to make sure that the *vakf* is managed in full compliance with the principles of Islamic law. In any event, provided that at least one co-trustee is resident in Cyprus, the trust can be governed by the Cyprus International Trusts Law.

Unlike a traditional trust, which is subject to the rule against perpetuities, a *vakf* must be perpetual. This can be easily accommodated under Section 5 of the Cyprus International Trusts Law, as amended in 2012, which provides that:

(a) there shall be no limit on the period for which a trust continues to be valid and enforceable, and

(b) no rule against perpetuities or remoteness of vesting ort any analogous rule applies to a trust or o any advancement, appointment, payment or application of property from a trust.

The main feature of a *vakf* is that it must have an ultimately charitable purpose, which is recognised as valid, lawful and charitable under Islamic law, and at the same time it may provide for the dedicator and his family across generations. Section 7 of the Cyprus International Trusts Law, as amended in 2012, provides for international trusts for a charitable purpose. Subsection 7(1) lists all the purposes that may considered to be charitable and expressly includes "(a) the prevention or relief of poverty" and "(c) the advancement of religion", which in the case of a *vakf* must obviously be the Muslim religion.

Subsection 7(2) expressly provides that:

An international trust established for one or more of the objects or purposes set out in subsection (1) shall be deemed to be charitable, notwithstanding that –

(a) The object or purposes are not of a public nature or for the benefit of the public, but may benefit a section of the public, or that it may also benefit privately one or more persons or objects or persons within a class of persons; or

...

(c) the trustee has the power to defer the distribution of the benefits to any charity of the trust for a period not exceeding the period of the trust.

On this basis, a *vakf* can be organised as an international charitable trust for a lawful purpose under Islam and simultaneously provide for the immediate benefit of the dedicator's family. The charitable nature of the trust is not affected by the circumstance that any payments for charitable purposes may not take place until the extinction of the dedicator's family. This is consistent with the practice of Islamic *vakfs*, as we have seen in a review of the corresponding experience in India.

This construction of a *vakf* provides that some of its beneficiaries may be unborn at the moment of the creation of the *vakf*. This may be a problem under the rule against perpetuities in the case of a Cypriot domestic trust under the Trustee Law 1955 (Cap 193), as discussed elsewhere in this book. Section 2 of the Cyprus International Trusts Law defines a 'beneficiary' as a legal or natural person "including a person not yet born at the time of the creation of the trust".

Another construction issue may relate to the doctrine under which the title to the *vakf* property does not vest in the *Mutevelli*, who is thus merely the manager or administrator of such property that ultimately belongs to Allah the Almighty. The definition of 'trustee' under Section 2 of the Cyprus International Trusts Law is flexible enough to include a person who "is deemed to hold or have had trust property transferred to him ... (a) for the benefit of a beneficiary irrespective of whether the trustee is also beneficiary of the trust; and/or (b) for any purpose which is not for the exclusive benefit of the trustee".

In other words, the transfer of legal title to the trustee is not mandatory for an international trust under Cypriot law and a different arrangement, as in the case of a *vakf*, can still be validly governed by the Cyprus International Trusts Law if the other conditions are met.

Section 4 of the Cyprus International Trusts Law introduces a presumption that an international trust is deemed to be irrevocable unless the trust instrument contains an express power of revocation. For the purposes of a valid *vakf* such a power cannot be reserved and the international trust will be deemed to be irrevocable by default.

Section 4A of the Cyprus International Trusts Law, which was inserted under the amending law of 2012, allows the settlor of an international trust to retain "any right or interest to the trust property" or any of the powers listed in subsection 4A(2). In particular, paragraph 4A(2)(e) allows the settlor to retain the power "to appoint or remove any trustee, enforcer, protector or beneficiary". Enforcers and protectors do not usually exist under a *vakf* but the power to appoint or remove trustees is equivalent to a dedicator's power to appoint and remove *Mutevellis* under the terms of a *vakf*.

This high-level analysis shows that the main features of a *vakf* can be carefully crafted under a properly drafted international trust governed by the

Cyprus International Trusts Law. This is still a largely unexplored path in the profession but it may have some potential to open a new market for Cyprus international trusts in the context of Islamic finance.

Charitable trusts and charitable organisations

Eleni Drakou
Michael Kyprianou & Co LLC

1. Charitable trusts

Estate planning and the preservation of family wealth can be managed through a Cyprus international trust (CIT). A CIT can also be established for the promotion of charitable and philanthropic purposes, ultimately benefiting the country, a particular community or even a smaller group of persons. The crucial element is to serve a noble and worthy project.

To establish a charitable CIT, the provisions of the Cyprus International Trusts Law 1992 (69(I)/1992), as amended, should be met. In addition to the rest of the provisions, the object of the charitable trust should be aligned with Section 7 of the law, which states specifically under which categories a trust can be deemed charitable.

Section 7 states that, subject to the provisions of the Constitution of the Republic of Cyprus and notwithstanding the provisions of any other law or regulations of Cyprus or any other country, an international trust will be deemed charitable where the trust has as its main purpose the achievement of one or more of the following:

- the prevention or relief of poverty;
- the advancement of education;
- the advancement of religion;
- the advancement of health or the saving of lives;
- the advancement of citizenship or community development;
- the advancement of the arts, culture, heritage or science;
- the advancement of amateur sport;
- the advancement of human rights, conflict resolution or reconciliation, or the promotion of religious or racial harmony or equality and diversity;
- the advancement of environmental protection or improvement;
- the relief of those in need by reason of youth, age, ill health, disability, financial hardship or other disadvantage;
- the advancement of animal welfare and the protection of animals; and
- any other purpose beneficial to the public in general or which may reasonably be considered relevant to any of the preceding points.

The international trust established for one or more of the objects or purposes set out above will be deemed to be charitable, notwithstanding that:

- the objects or purposes are not of a public nature or for the benefit of the public, but may benefit a section of the public, or that it may also benefit privately one or more persons or objects or persons within a class of persons;
- the international trust is liable to be amended or terminated, whether by the exercise of a power of appointment or disposition of assets;
- the trustee has the power to defer the distribution of the benefits to any charity of the trust for a period not exceeding the period of the trust; or
- the international trust is or is deemed to be in the class of discretionary trusts.[1]

Notwithstanding any legal provision to the contrary of Cyprus law or the law of any other country, an international trust will not be void or voidable by reason only that it is a trust for a purpose, provided that when the trust is not a perpetual trust or when it may be terminated, the instrument creating the trust will specify the event or events on which the trust terminates and provides for the disposition of the net assets of the trust on its termination. An international trust so created will be enforceable by the settlor or their personal representatives or enforcer.[2]

A charitable trust can be set up *inter vivos* by the settlor, as per the provisions of the Cyprus International Trusts Law, through a trust deed or following the settlor's death through a will. The trust deed is signed between the settlor and the trustees. It can indicate the conditions under which the trust property will be transferred to the trustee, as well as the purposes and objects of the trust, provided that they are in line with Section 7. The settlor can provide the trustees detailed or general guidance on how to serve the trust's causes. Such guidance can be further elaborated in a letter of wishes. Alternatively, the settlor may instruct the trustees to decide on how best to promote the trust's purposes.

The charitable trusts are considered purpose trusts since a particular cause is stated for the trust's establishment. Purpose trusts should specify the trust's termination event and include provisions for the disposition of the trust's assets on termination.

While the Trustee Law (Cap 193) limits the number of trustees to four, Cap 193 states specifically that such a limitation does not extend to charitable trusts, which can therefore have more than four trustees.[3]

Before its amendment in 2012,[4] the previous Cyprus International Trusts Law

---

1 The Cyprus International Trusts Law, 69(I)/1992, Section 7(2).
2 *Ibid*, Section 7(3).
3 The Trustee Law (Cap 193), Section 34.
4 The Cyprus International Trusts Law, amended, 20(I)/2012.

provided that international trusts were valid for a maximum period of 100 years from the date of their establishment. The charitable trusts and the purpose trusts were exempt from such a limitation, hence emphasising their significance for existence in perpetuity. However, with the amendment of Law 20(I)/2012, such limitation in duration has been lifted for all trust categories, as such there is no time limit regarding the duration that a trust may continue as valid and enforceable.[5]

While the Cyprus International Trusts Law states that 'international trust' means a trust in respect of which no beneficiary, whether a natural or legal person, is a resident of Cyprus during the calendar year immediately preceding the year in which the trust was created, charitable trusts are specifically exempt by law from such limitation.[6]

2. Charitable institutions

Besides the establishment of a charitable trust as per the Cyprus International Trusts Law, a charitable trust can be established by virtue of the Charities Law (Cap 41). The Charities Law aims at the operational and administrational aspects of a trust without targeting a holistic treatment of charitable trusts, hence it does not provide a definition for the term 'charity'. The charities or charitable trusts result from equity law and their definition and evolution is based on case law.[7]

The Charities Law provides that trustees of any charity promoting educational, literary, scientific or public charitable purposes, can apply to the Council of Ministers for a certificate of registration of the trustees of any such charity as a corporate body.[8] Therefore, the issuance of the certificate of incorporation aims to the functioning and representation of the charity, which through the certificate becomes a corporate body having continuous succession and power to sue and to be sued with its incorporation name, as well as to possess, acquire, transfer, assign and bequeath any movable or immovable property for the benefit of the charity.[9] If the Council of Ministers considers such incorporation expedient, it may grant the certificate of incorporation accordingly. The certificate may include conditions or directions with regard to the qualifications and number of trustees, their tenure or avoidance of office and the mode of appointing new trustees.

The trustees of an incorporated charity will consequently become a corporate body by the name described in the certificate of incorporation, and will have perpetual succession and a common seal, of which the device will be approved by the Council of Ministers. The trustees will have the power to sue and to be sued in their corporate name, and to hold, acquire, transfer, assign

5 The Cyprus International Trusts Law, Section 5(1).
6 *Ibid*, Section 2(c).
7 *Hadjinicolaou Theodora v the Ephorate of Greek Schools of Nicosia* ((2011) 1 AAD 789).
8 The Cyprus Charities Laws (Chapter 41), Section 2.
9 *Hadjinicolaou Theodora v the Ephorate of Greek Schools of Nicosia* ((2011) 1 AAD 789).

and bequeath any movable or immovable property for the purposes of the charity.[10]

The application to the Council of Ministers for a certificate of registration must be filed in writing and signed by the persons submitting the application. The application should include the following:

- the charity's objects, rules and regulations, together with the date of, and the parties of every deed, will or other instrument creating, constituting or regulating the charity;
- a statement and short description of the movable and immovable property, which is possessed by, belongs to or is held on behalf of the charity, at the date of the application;
- the names and places of residence of the trustees of such a charity;
- the proposed name of the corporate body; and
- the proposed device of the common seal, which will, in all cases, bear the name of the corporate body.[11]

The certificate of incorporation forms evidence of the charity's compliance with the Charities Law. The issued certificate is under the hand and official seal of the Council of Ministers and is published in the *Official Gazette of the Republic of Cyprus*, forming conclusive evidence that all the preliminary requisitions required in respect of such incorporation have been complied with. The date of incorporation stated in the certificate is deemed to be the date on which the incorporation took place.[12]

The registration benefits the trustees by creating an irrefutable presumption that the institution is indeed charitable and as such is entitled to the privileges conferred to such an institution. On the other hand, an institution that is not registered, in case its charitable status is being questioned, should obtain a decision to that end through a court.[13]

The charity that is created according to the provisions of the Charities Law and by receiving a certificate of incorporation by the Council of Ministers, forms a legal entity of private law. As such, the charity does not perform actions that fall within the domain of public law, irrespective of whether the government is involved in any way in the charity. Therefore, the definition of matters arising from the charity's actions or omissions fall within the jurisdiction of the Supreme Court by virtue of Section 13 of the Charities Law, not within the frame of Article 146 of the Constitution for appeal against public actions.[14]

---

10 The Cyprus Charities Laws (Chapter 41), Section 2.
11 *Ibid*, Section 4.
12 *Ibid*, Section 7.
13 *Hadjinicolaou Theodora v the Ephorate of Greek Schools of Nicosia* ((2011) 1 AAD 789).
14 *Florentia Petridou v Oncology Center Bank of Cyprus* ((2005) 3 AAD), www.cylaw.org/cgi-bin/open.pl?file=apofaseis/aad/meros_4/2002/rep/2002_4_0177.htm&qstring=%E1%E3%E1%E8%EF%E5%F1%E3%2A%20and%20%E9%E4%F1%F5%EC%E1%2A.

Before a certificate of incorporation is granted, the charity's trustees must have been effectually appointed in pursuance of the terms of any deed, will or other instrument creating the charity, to the satisfaction of the Council of Ministers. Following the issuance of the certificate of incorporation, any vacancies in the number of trustees that occur from time to time can be filled as required by the constitution or settlement of the charity, by such legal means as would have been available for the appointment of new trustees of the charity as though no certificate of incorporation had been granted. The appointment of each new trustee will be certified by, or by the direction of, the trustees to the administrative secretary on the completion of such appointment. Within one month after the expiration of a five-year period from the date of issuance of the certificate, or whenever required by the Council of Ministers, a report of the trustees' names and places of residence must be submitted by the trustees to the administrative secretary.[15]

Following the issuance of the certificate of incorporation, all trustees of the charity, notwithstanding their incorporation, will be liable and chargeable for any property that comes into their hands, and will be accountable for their own acts, receipts, neglects and defaults and for the due administration of the charity and of its property, in the same manner and to the same extent as if no such incorporation had taken place.[16]

As per Section 12 of the Charities Law, every deed, will or other instrument creating a charity will be enrolled by depositing the same, with the office of the Registrar of the Supreme Court. A true copy certified by the registrar of the instrument deposited in their office or a true copy of an instrument executed outside Cyprus and deposited in their office, will be received as evidence of the instrument's contents and of its enrolment. Nonetheless, there is no sanction in case the instrument creating the charity is not deposited with the registrar in such a way that it is considered the charity does not exist or that it is not charitable. Section 12 provides that the certification of the deposited instrument is considered in any case as evidence on the content of the instrument and that the same has been duly enrolled with the Registrar of the Supreme Court. Therefore, there should be no consequences on the content of the instrument from the non-enrolment to the Supreme Court provided that it is accepted that a charity has been established through the instrument. Nor does the issuance of a certificate of incorporation by the Council of Ministers on the charitable purposes of the institution affect it in any way, provided that the rest of the requirements on the establishment of the institution are met.[17]

Unincorporated charities can exist and cannot be invalidated by either the

15 The Cyprus Charities Laws (Chapter 41), Section 5.

16 *Ibid*, Section 6.

17 *Hadjinicolaou Theodora v the Ephorate of Greek Schools of Nicosia* ((2011) 1 AAD 789).

failure of the trustees to apply for incorporation or the rejection of an application by the Council of Ministers. Ultimately, it is the trustees' right whether to apply for incorporation, considering the advantages that they can enjoy, as well as their responsibilities (eg, bookkeeping and auditing their accounts).[18]

An essential requirement of any charity incorporated under the Charities Law is the obligation of its trustees to regularly maintain accurate books, full and true accounts of all moneys received and paid respectively on account of each charity, and to prepare and submit to the administrative secretary at the end of every year:

- an account of the gross income arising or which ought to have arisen for the benefit of the charity during the year ending 31 December last year;
- an account of all balances in hand at the commencement of every year, and of all moneys received during the same year, on account of the charity;
- an account for the same period of all payments; and
- an account of all moneys owing to or from the charity, so far as is convenient.[19]

The Council of Ministers may at any time order that the accounts of the trustees be audited by the director of audit or any other person that they may deem fit to appoint.[20]

The Cyprus Supreme Court has power and jurisdiction to enforce every trust created for a charitable purpose, to give all such directions and make all such orders as may appear necessary or expedient for the administration of any trust created for a charitable purpose, as well as to sanction the sale or other disposition of any property subject to a charitable trust on being satisfied that such sale or disposition is for the benefit and advantage of the charity.[21] The powers of the Supreme Court deriving from Section 13 are exercisable in all charities, incorporated or not. These powers were intended by the legislature to form a measure for the protection of charities, in addition to the incorporation and enrolment of deeds.[22] The provisions of Section 13 essentially grant the Supreme Court with power and jurisdiction, among other things, to implement every trust that is established for charitable purposes. By virtue of Article 21(1)(b) of Law 14/60 as amended with Law 51/1984, the jurisdiction of the Supreme Court will be read as the jurisdiction of the district courts.[23]

---

18 *Municipality of Nicosia v Constantinos Adamides* ((1980) JSC 158), www.cylaw.org/cgi-bin/open.pl?file=jsc/files/1980/1980_0158.html&qstring=charit%2A%20and%20trust.

19 The Cyprus Charities Laws (Chapter 41), Section 10.

20 *Ibid*, Section 11.

21 *Ibid*, Section 13.

22 *Municipality of Nicosia v Constantinos Adamides* ((1980) JSC 158), www.cylaw.org/cgi-bin/open.pl?file=jsc/files/1980/1980_0158.html&qstring=charit%2A%20and%20trust.

23 *Hadjinicolaou Theodora v the Ephorate of Greek Schools of Nicosia* ((2011) 1 AAD 789).

The attorney general will be a party to all proceedings under the Charities Law and may at any time stay such proceedings and compromise or authorise the compromising of any matters in dispute. No compromise made without the authority of the attorney general will be valid. All such proceedings will be instituted by the attorney general with regard to the enforcement of the charitable trust. Proceedings regarding the administration of the charitable trust or the sale or disposition of any property subject to the trust, can be instituted by the attorney general or by the trustees of the charity if authorised by the attorney general in writing, as per the provisions of the Charities Law.[24]

The provisions of Cap 41 are sufficiently clear, irrespective of the certificate by virtue of Section 2 or the filing of the instrument by virtue of Section 12 to the Supreme Court, the attorney general has extensive power over the procedures arising for the implementation of a charitable trust for the protection of the bequest, to exclude, among others, distant relatives or persons who have only an indirect interest in the protection of the bequest from initiating lawsuits affecting the proper functioning of the charitable institution. With regard to the charities, the attorney general seeks to implement the charity for the benefit of the public – or part of it – for which the charity was established and operating. Therefore, the attorney general acts as *parens patriae*, meaning that their involvement in the whole process is required. Besides, in general, in the law of trusts the initiator of the process should be a beneficiary or *cestui que* trust. To that end, Section 13(a) of the Charities Law provides power to the court to implement every trust established for a charitable purpose without limiting such implementation to trusts being registered under Cap 41 or for which their instrument has been submitted before the Registrar of the Supreme Court.[25]

Section 15 of the Charities Law states that all proceedings under this law will be instituted, heard and determined by the Supreme Court in accordance with the law relating to charitable trusts presently in force in England. However, as it was ruled by the Supreme Court, such provision will have no implementation following the establishment of the independent, sovereign Republic of Cyprus in 1960 and as such the legislation that led to the evolution of charities in England since then is not applicable.[26]

Ruling on a case of establishment of a charity through a will, the court found that a charitable bequest is not considered void for uncertainty merely because the body of persons for whose benefit it is given is large and fluctuating (*Re Brown* (1888) 1 Ir R423) or because it gives the testator's trustees a wide power of selection. Nor does the limited amount of the bequest make it void for uncertainty. The legacies are not conditional that the fund should be sufficient

24 The Cyprus Charities Laws (Chapter 41), Section 14.
25 *Hadjinicolaou Theodora v the Ephorate of Greek Schools of Nicosia* ((2011) 1 AAD 789).
26 *Ibid.*

to benefit all the objects of the charity. A scheme must be prepared and the regulations should include relevant provisions.[27]

3. Charitable organisations

Besides charitable trusts and charitable institutions, persons wishing to serve noble and worthy projects can do so through private organisations that can be registered to serve and promote non-profitable purposes. Cyprus legislation provides for different entities of organisation for charitable or non-profitable purposes, with each is subject to the relevant legislation.

Cyprus has been very active in the establishment of non-profitable organisations for the promotion of education, culture, the environment, community, and medical research, as well as the support of vulnerable groups or patients of particular diseases, professional and sports bodies and other worthy causes.

The main forms of charitable organisation that are used frequently in practice are the associations, foundations, federations and unions of organisations, organisations that are registered abroad and are active in Cyprus, and not-for-profit companies. These organisations, besides being non-profitable, are established on a voluntary basis and are non-governmental organisations.

3.1 Clubs

The Associations and Foundations and Other Related Issues Law 2017 (104(I)/2017) was voted for by Parliament, replacing the previous Law on Associations and Foundations of 1972 (N 57/1972) and abolishing the Clubs (Registration) Law (Cap 112). Therefore, legal entities that were established and registered as a club had to make the relevant administration procedures and proceed with their re-registration, this time in the form of an association, a foundation, a federation or a union of organisations, or a not-for-profit company, in order to continue conducting their activities. With the abolishment of the Clubs (Registration) Law (Cap 112), registering a club is no longer available under Cyprus laws.

3.2 Associations, foundations, federations and/or unions of organisations

The Associations and Foundations and Other Related Issues Law defines the non-profit character in relation to an association or foundation, stating that such an association or foundation does not distribute any profits that may arise from its activities to its members, founders, board of directors or officials, but

27 *Christakis Michael Christopoulou v Maria Marianthi Christopoulou and the Attorney-General of the Republic* ((1972) JSC 555), www.cylaw.org/cgi-bin/open.pl?file=jsc/files/1972/1972_0555.html&qstring=charit%2A%20and%20international%20and%20trust.

rather invests or uses those profits towards the continuation and achievement of the association's or foundation's objectives.[28]

As per the provisions of Law 104(I)/2017, the registrar is the district officer who is responsible for the registration and operation of associations, foundations, federations and/or unions of organisations, as well as branches that have their headquarters in the registrar's district. The position of general registrar refers to the permanent secretary of the Ministry of Interior, who is responsible for the implementation of the provisions of Law 104(I)/2017 and the coordination of the registrars, aiming at a cohesive interpretation and implementation of Law 104(I)/2017. The registrar maintains a registry, in which associations, foundations, federations and/or unions are registered under the provisions of Law 104(I)/2017. The registry must be kept updated in electronic form and part of its information must be uploaded to a relevant website.[29]

An association or foundation or federation and/or union acquires its legal personality on its entry into the registry and the issuance of the relevant certificate by the registrar. The legal personality is lost on the organisation's dissolution. The capacity of an association or foundation or federation and/or union that has acquired a legal personality does not extend to legal relationships that require the attributes of a natural person.[30]

An association or foundation or federation and/or union that constitutes an unlawful organisation,[31] or whose objectives or operation aim or tend to undermine Cyprus, the democratic institutions, the safety of Cyprus, the public order, public safety, public health, public morals, the fundamental rights and freedoms of the individual, or the rights of people with disabilities, will have no legal existence and cannot be registered, or if it is already registered, may be dissolved by an order of the court ruling the organisation unlawful.[32]

In particular, as defined by the Criminal Code, 'unlawful organisation' means:

- any group of persons with or without legal personality, which by its constitution or propaganda or that it otherwise advocates, incites or encourages to overthrow the constitution of Cyprus by revolution or sabotage;
- the overthrow by force or violence of the established government of Cyprus, or of any other civilised country, or of organised government; or
- the destruction or injury of property of Cyprus or of property used in trade or commerce with other countries or in Cyprus.

28 Law 104(I)/2017, Section 2.
29 *Ibid*, Section 2.
30 *Ibid*, Section 5.
31 As defined in Article 63 of the Criminal Code.
32 Law 104(I)/2017, Section 4(1).

The organisation might be deemed unlawful even if it is or appears to be affiliated or in any way connected with such groups of persons[33] and as a result cannot be registered.

In order to ensure transparency and good governance of organisations, Law 104(I)/2017 introduced a new provision stating that the members of the board of directors cannot be permanent employees of the organisation and cannot receive remuneration for any services rendered.[34] However, members of the board of directors may claim the reimbursement of reasonable expenses incurred during the implementation of their duties, and may participate and receive payment from research projects or other projects funded or co-funded by third parties, provided that a relevant provision is included in the organisation's articles of association.

Law 104(I)/2017 provides for the replacement of a member of the board of directors in case such a member has been convicted of a criminal offence involving lack of integrity or moral obscenity. If the organisation itself does not proceed to replace the person in question, the registrar may do so, either on their own initiative or following a complaint.[35]

Moreover, Law 104(I)/2017 provides for exclusion of a member of the board of directors from procedures in cases of impediment or conflict of interest and, in particular, exclusion from a discussion or a vote during which a decision must be taken in relation to a legal transaction or the filing or cancelling of a lawsuit between the organisation and that member or their spouse or a blood relative or relative by matrimony up to the third degree. If a decision is taken against these provisions, then such a decision may be declared void.[36]

The members of the administration of associations, foundations and federations and/or unions are bound to keep accurate and detailed accounting books, in which all the movements of the organisations' funds are recorded. Moreover, at the end of every financial year, they are bound to prepare:

- the gross income accounts of the organisation for the duration of the financial year;
- the credit balance account as it appeared at the start of the financial year; and
- all the amounts received during the financial year, as well as an account of all the amounts due and owed, and of all the payments made during the financial year.

The accounts of the organisations are audited by a certified accountant at the organisation's own expense. Associations, federations and/or unions with

33 The Criminal Code, Article 63.
34 Law 104(I)/2017, Sections 18A, 26(2), 44(3)(g).
35 *Ibid*, Sections 16(2), 32(2).
36 *Ibid*, Sections 17(1), 21(3), 33(1).

an annual income lower than €40,000 are not required to submit accounts certified by an accountant. The accounts and the audited reports must be filed with the registrar within seven months of the end of each financial year, at the latest.[37]

Law 104(I)/2017 states in detail the required content of the articles of association of each organisation.[38] In particular, the articles of association should include the organisation's name, address, scope, terms of admission, withdrawal and expulsion for members, the members' rights and obligations, its financial resources, provisions for in-court and out-of-court representation, its administrative bodies and their election terms.

3.3 Associations

An association is an organised union comprising at least 20 people, aiming to achieve a not-for-profit common objective, and does not include political parties or trade unions.[39] The association's objectives must be stated in detail in its articles of association.

It is essential at all times to maintain 20 members, otherwise the association might be dissolved. In such a case, the dissolution will not be concluded automatically, but it can be concluded after six months have lapsed since its membership fell below 20, and provided that within that period the names of no new members have been given to the registrar to achieve the required minimum number.[40]

For the establishment of a new association, the (minimum) 20 founding members must sign the founding act and appoint the board of directors.

For the purpose of the registration of associations in the registry, an application in writing is made to the registrar by the founders or the administration of such an association, to which are attached the act of incorporation, the names, addresses and contact details of the members of the administration, the articles of association signed and date by the founding members, the logo of the association (if it exists), and a description of the movable and immovable property possessed by or belonging to the association at the time of the registration.[41] On approval of the application for registration by the registrar, the association's name will be published in the *Official Gazette of the Republic of Cyprus* and will be included in the Registry of Associations. The association will receive a certificate of registration stating the association's registry number.

The associations are administered by a board of directors consisting of at

37 *Ibid*, Section 49.
38 *Ibid*, Sections 8, 44.
39 *Ibid*, Section 2.
40 *Ibid*, Section 24(1)(b).
41 *Ibid*, Section 7(2).

least five persons who, unless otherwise stated in the articles of association, are members of the association. Decisions are taken by absolute majority of the members present, unless otherwise stated in the articles of association.[42] The board of directors must attend to the affairs of the association with due care and with respect to the laws of Cyprus. The board represents the association in court and out of court, unless otherwise stated in the act of incorporation or the articles of association. Any legal action undertaken by the board of directors within the scope of its powers is binding to the association. The board of directors is obliged to maintain a registry of members available for inspection by the registrar and by any third party with a legitimate interest, fully updated at least once a year.[43]

Law 104(I)/2017 introduced a new obligation of the registered associations to inform the registrar of any changes within the first three months of every calendar year. Such changes could relate to the association's postal address, members of its board of directors (including titles and contact details), any new registrations, withdrawals or expulsions of its members, and the convergence of the annual general meeting, including the date, procedure followed and information on the number of members present and quorum. In case the association does not comply, the registrar may put in motion, after giving a notice to that end, the process of dissolution of the organisation.[44]

Moreover, a limitation has been introduced on the members' option to be represented by giving a relevant authorisation and, as such, it is now specifically stated that the membership status cannot be represented, transferred or inherited.[45]

In the event of the association's dissolution for any reason, the redistribution of the association's property among its members is strictly forbidden.[46] Once an association has been, for any reason, dissolved, it is automatically under liquidation. During the liquidation, the property included in the association's assets will be transferred to another entity whose objectives are in line with those of the association under liquidation, as these are stated in the latter's articles of association. Subject to the provisions of any law pertaining to matters of justice, in case the dissolution is not voluntary, the registrar has the right to intervene in the process to ensure the better distribution of the association's property for public benefit.[47]

Any member of the association who withdraws has no right over the property of the association and, moreover, is liable to pay any due subscription fees, unless the articles of association state otherwise.[48]

42 Law 104(I)/2017, Section 16(1).
43 *Ibid*, Section 18.
44 *Ibid*, Section 10.
45 *Ibid*, Section 15.
46 *Ibid*, Section 8(i).
47 *Ibid*, Section 25.
48 *Ibid*, Section 14(1).

3.4 Foundations

A foundation is the totality of the property intended to serve the implementation of a particular not-for-profit objective; for the purposes of the foundation's establishment, the dedicated property cannot amount to less than €1,000.[49]

A foundation may be registered if its main purpose is to achieve:

- the determent or alleviation of poverty;
- the promotion of education;
- the promotion of health or the saving of lives;
- the promotion of the development of citizens and of the community;
- the promotion of the arts, culture, cultural heritage or science;
- the promotion of amateur sports;
- the promotion of human rights or of conflict resolution or reconciliation, or the promotion of religious or ethnic harmony or of equality and of diversity;
- the promotion of the protection or improvement of the environment;
- the relief of the needs resulting from young or advanced age, health problems, disability, economic difficulties or other disadvantage;
- the promotion of the welfare and protection of animals; and
- any other objective that aims at benefiting the public in general.[50]

The incorporation of a foundation is achieved with its registration in the Registry of Foundations kept by the registrar, and with the issuance of a certificate of registration by the registrar. The registration of a foundation is carried out following an application by the founders, or by the trustees or the executors of a will, written in the prescribed form and submitted together with the founding act, as well as the corresponding articles of association.[51]

The founding act includes all contracts, wills or other instruments by which a foundation is incorporated. The founding act is brought about through either a legal action when the founder is still alive or a will. The act must state the name and the objective of the foundation, its seat, its logo, the property allocated thereto, the names, addresses and contact details of the members of its board of directors, and the mode of succession thereof, as well as its articles of association.[52]

On approval of the application for registration, the foundation's name will be published in the *Official Gazette of the Republic of Cyprus*. The foundation's establishment is concluded with its registration in the Registry of Foundations, which is kept by the registrar and with the issuance of the certificate of registration of a foundation by the registrar.[53]

---

49 *Ibid*, Section 2.
50 *Ibid*, Section 26(3).
51 *Ibid*, Section 26.
52 *Ibid*, Section 27.
53 *Ibid*, Section 26(1).

Unless otherwise stated in the founding act, or unless otherwise decided by the registrar, the property of a dissolved foundation comes under the possession of the Republic of Cyprus, which must put it to use in order to serve the objective of the foundation or any other related objective.[54]

As it has been reinstated by the Administrative Court, the foundation is an entity of private law and does not form a public authority, body or person. The state's involvement in the foundation's incorporation, structure, provision of guarantee or funding or even the state's participation in the implementation of public law rules in its activities (eg, procurement for recruitment of its employees under private employment status), does not alter the fact that it is a private law entity and as such does not exercise power or take decisions falling in the scope of public law. Therefore, any omissions by the foundation do not fall within the scope of public law and as such do not fall within the jurisdiction of the Administrative Court.[55] The competent courts for the foundation's acts or omissions will be the district courts.

3.5 Federations and/or unions of organisations

Three or more associations, foundations, not-for-profit companies or other similar not-for-profit legal entities, whether foreign or domestic, that share common objectives, subject to the provisions of the law that governs them, may establish federations and/or unions and be registered as such in a registry kept by the registrar, provided that the applicable law named in their articles of association is the law implemented in Cyprus.

For the registration of a federation and/or union in the registry, a written application by the founders or representatives of the interested organisations comprising the federation and/or union must be submitted to the registrar, including:

- the articles of association of the federation and/or union signed by the founding members and stating the founding date;
- the articles of association of the interested organisations;
- the founding act;
- the names, addresses and contact details of the members of the administration of the federation and/or union;
- the logo of the federation and/or union, if it exists; and
- a description of the movable or immovable property owned by or to be transferred to the federation and/or union after its registration.[56]

---

54 Law 104(I)/2017, Section 43.

55 *Koptides v The Cyprus Institute of Neurology and Genetics* ((2022) 1226/2019), 31 May 2022, www.cylaw.org/cgi-bin/open.pl?file=administrative/2022/202205-1226-19.html&qstring=charit%2A%20and%20%E1%E3%E1%E8%EF%E5%F1%E3%2A%20and%20%E9%E4%F1%F5%EC%E1%2A.

56 Law 104(I)/2017, Section 44.

On approval of the application for registration, the federation and/or union's name will be published in the *Official Gazette of the Republic of Cyprus* and will be included in the registry of federations and/or unions of organisations. The federation and/or union will receive a certificate of registration stating the federation and/or union's registry number. Every federation and/or union established and registered acquires its own legal personality and its own administration, which is different from those of constituent organisations, on issuance of a certificate of registration.[57]

The administration of federations and/or unions is composed of at least three members.

On dissolution of a federation and/or union, it is possible to distribute its property to its members.[58]

3.6 Recognition of organisations registered abroad

Law 104(I)/2017 allows for the registration in Cyprus of organisations that are registered abroad. Such organisations, including associations, foundations, federations or unions of organisations or any non-governmental organisation, should have been registered in a state that has concluded and ratified the European Convention on the Recognition of the Legal Personality of International Non-Governmental Organisations (Treaty 124).

The applicant's legal personality and capacity in Cyprus will be recognised provided that the registration does not collide with national and public safety, crime prevention, the protection of health and public morals, as well as the protection of the freedoms and rights of third parties, and may not jeopardise transnational relations or the maintenance of international peace and security.[59]

3.7 Private non-profit companies

A Cyprus private limited company aiming to serve charitable and non-profitable purposes, can be incorporated as per the provisions of the Companies Law (Cap 113).

To be considered a non-profitable company, such company should prove that its objectives will be the promotion of:

- commerce;
- art;
- science;
- religion;
- charity; or
- any other useful object.

57 *Ibid*, Section 44(4).
58 *Ibid*, Section 45(6).
59 *Ibid*, Section 46.

In case it is proved to the satisfaction of the Council of Ministers that such company further intends to apply its profits or other income in promoting such objects, and prohibits the payment of any dividend to its members, the Council of Ministers may, by licence, direct that the association may be registered as a company with limited liability without the addition of the word 'limited' to its name, enjoying all the privileges and being subject to all the obligations of limited companies.[60]

Therefore, non-profitable companies are obliged to comply with all the obligations of limited companies, including the filing of audited financial statements and annual returns with the Registrar of Companies every year.

Such companies can be incorporated as limited liability companies by guarantee, without share capital. This type of company does not have a share capital and its members act as guarantors rather than shareholders. The liability of the company's members is limited by its memorandum of association, up to the amount that the members have undertaken to contribute respectively to the assets of the company, in case of dissolution.

It is further possible to lift the word 'limited' in the name of an existing company, provided that the above conditions are met. To that end, the company may submit a relevant request to the Registrar of Companies for the omission of the word 'limited' from the company's name due to the company's non-profitable purposes and activities.

The company's memorandum of association should state explicitly that it is a non-profit company. Moreover, the memorandum of association should mention that in the event of the company's dissolution, any surpluses will be distributed exclusively to other non-profit organisations, having similar purposes or comparable to the objects of the company under dissolution.

3.8 Ultimate beneficial owners registry

Establishing and registering charitable organisations is usually straightforward, as the competent laws might set the criteria and the processes to be followed in a comprehensive way. However, charitable organisations are subject to enhanced due diligence and the relevant legislation has been amended recently to reflect the new requirements for compliance.

Aiming to implement the provisions of the Fifth Anti-Money Laundering Directive (EU) 2018/843 of the European Parliament and of the Council, 30 May 2018, amending the Directive (EU) 2015/849 on the prevention of the use of the financial system for the purposes of money laundering or terrorist financing, and amending Directives 2009/138/EC and 2013/36/EU, the Directive on the Prevention and Combating of Money Laundering Activities (Register of Beneficial Owners of Associations, Foundations, Federations or Associations, Charitable

60 The Companies Law (Cap 113), Section 20.

Foundations and Non-Governmental Organisations with legal personality in another state) was published in the *Official Gazette of the Republic of Cyprus* on 19 March 2021.[61] By virtue of this directive, a central registry has been established and is being maintained by the general registrar, a position held by the general director of the Ministry of Interior. The registry records information on the ultimate beneficial owners of non-profitable legal entities, including associations, foundations, federations and unions of organisations, organisations established abroad and recognised in Cyprus by virtue of Section 46 of Law 104(I)/2017, as well as charitable institutions as per the provisions of the Charities Law (Cap 41).

Section 2 of the Prevention and Suppression of Money Laundering and Terrorist Financing Law 188(I)/2007, states that the term 'beneficial owner' refers to the natural person who ultimately owns or controls the customer and/or the natural person on whose behalf a transaction or activity is being conducted and includes at least the following:

a) In the case of corporate entities:

(i) The natural person who ultimately owns or controls a corporate entity through direct or indirect ownership of a sufficient percentage of the shares or voting rights or ownership interest in that corporate entity, including through bearer shareholdings, or through control via other means, other than a company listed on a regulated market that is subject to disclosure requirements consistent with EU law or subject to equivalent international standards that ensure adequate transparency of ownership information. Provided that:

- an indication of direct shareholding will be a shareholding of 25% plus one share or an ownership interest of more than 25% in the customer held by a natural person; and
- an indication of indirect ownership will be a shareholding of 25% plus one share or an ownership interest of more than 25% in the customer held by a corporate entity, which is under the control of a natural person, or by multiple corporate entities, which are under the control of the same natural person or persons.[62]

(ii) The natural person who holds the position of senior managing official if, after having exhausted all possible means and provided that there are no grounds for suspicion, no person under point (i) (above) is identified, or if there is any doubt that the person identified is the beneficial owner – provided that the obliged entity keeps a record of the actions taken in order to identify the beneficial ownership under points (i) and (ii).

61 RAA 119/2021.

62 Provided further that the control by other means can be verified based on, among other things, the criteria provided for in Section 142(1)(b) and Section 148 of the Companies Law (Cap 113).

b) In the case of trusts:
   (i) the settlor;
   (ii) the trustee or commissioner;
   (iii) the protector, if any;
   (iv) the beneficiary, or where the individual benefiting from the legal arrangement or legal entity have yet to be determined, the class of persons in whose main interest the legal arrangement or entity is set up or operates; and
   (v) any other natural person exercising ultimate control over the trust by means of direct or indirect ownership or by other means.

c) In the case of legal entities, such as foundations and legal arrangements similar to trusts, the natural person holding equivalent or similar positions to the person referred to in point b).

4. Taxation

As per the Cyprus Income Tax Law 2002 (118(I)/2002), the income of a religious, charitable or educational institution of public character is exempt from tax.[63]

Moreover, donations or contributions made for educational, cultural or other charitable purposes to charitable institutions that have been licensed as such by the Council of Ministers, will be deducted from the taxable income of a person, legal or natural.[64] Provided that, notwithstanding any provisions of the Income Tax Law to the contrary, in the event of a loss incurred in the year in which such a donation or contribution was made, any part of the loss up to the amount of the donation or contribution will not be carried forward and will not be set off against the income of subsequent years.

A donation contributed for educational, cultural or other charitable purposes to any charitable institution in Cyprus, which is approved by the Council of Ministers to that end, will not be considered as a disposal of property, and as such will be exempt from capital gains tax.[65]

No immovable property tax will be imposed or collected on buildings that are being used solely for the main purposes of any charitable institutions of public character supported mainly through donations or voluntary contributions.[66]

---

63 The Income Tax Law 2002 (118(I)/2002), Section 8(13).
64 *Ibid*, Section 9(f).
65 The Capital Gains Tax Law (52/1980), Section 10(f).
66 The Immovable Property Tax Law 1980 (24/1980), Section 18(e).

The Cyprus International Trusts Law 1992–2012: new dynamics

Chrysthia Papacleovoulou-Vassiliou
Open University of Cyprus

1. Introduction

The evolution of the Cyprus International Trusts Law has been guided by English law and driven by international developments. Cypriot trusts are regulated and governed by the Trustees Law (Cap 193), enacted in 1955, and based on the English Trustees Act 1925, the doctrine of equity,[1] case law as it applied in England and Wales before 1960,[2] and the case law of the Supreme Court of Cyprus. According to established case law, in cases where there is no express or specific legal provision for a particular matter, the Supreme Court has held that reliance may be placed on common law or doctrine of equity as it is applied in England.[3] This is of particular importance for the purposes of interpretation or guidance where no express provision under Cyprus law exists.

Until 1992 it was a valid criticism that Cyprus lacked an international trust law framework. The legislation was outdated and not in synchronicity with international developments, and therefore did not serve the needs of those who wished to use an international trust vehicle.

The need for more attractive and modern trust legislation that would put Cyprus on the map of desirable international trust jurisdictions soon became compelling. To this end, in 1992 Cyprus enacted the Cyprus International Trusts Law 69(I)/1992, establishing the legal framework for the formation and administration of Cypriot international trusts ('CITs'),[4] introducing "certain novel provisions designed to make Cyprus an attractive centre for international trusts".[5]

---

1 Section 29(1)(c) of the Courts of Justice Law 14/1960. Civil and criminal courts were instructed to adhere to the common law and doctrine of equity, "save in so far as other provision has been or shall be made by any law and so long as not inconsistent with the constitution". See A Neocleous and Co, *Introduction to Cyprus Law* (Yorkhill Law Publishing, 2000), p852. In *National Bank of Greece v Masonou* ((1980) 1 CLR 195 (ca)), it was held that equity intervenes to stop the abuse of a legal right and ameliorate the rigidity of contract law, and that equity would be applied where the strict application of contractual rights would manifest injustice. In *Iranian Tanker v Pastella* ((1987) 1 CLR 120), the court affirmed that equity applies as part of national law by virtue of Section 29(1)(c) of Law 14/60. In *Limmare Shipping v Boustani* ((1981) 1 CLR 386), the court upheld the doctrine of promissory estoppel.

2 In 1960 Cyprus became an independent republic. Section 29(1)(c) of the Courts of Justice Law 14/1960 identifies the sources of Cyprus law.

3 *Solomos Stylianou v The Police* ((1962) CLR 152); *A Mouzouris v Xylofagou Plantations Ltd* ((1977) 1 CLR

As new opportunities and investment practices emerged and competition from other trust jurisdictions grew, it transpired that some provisions of the Cyprus International Trusts Law 1992 contained restrictions and limitations that were no longer workable. It was therefore with much enthusiasm that the reform of the Cyprus International Trusts Law was introduced through the enactment of the amending Cyprus International Trusts Law 20(I)/2012 on 9 March 2012. As a result, while the basic structure provided by the Cyprus International Trusts Law 1992 remained, essential amendments were introduced. Most importantly, the amending Cyprus International Trusts Law 2012 extensively modernised the legal regime, aligning it with the needs of the international economy, while maintaining compliance with EU law.

In combination with the stability of the legal system, the established network of double tax treaties, numerous tax arrangements including low corporate tax and favourable taxation for trusts, it is no surprise that Cyprus grew to be regarded as a preferred jurisdiction for the establishment and maintenance of international trusts. CITs are used increasingly for international wealth management, inheritance and succession planning, family and matrimonial arrangements, asset protection, business structuring, tax organisation and planning.

The first part of this chapter presents the Cyprus International Trusts Law 1992, offering critical analysis of the main provisions. The second part of the chapter explains the amendments introduced by the amending Cyprus International Trusts Law 2012 and identifies the major reforms and the new dynamic that further enhanced Cyprus as an international trust jurisdiction. The third part of the chapter considers recent legislative enactments, case law of the Cyprus courts, as well as international and European law developments that affect CITs.

2. Cyprus International Trusts Law 69(I)/1992

The Cyprus International Trusts Law 1992 introduced for the first time the legal framework for the formation and administration of CITs, offering incentives for their establishment.[6] At the material time of the introduction of the 1992 law, the exchange control and income tax laws exempted CITs from income tax, capital gains tax and estate duty tax, making them attractive tax-planning

---

287) at p300. *Constantinou v Democritos Publishers Ltd* ((1996) 1 AAD 206.o), Neocleous, *Introduction to Cyprus Law*, p852. It is also well established that English case law and the case law of the Privy Council and other commonwealth jurisdictions have persuasive weight and are considered by Cyprus courts.

4 In accordance with Section 15 of the Cyprus International Trusts Law 69(I), the provisions of the Cyprus Trustees Law (Cap 193) 1955 will remain in force except insofar as they are inconsistent with or have been modified by the provisions of the Cyprus International Trusts Law 69(I), therefore maintaining the rights and obligations as provided in the Cyprus Trustees Law (Cap 193) and applicable case law.

5 According to the explanatory note to the English translation of the Cyprus International Trusts Law 1992 prepared by the Central Bank of Cyprus, see http://cypruslaw.narod.ru/laws/ITLWE_ITCSLAW.pdf.

6 http://cypruslaw.narod.ru/laws/ITLWE_ITCSLAW.pdf.

vehicles to non-resident settlors for asset protection and tax planning. The 1992 law is applicable to all CITs created after its enactment.[7] The 1992 law builds on existing trust legislation, the Trustees Law (Cap 193), the provisions of the latter remain in force except insofar as they are inconsistent or modified by the 1992 law.[8] Therefore, as Neocleous suggests, the 1992 law "is not a self-contained statute, but rather a law which builds on the existing statutory base".[9]

It is important to highlight that the 1992 law, as amended from time to time, is regarded as a specific legislation on a particular area of law. It is well established by Supreme Court case law that where a specific law or secondary legislation provides for special consideration on specific issues, then the specific provision applies and supersedes any other contrary provisions of the general laws of Cyprus.[10]

3. Revisions by the amending law

3.1 The settlor's and the beneficiary's place of residency

Before the 2012 amendments, the use of CITs was restricted to non-Cyprus residents (settlors and beneficiaries) and for assets situated outside Cyprus. It was unclear whether, after establishing a CIT, settlors or beneficiaries could relocate or take residency in Cyprus, discouraging many from setting up a CIT. The 2012 amendments removed this ambiguity by changing the criterion of the CIT that the settlor and beneficiary must not be residents in the calendar year proceeding the year of creation of the trust.

3.2 Investing in Cyprus movable or immovable property

The 1992 law expressly excluded immovable property in Cyprus from being part of the trust property. One of the reasons was the taxation of the trust that held immovable property. Since the amending law makes provisions as to the taxation of trusts, it is possible now for the trust property to comprise movable and immovable property in Cyprus and abroad, including shares in Cyprus companies.

3.3 Asset protection

A CIT is not void or voidable and no claim can be brought in respect of assets transferred to a CIT in the event of the settlor's bankruptcy or liquidation or in

---

7 Section 13.

8 According to Section 15 of the Cyprus International Trusts Law 69(I)/1992, the provisions of the Cyprus Trustees Law (Cap 193) 1955 will remain in force except insofar as they are inconsistent with or have been modified by the provisions of the Cyprus International Trusts Law 69(I), therefore maintaining the rights and obligations as provided in the Cyprus Trustees Law (Cap 193) and applicable case law.

9 A Neocleous and Co, *Introduction to Cyprus Law* (Yorkhill Law Publishing, 2000), p861.

10 *Port Authority of Cyprus v Larnaca Municipality* ((1998) 4B AAD 1081); και *Tv and Radio Broadcasting Authority of Cyprus v Antenna Ltd* ((2005) 3 AAD 583).

any action or proceedings against the settlor or at the suit of their creditors notwithstanding any provision of the law of Cyprus or of any other country. Any claim can be brought only within a two-year period from the date when the assets have been disposed of under the control of the trustees of the CIT.

3.4 Taxation

Taxation of CITs remains favourable. The 2012 law expressly provides that income and gains from an international trust sourced in or outside Cyprus will be taxed in Cyprus provided that the beneficiary is a Cyprus tax resident. Further, a non-Cyprus tax resident beneficiary will be subject to Cyprus tax only on Cyprus-sourced income. A CIT with non-Cyprus resident beneficiaries and income from non-Cyprus sources continues to be exempt. The new regime may be combined with the non-domiciled tax residency, which offers considerable tax advantages.

3.5 Validity of an international trust and exclusion of foreign law

The new provisions further reinforce the already formidable asset protection features of the CIT and enhanced the exclusive jurisdiction of Cyprus law and Cyprus courts to determine matters in relation to CITs. The law as amended explicitly provides that:

- any question relating to the validity or administration of an international trust or a disposition to an international trust will be determined by the laws of Cyprus, without reference to the law of any other jurisdiction;
- the law relating to inheritance or succession in force in Cyprus, or any other country, will not in any way affect the validity of the international trust or any transfer or disposition of property to it;
- the trustees' fiduciary powers and duties, and the powers and duties of any protectors of the trusts, are governed exclusively by Cyprus law; and
- dispositions to a trust may not be challenged on the grounds that they are inconsistent with the laws of another jurisdiction (eg, regarding family and succession issues) or on the grounds that the other jurisdiction does not recognise the concept of trusts.

3.6 Reserved powers of the settlor

A new section has now been introduced enabling the settlor to reserve powers, retain rights over, or interest in, the trust property, even to act as a protector or enforcer of the trust without these affecting the validity of the trust. Such reserved powers give settlors great flexibility and include:

- the right to revoke, vary or amend the terms of the trust;
- the right to apply trust income or capital or to give directions to this effect;
- the right to act as a director or officer or to give binding directions for the appointment or removal of directors or officers of a company belonging to a trust;

- the right to give binding directions to the trustee in connection with the trust property;
- the right to appoint or remove any trustee, enforcer, protector or beneficiary, investment manager or investment consultant;
- the right to change the governing law or forum of administration of the trust; and
- the right to limit the powers of the trustees by stipulating that these are exercisable only with the consent of the settlor or any other person so specified in the terms of the trust.

3.7 Appointment of protector

Under the new law, it is possible to appoint a protector, which brings CITs in lie with international practices.

3.8 Duration of the trusts: abolition of restrictions

CITs may now be valid indefinitely, avoiding the rule against perpetuities and the 100-year lifespan of trusts under the old law.

3.9 Authorised investments: extension of trustees' investment powers

Before the current amendments of the law, trustees had freedom in terms of investment powers, merely requiring that such powers be exercised in accordance with the trust instrument and with the diligence and prudence that a reasonable person would be expected to exercise when making investments.

The newly amended law gives trustees the same investment powers as those of an absolute owner, allowing them to invest in a broader range of investments for the best interests of the beneficiaries. This brings trustees' investment powers into line with those of a trustee in other international jurisdictions.

3.10 Choice of law clause and public policy

The amending law ensures and guarantees jurisdictional protection of the trust's legal status by providing that an international trust that contains a choice of law clause in favour of Cyprus law is fully protected from unfounded foreign judicial claims as a matter of 'public policy and order'.

3.11 No foreign law can invalidate the transfer or disposition

The Cyprus International Trusts Law provides that no foreign law relating to inheritance or succession will invalidate the transfer or disposition relating to the creation of such trust.

It is useful to analyse the provisions one by one to understand the basic provisions of the original law and grasp the importance and impact of the amendments introduced by the amending law of 2012.

4. Basic provisions under the 1992 law

4.1 Definitions and conditions

The Cyprus International Trusts Law 1992 introduced for the first time both the concept and the definition of a CIT. A CIT is created when the four pre-requisite conditions set out in Section 2 are met. Accordingly, a CIT is a trust where:

- the settlor is not a permanent resident of Cyprus;
- at least one of the trustees of the CIT for the duration of the CIT is a permanent resident of Cyprus;
- none of the beneficiaries, with the exemption of a charitable institution, is a permanent resident of Cyprus; and
- its property does not include immovable property in Cyprus.

The Cyprus International Trusts Law applies to 'international trusts', which are broadly defined as those trusts whose settlor and beneficiary or beneficiaries are not permanent residents of Cyprus and satisfy the dual statutory requirements of:

- at least one resident trustee; and
- no immovable property in Cyprus to be included in the trust assets.

The statutory requirement for the resident trustee in Cyprus ensures that the Cyprus courts have effective jurisdiction over the CIT. Theoretically, the settlor could also be a trustee (the statutory requirement being that at least one of the trustees is a resident) or beneficiary, although this is not recommended.

4.2 Offshore company or partnership as trustee/settlor/beneficiary

'Trustee' means the trustee of the trust and includes a natural or legal person.[11] A Cyprus offshore company or partnership may be the settlor or a trustee, or in fact one or more of the beneficiaries of the CIT.[12] These provisions enhance the attractiveness of the CIT in terms of its administration and tax efficiency.[13]

4.3 Capacity of the settlor

There is a presumption that the settlor has the power to transfer or in any other way to dispose of property assets in a CIT provided that, at the time of such

---

11 Section 2 of the Cyprus International Trusts Law 1992.

12 *Ibid.*

13 Before Cyprus' accession to the European Union in 2004, it was possible for the settlor to set up a Cyprus offshore company or partnership that would be appointed as the trustee of the CIT or one of the beneficiaries. The exemptions and tax incentives that were available to Cyprus offshore companies have been abolished. Currently, there are local Cyprus companies, overseas companies and European companies. A company that is tax resident in Cyprus is taxed on income accruing or arising from sources both within and outside Cyprus. A company that is not tax resident in Cyprus is taxed only on income accruing or arising from sources within Cyprus. A company is tax resident in Cyprus if it is managed and controlled from Cyprus, or it is incorporated or registered in Cyprus but is managed and controlled from outside Cyprus, as long as the company is not considered a tax resident of any other country (this applies from 31 December 2022). The headline corporate income tax rate is 12.5%, certain income is subject to exemptions.

transfer, the settlor is of full age and of sound mind, according to the applicable laws of the jurisdiction where the settlor is a permanent resident.[14]

4.4 Validity of a CIT

The validity of a CIT created by any person who is of full age and sound mind, will be upheld regardless of any other provision of the law of Cyprus or the law of any other country.[15]

4.5 Asset protection and immunity from creditor claims

A trust intended to protect, preserve and insulate the settlor's assets against their creditors or potentially other persons who may have a claim against them, is called an 'asset protection trust'.[16] The Cyprus International Trusts Law 1992 makes specific provision to asset protection trusts. The validity of the CIT is immune from challenges relating to inheritance or succession, the settlor's bankruptcy or liquidation of their property or any action or proceedings against the settlor at the suit of their creditors:

- Although some civil law jurisdictions have rules of inheritance law or succession that potentially conflict with the trust concept, it is expressly provided that the law of inheritance or succession that is applicable in Cyprus or in any other country, will not affect the transfer or disposition or the validity of the CIT.
- Notwithstanding any contrary provisions under Cyprus law or any other country, the settlor's bankruptcy or liquidation of their property or in any action or proceedings against the settlor by creditors will not invalidate the CIT or render it void, even where the CIT is voluntary and without consideration, or is made for the benefit of the settlor, the spouse or children of the settlor, unless and to the extent that it is judicially proven[17] that the CIT was created with the intent to defraud the settlor's creditors at the time of transfer of the settlor's assets to the CIT, and that they were creditors at the time of making the CIT. The onus of proof of such intent on the part of the settlor falls on the creditors.[18]

---

14 Section 3(1) of the Cyprus International Trusts Law 1992.

15 *Ibid.*

16 Three essential features usually differentiate asset protection trusts from normal tax planning trusts: (a) the settlor remains the beneficiary and is very much in control of the 'protected' assets; (b) asset protection trusts are situated in low-tax jurisdictions with particularly favourable legislative provisions for asset protection; and (c) the legislation in question usually allows for a change of the proper/applicable law of the trust. In my opinion, there are at least two more important features: (i) creditors must prove that the trust was created specifically to harm them (burden of proof); and (ii) creditors can bring an action within a specified period (limitation period).

17 In the Greek text of Section 3(2) of the Cyprus International Trusts Law 1992, the term used is "εκτός αν και σε όση έκταση δικαστικά αποδεικνύεται", which could be interpreted as 'the creditor must prove successfully before a Cyprus court of law that the trust was created with the intention to defraud creditors of the settlor at the time of the transfer of the assets of the settlor to the trust'. The unofficial translation in English prepared by the Central Bank of Cyprus at the time reads: "to the extent that it is proven to the satisfaction of the Court."

18 Section 3(2) of the Cyprus International Trusts Law 1992.

Neocleous comments that Section 3 contains specific provisions that allow the CIT to be used as an asset protection vehicle. The combined effect of Section 3 and Section 9, which is the power to determine the proper or applicable law of the trust, "is to render the CIT immune, or at least to a large extent immune, from forced heirship and 'claw back' rules, especially in those cases where the settlor is domiciled in a civil jurisdiction which has forced heirship rules applicable on death".[19] Provisions in other jurisdictions, such as the Statute of Elizabeth, which cuts through arrangements made to hide assets from future creditors, again according to Neocleous, are expressly negated in Cyprus.[20]

A CIT may not be set aside by the settlor's creditors unless there is an intention to defraud creditors at the material time of the transfer of the assets into the CIT and this is proven by the aggrieved. Ostensibly, the Cyprus International Trusts Law 1992 will not shield the settlor from creditors who have pre-existing, prior, current, pending claims or contingent claims against the settlor at the time of creation of the CIT.[21] According to Neocleous, "subsequent creditors, i.e. those who may entertain a claim in respect of future dealings are, however, clearly excluded from the ambit of this provision",[22] if their claim is brought after the two-year time bar. Neocleous suggests that:

> *the key element is whether, at the time of the transfer, the settlor had sufficient property to meet all his liabilities, the property to be transferred to the trust not being included. If this test is satisfied, and, assuming that, the settlor did not anticipate bankruptcy at the time of the setting up of the trust and transferring the property to it, an intention to defraud cannot be proven.*[23]

The Cyprus courts, however, could be willing to accept other evidence by creditors that may suggest such an intention, but it would be necessary to discharge the civil burden of proof for the 'intent to defraud' test at the time of the transfer of the assets into the CIT.

The validity of the CIT may be challenged under this provision by a creditor and not any other person such as an aggrieved family member who is unhappy with the settlement. The creditor will bring such an action to invalidate the CIT against the trustee of the trust, as provided by Section 3(2), within the two-year limitation period.

Section 4(c) does not define who the eligible creditor is, leaving it to the court to determine whether a creditor is a natural or legal person with (i) liquidated claims at the time of the transfer of assets by the settlor into the CIT,

19 A Neocleous and Co, *Introduction to Cyprus Law* (Yorkhill Law Publishing, 2000), p862.
20 *Ibid.*
21 *Ibid.*
22 *Ibid.* Neocleous suggests that the post transfer insolvency of the settlor is irrelevant to the fraudulent transfer issue and that this provision would be treated in a similar way as the Fraudulent Transfer Avoidance Law (Cap 6) was applied and interpreted in *Andreas Mailos v Constantinides* ((1979) 1 SC 242).
23 *Ibid*, p863.

but also (ii) creditors with claims that were contingent on a future event or fulfilment of a future condition.

An important caveat must be made. These provisions stand unchallenged in court to date, and it is unclear whether they provide effective insulation, particularly in cases where trust property is located in multiple jurisdictions.

4.6 Time bar for actions against the trustee

An action against a trustee of a CIT is time barred after two years from the date when the transfer or disposal of assets was made to the CIT.[24]

Many domestic bankruptcy laws (including that of Cyprus) provide that any trust is automatically void if the settlor becomes bankrupt within two years, and if they become bankrupt within a further eight years the creditors may still be able to set aside the trust unless the beneficiaries can show that the settlor could discharge their debts without recourse to the trust funds. Section 3(3) introduces a two-year limitation period for initiating any action by a creditor. This period will run from the date when the relevant transfer of assets is made to the trust. It is intended to offer a legitimate protection to settlors against future undetermined claims at the time of the creation of the trust, while maintaining creditor protection.

4.7 Presumption of irrevocability of a CIT

If a CIT contains no express power of revocation it will be deemed to be irrevocable by the settlor or their legal representatives notwithstanding that it is voluntary.[25]

4.8 Duration of a CIT

The Cyprus International Trusts Law 1992 provides for a modern perpetuity period so that a CIT may have duration of up to 100 years from the date of its creation, unless it is terminated earlier in pursuance to any provision in the CIT itself.[26] This is notwithstanding any contrary legal provision or rule of law of Cyprus or any other country. If it is a charitable or purpose trust, it may continue indefinitely.[27]

4.9 Power of accumulation of income

This provision merely reflects the existing law in Cyprus that allows for trust

24 Section 3(3) of the Cyprus International Trusts Law 1992.

25 Section 4 of the Cyprus International Trusts Law 1992. Trusts are presumed to be irrevocable because deeds are presumed to be irrevocable. This is now expressly provided in Section 4. Wills, on the other hand, may be revoked without containing an express power of revocation simply by the testator making a new will (subject to satisfying the formalities for the capacity and signature of the testator, and attestation of the signature of the testator by two witnesses who have capacity).

26 Section 5(1) of the Cyprus International Trusts Law 1992.

27 Section 5(2) of the Cyprus International Trusts Law 1992.

income to be accumulated throughout the life of the trust. Income may be accumulated throughout the duration of a CIT, and any provision of the trust instrument creating the CIT will be valid for any term during the life of the CIT.[28]

4.10 Charitable trusts and purpose trusts

The Cyprus International Trusts Law 1992 provides for the creation of charitable trusts and purpose trusts.[29]

4.11 Authorised investments

At the time of the adoption of the Cyprus International Trusts Law 1992 there were currency exchange controls, limitations on participation and capital requirements for companies, as well as restrictions in relation to investments. The 1992 law expressly provides that the trustee, subject to the provisions of the instrument creating a CIT, may at any time invest the whole or any part of the trust funds in any kind of investment:

- wherever the investment is situated; and
- whether the funds have already been invested or not.

The trustee may vary the investment or retain it in its original state, as long as they exercise the diligence and the prudence that a reasonable person would be expected to exercise when they make investments. These wider powers are essentially similar to the 'prudent man' test or rules found in other jurisdictions.[30]

4.12 Power to determine the applicable law of a CIT

Where the provisions of a CIT instrument so allow, the law governing or applicable to the CIT may be changed to a foreign law, and a foreign trust may change the applicable law and adopt Cyprus law, provided that:

- in the event of change from the law of Cyprus to a foreign law, the new law that will govern the CIT will recognise the validity of the trust and the respective interests of the beneficiaries; and
- in the event of a change from a foreign law to the law of Cyprus, this change will be recognised by the applicable foreign law that previously governed the trust.[31]

This is a useful option, common in most modern offshore trust laws and aligns Cyprus law to the international standard.

---

28 Section 6.

29 Section 7. These are analysed in detail in the "Charitable trusts and charitable organisations" chapter by Eleni Drakou and are therefore only briefly referred to herein.

30 Section 8. These are analysed in detail in the "Trustee investment powers and delegation" chapter by Savvas Georgiou and are therefore only briefly referred to herein.

31 To or from choice of law provision, see Section 9.

4.13 Variation of a CIT by the court

Section 10 provides for the mechanism to vary or amend the CIT by way of an application to the Cyprus court. This section empowers the court to approve a variation of the terms of a trust. The wording follows closely that of the United Kingdom's Variation of Trusts Act 1958. Accordingly, by way of a court order, the court may grant any arrangement amending or revoking the provisions of a CIT or expanding or amending the powers of management or administration of the trustees, on behalf of the people below, notwithstanding whether there is another beneficiary that has capacity to consent to the arrangement:

- any person incapacitated at law having an interest, directly or indirectly, whether vested or contingent, under an international trust;
- any person, whether ascertained or not, who may become entitled, directly or indirectly, to an interest under an international trust as being the person, which at a future date or on the occasion of a future event, will be a person of any specified description or a member of any specified class of persons referred to in the instrument creating the international trust;
- any person unborn;
- any person in respect of any interest that may arise by reason of any discretionary power given to anyone on the failure of determination of an existing interest that has yet to fail or be determined; or
- any other person with permission of the court.

4.14 Confidentiality relating to a CIT

The confidentiality of a CIT against the disclosure of information is statutorily protected, since the trustee as well as any other person including government officials and officers of the Central Bank of Cyprus, cannot disclose any information or documents to a person that is not legally entitled by law, unless there is a court order to disclose.[32] The protected confidential information is the following:

- the names of the settlor or any beneficiary;
- the trustee's deliberations as to the manner in which a power or discretion was exercised or a duty conferred or imposed by law or by the terms of the CIT was performed;
- the reason for any particular exercise of such power or discretion or performance of duty or the material on which such reason had been or might have been based;
- the exercise or proposed exercise of such power or discretion or the performance or proposed performance of such duty; or
- relating to or forming part of the accounts of the CIT.[33]

32 Section 11.

However, if the request to disclose any document or information that relates or forms part of the accounts of the CIT is made by a beneficiary or a charitable institution that is the named beneficiary of the CIT, then the trustee is obliged to disclose these.[34]

The protection of confidential information is not absolute. The court, following an application that is filed by a party in a civil or criminal procedure, may, by way of a court order, allow the disclosure of the aforementioned documents or information,[35] provided that the court will be convinced that the disclosure of such document or information is paramount to the outcome of the case.[36]

4.15 Taxation of a CIT

It is expressly provided that CITs are exempt from all tax in Cyprus. The income and gains of a CIT derived or deemed to be derived from sources outside Cyprus are exempt from all tax imposed in Cyprus and no estate duty will be chargeable in respect of its assets, except stamp duty at a fixed rate of C£250.

4.16 Registration duty on a CIT

Stamp duty of C£250 is levied on the instrument creating the CIT. This duty is payable within 30 days from the date of the creation of the instrument creating the CIT.

4.17 Saving existing laws

All existing laws that pertain to trusts and the transfer of assets to trusts in force before the enactment of the Cyprus International Trusts Law 1992 remain in force and apply to CITs to the extent that they are not inconsistent or modified by the provisions of the new law.[37] Moreover, the laws and regulations that, from time to time, are applicable to investments made in Cyprus by non-permanent residents of Cyprus will also apply to any investments of a CIT in Cyprus.[38]

4.18 Registration requirements

Under the Cyprus International Trusts Law 1992, CITs were exempt from the requirement of registration. Trust or trustee companies were obliged to inform the Central Bank of Cyprus in order to obtain the exchange control permit and,

---

33 Section 11(1). Also, Section 11(4) clarifies that the confidential information or documents include information or documents stored in a computer, and in this case an order for disclosure is executed with the disclosure or the supply of the information or the document in a visible, legible and portable form.

34 Section 11(1).

35 Section 11(2).

36 Section 11(3).

37 Section 14(1).

38 Section 14(2).

pursuant to the Exchange Control Law (Cap 199), to operate external bank accounts. This requirement was abolished in anticipation of Cyprus' accession to the European Union.

Presently, the Fiduciaries Law obliges Cyprus resident trustees to register all Cyprus trusts with one of the three competent authorities: the Cyprus Bar Association (CyBar), the Cyprus Securities and Exchange Commission (CySEC) and the Institute of Certified Public Accountants of Cyprus (ICPAC) – this is compulsory for all fiduciary service providers that offer nominee directorship or nominee shareholding services or other trust services. Also, the Ultimate Beneficial Owner (UBO) Register is now maintained under the CySEC.[39]

5. The amending Cyprus International Trusts Law 2012

The CIT regime proved very popular with high-net-worth individuals who set up their asset protection structures through the jurisdiction of Cyprus. International developments associated with globalisation, expansion, reduction of barriers to trade and capital movements increased cross border transactions and encouraged tax planning and corporate structuring. At the same time, growing competition from other jurisdictions that also offered similar structures, revealed that "the Cyprus international trust regime had fallen behind those of its competitors".[40]

The long-awaited reform of the Cyprus International Trusts Law 69(I)/1992 was brought about by the enactment of the Cyprus International Trusts Law 20(I)/2012 on 9 March 2012, which addressed the perceived deficiencies and extensively modernised the CIT regime to align with the needs of the globalising economy. This new legislation now governs CITs under revised and updated provisions that are based on greater certainty, clarity and stability. Ostensibly, the amending law introduced provisions that make CITs more workable and accessible, and it effectively transformed the Cypriot trust regime into a modern, favourable trust regime, one of the most dynamic in Europe.

The amending Law 20(I)/2012 made numerous changes to the 1992 law, many of which were of a relatively technical nature.

5.1 New definitions included and existing definitions clarified

The amending law introduces clarity and offers express descriptions of key terms that were previously undefined or ambiguous:

- 'Trust' is defined as having the meaning assigned to such term by the Trustee Law and also includes the bequest.
- 'International trust' is redefined and the test is revamped to allow

39 These are analysed in detail in the "Trusts and ultimate beneficial ownership registers in Cyprus" chapter by Eleni Drakou, and below.

40 See E Neocleous and E Kollatou, "Cyprus", in *The Private Wealth and Private Client Review*, 9th edn (Law Business Research Ltd, 2020), p136.

settlors the right to reside in Cyprus, even to become tax residents, so long as the settlor and the beneficiary (other than a charitable institution) is not a resident in Cyprus (under the residency test defined under the new law) for a calendar year immediately preceding the creation of the trust. The settlor or the trustee or any beneficiary may be a partnership or company.

- 'Trust property' means property that is held on trust at the relevant time.
- 'Trustee' has been given a much broader definition and is provided to mean a legal or natural person who holds or has had trust property transferred to them, or is deemed to hold or have had trust property transferred to them, or is expected to have trust property delivered or transferred to them, to be held by them:
  - for the benefit of a beneficiary irrespective of whether the trustee is also beneficiary of the trust; and/or
  - for any purpose that is not for the exclusive benefit of the trustee.
- 'Beneficiary' means a legal or natural person including a person not yet born at the time of the creation of the trust, or a person who is part of a class of people entitled to a right or interest in property that is subject to the trust. This is a very important revision as it expressly clarifies the issue of an unborn beneficiary, avoiding challenges with respect to the certainty of beneficiaries. A new definition is introduced with respect to 'object of discretionary trust' to mean a legal person or individual who forms part of a class of persons to whom a distribution may be made in accordance with a discretionary trust or on the basis of the discretionary power of the trustee or of the holder of the power.
- 'Court' means the president of a district court or a senior district judge of the district where the trustees or the trustee of the international trust or any one of them who is a resident of Cyprus have their residence. This definition clarifies the issue of which court has jurisdiction to hear any applications in relation to CITs, as it determines that the competent court will be the district court where the trustee or any one of them has residency. It also expressly provides that a senior judge or president of the district court will adjudicate the case, clarifying an important issue that remained vague as to which was the competent court to hear an application or dispute pertaining to a CIT.
- 'Creditor' means any legal or natural person or persons to whom the settlor owes a debt or other obligation at the time when a trust is created or a disposition of the property held on trust, which clarifies and resolves an important ambiguity.
- 'Disposition' means any disposition or number of dispositions carried out in any manner and includes any transaction, gift, grant or transfer of property of any nature.

- 'Enforcer' means a person or persons whose duty is to enforce an international trust, with the exception of trusts for charitable purposes in accordance with Section 7(3). The enforcer is a new provision and addition to the law.
- 'Immovable' is clarified so that it has the meaning assigned to this term by the Trustee Law and therefore the definitions in other legislative provisions do not apply. This is an important clarification.[41]
- 'Intent to defraud' is clarified to mean the intention of a settlor to 'dishonestly avoid' any obligation that they owe to a creditor, thus clarifying that the standard the creditor must prove is that the settlor, at the time of creating the trust or making a disposition into the trust, intended to dishonestly avoid any obligation that they owe to a current creditor to whom the settlor owes a debt. This definition is directly linked with the asset protection provisions and validity of the CIT.
- 'Judgment' means any judgment or award of arbitration issued by a court, or arbitrator or administrative body in any country, irrespective of what any judgment may be called, including an order, decision or writ of execution, as well as the determination of costs or expenses of the court or tribunal by the court or arbitrator.
- 'Obligation' means an obligation or liability that existed on or prior to the date of a relevant disposition and of which the transferor had knowledge.
- 'Personal relationship' is introduced as a term to ensure that Cyprus is aligned with current developments as they pertain to relationships so that the new term includes all forms of relationship either by blood or marriage, including present or former marriage and every form of cohabitation, and in particular a personal relationship between two persons, if:
  - one is the natural or adopted child of the other, irrespective of whether paternity or the adoption is recognised by law in force in Cyprus or elsewhere, and whether such child is born during or outside marriage;
  - one is married to the other, irrespective of whether the marriage is recognised by the law in force in Cyprus or elsewhere;
  - one cohabits with the other, or by virtue of their behaviour towards the other, there arises, in any jurisdiction, any rights, obligations or

41 Section 3 of the Trustees Law (Cap 193) states that immovable property includes: (a) land; (b) buildings and other edifices, structures or appurtenances permanently attached to any land or any building or other edifice or structure; (c) trees, vines and anything else planted or cultivated on any land and any produce thereof before the cutting down; (d) springs, wells, water and water rights, whether these are held with, or independently of, any land; (e) privileges, liberties, easements and any other rights and advantages belonging or deemed to belong to any land or any building or other structure or construction; and (f) an undivided interest in any property referred to in the foregoing.

    responsibilities analogous to those of a parent and child or husband and wife between them; or
  - a personal relationship exists between any of these persons and any third person.
- 'Protector' has been introduced and is a person other than the trustee to whom powers of any nature are conferred by the trust instrument creating or evidencing the trust including the power to advise a trustee as to the exercise of the trustee's powers or as to the trustee's right in respect of a consent or veto and includes the power to appoint or remove a trustee.
- 'Purpose trust' or 'trust for a purpose' is redefined and means a trust other than:
  - a trust with beneficiaries that are certain individual or legal persons readily ascertainable or not; and
  - a trust with beneficiaries that are the whole of certain individuals or legal persons that are ascertained with reference to some personal relation or affinity.
- 'Right to inheritance' is defined to mean any right, claim or interest arising under the law of any jurisdiction other than that of Cyprus in relation to, or against the property of any person that arose, accrued or exists as a consequence of, or in anticipation of, that person's death, other than a right, claim or interest created by a will or expressed in any other voluntary disposition by that person or resulting from an express limitation in the disposition of the property to that person.

5.2 Cyprus International Trusts Law upholds powers and authorities

The new law introduces an important clarification in relation to the interpretation of the powers and authorities conferred on the trustee, protector, settlor and enforcer. The new Section 2A expressly states that the provisions of the Cyprus International Trusts Law as amended "shall be supplemental to the powers and authorities which may be conferred on them in accordance with the terms of an international trust", which potentially allows the provisions of trust instruments to expand these powers and extend even beyond the statutorily defined scope. Section 2A provides that "the powers and authorities of this Law apply if and so far only as a contrary intention is not expressed in the terms of the trust and shall have effect subject to the terms of the trust and shall be subject to the terms of the same".

5.3 Revised criteria for the creation of a CIT

(a) Old law

CITs were restricted to non-resident settlors and beneficiaries, since it was a requirement that the settlor and the beneficiaries should not be permanent residents of Cyprus. While this prevented the use of CITs by Cyprus residents, it remained unclear whether settlors or beneficiaries could relocate to Cyprus after establishing a CIT. In fact, this discouraged the taking up of residency. According to the old law, the last criterion was that a CIT did not include immovable property in Cyprus. Since Cyprus' accession to the European Union, exchange controls were lifted and investment restrictions were gradually abolished. Cyprus introduced new schemes to attract foreign direct investment (FDI) such as permanent residency or temporary residency schemes, even citizenship by investment, which involved the acquisition of immovable property as a criterion. It soon became apparent that the CIT regime, especially the criteria for its creation, had to be revised to align and integrate with the FDI policy and the strategy of Cyprus.

(b) *New law*

The 2012 law provides three amended criteria:

- the settlor must not be a Cyprus tax resident in the calendar year preceding the year of creation of the trust;
- at least one of the trustees must be a permanent resident of Cyprus during the whole duration of the trust (same as the old law); and
- none of the beneficiaries can be a Cyprus tax resident in the calendar year preceding the year of creation of the trust.

The new criteria resolve a very important irregularity in the old law that required that the settlor and beneficiaries should not be residents in Cyprus. Arguably, the removal of the prohibition against the residency in Cyprus for the settlor and beneficiary after one year from the creation of the CIT ensures full compliance with fundamental EU treaty freedoms; namely, the freedom of movement and the freedom of establishment. Considering that permanent residency requirements (eg, those under Regulation 6(2)) include as an investment criterion the acquisition of immovable property in Cyprus of €300,000 or more,[42] issues where the settlor or the beneficiary subsequently take up residency in Cyprus are also resolved.

42 Investment in real estate or the purchase of a house or apartment is included in the criteria for granting an immigration permit within the scope of the expedited procedure to applicants who are third country nationals and invest in Cyprus – 3rd Revision, 24 March 2021 to 7 April 2021. See www.moi.gov.cy/moi/crmd/crmd.nsf/All/1BA4BAD03702D2D1C22586B00026CE26#:~:text=According%20to%20the%20provisions%20of%20Regulation%206%20%282%29,obliged%20to%20become%20a%20permanent%20resident%20in%20Cyprus. In pursuance of the provisions of Regulation 6(2) of the Aliens and Immigration Regulations, the Minister of Interior, having notified the Council of Ministers, has decided to issue an immigration permit to third country applicants in cases of investment that meet the requirements of this policy. The applicant must meet one of the investment criteria in Section 2.1, as well as the quality criteria in Section 3. Money used for the investment must be proven to have been transferred to Cyprus from abroad. Under section 2.1, the applicant must invest at least €300,000 in one of the following investment categories: (a) Investment in a house/apartment through acquisition from a development company, which should concern a first sale of minimum of €300,000 (plus VAT); (b) Investment in real estate (excluding houses/apartments): purchase of other types of real estate such as offices, shops, hotels

The new law introduces a clear definition of 'resident in Cyprus', which is necessary for the taxation aspect of the CIT, since certain aspects of the CIT are now taxable in Cyprus. When applied to an individual, it means that an individual who stays in Cyprus for a period or periods exceeding in aggregate 183 days in the year of assessment. When applied to a company, it means a company whose management and control is exercised in Cyprus and 'non-resident or resident outside Cyprus' will be construed accordingly, provided that the presence of an individual in Cyprus for part of a day is counted as one day.[43]

5.4 Capacity of the settlor

The provision remains unchanged by the amending law.[44]

5.5 Cyprus law to determine matters in respect of CIT validity

The new law introduces Section 3(1A), according to which all matters arising in respect of a CIT or any disposition of property under such trust will be determined under the laws of Cyprus, including but not limited to:

- the validity, interpretation or effect of any trust or disposition or any variation;
- the validity or effect of any transfer or other disposition of property in trust;
- the management of the trust wherever it is carried out, including the functions, appointment or removal of trustees, protectors and enforcers;
- the existence and extent of any functions in relation to the trust such as the powers to vary, revoke and make any appointment and the validity of the performance of such functions; and
- the powers, obligations or duties or rights of trustees, protectors or enforcers of a trust.

---

or related estate developments or a combination of these with a total value of €300,000 plus VAT, if applicable. The purchase of interest can be the result of a resale. (c) Investment in a Cyprus company's share capital, with business activities and personnel in Cyprus: investment worth €300,000 in the share capital of a company registered in Cyprus, based and operating in Cyprus and having a proven physical presence in Cyprus and employing at least five people; (d) Investment in units of Cyprus investment organisation of collective investments (forms of AIF, AIFLNP, RAIF): investment worth €300,000 in units of Cyprus investment organisation collective investments. The applicant may not alienate the investment without its immediate replacement with another of the same or greater value that must meet the conditions set out in the present procedure, otherwise any permit granted will be cancelled. Under Section 2.2, the applicant should, in addition to the investment under Section 2.1, be able to prove that that they have at their disposal a secure annual income of at least €30,000. This annual income increases by €5,000 for each dependent family member and €8,000 for each dependent parent (of the applicant and/or their spouse). This income should derive from abroad and may include salaries or wages, pensions, dividends from shares, fixed deposits and rents, among other things, in cases where the applicant chooses to invest as Section 2.1(A). In calculating the total amount of income, the spouse's income may also be taken into account. In cases where the applicant chooses to invest as Sections 2.1(B), 2.1(C) or 2.1(D), their total income or part of it may also come from sources coming from activities within Cyprus. The applicant must meet the quality criteria under Section 3 as well as other requirements as stipulated in Regulation 6(2).

43 According to the Income Tax Law 2002, 118(I)/2002, 15 July 2002.

44 Section 3(1) of the Cyprus International Trusts Law 1992.

It is also expressly provided that the inheritance or succession laws of Cyprus or any other country will not affect the transfer or disposition or validity of any international trust.[45]

5.6 Asset protection and immunity from creditor claims

The main provisions of the Cyprus International Trusts Law 1992 are maintained with the amendments. Most importantly, the term 'creditor' is defined to mean any legal or natural person or persons "to whom the settlor owes a debt or other obligation at the time when a trust is created or a disposition of the property held on trust". Again, another important matter is clarified and resolved, as the definition arguably excludes contingent or future creditor claims.

The creditor definition enhances the CIT as an asset protection trust that ringfences the settlor's assets from persons who may have a claim against them. The CIT law regime contains a strong presumption against avoidance of the trust; unless the court is satisfied that the trust was made with the intent to defraud creditors, the CIT will not be void or voidable. The burden of proof of the settlor's intent to defraud lies with the person seeking to set aside the transfer, which must be applied before the Cyprus courts not later than two years after the trust was created or the assets were transferred to the trust. The standard of proof for the intention to defraud is on the balance of probabilities, but the claimant must establish that the trust was more likely than not a fraud. In practice, there may be evidentiary difficulties to justify or prove that the settlor created the trust with the intent to defraud their creditors. Moreover, a claimant domiciled outside the European Union and without assets in Cyprus may be required to provide security of costs in pursuing such claim.[46]

The anti-avoidance provision emphasises the new dynamics of CITs as they add another layer of protection to persons contemplating setting up a trust. According to Neocleous and Kollatou, notwithstanding professional indemnity insurance, some professions still involve high-risk claims that could be financially disastrous, and not just in case they prove successful.[47] Freezing orders may be issued, which may restrict the cash flow of settlors. Personal affairs, such as the breakdown of a marriage or civil partnership, may necessitate an added layer of asset protection. In certain jurisdictions, such as Cyprus, where prenuptial agreements are ineffective or invalid by operation of the law as agreements to agree or against the institution of marriage, CITs may provide

45 Section 3(1A) of the Cyprus International Trusts Law 1992.

46 The defendant may apply to the court so that a security of costs or payment into court is made by the claimant under Order 60 of the Civil Procedure Rules. Furthermore, Cyprus is not a party to the arrangements set out in Sections 426(4) and (5) of the Insolvency Act 1986, unlike other commonwealth jurisdictions, and therefore is not required to assist in insolvency cases. The Statute of Elizabeth, which invalidates arrangements made to hide assets from future creditors, is also not applicable to CITs.

47 E Neocleous and E Kollatou, "Cyprus", in *The Private Wealth and Private Client Review*, 9th edn (Law Business Research Ltd, 2020), p136.

the solution. Many countries, including Cyprus and most of the European Union, have forced heirship rules or provisions for their succession law leaving little or no scope for bequeathing more than a specified and usually small portion of the testator's estate to relatives or other beneficiaries. In all these cases, a CIT can provide a means of regaining freedom of testation, as there is a clearly provided protection against forced heirship and similar claims.[48]

The asset protection provisions of the amending Cyprus International Trusts Law 2012 are further enhanced by the explicit provision that any matter relating to the validity or administration of a CIT will be determined by the laws of Cyprus without reference to any other jurisdiction. This extends to fiduciary powers and duties of trustees as well as powers and duties of protectors. The amending Cyprus International Trusts Law 2012 expressly provides that no CIT and no disposition of property to or under such a trust, will be void, voidable or liable to be set aside or subject to any implied term, nor will the capacity of any settlor, trustee, enforcer, protector or beneficiary be questioned, and no settlor, trustee, enforcer, protector, beneficiary or third party will be subject to any obligation or liability or be deprived of any right, claim or interest, by reason that:

- the applicable laws of any jurisdiction prohibit or do not recognise the concept of a trust; or
- the trust or disposition will not be invalidated and the rights, claims, interests, obligations or liabilities conferred or imposed will not be eliminated or potentially invalidated by reason of the personal relationship to a settlor or any beneficiary or the right to inheritance.[49]

Section 3 of the Cyprus International Trusts Law is complemented by the provisions entrenching the jurisdictional protection of the Cyprus law as the governing law of the CIT, since the choice of applicable law provision is protected from foreign judicial claims as a matter of public policy and order.[50]

---

48 Section 3(1).

49 Section 3(4).

50 See E Neocleous and E Kollatou, "Cyprus", in *The Private Wealth and Private Client Review*, 9th edn (Law Business Research Ltd, 2020), p165. Section 12B provides:

Without prejudice to the provisions of Council Regulation (EC) No. 44/2001 of 22 December 2000 on jurisdiction and the recognition and enforcement of judgments in civil and commercial matters, the Court shall have jurisdiction where:

(a) the governing law of a trust or a particular aspect of a trust is the law of the Republic;

(b) the trustee of any trust is resident in the Republic;

(c) in the case of a company acting as a trustee company offering administrative services, provided that it is incorporated in the Republic;

(d) any trust property is situated in the Republic;

(e) the administration of any trust is carried out in the Republic;

(f) the parties submit to the jurisdiction of the Court;

(g) the instrument creating or evidencing the trust contains provision for the referral of any dispute to the jurisdiction of the courts of the Republic:

Provided that such jurisdiction will be exclusive unless the instrument creating or evidencing the trust provides otherwise.

5.7 Reserved powers of the settlor

(a) Old law

The old law was silent on whether the settlor could retain powers when surrendering control to the trustees by creating a CIT. The lack of express provisions as to whether the settlor could reserve powers, created ambiguities where the CIT instrument did provide for such reserved powers.

(b) New law

The new Section 4A allows the settlor of a trust to reserve powers to retain a beneficial interest in trust property, or to act as the protector or enforcer of the trust without affecting the validity of the trust. The powers that may be reserved are extensive:

- to revoke, vary or amend the terms of a trust;
- to advance, appoint, pay, apply income or capital of the trust assets or to give directions;
- to act as, or to give binding directions as to the appointment or removal of a director or officer of any company wholly or partly owned by the trust;
- to give binding directions to the trustee in connection with the purchase, retention, sale, management, lending, pledging or charging of the trust assets;
- to appoint or remove any trustee, enforcer, protector or beneficiary;
- to appoint or remove any investment manager or investment adviser;
- to change the proper law of the trust or the forum of administration of the trust; and
- to restrict the exercise of any power or discretions of a trustee by requiring that they will be exercisable only with the consent of the settlor.

The settlor will not be deemed to be acting in breach of the trust in exercising these powers.

The reserved power provisions, which are similar to corresponding provisions in other trust jurisdictions, offer settlors great flexibility to adapt to changes in circumstances or objectives and a sense of control over the trust property of the CIT. It is expressly provided by the new law that where a power has been reserved by the settlor or conferred on them in their capacity as protector or enforcer, no intention to defraud may be imputed to the settlor.[51]

51 Similar provisions can be found in other jurisdictions – for example: Section 86 of the British Virgin Islands Trustee Act; Section 15 of the Trusts Guernsey Law 2007; Section 47 of the Nevis International Exempt Trust Ordinance; Section 9A of the Trust (Jersey) Law 1984, as amended in 2006; Part III of the Cayman Trusts Law (2021 Revision) to the Trusts (Amendment) (Immediate Effect and Reserved Powers) Law 1998; Sections 3 and 81(2) of the Bahamas Trustee Act 1998.

Reserved powers are affirmed by Article 2 of the Hague Convention (1 July 1985) on the Law Applicable to Trusts and on their Recognition, which provides that "the reservation by the settlor of *certain* rights and powers is not *necessarily* inconsistent with the existence of a trust"[52] (the key words are emphasised). Therefore, the settlor who creates a CIT, and indeed a lawyer or professional who will advise on or be responsible for drafting the trust instrument, must carefully advise settlors as to the extent of reserved powers in the trust instrument.

In a similar vein, international case law cautions against reserving powers to the settlor, as this alone may provide sufficient grounds to invalidate an international trust by a list of potential litigants such as a divorcing spouse or partner, a discontented beneficiary, a tax authority or a creditor, to name a few, who may apply to the court for satisfaction and claim to set the trust aside.[53] Recently, in *Webb v Webb*, the Privy Council held, among other things, that the reservation of powers by the settlor of the two discretionary trusts was so extensive that the trusts had never come into existence.[54] Although this is untested under Cyprus law, reserved powers should be used with caution, if not sparingly.[55]

5.8 Distribution does not invalidate a CIT

A direction in an instrument creating an international trust for non-distribution of income is valid for any period within the duration of the trust.[56]

5.9 Investment powers of trustees

(a) Old law

Trustees had the freedom in terms of investment powers, provided that such powers were exercised in accordance with the trust instrument and with the diligence and prudence that a reasonable person would be expected to exercise when making investments.

---

52 The Convention of 1 July 1985 on the Law Applicable to Trusts and on their Recognition. While Cyprus signed the Hague Trusts Convention in 1998, it only entered into force in 2017.

53 In the following cases the international trusts were set aside: *In Re Stephen J Lawrence* (279 F3d 1294 (11th Cir 2002) (United States)), it was held that the settlor retained *de facto* control over the trust though his power to appoint trustees. *In the marriage of Ashton* ((1986) 11 FamLR 457, 461 (Australia)), the husband who had retained the power to appoint and remove trustees replaced himself as trustee with a corporate trustee and received trust income although he was not a beneficiary. He was deemed to be "in full control of the assets of the trust" as he applied the assets and income from them as he wished and for his own benefit. *In the marriage of Goodwin* (Appeal 172 of 1989 (Iowa, United States)), the court determined that "that no person other than the husband had any real interest in the property or income of the trust except at the will of the husband" and "the husband had the sole power of appointment of the trustee, which was a creature under his control, and he was a beneficiary to whom the trustee could make payment exclusively of other beneficiaries as the husband saw fit".

54 *Webb v Webb* ([2020] UKPC 22).

55 These are analysed in detail in the "Settlor reserved powers trusts" chapter by Emily Yiolitis, and are therefore only briefly referred to herein.

56 Section 6.

(b) ***New law***

Investment powers of trustees are extended to be the same as if the trustee were absolutely entitled to the assets of the trust, wherever the investment is situated and whether or not the funds have already been invested.[57] The power to vary the investment or retain it in the original state is again subject to the duty to exercise it with the diligence and prudence that a reasonable person would be expected to exercise in making investments. The power of investment is expressly extended to include the power to invest in movable or immovable property in Cyprus and overseas including shares in companies incorporated in Cyprus.[58] The abolition of the prohibition on investment in Cyprus to inward investment covering movable or immovable property, provides a boost to the real estate market.

5.10 Duration of trusts

(a) ***Old law***

The old law provided against perpetuities and determining the maximum duration of a CIT to 100 years from the date on which the trust came into existence,[59] as was the common practice in various trust jurisdictions at the time. Over time, the duration limitation grew to be regarded as disadvantageous, as other jurisdictions removed the restriction.

(b) ***New law***

All CITs created on or after the enactment of the amending Cyprus International Trusts Law 2012, provided that the trust instrument so provides, may be established with unlimited duration and will continue to be valid and enforceable. No rule against perpetuities or remoteness of vesting or any analogous rule will apply to a trust or to any advancement, appointment, payment or application of property from a trust.[60] Except where the terms of a trust provide expressly to the contrary, no advancement, distribution, appointment, payment or application of income or capital from the trust to another trust will be invalidated solely because the other trust continues to be valid and enforceable beyond the date on which the first trust must terminate.[61]

5.11 Confidentiality

The new law extends confidentiality duties to the trustee, protector, enforcer of

---

57 Section 8(1) of the Cyprus International Trusts Law 2012. Trustees' investment powers are now in line with those of a trustee in England and Wales, and other trust jurisdictions that have followed the English Trustee Act 2000, including Malta.

58 Section 8(3) of the Cyprus International Trusts Law 2012.

59 Except charitable trusts and non-charitable purpose trusts, which were allowed to exist in perpetuity.

60 Section 5(1).

61 Section 5(2).

the performance of the trust or any other person, forbidding them from disclosing to any person not legally entitled to any documents or information regarding the trust. The 2012 law specifically provides that disclosure can be made only where the instrument creating the trust provides otherwise, when a court order for disclosure is issued, or where a request is submitted by a beneficiary to the trustee for the disclosure of accounts of the trust or for any documents or information relating to the proceeds and payment is made by the trustees that form part of the said accounts. In such a case, the trustee will have the power to make such disclosure only if, in their opinion, it is necessary and in the best interest of the trust.[62]

While the new law preserves confidentiality and even extends it, this is undercut by several provisions of the anti-money laundering directives as implemented and adopted under Cyprus law.[63] In 2012, Cyprus introduced the Fiduciary Services Providers Law, whereby any fiduciary providing the professional service of a trustee or fiduciary was obliged to disclose the name of the trust, the name of the trustee and the UBOs to one of the following registries held by the CyBar (if the trustee is a lawyer), the ICPAC (if the trustee is an accountant/auditor) or the CySEC (in case of other licensed providers of fiduciary services).[64] In addition, trusts must now comply with the UBO registration requirements.

5.12 Registration requirements

Before 2003, trusts deeds would be filed with the Central Bank of Cyprus as part of the currency exchange control legislation. As of Cyprus' accession to the European Union and the reduction of the powers of the Central Bank, this was abolished. Section 15 of the Cyprus International Trusts Law 1992, which provided for the registration requirement of CITs, was abolished by the new 2012 law. Although the amending 2012 law does not provide for a registration requirement, the Fiduciary Services Providers Law and the UBO Registry impose obligations of registration. More importantly, Section 12E explicitly states that

62 Section 11 of the Cyprus International Trusts Law.

63 The Prevention and Suppression of Money Laundering and Terrorist Financing Law 188(I)/2007 as amended.

64 The provisions of Directive 2005/60/EC were transposed into national law by the law regulating the professional activities provided in the framework of administrating private companies by other companies the Law on the Regulation of Fiduciaries, Administration Businesses and Company Directors, which was enacted by the Cyprus Parliament on 21 December 2012. The law applies to persons and companies providing relevant fiduciary and other corporate services relating to the administration or management of trusts and companies in or from Cyprus, including: (a) directorship and secretarial services provided by a legal person, including acting as an alternate director or secretary; (b) services such as holding of shares of legal persons in a nominee or trustee capacity; (c) provision of a registered office; (d) opening or managing bank accounts; and (d) safe keeping of financial instruments on behalf of clients. The law purports to regulate the provision of management and administration services to corporate entities and trusts, the provision of nominee and protector services for corporate entities and trusts. The provision of a registered office in Cyprus, the opening and administration of bank accounts, will also be deemed as regulated activity.

"the trustee shall be bound to comply with and implement the provisions of the Prevention and Suppression of Money Laundering Activities Law".

In December 2012, Cyprus put in place a new regulatory regime for professional trustees and providers of company management services under the Regulation of Fiduciaries, Administration Businesses and Company Directors Law 2012. The Fiduciaries Law requires all individuals or companies offering trustee, administration or related services to be authorised as 'fit and proper' and licensed by the CySEC. Registered lawyers and auditors/accountants in Cyprus who have provided fiduciary and corporate services via their respective firms and associated companies have been regulated throughout by their respective professional bodies (the CyBar and the ICPAC, respectively). Regulated service providers are required to put in place adequate internal controls, policies and procedures, as the Fiduciaries Law sets out accounting and reporting requirements and ensures that the authorities have accurate and up-to-date information on settlors, trustees and beneficiaries of trusts. These regulatory obligations are complemented by the obligation for service providers to adhere to the obligations and regulations of the anti-money laundering directives as transposed into national law.

The Fiduciaries Law provides an exemption for persons acting as trustee of a trust of which the person concerned is the settlor and where the only beneficiaries of the trust are the person concerned or members of their family. It is apparent that the exemption granted is quite limited and narrow. A typical family trust structure not involving a professional trustee company would involve a private trust company (PTC), the shares of which are owned by the settlor and their family or, if offshore, by a trust or other entity such as a foundation established for the purpose. The PTC is formed for the purpose of acting as trustee of one or more specific trusts. The directors of the PTC will usually be or include members of the settlor's family, who may also be beneficiaries of the trust or advisers to the family. The power to appoint directors is likely to be put under the control of the settlor or the protector.

Under section 25A of the Fiduciaries Law, there are three registers: the CySEC, the CyBar and the ICPAC, each establishes and keeps a trust register. The CySEC maintains the default register as it keeps a register of trusts with respect to every trust governed by Cyprus law that would not be registered with the CyBar register or the ICPAC register.[65]

Section 25A(3) of the Fiduciaries Law obliges each trustee, resident of Cyprus and of a trust governed by Cyprus law, that within 15 days from the

65 A trust is kept in the trust registers for as long as it is governed by Cyprus Law. The trust registers are not available to the public but will be available for inspection by the competent authorities and must contain the following information: the name of the trust; the name and full address of every trustee at all relevant times; date of establishment of the trust; the date of any change in the law governing the trust; and the date of termination of the trust.

establishment of the trust or the adoption of Cyprus law as the applicable law governing the trust, or any change in the information filed, to notify the competent authority that keeps the relevant trust register. Failure to comply is a serious offence punishable by a fine or imprisonment.[66]

5.13 Clear provisions for court assistance

The new law introduces a mechanism whereby a trustee may file an application to the court for directions regarding:

- the manner in which they may or should act in respect of any matter concerning an international trust and the court may issue any order in relation to execution or the administration, exercise of any power, discretion or duty of the trustee or of the protector, the appointment or removal of a trustee or protector, the remuneration of a trustee or protector, the filing of accounts, the conduct of the trustee or protector, payments to the court, the beneficiary or any person with a connection to the trust;
- a decision or declaration as to the validity or the enforceability of a trust; or
- rescinding or varying any order or declaration made under this law, or making any new, subsequent or further orders or decisions.[67]

Such application to the court may be submitted by a trustee, beneficiary or protector and by any other person with the permission of the court. The applications are filed either with the president of the district court or a senior judge of the district court where the trustee or one of the trustees is resident.

5.14 Taxation

(a) Old law

The 1992 law provided for an all-embracing clause exempting income earned from sources outside Cyprus from Cyprus tax. Now that either the settlor or beneficiaries may become residents in Cyprus, or the trust property may include immovable property in Cyprus, the taxation of CITs has become more complex.

---

66 109(I) of 2013 amending the Fiduciaries Law, introduces onerous obligations for non-compliance: *26. (1) A person who is in violation of or does not comply with article 5 and or article 24 and or article 25A, is guilty of a criminal offence, punishable, in the event of conviction, by a term of imprisonment not exceeding five (5) years or by a fine, not exceeding three hundred and fifty thousand euro (€350.000) or both. (2) Where the offence of paragraph (1) is committed by a legal person, the criminal liability also rests, besides the legal person, on any member of the board of directors, of the managerial, supervisory or auditory bodies where it is established that he has consented, or is party to the offence.*

67 Section 11A of the Cyprus International Trusts Law.

(b) ***New law***

The 2012 law amends Section 12, which provides for the taxation of CITs. According to Section 12(1)(a), the income and profits of an international trust that are earned or deemed to have been earned from sources within and outside Cyprus will be subject to every form of tax imposed in Cyprus in the case of a beneficiary who is resident in Cyprus. In the case of a beneficiary who is not resident in Cyprus, the income and profits of an international trust that are earned or deemed to have been earned from sources within Cyprus will be subject to every form of tax imposed in Cyprus. These tax provisions mean that a trust with non-Cyprus residents and income from non-Cyprus sources will be exempt from Cyprus tax. Only Cyprus-sourced income and profits are subject to Cyprus tax. The new provisions ensure that there will be no discriminatory tax or undue tax advantages open to any person. Although the application of Section 12 is clear in the case of trusts whose beneficiaries are exclusively non-resident, in practice, many trusts may have a mixture of resident and non-resident beneficiaries and the apportionment of the various forms and sources of income, which renders the taxation of CITs complicated. The "Taxation" chapter by George Economides provides further analysis on the taxation of CITs.

5.15 Stamp duty

The instrument creating a CIT must be legalised with the payment of the stamp duty at a fixed rate of €430.[68]

5.16 Choice of applicable law

The 2012 law provides that any trust will be governed by the law chosen by the settlor. This choice must be express or implied in the terms of the instrument creating or evidencing the trust, which will be interpreted in light of the circumstances of each case.[69] The new provision holds that an express or implied choice of Cyprus law is valid, effective and conclusive irrespective of the circumstances.[70] Where the choice of law is not applied, the trust will be governed by the law with which it is most closely connected, taking into consideration certain factors, such as:

- the country where the settlor is designated for the administration of the trust;
- the country where the trust assets are located;
- the trustee's country of residence (this is the same position as under the Hague Trust Convention and, hence, an important provision as it is

68 Section 12 (2). According to the previous provisions, the stamp duty was C£250. With Cyprus' accession to the Eurozone in 2008, Cyprus now has the euro currency.

69 Section 12A(1).

70 Section 12A(2).

persuasive in favour of the jurisdiction of Cyprus as the choice of law even where there is no determined choice of law); and
- the objects of the trust and the countries where they are to be fulfilled.[71]

Where the law most closely connected to the trust is the law of Cyprus, then the application of Cyprus law is valid, effective and conclusive, irrespective of other circumstances.[72]

5.17 Jurisdiction

The new Section 12B as amended explicitly provides that the Cyprus courts have jurisdiction (except where the trust instrument provides otherwise) without prejudice to the provisions of EC Council Regulation 22/2001 on jurisdiction and enforcement of judgments in civil and commercial matters. Unless the trust instrument provides otherwise, the exclusive jurisdiction of the Cyprus courts is reserved by a widely defined jurisdiction criteria, any of which can apply:

- Cyprus is the governing law of a trust or a particular aspect of a trust;
- the trustee is resident (which applies to all CITs);
- where the trustee is a trustee company incorporated in Cyprus and offering administrative services;
- the trust property is situated in Cyprus;
- the administration of the trust is carried out in Cyprus;
- the parties submit to the jurisdiction of the court; and
- the instrument creating or evidencing the trust contains provision for the referral of any dispute to Cyprus courts.[73]

Effectively, any matters regarding the validity, interpretation or effect of any trust or transfer will be adjudicated before the Cyprus courts and decided in accordance with Cyprus law.

5.18 Choice of laws

According to the new Section 12C, the Cyprus International Trusts Law 1992 as amended applies to international trusts containing a choice of law determining Cyprus as governing law, irrespective of any conflict of law rules that apply in Cyprus, and that upholding Cyprus as a choice of law constitutes a fundamental rule of law, adherence to which is a matter of public order.

The combined effect of the jurisdiction and choice of law provisions ensure that any challenges to the validity or administration of a CIT or disposition will

---

71 Section 12A(4).
72 Section 12A(5).
73 Section 12B.

be determined by the Cyprus courts without reference to the applicable law of any other jurisdiction, and that the Cyprus International Trusts Law 1992 will apply despite any contrary provision of the Cyprus inheritance or succession laws in Cyprus or any other country. This extends to the exercise of the trustee's powers and duties, including dispositions, which may not be challenged on the grounds that they are inconsistent with the laws of another jurisdiction, or on the grounds that the other jurisdiction does not recognise the concept of trusts. These provisions further reinforce the strong asset-protection provisions.

5.19 Foreign trusts

The new law stipulates that a foreign trust is governed by and will be interpreted in accordance with the law applicable in the country of its governance,[74] but that a foreign trust will be unenforceable in Cyprus where the court declares that it is contrary to public interest.[75]

5.20 Variation of trusts

A trust may be varied in any way provided by its instrument or following an application to the court and where the court exercising its discretion approves any arrangement that varies or revokes the terms of the international trust or modifies the powers of management of administration of trustees.

5.21 Retrospective application of amending the 2012 law

The amendments introduced by the amending Cyprus International Trusts Law 2012 apply to all CITs retrospectively,[76] as well as to all CITs created after the commencement of the amending law.[77] It is further provided that the new law does not in any way affect the validity of any distribution or transfer or investment that took place prior to the enactment of the amending law, as the laws and regulations that were applicable before the enactment of the amending law remain in force and apply to the extent that they are not inconsistent.[78]

5.22 The Fiduciaries Law

Non-compliance with the Fiduciaries Law must be expressly referred to in any application or civil action. The courts may be unwilling to make any determination on the compliance or conformity with the provisions of the Fiduciaries Law if pleaded at the pleadings stage, but not expressly stipulated in the judicial documents filed.[79]

---

74 Section 12D(1).
75 Section 12D(2).
76 Section 15.
77 Section 13.
78 Sections 14(1) and 14(2).
79 Writ of summons, statement of claim, or in the body of the application or originating summons application.

5.23 Stamp duty on trust instruments filed in court proceedings

Any trust instruments presented as evidence in court proceedings before the Cyprus courts must be legalised in accordance with the Stamp Duty Law 19/63 and Section 12(2) of the Cyprus International Trusts Law 1992 as amended. In the event that trust instruments are presented as evidence in court proceedings and are not stamped, the court may order that these be stamped by the payment of the stamp duty, as well as the payment of interest and a penalty, as this will be assessed by the tax department.

6. Reform of the Civil Procedure Rules

The reformed Civil Procedure Rules set to be enforced on 1 September 2023 lack any express provision regarding CITs. According to the new rules, the judicial procedure commences with the filing of a claim form when there is a material dispute of facts, the ordinary procedure of Part 7 of the rules will be followed. Part 8 provides for an alternative procedure that is intended for cases where there is no material dispute of facts, or for any claim or in relation to any claim for which a legislative provision or rule provides that this should be filed by way of an originating summons application. Part 8 contains a non-exhaustive list of claims that the procedure under Part 8 would be most appropriate such as the interpretation of a will, deed or a contract; a claim of the trustee for permission of the court in relation to the performance of any step where there is no dispute or no material dispute of facts.

The new Civil Procedure Rules expressly refer to trusts in relation to Part 5:

- it is a service out of jurisdiction, where service of a claim under Part 7 or Part 8 may be allowed by the court where there is a claim in relation to a trust created by law, or in writing or verbally and affirmed in writing, and which is governed by the laws of Cyprus;[80]
- it is stipulated that the Cyprus courts have jurisdiction over the dispute;[81] or
- it relates to a claim against a defendant in a resulting or constructive trust when the claim emanates from acts that took place within the jurisdiction of Cyprus or relates to proprietary assets within the jurisdiction of Cyprus.[82]

The new rules expressly refer to trusts in relation to Part 2: representative parties. Rule 20.8 governs the representation of interested parties that cannot be determined and the claim relates to property that is under trust.[83] Unless otherwise provided by law or rule, a claim will be filed by or against trustees,

80 New Civil Procedure Rules, Rule 6.8(1)(ν).
81 New Civil Procedure Rules, Rule 6.8(1)(ξ).
82 New Civil Procedure Rules, Rule 6.8(1)(ϱ).
83 New Civil Procedure Rules, Rule 20.8(1)(β).

executors or administrators under this capacity, without adding as parties persons that have an interest in the trust or the property.[84] Where a property is under trust, the court has the authority to issue binding judgments to non-parties to the litigation.[85]

The new rules expressly refer to trusts in relation to Part 36: payment into court. They describe the steps for the payment into court by the trustee in accordance with Section 60 of the Trustees Law (Cap 193) and that an affidavit or witness statement must be filed with a brief description of the trust deed or the circumstances that create the trust, the names of the persons with interest in the moneys or bond to be deposited into court and their address, to the extent that this is known, and a declaration by the trustee that they agree to answer any questions of the court. The trustee who deposits funds or bonds into court, unless the court orders otherwise, will serve the deposit receipt to the person who has an interest in or is entitled to the funds or bonds.[86] An application for the payment from any amount or bond paid into court must be made in accordance with Part 36, and the application may be filed *ex parte*, although the court may give directions for the service of notice to any person.[87]

The new rules expressly refer to trusts in relation to Part 38: judgments and orders. Where the interested personal representatives or trustees were not the parties that received directions from the court to examine a claim, the court may give them instructions to join with any party that received such instructions to review claims for the purpose of submitting written testimony as required under Rule 38.[88] Consequently, a litigant intending to initiate legal proceedings in relation to CITs should consider carefully whether to file an originating summons application or a writ of summons and to include the correct legal basis.

84 New Civil Procedure Rules, Rule 20.9(1).
85 New Civil Procedure Rules, Rule 20.11.
86 New Civil Procedure Rules, Rule 36.5.
87 New Civil Procedure Rules, Rule 36.6.
88 New Civil Procedure Rules, Rule 38.15(3).

Settlor reserved powers trusts

Emily Yiolitis
Anemi Trustees Limited

1. Introduction

One of the most important considerations, or rather hesitations, of a prospective settlor when setting up a trust is that they are propelled to relinquish legal ownership and control over hard-earned assets to trustees that they may never have met in a jurisdiction that they may never have visited. Having accumulated wealth over what are often generations of labour and sacrifice, it is unsurprising that settlors are loath to part with it and will often seek ways to retain some control over the settled assets. On the one hand, settlors want to set up a trust and segregate themselves from their estate for tax, asset protection, seamless succession and other reasons; while on the other hand, they are reluctant to hand over control of what they consider to be their property to trustees who have little, if any, business know-how of the industry in which the settlors have built their empire. They want to have their cake and eat it too.

Modern trust jurisdictions make this easy for them:

- they will permit the settlor to write a letter of wishes to the trustees outlining how they would like to see their assets utilised (which, although non-binding, is a soft point of reference for trustees);
- it will be proposed to them to appoint a protector who may have far-wielding powers over how the trustees use (or do not use) their powers;
- they will be appeased with legislative security via firewall provisions that, despite their property and business and heirs being located in a multitude of jurisdictions, only their chosen law and forum will apply;
- they may be offered a place on the board of a trust underlying the company; and
- most recently, they will be permitted by legislation to specifically reserve powers under the trust deed, so that they can continue to 'run the show' unfettered by interfering trustees.

It is, however, important from the outset to take into account that reasonable parameters should be set for the utilisation by settlors of such facilitative mechanisms, including settlor reserved powers, to ensure that the fundamental concept of a trust, under which the trustees owe fiduciary duties and are accountable to the beneficiaries, is not compromised by these mechanisms.

2. Cyprus International Trusts Law

Section 4A of the Cyprus International Trusts Law permits a settlor to reserve powers, to retain a beneficial interest in the trust property and to act as protector or enforcer of the trust. The list of powers that may be reserved is extensive and includes the powers to:

- revoke, vary or amend the terms of a trust;
- advance income or capital of the trust property or to give directions for the making of such advancement;
- give binding directions as to the appointment or removal of a director of any company wholly or partly owned by the trust;
- appoint or remove any trustee, enforcer, protector or beneficiary; and
- restrict the exercise of any powers or discretions of a trustee by requiring that they will be exercisable only with the consent of the settlor.

There is also an explicit provision that where a power listed above has been reserved by or granted to the settlor, a trustee who acts in accordance with the exercise of the power is not acting in breach of trust. Further, the reservation of any powers will not be construed as an 'intent to defraud' the settlor's creditors, and that intent must therefore be independently proven.

3. Settlor reserved powers in other legislation

Cyprus, of course, is not alone in enacting legislation in the form of settlor reserved powers. The British Virgin Islands enshrine these powers in Section 86 of the British Virgin Islands Trustee Act. Section 15 of the Trusts (Guernsey) Law 2007 and Section 47 of the Nevis International Exempt Trust Ordinance make similar provisions. Jersey relies on Section 9A of the Trusts (Jersey) Law 1984, as amended in 2006. The Cayman Islands have Part III of the Trusts Law (2001 Revision), which was introduced as early as 1998 by the Trusts (Amendment) (Immediate Effect and Reserved Powers) Law 1998. Sections 3 and 81(2) of the Bahamas Trustee Act 1998 also provide for the reservation of such powers, as does Section 90(5) of the Singapore Trustees Act (Cap 337), as amended and Part IVD, and Section 41X of the Hong Kong Trustee Ordinance (Cap 29), as amended.

This jurisdictional parade of settlor reserved powers has been introduced specifically to lure hesitant settlors, particularly from civil law jurisdictions, who are accustomed to exerting full control over their assets and for whom the creation of a trust involves a considerable leap of faith, to take that leap. Each jurisdiction wants to remain competitive by making their legislation attractive to prospective high-net-worth settlors who wish to remain involved (often at the helm) in managing the settled trust assets.

Article 2 of the Hague Trusts Convention[1] buttresses this position by declaring that "the reservation by the settlor of certain rights and powers is not necessarily inconsistent with the existence of a trust". However, despite the widespread legislation and the nod to the practice by the Hague Trusts Convention, there is little guidance on which 'certain rights and powers' it is acceptable for a settlor to reserve and at what point the reservation becomes tantamount to a settlor not relinquishing a proprietary interest to the trustees at all. Because despite each jurisdiction wanting to appear more settlor-friendly, shinier and brighter than the rest, the basic test for the valid creation of a trust remains a test of Millet LJ in the English Court of Appeal case of *Armitage v Nurse*,[2] where it was held that there is an irreducible core of obligations owed by the trustee to the beneficiaries and enforceable by them, which is fundamental to the concept of a trust. If the beneficiaries have no rights enforceable against the trustees, there is no trust.

This core content of obligations represents the minimum set of duties that must be present and exercised by the trustees if the very validity of the trust is to be preserved. If the reserved powers that the settlor purports to reserve, albeit permissible by legislation, overreach the irreducible core needed for a valid trust to be present, there is no trust.

4. The risk of sham

A trust will be held to be invalid if it is found that the arrangement between the trust parties is actually a 'sham', which is a trust resulting out of actions between a settlor and trustees, whereby they execute acts or documents in a manner that is "intended by them to give to third parties or to court the appearance of creating between the parties legal rights and obligations different from the actual legal rights and obligations (if any) which the parties intended to create".[3] In order to determine whether a trust is a sham, a court must consider the subjective intentions of the parties involved. A court, for example, may hold that a trust is a sham when a settlor purports to create a trust for the benefit of stipulated beneficiaries, but at the same time reserves an inordinate amount of powers to themselves, which permit them to secure that the trust is administered by the trustees in accordance with their wishes and interests rather than in the interests of the stipulated beneficiaries and the trustee implicitly or explicitly shares the common intention with the settlor to relinquish core fiduciary duties. As far as settlor reserved powers are concerned, at a minimum, the nature and extent of such powers, if used, must be such so

---

1 The Convention of 1 July 1985 on the Law Applicable to Trusts and on their Recognition (HCCH 1985 Trusts Convention).

2 *Armitage v Nurse* ([1998] Ch 241 (CA)).

3 *Snook v London and West Riding Investments Ltd* ([1967] 2 QB 786).

as not to exclude the trustee's exercise of their duties in good faith in the best interests of all the beneficiaries. Where the settlor reserved powers are such that they preclude the exercise of this 'irreducible core' of trustee duties and the trustee concedes and shares this common intention with the settlor to create an illusory trust relationship, the trust will be held to be a sham trust.

In *Rahman v Chase Bank*[4] the Royal Court of Jersey considered a trust settlement under which a trust corporation was appointed as trustee to hold the trust fund and income on such trusts as the settlor should appoint during his lifetime, with the trustee's consent. The settlor, under the terms of the trust deed, could in any 12-month period distribute one-third of the capital of the trust fund to himself without the consent of the trustee. Moreover, the trust deed granted the trustees absolute discretion to pay, transfer or apply part or the whole of the trust capital fund to the settlor, having "regard exclusively to the interests of the settlor". The court held that the settlor retained such concentration of powers that he could, whether directly or indirectly, "revoke or otherwise terminate the settlement for his own absolute benefit". The court further examined the practice of the trust administration from evidence showing that the settlor effected gifts and loans to himself or made investments without the trustee's consent concluding that the trust was a sham because the settlor had exercised "dominion and control" over the trustee in the management and administration of the settlement.

In a similar vein, in *Minwalla v Minwalla*[5] the actions of the settlor, who withdrew and transferred trust funds as if they were his own, led the court to infer that the settlor's purpose was "only to set up a screen to shield his resources from other claims or unwelcome scrutiny and investigation".

A prerequisite for the creation of a trust is transfer of legal ownership to the trustee. If it can be shown from either the nature or the amount of powers reserved to the settlor that the transfer cannot be said to have occurred because the intention of the parties was for the settlor to remain as the effective legal owner, to do as they please with the assets and the trustee implicitly or explicitly agrees with this arrangement relinquishing core fiduciary duties, the trust will be held void *ab initio*. The problem lies in identifying the point at which the settlor has retained so much control that it can hardly be said that they have relinquished any proprietary interest to the trustees. It is not only the number but also the nature of the powers, cumulatively, that may imply a sham trust. So, a settlor power to remove and replace trustees may alone cause a court to hold that the trust is a sham, whereas a settlor reserving the power to add to the class of beneficiaries and change the governing law may, together, be held to be reasonable and permissible reservations.

---

4 *Rahman v Chase Bank (CI) Trust Co Ltd* ([1991] JLR 103).
5 *Minwalla v Minwalla* ([2004] EWHC 2823 (Fam)).

The Bermudan case of *Re the AQ Revocable Trust*[6] demonstrates clearly that while a settlor can validly reserve certain powers, there comes a point where the extent of the powers can subsume the irreducible core needed for the existence of a valid trust. In this case, the settlor, who was also sole trustee, was given a power to remove and appoint trustees and to provide written approval for any transaction that would be "a complete release of the trustee (including the settlor) of any liability or responsibility of the trustee to any person in respect of this transaction". The court held that the concatenation of powers in the settlor, in conjunction with the fact that he was the sole trustee, rendered the trusts he purported to create illusory during his lifetime.

In 2017 the English High Court decision of *Mezhprom Bank v Pugachev*[7] considered the validity of five New Zealand trusts that the settlor retained extensive powers over (he was also a beneficiary and protector of the trusts with powers as wide as appointing and removing trustees and directing a sale of trust property). It was held that although the trustees were properly appointed the facts of the case pointed towards an undue concentration of power in the person of the settlor, who remained, in his various capacities, in effective control of the assets. The extensive powers that Mr Pugachev kept for himself meant he could act for his own interest rather than that of the beneficiaries, and the trusts were thus held to be shams.

Similarly, in a more recent case, *Webb v Webb*,[8] where the settlor had retained a number of powers, including the power to remove and appoint beneficiaries, the Privy Council held that the reservation of powers by the settlor of two discretionary trusts was so extensive that the trusts were invalid. The facts in this case were that shortly after his second marriage, a New Zealand individual, Mr Webb, set up a trust in the Cook Islands for the benefit of himself and his son from his first marriage and appointed himself as the sole trustee. Mr Webb had a daughter with his second wife and subsequently the marriage broke down. Mr Webb set up a new trust in New Zealand for the benefit of himself and his children, appointing himself and his then girlfriend as trustees. He then transferred the assets from the Cook Islands Trust to the New Zealand Trust for nominal consideration. Mr Webb's second wife commenced proceedings in the Cook Islands seeking a matrimonial property order on the basis that the trust assets should be taken into account in the divorce apportionment. Mr Webb's position was that the assets were held in trust and should not be included in the matrimonial division. The first-instance court agreed with Mr Webb. However, this decision was reversed by the Court of Appeal, which struck down the trusts because, among other things, Mr Webb retained powers under the trust deeds

6 *Re the AQ Revocable Trust* ((2010) 13 ITELR 260).
7 *JSC Mezhdunarodniy Promyshlenniy Bank v Pugachev* ([2017] EWHC 2426).
8 *Webb v Webb* ([2020] UKPC 22).

that allowed him to recover the property purportedly settled on trust at any time he wished. Mr Webb appealed to the Privy Council, which dismissed his appeal, holding that he "had the power at any time to secure the benefit of all of the trust property to himself and to do so regardless of the interests of the other beneficiaries". Interestingly, the Privy Council also held that the trusts were invalid *ab initio* because "the bundle of rights which he retained is indistinguishable from ownership".

5. Court-compelled actions of a power-enabled settlor

A court, particularly a court in a country that has personal jurisdiction over a settlor (eg, because the settlor may be resident or domiciled there or the situs of the trust property may be located there), may rely on settlor reserved powers entrenched in a trust deed to compel the settlor's use of them in favour of a claimant, defeating any purpose, particularly with respect to asset protection, for which the trust is created. This consideration is becoming particularly relevant, not only for creditors and disgruntled beneficiaries, but also for divorcing spouses, too.

A case where the use of reserved powers resulted in a loss of the asset protection that the trusts sought to achieve is that of *Clayton v Clayton*.[9] Mrs Clayton claimed that Mr Clayton's rights and powers under the trust deed amounted to relationship property under the New Zealand Property (Relationships) Act 1976. Under the trust deed Mr Clayton had broad powers including the power to exercise any power without considering the interests of the beneficiaries, to exercise discretion in his favour, to resettle the trust fund, and to exercise a power of appointment to remove beneficiaries. The Supreme Court held that a general power of appointment is usually viewed as equivalent to ownership and can be treated as property for a variety of purposes. Thus, the Supreme Court held that, while the relevant power under consideration was not a general power of appointment in and of itself that would allow Mr Clayton to effectively revoke the trust, the combination of Mr Clayton's powers and entitlements as principal family member, trustee, and discretionary beneficiary of the trust amounted to a general power of appointment in relation to the trusts' assets. These powers were considered property, and because the trust was established during the relationship and the powers were acquired at that time, the property became relationship property, to be shared by Mr and Mrs Clayton.

In the US case of *Re Stephen J Lawrence*,[10] the settlor, who had reserved powers, claimed it was impossible to comply with a court order to return assets from an offshore trust, and failed to comply. The settlor was held in contempt of court and was therefore jailed. On appeal, it was held that the bankruptcy

---

9 *Clayton v Clayton* ([2016] NZSC 29) and *Clayton v Clayton* ([2016] NZSC 30).
10 *Re Stephen J Lawrence* (279 F3d 1294) (11th Cir 2002).

court did not err in holding that the settlor failed to establish his defence of impossibility because, as a settlor and a prospective beneficiary, he retained *de facto* control over the offshore trust through his ability to appoint trustees who could reinstate the settlor as a beneficiary under the trust and assign the entire proceeds to him. The defence was invalid because the impossibility that the settlor claimed was created by the settlor himself.

6. Tax migration

Settlors who set up trusts in tax-friendly trust jurisdictions with an aim to accumulate assets tax free, but who retain extensive powers over such assets, risk being taxed in their jurisdiction of residence. With an increasing number of courts around the world finding *de facto* directors and taxing accordingly, similarly for trusts, it is feasible that a settlor who has reserved wide-ranging powers to themself may find their actions taxable in their jurisdiction of residence.

In *Ingle v McGowan*[11] the court found that the settlor's power of disposition, which allowed him to amend the trust instrument, gave him a control very close to that of complete owner. The court found that a settlor who can control the spending of the trust fund in every respect except spending it for themself is sufficiently the 'owner' of the trust fund to make its income attributable and taxable to them.

7. Trustee liability

Regardless of powers being reserved to settlors, it is imperative to keep in mind that the overriding common law fiduciary duty lies with the trustees to act in the best interests of the beneficiaries. So, while the legislation, as in Cyprus, may permit settlors to give binding directions to the trustees in connection with the trust property, trustees must ensure that they apply their mind independently to the usefulness of such directions and to the wider benefit of the beneficiaries. They must not just sit back and watch a calamity befall the trust assets by acting as mere nominees. That said, Clause 4A(3) of the Cyprus International Trusts Law explicitly exonerates trustees from breach in such circumstances by providing that, notwithstanding where powers have been preserved or granted to the settlor under either their capacity as such or their capacity as protector or enforcer, the trustee who acts in accordance with the exercise of such power is not considered to be acting in breach of the trust.

8. Conclusion

While settlor reserved powers have become popular and, if used cautiously, are a useful tool to provide some security to settlors who reluctantly part with their

11 *Ingle v McGowan, Collector of Internal Revenue* (189 F2d 785 (1951)).

property, it is important to adopt a conservative approach to avoid defeating the very purpose for which a trust is set up in the first place: to relinquish control and separate the trust assets from the settlor's assets. Great care must be taken to ensure that the use of settlor reserved powers does not jeopardise the asset-protection features of a Cyprus international trust. When viewed cumulatively, the reserved powers should not, in nature or number, overwhelmingly support a finding that there is in fact no trust. Settlors should be made aware of the risk of reserving too many powers from the outset or relying too heavily on jurisdictional firewall provisions to protect their use of powers. It is vital to look beyond the jurisdiction in which the trust is established (which may itself permit settlor reserved powers to the jurisdiction of domicile of the settlor, the settlor's spouse, the beneficiaries as well as the situs of the trust assets), which may have less accommodating legislation. Settlors must remember that there are minimum requirements to ensure that the use of control mechanisms, particularly in the form of settlor reserved powers, will not jeopardise the very existence of the trust they seek to establish and control. So, to answer the perennial question of 'to reserve or not reserve', the most apt reply would be: reserve conservatively and defer to the proverbial impossibility of both having your cake and eating it.

Beneficiaries' right to information

Nicky Xenofontos
N Xenofontos LLC

1. Introduction

This chapter gives an overview of the rights that trust beneficiaries have under Cyprus law, but that are also applied in other jurisdictions, and how they vary.

A beneficiary is quite frequently referred to as the true owner of trust property. This is the generally accepted position in all common law jurisdictions recognising trusts, including Cyprus. Beneficiaries' rights may consist of a bundle of tangible property, non-tangible property and personal rights. The nature of a trust itself, being a very flexible arrangement, allows for beneficiaries' rights to be moulded as the settlor thinks best for the trust's beneficiaries in the instrument that creates the trust, known as the 'trust deed'. Although beneficiaries have a number of rights, this chapter will focus on the specific and perhaps the most vital and valuable right to trust information that beneficiaries are most concerned about.

The basic right of a beneficiary of a trust is to have the trust administered properly in accordance with general law and the provisions of the trust instrument. Beneficiaries are entitled to know of the existence of the trust and the nature of their interest in it (whether it is fixed, remainder or contingent), but it may be the case, especially where minor beneficiaries are concerned, not to have any trust information disclosed.

If there are members of a class of beneficiaries named in a discretionary trust, known as 'objects', they are only potential beneficiaries as the trustees have complete discretion as to when and to whom distributions are made (provided that they act in accordance with their powers and duties). Objects of a discretionary trust are therefore only entitled to be informed of the trust if they are likely to benefit under it. In the 2012 amendment of the Cyprus International Trusts Law, a statutory definition of 'objects of a discretionary trust' was introduced, where such objects were defined to be "a legal or natural person forming part of a class of persons to whom distributions may be made according to the terms of the discretionary trust or based on the discretionary powers conferred to the trustee or power holder". In addition, a definition of those who are considered beneficiaries was also included: "a legal or natural person including a person not yet born at the time of the creation of the trust, or a person who is part of a class of people entitled to a right or interest in property which is subject to the trust."

2. General beneficiaries' rights under common law principles of equity and precedent

It is a deep-rooted principle of trust law that a beneficiary must be able to enforce the trust and to make the trustee account for their conduct in the administration of the trust.

2.1 Right to information

For a beneficiary to be permitted to pursue the enforcement of the trust, they must be able to receive adequate information about the trust assets. A trustee therefore has the duty to provide certain information to beneficiaries, which usually, in other common law jurisdictions apart from Cyprus, includes a copy of the trust document,[1] any deeds of variation of the trust, deeds of appointment and trust accounts. However, there may be occasions where a beneficiary may seek further information or documentation from the trustee; for example, trustees' correspondence and other evidence of how the trustees have managed the trust. A beneficiary has no entitlement as of right to such documentation – it is usually at the trustee's discretion to disclose any requested information.

The extent of a beneficiary's right to trust information was clarified in the case of *Schmidt v Rosewood*.[2] The Judicial Committee of the Privy Council held that the right to information is based on the fiduciary duty of the trustees to keep the beneficiaries informed, rather than on any ownership right of the documents and information: it is not a question of whether a document is a 'trust document' or whether the beneficiary has an interest in the document, the right to trust information arises under the court's inherent jurisdiction to oversee and, if necessary, to intervene on behalf of the beneficiary to enforce the trust against the trustee. The case has excited great interest among trust practitioners because it considers the approach to be taken to the question of disclosure of information by trustees to beneficiaries. The decision is likely to be regarded as authoritative under English law (although it is an Isle of Man case).

Since *Schmidt* a document will be ordered to be disclosed if disclosure will be "conducive to the proper administration of the trust". Therefore, when trustees are faced with a request for disclosure, they must balance such requests on a case-by-case basis made by a beneficiary to have access to trust information, rather than whether a document can be classified as a trust document.

---

1 In Cyprus this is not generally the position regarding the trust deed, trustee resolutions or any other deeds, supplemental or not.

2 [2003] UKPC 26, 2 AC 709.

Although it is helpful that the court gave an authoritative ruling on the nature of the right, it does mean that the parties will in effect have to second guess what the court may decide should be disclosed if an application were to be made to court. When facing a request for disclosure of information from a beneficiary, trustees should consider the purpose of the request and, of course, the interest of the beneficiary. Some points that trustees should take into consideration include:

- the nature of the beneficiary's interest;
- the information that the beneficiary is requesting;
- the reasons for the request for information; and
- whether the information may be commercially sensitive.

The grounds on which trustees may be able to refuse disclosure include where:

- there is a legal reason to refuse (eg, if it contains privileged legal advice);
- the document is confidential (eg, if relevant to one beneficiary but not the other);
- the beneficiary only has a theoretical possibility of benefiting from the trust (eg, the possible interest is too remote, especially when a discretionary trust is concerned);
- the information is requested for an adverse purpose (eg, challenging the validity of the trust itself – which will not be in the interest of the beneficiaries as a whole); and
- disclosure is impractical or too costly.

In the New Zealand Supreme Court case *Erceg v Erceg*,[3] the appellant was a class beneficiary of two trusts established by his late brother. At the time when the trusts were wound up, in December 2010, the appellant was an undischarged bankrupt and received no distribution from either trust. Later, the appellant requested certain trust documents be provided to him, which the trustees refused. The matter was then brought before the High Court, the Court of Appeal and finally the Supreme Court, where a decision was reached regarding the trust documents.

After the High Court finding that he had no standing as an undischarged bankrupt at the time the trusts were distributed, and the Court of Appeal finding that he had standing to request trust documents, the appellant finally appealed to the Supreme Court. The Supreme Court held that the court must exercise its supervisory judgment regarding disclosure to beneficiaries in the given circumstances and further said that basic trust information should be disclosed to a close beneficiary, dependant on a number of factors. It was not

3 [2017] NZSC 28.

determined who would be considered a 'close' beneficiary – something that is likely to be different in every circumstance.

The following list of criteria for evaluating an application for disclosure of documents was established by the Supreme Court:

- the reason the documents are being sought;
- the nature of the interest held by the beneficiary seeking access;
- whether there is any practical difficulty in providing the information;
- whether the documents sought disclose the trustees' reasons for decisions made by the trustees;
- the likely impact on the trustees and other beneficiaries if disclosure is made;
- whether disclosure can be made while still protecting confidentiality; and
- whether safeguards can be imposed on the use of the trust documentation, if disclosed to the beneficiary.

The court also noted that bankruptcy does not affect an individual's capacity to seek disclosure of trust information from either the court or trustees of the trust to which they are a beneficiary.

The court dismissed the appeal having determined that disclosure should not be ordered due to the potential threat to confidentiality, future litigation and lack of necessity.

In addition, before refusing disclosure, trustees should consider whether they are able to offer part of the document or information requested or ask for an undertaking in relation to the use of the information disclosed. Outright refusal of disclosure is not always the only option. Trustees should consider any request for information carefully, because should the court discover that there is no good reason for the trustees' refusal, they are at risk of an order for costs (as was the case in *Schmidt*), which could mean a significant, personal financial penalty.

In *Lewis v Tamplin*[4] the High Court was asked to exercise its jurisdiction to supervise trustees in the performance of their obligations by requiring trustees to give disclosure of documents requested by three of the nine beneficiaries. The case also serves as a reminder of the rules regarding privilege between trustees and beneficiaries.

The central issue in this case was whether, following a request from the beneficiaries, the trustees were obliged to disclose documentation regarding the trustees' decisions in managing the trust, such as letters regarding tax advice, the occupiers of the immovable property (a farm) and what income was being generated from the farm. The claimants' rationale for seeking the documents stemmed from alleged concerns about option agreements in respect of the land, which had been entered into by the trustees with potential developers.

4 [2018] EWHC 777 Ch.

Although the trustees had responded to the claimants' information requests, they did so some 10 months after the request had been made and, besides, the claimants alleged that the information provided was unsatisfactory. The claimants therefore sought an order that the defendants disclose the information sought. In reaching its judgment, the court considered the general rules regarding the disclosure of information by trustees applied by the Privy Council in the case of *Schmidt*,[5] confirming the principle that trustees owe a fiduciary duty to keep beneficiaries informed and this includes providing trust accounts and while beneficiaries are not entitled to disclosure *per se*, they do have a legitimate expectation to see trust documents so as to hold trustees to account. The power to order to disclosure though remains with the court's inherent jurisdiction to oversee the trustees' performance of their duties. On the other hand, the trustees arguments for rejecting disclosure were based on the fact that the claimant beneficiaries had sufficient information about the trustees' stewardship of the trust, that any further disclosure of information may potentially reveal the reasons why the trustees had made some management decisions[6] that would effectively mean that the Londonderry principle[7] would apply, implying that legal professional privilege may also apply, and that there was a distinction to be drawn between a request by one beneficiary, in which case an individual beneficiary would not be entitled to review the disclosure, and a request by all beneficiaries, where as a collective the beneficiaries could apply to review documents.[8] In summary, the court was satisfied that the beneficiaries' claim was for good reason and did not look favourably on the fact that the trustees had thus far provided insufficient disclosure, which was disclosed only as a result of the threat of legal proceedings. It was also highlighted that trustees cannot simply serve limited disclosure as a means of avoiding the application of this rule. The judge concluded that a *prima facie* case had been established and therefore ordered the documents be disclosed (although disclosure was not ordered in relation to all the categories sought).

2.2 Right to distribution

A beneficiary under a Cyprus trust is entitled to benefit from the trust property and therefore to possession of the trust property provided that it is not inconsistent with the trust deed and subject to the trustee exercising its power of distribution suitably. Subject to the terms of the trust deed and type of trust, beneficiaries are entitled to the beneficial, equitable interest of the trust property. To explain this further and to distinguish between the various types of trust, in a fixed or bare trust beneficiaries' have an *in rem* right to property,

---

5 Referred to above.
6 This is the position in Cyprus, Section 11A of the Cyprus International Trusts Law.
7 *Re Londonderry's Settlement* ([1965] Ch 918).
8 *Saunders v Vautier* ([1841] EWHC J82, (1841) 4 Beav 115).

whereas under a discretionary trust, beneficiaries have no 'proprietary interest' in the trust fund unless the trustees decide on a distribution. This means that they do not own the beneficial interest under the trust – merely a hope that they will benefit. They may never do so. The trustees are the legal owners of the trust property. When trustees are replaced following death, where a natural person is a trustee, or on insolvency or dissolution of a corporate trustee, this right to distribution in no way affects beneficiaries' right to the property.

2.3 Right to equitable remedies and equitable rules of evidence for breach of trust

In case of a breach of trust, beneficiaries have a right to:

- follow the trust property in the hands of a third party and claim it back from the third party, if that third party is not a *bona fide* purchaser for value without notice of the breach;
- trace the converted value of the trust property into a new asset; and
- seek proprietary as well as personal equitable remedies such as rescission, equitable compensation, account of profits against the trustee, their representatives and third parties who acted dishonestly or received trust property without consideration.

2.4 Right to apply to court

While beneficiaries have no general right to direct trustees on how to exercise its discretion, in case of breach by the trustee of any of the terms of the trust deed, beneficiaries may apply to the competent court to seek an order to remedy that breach and compel the trustees to act and administer the trust in accordance with the trust deed and the law.

2.5 Right to call for the transfer of trust property

Beneficiaries have the right to call for a transfer where they are absolutely entitled to trust property. Consequently, beneficiaries can compel the trustees to distribute and transfer trust property where they hold an absolute entitlement thereto. This right does not extend to beneficiaries (or call of beneficiaries) of a discretionary trust.

2.6 Right to bring the trust itself to an end

Beneficiaries of a trust who have an interest in the trust can end a trust and request the transfer of the property to them, even if this request overrides the wishes of the settlor.

As established by the leading English trusts law case, *Saunders v Vautier*,[9] the rule of equity provides that if all the beneficiaries in the trust are of legal age

9 [1841] EWHC J82, (1841) 4 Beav 115.

and under no disability they may require the trustee to transfer the legal estate to them and thereafter the trust is terminated due to lack of subject matter, which is one of the three certainties that must be fulfilled in order for a trust to be validly established. The rule has been repeatedly affirmed in common law jurisdictions. Subsequent to this case, it has also been held that the rule applies to discretionary trusts as well as fixed trusts. The principle in *Saunders v Vautier* is not a rule of construction but depends on the fundamental proposition that the beneficiaries are collectively the beneficial proprietors of the trust fund.

2.7 Right to have the trust administered properly

One basic right that beneficiaries have is to have the trust administered properly in accordance with the general law, common law principles of equity, and the provisions of the trust instrument. Under the current legal framework in Cyprus, beneficiaries have no general right *per se* to know of the existence of the trust and the nature of their interest in it (whether it is fixed, remainder or contingent).

Where beneficiaries are members of a class of beneficiaries named in a discretionary trust, referred to as 'objects', they are only potential beneficiaries as the trustees have complete discretion as to when and to whom distributions are made (provided that they act in accordance with their powers and duties). Therefore, objects of a discretionary trust will become aware of the existence of the trust only at the time of receiving any distribution, not at any stage prior to that.

2.8 Right to be treated impartially

Under Section 5 of the Trustee Law (Cap 193), trustees have general discretionary power whereby any powers they possess under the trust deed and applicable laws can be exercised at their discretion, but subject to any consent or direction in relation to investment required by the trust deed (if any, or by any other applicable law). This right is only in relation to the power of investment of trust property and in exercise of this power of investment, the trustees should apply such investment decision by acting impartially towards the beneficiaries and in a fair manner so as investments that may accumulate are in the best interests and for the benefit of all beneficiaries as a whole, as well as the trust itself. Moreover, the general common law duty of impartiality imposes a duty on trustees during the management and administration of the trust to act impartially at all times in relation to the beneficiaries and to not be unfairly partial to one beneficiary or group of beneficiaries to the detriment of the others.

This duty is clearly relevant when managing trust assets. Trustees must actively manage the trust assets on behalf of all the trust's beneficiaries. Individual beneficiaries have no rights to assets until the trustees exercise a discretion in their favour. Consequently, an obligation for trustees to act impartially while managing trust assets for the benefit of all beneficiaries is reasonable and appropriate.

In this context, the duty of impartiality provides useful guidance for trustees about balancing the potential interests of various beneficiaries, particularly when there are different classes of beneficiary that benefit from trust capital. For example, some trusts have beneficiaries that benefit from trust income and other beneficiaries that benefit from trust capital. In this situation, the duty of impartiality means that the trustees need to fairly and even-handedly balance the interests of the beneficiaries who receive income distributions with the beneficiaries who receive capital distributions.

2.9 Right to confidentiality

Confidentiality is perhaps the supreme concern regarding trust information, especially so far as disclosure to outsiders is concerned. The general position is that by virtue of the nature of the information that trustees hold and their fiduciary function, the law of confidence requires trustees to keep trust information and documents confidential.

The English law of confidence has been developed through common law,[10] which is the part of English law that is derived from case law rather than statutes.

The common law of confidentiality is a broad principle of law that a person who receives information from another party in confidence cannot take advantage of it. That person must not make use of it to the prejudice of the person who gave the information without obtaining their consent.

The position in Cyprus regarding confidentiality issues are two-fold: on the one hand, protection of information is safeguarded by the law,[11] while on the other hand, with the implementation of the Fifth Anti-Money Laundering Directive,[12] disclosure of certain trust information to the competent regulators[13] of each obliged entity is now mandatory following the establishment of the Trusts and Other Similar Arrangements Ultimate Beneficial Owners (UBO) Registry.[14] Regarding the information required to be submitted by a professional fiduciary acting as a trustee on establishing a Cypriot trust to the competent regulators with regard to only the name of the trust, its date of establishment, the names and contact details of the trustee, the date of change of the proper

10 Most Cypriot law has been modelled on English common law, the basic principles of which are applied directly by Cyprus courts, Section 29, Courts of Justice Law 14/60, as amended from time to time.

11 Section 11, Cyprus International Trusts Law 69(I)/1992, as amended from time to time.

12 Directive (EU) 2018/843.

13 Cyprus Securities and Exchange Commission, Institute of Certified Public Accountants of Cyprus and Cyprus Bar Association.

14 Referred to as the 'UBO Registry' for ease of reference, Section 61C of the Anti-Money Laundering and Suppression of Financing of Terrorist Activities Law, N 188(I)/2007, as amended from time to time.

law of the trust, if any and the date of termination of the trust once (and if) the trust has been terminated. Neither the trust instrument nor the names of the settlor, beneficiaries and protector (if any) are disclosed. The obligation to submit information that must be submitted to these competent authorities derives from the Law Regulating Companies Providing Administrative Services and Other Related Matters.[15] By strict interpretation of the Fiduciaries Law, it is worth mentioning that the information held by the competent regulators is not open to the public, only to the competent state authorities.

Moreover, the Cyprus International Trusts Law imposes a stringent obligation of confidentiality on the professionals appointed to assume trusteeship and protectorship during the administration and management of the trust.

3. The Fifth Anti-Money Laundering Directive and the UBO Registry

With the implementation[16] of the Fifth Anti-Money Laundering Directive into national law, UBO registries were established for legal entities (companies), trusts and other similar legal arrangements. The creation of the Cyprus Trusts Beneficial Owners Registry (CyTBOR) is administered and operated by the Cyprus Securities and Exchange Commission (CySec).

On 18 June 2021, CySEC published its regulations with immediate effect, for the prevention and suppression of money laundering and terrorist financing in regard to the register of beneficial owners of express trusts and similar legal arrangements, which sets out the *modus operandi* of CyTBOR, the timeframes when information must be submitted on the establishment of a new trust, any changes pertaining to a trust, subscription fees, penalties for non-compliance, exceptions to submit information, access and the details of the UBOs of the trust.

As per CySec's regulations, the information that must be disclosed is the name of the trust, country and date of creation and/or establishment, termination date (if applicable), for similar legal arrangements, the type of such arrangement, country in which the trustee is located or resides and their residential address, date of commencement of the business relationship, the name of the person with whom such relationship is established together with the document that governs the relationship (applicable only in cases where the trustee resides outside the European Union and establishes a business relationship on behalf of the trust in Cyprus), registration number and address of any immovable property together with the title deed of the property (applicable only in cases where the trustee resides outside the European Union

15 Section 25A (Fiduciaries Law), N 196(I)/2012, as amended from time to time.

16 18 February 2022, Directive 2018/843 by amending the Prevention and Suppression of Money Laundering and Terrorist Financing Law 188(I)/2007.

and acquires immovable property on behalf of the express trust in Cyprus), any other information and/or supporting documentation requested by CySEC for identification purposes of the UBOs of the trust, the name and surname together with the father's name, date and place of birth, nationality(ies), residential address, number, type and country of issuance of identification document.

For the purposes of disclosure, UBOs are considered to be the trustee, settlor, beneficiaries (and/or class of beneficiaries) and the protector (if any). The respective entitlement of each beneficiary must also be disclosed along with the above information.

In contrast to the Companies UBO Register, CyTBOR is not open to the public and only the relevant competent authorities have access, as well as obliged entities who must submit information to be compliant with the anti-money laundering laws. The conditions for a third person to have access to CyTBOR, according to the regulations, is based on the 'legitimate interest' notion (ie, those who can demonstrate that they have a legitimate interest and prove the same). Notably, there is no outright definition of what such legitimate interest is, but such interest should be in light of the Anti-Money Laundering Law that the reason for requesting access is that the person believes that the structure is being used for the purposes of money laundering and/or terrorist financing. The conditions for the 'legitimate interest' test must be defined in the law by each individual member state.

4. Right to information and the position in Cyprus

The Cyprus International Trusts Law[17] places strict confidentiality on the disclosure of documents or information related to a Cyprus international trust. That said, the general position is that any disclosure of documents or information, to any person not entitled to receive any such documents or information by a trustee or a protector, or trust enforcement supervisor or any other person dealing with a Cyprus international trust is stringently prohibited. On reading the relevant section of the Cyprus International Trusts Law, one can comprehend the prominence of this strict confidentiality. Section 11 (free, unofficial translation) specifically provides that:

(1) Subject to the terms of the instrument creating an international trust and if the court does not issue an order for disclosure according to the provisions of subsection (2), the trustee, protector, enforcer or any other person, cannot disclose to any person who has no right by law to know documents or information:

(a) By which the name of the settlor or of any beneficiaries is disclosed;

(b) By which the trustee's deliberations as to the manner in which a power or

17 Section 11 of the Cyprus International Trusts Law.

discretion was exercised or a duty conferred or imposed by the law or by the terms of the international trust was performed are disclosed;

(c) By which the reason for any particular exercise of such power or discretion or performance of duty or the material upon which such reason has been or might have been based is disclosed;

(d) By which any documents or information relate to the exercise or proposed exercise of such powers or discretions or the performance or proposed performance of such duty is disclosed; and

(e) Which relate to or form part of the accounts of the international trust: Provided that where a request is made by a beneficiary to the trustee for the disclosure of the accounts of an international trust or any documents or information relating to proceeds and payments made by the trustees forming part of the said accounts, the trustee shall have the power to disclose those accounts, documents or information to the beneficiary only if in his opinion such disclosure is necessary and secures the lawful interests of the trust.

(2) Notwithstanding the provisions of any other law and subject to the provisions of subsection (3), a court before which civil or criminal proceedings are pending may by order allow the disclosure of the documents or information referred to in subsection (1) after an application submitted by a party in the said civil or criminal proceedings, as the case may be.

(3) The court issues an order under subsection (2), if satisfied that the disclosure of the documents or information referred to in subsection (1) is material for the outcome of the proceedings.

(4) For the purposes of this section 'documents or information' includes documents or information stored in electronic computers and in such a case an order for disclosure is executed by the disclosure or giving of the documents or information in visible, readable, and portable form.

In interpreting the above points, and especially with regard to the accounts of a trust or any payments, any documents or information relating to proceeds and payments made by the trustees forming part of the said accounts, the trustee despite having the power to disclose such information to the beneficiaries, this power can be strictly exercised only if the trustee is of the opinion and considers that any such disclosure safeguards the best interests of the trust. Thus, even when a beneficiary requests such disclosure, nevertheless, the trustee can refuse to provide such information or documents. Where a beneficiary is aggrieved by any refusal, the beneficiary may opt to file an application to the relevant competent judicial court seeking an order for disclosure. Notwithstanding the above, where, within the knowledge of the trustee and/or the court, there are any pending criminal prosecution or civil litigation proceedings, the court may grant an order for disclosure if it is satisfied that such an order is paramount to the outcome of any such pending proceedings. With this provision, the Cyprus International Trusts Law has imposed further conditions when a court should consider issuing a disclosure order and the above conditions must be met.

There are not enough case law precedents in Cyprus regarding ordering by a court for providing access to information and/or documentation to beneficiaries; however, there is some guidance.

In *The HPH Settlement v HPH Cayman Limited,*[18] one of the sought remedies, *inter alia*, filed by application by the trustees of the settlement was for the court to instruct and/or grant an order for the original, initial trustee regarding its conduct and accountability during its appointment and to order the disclosure of the accounts of the settlement and submission of the same to the new trustees from the date of the settlement's establishment until the cessation of the trustees' appointment (which was another sought remedy in this application), to instruct and/or order the initial trustee to present and provide a detailed statement of expenses to the applicant that were incurred by the trust's assets during the administration and to deliver to the new trustee (ie, the applicant) copies of all receipts and expenses paid out of the settlement's trust assets. In addition, the applicant requested that the court instructs and/or orders and/or issues a judgment for the initial, original trustee and/or any of its representatives to hand over free possession of all the assets of the trust to the applicant. Following a hearing and based on the testimony provided by the witnesses of each side and the weight given to each, the court rejected the application. In the co-related and co-tried second and first-instance cases,[19] the applicants sought a remedy from the court against the respondents for an order and/or instructions and/or judgment ordering the respondent to provide them with a detailed statement of the assets held by the trustees in a number of trusts within the structures of each that were interlinked and also concerning previous distributions to the beneficiaries of assets, which in their view were not analogous according to the accounts and terms of each of the trusts. During the hearings, it appeared from the court's files that the position of one of the witnesses was correct in the context of previously tried law suits back in 2003 and decrees were issued by mutual agreement by which the respondent and its directors were ordered to submit a detailed account with regard to dividends, interest, income received or reaped by another person by order and for the benefit of the respondents acting as trustees. In its findings, the court ordered the distributions of certain amounts to the beneficiaries that they were entitled to.

There is a plethora of well-established precedent that when an applicant files an application for an order of disclosure of documents and/or information

---

18 Nicosia District Court case, 15 June 2017; General Applications 1036/13 and 1037/13.

19 *Frabran Holdings Co Limited v Daventree Trustees Limited,* 25 April 2017, *Husky Trading Co Ltd v Daventree Trustees Limited,* case numbers 13792/03 και 13842/03.

and/or statement of the financial position and accounts of a trust, the court will first consider whether the applicant has a right to such information and whether the three conditions[20] for the issue of an order are satisfied. The above conditions were considered by the court in *Ammar Al Assam et al v Latimer (Management Services) Limited*[21] where the applicants, sought a number of orders instructing the respondents (acting as trustees of the trust) to prepare, and serve, by affidavit information listing the current assets of the trust, specifying the type and nature of each asset, the name and bank account number, value and location where the assets are held as well as copies of the latest available financial statements of the trusts and any of its subsidiaries, copies of bank statements relating to any bank accounts in the name of the respondents and the beneficiaries themselves and finally to file this list with the district court. In its judgment, the court ruled that the conditions were not satisfied and rejected the application.

In an interim judgment,[22] the court was asked to grant orders for the disclosure by the respondents of information (among other orders that we are not concerned with for the purposes of this chapter) relating to any payment or transfer of money to the respondents or to any subsidiary of the respondents to any other company controlled by the respondents made by or on behalf of them in connection with services provided by respondents including bank account details where any such payment, transfer and remittances to the relevant payments was made, the date and purpose of any such payment or remittance. Most interesting is the request for an order for the respondents to disclose and provide the applicant with all details regarding the terms of that trust, all information and documents relating to the creation of that trust or the applicant's interest in that trust, full accounts relating to that trust, all details of the exercise of any powers by the trustee or trustees under the terms of that trust and all details concerning the rights of the beneficiaries.

Once again, the main issue for consideration by the court was whether the conditions were satisfied. In its analysis, the court referred to an excerpt from the English case[23] where the presiding judge quoted:

> *(21) The three conditions to be satisfied for the court to exercise the power to order Norwich Pharmacal relief are: (i) a wrong must have been carried out, or arguably carried out, by an ultimate wrongdoer; (ii) there must be the need for an order to enable action to be brought against the ultimate wrongdoer; (iii) the person against whom the order is sought must: (a) be mixed up in so as to have facilitated the wrongdoing; And (b) be able or likely to be able to provide the information necessary to enable the ultimate wrongdoer to be sued.*

20 Section 32 of the Courts of Law, N 14/60.

21 (2022) EWHC 451 (Ch), 13/2019, 16 June 2019.

22 *OJSC Bank of Moscow v Oneworld Limited* (6029/2012, 23 January 2015).

23 *Mitsui & Co v Nexen Petroleum UK Ltd* ([2005] 3 All ER 511).

> ...
>
> *I consider first whether the second condition is satisfied. I proceed in this judgment on the basis that the claimant needs further information which the defendant is likely to be able to provide before it can fully and properly plead a breach of the first limb. In a word the information sought is necessary to enable the action to be brought.*
>
> ...
>
> *In my judgment, it is clear that the exercise of the jurisdiction of the court under Norwich Pharmacal against third parties who are mere witnesses innocent of any participation in the wrongdoing being investigated is a remedy of last resort. The jurisdiction is only to be exercised if the innocent third parties are the only practicable source of information. The whole basis of the jurisdiction against them is that, unless and until they disclose what they know, there can be no litigation in which they can give evidence: see, eg, Lord Kilbrandon in* Norwich Pharmacal[24] *(1973). Whilst there is a public interest in achieving justice between disputing parties, there is also a public interest in not involving third parties if this can be avoided: see John Donaldson MR in* Harrington v North London Polytechnic *(1984) 3 All E.R. 666 at 670-671, (1984) 1 WLR 1293 at 1299. The Jurisdiction is both exceptional and only to be exercised when it is necessary: Lord Woolf CJ in* Ashworth Hospital Authority v MGN Ltd.[25] *The necessity required to justify exercise of this intrusive jurisdiction is a necessity arising from the absence of any other practicable means of obtaining the essential information.*

In delivering its judgment, the judge was satisfied that the three conditions were indeed satisfied: "All three criteria set by article 32 of Law 14/60 are met, while the balance of power is inclined in favour of the issuance of the requested orders. The conditions set by Norwich Pharmacal and coded by *Mitsui & Co v Nexen Pertroleum UK Ltd* (above) are also met. On the foregoing, the orders were subsequently granted."

5. Norwich Pharmacal orders

With Cyprus being a common law jurisdiction, the adoption by the Cyprus courts of judge-made remedies (as such may be the request for a beneficiary to request information and documents analysed above) that the English Courts have created for the needs of victims of fraud, was an important evolution to the Cyprus legal system in its battle against civil fraud. The principles initially laid down in the landmark decision[26] have been adopted and followed by the

24 2 All ER 943, at 973, 975, (1974) AC at 203, 205.
25 [2002] 4 All ER 193 at (75).
26 *Norwich Pharmacal v Customs and Excise Commissioners* ([1974] AC 133).

Cypriot Supreme Court in *Avila Management Services Ltd v Stepanek*[27] where it was decided that a victim of fraud can oblige, for example, a bank to disclose beneficial ownership, signatory details and account movements to assist in identifying the offender of a suspected fraud, the source of funds, the destination of any funds paid out of the account and any other persons participating in a fraudulent scheme. While these two cases were concerned with fraud, the principles could perhaps be applied when an application to the court is filed by a beneficiary if such beneficiary believes that the trustee has misappropriated or misused trust funds and therefore seeks disclosure of the trust's accounts.

6. Conclusion

Although there is little case law in Cyprus regarding the disclosure of information to a beneficiary (or other interested applicant), the courts are somewhat reluctant to grant disclosure orders. The main element that the courts consider and take into account is whether the conditions set out by Section 32 of the Courts of Law are satisfied. Especially where trusts are concerned, the nature and purpose for which a trust is usually set up, information relating to the same is, as a matter of protection, confidential and it seems that the courts are protective of securing this confidentiality. Being a common law system based on the principles of equity and following English case law precedent, the Cypriot courts will look to English precedent when trying a case for disclosure and apply the same principles.

Cypriot, but mainly English, case law has determined that disclosure of documents or information to beneficiaries is a matter for the trustees; the beneficiaries have no automatic entitlement. However, trustees do have a duty to account to beneficiaries and so beneficiaries should expect trustees to respond positively to legitimate requests for information.

Beneficiaries must be able to enforce the trust and the court has an inherent jurisdiction to supervise and, where necessary, to intervene to assist them to ensure the proper administration of a trust; so, information should be disclosed if conducive to the proper administration of the trust.

In general, trustees should disclose, and beneficiaries should expect to have sight of or receive copies of:

- documents that set out the terms of the trust (ie, the will or trust instrument and any variations);
- documents that confirm the identity of the trustees (ie, deeds of appointment or retirement); and
- documents that confirm the extent of the trust assets (ie, trust accounts); however, the trustees could specifically exclude by way of redaction of

27 (2020) 1 CLR 1403.

the documents any assets that other beneficiaries would be entitled to, and therefore disclose only the actual benefit that the particular beneficiary requesting the information is entitled to.

However, beneficiaries are not generally entitled to documents pertaining to the trustees' decision making, such as:

- letters of wishes;
- correspondence between trustees or with other beneficiaries;
- correspondence with professional advisers or advice obtained; and
- agendas for and minutes of trustee meetings.

This is because trustees are not required to give reasons behind the exercise of their powers or discretions and letters of wishes are generally accepted as being confidential to the trustees, as is the general position adopted by Section 11 of the Cyprus International Trusts Law.

If a beneficiary wishes to receive information about a trust, they should first request it from the trustees. On receipt of such a request, trustees should conduct a balancing exercise, considering all the relevant circumstances. They should consider what is in the best interests of all the beneficiaries. Trustees should generally provide beneficiaries with the items listed above on request and would need a very good reason to refuse.

There are, however, reasons why trustees may reasonably refuse requests, such as:

- legal privilege;
- commercial sensitivity or confidentiality;
- disclosure being impractical or costly;
- if the request came from a non-beneficiary or an object not intended to benefit, or for an improper purpose; and
- the rationale and justification for the actual purpose of a request (ie, is the request justified based on the requestor's standing or is the request merely a tool for holding a trustee 'potentially' accountable for their trusteeship or because there may be a family vendetta and a person is requesting information 'to get back' at someone else?).

Trustees should consider alternatives if and where possible, such as:

- access for inspection;
- disclosure of part of or redacted documents; and
- offering to legal advisers rather than to beneficiaries themselves.

Trustees may take comfort from undertakings regarding use, such as keeping the information or documents confidential. If unsure, trustees have the option to seek direction from the court, as provided by Section 11A of the Cyprus

International Trusts Law and it is urged that such option is exercised by trustees when unsure how to act in a particular circumstance. Conversely, beneficiaries faced with trustees' refusal to disclose may apply to the court.

Trustee investment powers and delegation

Savvas Georgiou
Christodoulos G Vassiliades & Co LLC

1. Introduction

Trustees have several duties by virtue of common law, statute and of course by the terms included in the trust instrument itself. One of the most fundamental duties of the trustees is associated with the power to invest the trust fund. When investing the trust fund the trustees must ensure that they act reasonably, impartially and loyally for the benefit of the beneficiaries. The reason that the trustees are under this obligation to invest is to ensure that the benefit that they were supposed to obtain does not stagnate and depreciate. The issue is that these three obligations may in certain circumstances conflict with each other. For example, it is well known that higher risk investments usually have a significantly higher return. Naturally, the trustee would like to ensure the highest possible gains for the beneficiaries, but the trustee must balance the risk accordingly and ensure that they are acting reasonably in the circumstances. For the purposes of this chapter, we will review the relevant legal provisions that permit the trustees to invest, what is considered as an investment, what duty of care is applicable to trustees and whether the trustees are permitted to delegate their powers of investment.

2. Legislation

In terms of Cyprus law, the trustees' initial investment powers are derived from the Trustees Law, Chapter 193. As was also provided in the original UK legislation, the investment powers of the trustees are restricted. The Trustees Law provides that the trustees can invest the trust funds:

- *in any securities in which trustees in England are for the time being authorised by the law of England to invest trust funds;*
- *in any securities where the interest on which is guaranteed by the government;*
- *in any debentures, bonds, stocks or securities issued under the authority of any law or in respect of any loan raised by the government;*
- *in any debentures, bonds, stocks or securities of any public body or local authority in the Colony, the revenues of which are under the control of the government; and*
- *on the security of a charge on immovable property, unless expressly prohibited*

> *by the instrument creating the trust, provided that such property will be situated within the limits of a municipal corporation and the sum to be invested is not more than two-thirds of the value of such property.*[1]

The trustees' investment powers are restricted to safeguard the interests of the beneficiaries. However, such restrictions are unsuitable in the current economic climate when taking into consideration the many investment products now available. The Cyprus International Trusts Law 69(I)/92, on the other hand, permits the trustees to make any investments. This is consistent with the provisions adopted pursuant to the amendments under the UK Trustee Act 2000. The Cyprus International Trusts Law provides that, subject to the provisions of the trust instrument, a trustee may at any time invest the whole or any part of the trust fund in any kind of investment as they would have done if they were the absolute beneficiary of the assets of the trust wherever the investment is situated and whether or not the funds have already been invested. There is no further guidance either in the law or the relevant case law of Cyprus regarding these provisions. Therefore, in the event that a claim is brought in relation to the investment powers, the relevant common law of other jurisdictions will be considered. For trustees this provision raises two important questions: first, what is considered to be an investment; and second, how can a trustee demonstrate that an investment was made in the same way as though the trustee had been the beneficiary?

3. Investments

It is presumed that the reasons why the term 'investment' is not defined in the law are twofold. First, certain transactions, when considered independently, would not appear as an investment. An example would be if a trustee holds shares worth €100 each and sells to X an option to purchase the shares if their value reaches €100 per share. The sale of the option on its own cannot be considered an investment; however, when considered alongside another investment (namely, that of the shares themselves) then it can be considered an investment. The reason is because the option would permit the trustee to set-off the loss that occurred to the trust fund in the event that those shares fell in value.[2] Second, the notion of what constitutes an investment is an evolving concept to be interpreted by the courts.[3]

The meaning of 'investment' has been interpreted by the judiciary in a number of cases without providing an exact definition. For example, in *Re Wragg, Wragg v Palmer*[4] it was stated that 'to invest' means "to apply money in the purchase of some property from which interest or profit is expected and

1 The Trustees Law (Cap 193) 1955, Section 4.
2 Gary Watt, *Trust and Equity* (Oxford University Press, 2020) at p423.
3 Trustees' Powers and Duties (Law Com No 260) (1999) para 2.28.
4 [1919] 2 Ch 58 at 65.

which property is purchased in order to be held for the sake of the income which it will yield". Therefore, according to *Wragg*, an investment is strictly something that is purchased for the purpose of generating income. However, such a definition does not consider any property that will yield a capital growth. In *Harries v Church Commissioners for England*[5] it was decided that "where property is so held ... the purposes of the trust will be best served by the trustees seeking to obtain therefrom the maximum return, whether by way of income or capital growth, which is consistent with commercial prudence". Consequently, any property or transaction that will generate an income or capital growth or both for the trust will be considered an investment.

4. Prudence

As stated in the Cyprus International Trusts Law, the trustees will make an investment as they would have done if they were the absolute beneficial owners of the assets. Against this backdrop resonates the general concept of acting prudently as developed through common law. Taking into consideration common law, I believe that it would be incorrect to interpret the law so as to consider that the trustees should deal with the trust fund in a way that they had only themselves to consider. Rather the interpretation adopted pursuant to *Re Whiteley*[6] should be applied by the trustees of a Cyprus international trust as well as a domestic trust. This being that the duty of the trustees is to "take such care as an ordinary prudent man would take if he were minded to make an investment for the benefit of other people for whom he felt morally bound to provide". Therefore, when considering an investment, the trustees should consider the interests of the beneficiaries as a whole.

Further, it is important to note that there is not only one standard of care that is applicable, there are various standards of care according to the expertise of the trustees. This is extremely important to consider when professional trustees have been tasked with managing the trust fund. In *Re Waterman's Will Trust*[7] it was ruled that a paid trustee is expected to exercise a higher standard of diligence and knowledge than an unpaid trustee. This concept was developed further in *Bartlett v Barclays Bank Trust Co Ltd.*[8] This case was in relation to a trust set up by Sir Herbert Bartlett regarding the shares in a property investment company called Bartlett Trust Ltd. Initially the company was involved in managing freehold and leasehold properties. These properties would generate income that would be distributed to the shareholder as dividends. The trust appointed merchant bankers to consider taking the company public. The bankers advised that a public offering would be much more successful if the

---

5 [1993] 2 All ER 300 at 304.
6 (1886) LR 33 ChD 347.
7 [1952] 2 All ER 1054.
8 [1980] 1 All ER 139.

company expanded its business from managing property to developing property as well. Barclays Bank, as trustee, agreed to this policy. The board approved certain questionable developments that resulted in the trust sustaining significant losses. The beneficiaries of the trust brought an action against Barclays Bank Trust Company Ltd, arguing that it was guilty of a breach of trust by permitting the company to engage in the speculative business of property development. It was decided that:

> *I am of opinion that a higher duty of care is plainly due from someone like a trust corporation which carries on a specialised business of trust management. A trust corporation holds itself out in its advertising literature as being above ordinary mortals. With a specialist staff of trained trust officers and managers, with ready access to financial information and professional advice, dealing with and solving trust problems day after day, the trust corporation holds itself out, and rightly, as capable of providing an expertise which it would be unrealistic to expect and unjust to demand from the ordinary prudent man or woman who accepts, probably unpaid and sometimes reluctantly from a sense of family duty, the burdens of a trusteeship. Just as, under the law of contract, a professional person possessed of a particular skill is liable for breach of contract if he neglects to use the skill and experience which he professes, so I think that a professional corporate trustee is liable for breach of trust if loss is caused to the trust fund because it neglects to exercise the special care and skill which it professes to have.*[9]

Therefore, corporate and professional trustees should be wary of this case as they will be subject to a higher standard of care than a prudent man and they should take the necessary steps to ensure that they are acting in the best interest of the beneficiaries.

Corporate trustees can at least rest assured that their directors are safe from personal liability as per *Gregson v HAE Trustees Ltd.*[10] Ms Gregson was a beneficiary of a trust set up by members of the family that had acquired the furniture company that later became Courts plc. The whole of the trust fund consisted of shares in Courts; the trustee was a company, HAE, set up specifically to act as an executor or administrator of estates of the family members, or as a trustee of the family trusts. In 2004, Courts went into administration and the trust fund became worthless. Considering that the trust company, set up specifically for this purpose, had no funds, it would be of no consequence to Ms Gregson to sue the company; she therefore attempted to sue the directors of the trust company. It was argued that HAE had breached its duty as trustee by failing to consider the need to diversify the content of the trust fund. It was claimed that:

- the directors had breached their duties to HAE;

---

9 *Bartlett v Barclays Bank Trust Co Ltd* ([1980] 1 All ER 139 at 152).
10 [2008] EWHC 1006.

- as HAE was a trustee, its rights against the directors were held on trust for the beneficiaries of the settlement; and
- the claimant could therefore force HAE to use those rights for her benefit.

Such a claim is considered a 'dog leg' claim as it was not based on a direct duty owed by the directors to the beneficiaries but rather on the proposition that a corporate trustee's claims against its directors are themselves held on trust. This claim was rejected, and it was held that the fiduciary duties owed by the directors were owed to the company, not to the beneficiaries. Deputy Judge Robert Miles QC stated that to allow such a claim "would for all practical purposes, circumvent the clear and established principle that no direct duty is owed by the directors to the beneficiaries".[11] However, a direct duty can arise in the situation where a director represents directly to a beneficiary that the trustee is undertaking a personal duty of loyalty to that beneficiary and has acted dishonestly.[12]

5. Duty of care

It is clear that the trustees must invest the trust fund. When they are exercising this duty to invest, they must ensure that the trust fund is preserved from risk while a reasonable return on capital is made and that any investment should be 'even handed' between the different classes of beneficiaries. Unlike the UK Trustees Act 2000, the Cyprus International Trusts Law includes no standard investment criteria for the trustees to consult. The trustees should therefore be aware of the relevant case law when making their investments to ensure that they do not breach their duty that they owe to the beneficiaries.

An investor's goal is usually to obtain the highest possible return on the investment, a higher return naturally involves a higher risk. Although this might be acceptable for an investor, a trustee must consider whether such a risk is reasonable in the circumstances. Thus, although the trustees are obliged to make the optimum return for the trust, they do need to safeguard the trust fund. This concept was examined in *Cowan v Scargill*,[13] where the defendant was the president of the National Union of Mineworkers and a trustee of the miners' pensions fund. The board of trustees was divided between executives of the trade union and executives from the coal board. The trustees identified the oil industry and investments in South Africa as being most profitable. The defendant refused to make such investments on the grounds that it was ethically wrong for the fund to invest in South Africa considering that apartheid

11 *Gregson v HAE Trustees Ltd* ([2008] EWHC 1006).
12 *Sinclair Investment Holdings SA v Versailles Trade Finance Ltd* ([2007] All ER (D) 283 (Apr)).
13 [1985] Ch 270.

was still in place and that it was contrary to the interests of the beneficiaries to invest in the oil industry (which can be considered a competitor of the coal industry) in which all the beneficiaries worked or had worked previously.

The court decided that:

When the purpose of the trust is to provide financial benefits for the beneficiaries, as is usually the case, the best interests of the beneficiaries are normally their best financial interests. In the case of a power of investment, as in the present case, the power must be exercised so as to yield the best return for the beneficiaries, judged in relation to the risks of the investments in question; and the prospects of the yield of income and capital appreciation both have to be considered in judging the return from the investment.[14]

Therefore, it is clear that the duty of the trustees is to obtain the best available return for the trust fund regardless of other considerations except the possible risk. In addition, it was stated that the trustees should put aside their own personal interests and views in the event that the investments would be more beneficial to the beneficiaries than other investments, the trustees should not refrain from making an investment based on the views that they have. "Trustees may even have to act dishonourably (though not illegally) if the interests of their beneficiaries require it."[15]

Thus, there is a positive duty to invest, taking into consideration the various risks, regardless of ethics. Trustees are therefore not permitted to subordinate consideration of financial returns to non-financial criteria such as politics, morals or ethics. The only exception is when dealing with charitable trusts where the trustee can decide not to proceed with an investment where such an investment would conflict with the objects of the charity (eg, a cancer charity investing in tobacco products).[16]

When considering risk, the trustees should keep *Learoyd v Whiteley*[17] in mind, in which it was decided that the trusteed should "avoid all investments of that class which are attended with hazard". Trustees should essentially focus on protecting and maintaining the trust fund, while allowing a certain level of capital growth.

In relation to trusts that have different classes of beneficiaries, trustees must act fairly between all beneficiaries. However, in certain instances the interest of different classes of beneficiaries may conflict with each other. A beneficiary who has a life interest in the trust is more concerned with high-income assets with limited scope for capital appreciation, while a remainder beneficiary is more interested in capital retention at the expense of income. With this in mind, trustees have a duty to act fairly in relation to investments and to look to the

14 *Cowan v Scargill* ([1985] Ch 270 at 287).
15 *Ibid.*
16 Graham Moffat, *Trusts Law*, 3rd edn (Cambridge University Press, 2005) at p359.
17 (1887) 12 App Cas 727 at 733.

"interests of all, and not of any particular member or class".[18] This concept was reviewed in *Nestle v National Westminster Bank PLC*,[19] where Hoffman J stated that:

> *The trustees have in my judgment a wide discretion. They are for example entitled to take into account the income needs of the tenant for life or the fact that the tenant for life was a person known to the settlor and a primary object of the trust whereas the remainderman is a remoter relative or a stranger ... It would be an inhuman law which required trustees to adhere to some mechanical rule for preserving the real value of the capital when the tenant for life was the testator's widow who had fallen upon hard times and the remainderman was young and well off.*[20]

This was also a significant case as it was held that the modern portfolio theory was applicable to trustees and that "modern trustees acting within their investment powers are entitled to be judged by the standard of current portfolio theory, which emphasises the risk level of the entire portfolio rather than the risk attaching to each investment taken in isolation".[21] Therefore, trustees can mitigate their risk by diversifying.

It is certainly clear that when trustees acting under Cyprus law are entrusted with a trust fund, they must be extremely careful when exercising their wide powers of investment. First and foremost, trustees should consider whether it is necessary to obtain advice regarding the investments. Thereafter, as stated in *Lewin on Trusts*, the trustees should:[22]

- act with a single eye to the benefit of their beneficiaries;
- exclude all ulterior purposes;
- exercise the appropriate duty of care in the selection of investments from among those authorised;
- have regard to their suitability and the need for diversification;
- obtain all necessary consents;
- act fairly and impartially as between beneficiaries with different interests, particularly between those interested in current income, among others; and
- review their investment on the same basis at suitable intervals thereafter.

6. Delegation of the power of investment

There are a number of factors for a trustee to consider in relation to investing the trust fund. In certain circumstances they may believe that it is preferable to delegate such power to a third party. However, the courts usually consider that

---

18 *Re Tempest* ([1866] LR 1 Ch App 485).
19 [1988] Lexis Citation 2473.
20 *Nestle v National Westminster Bank PLC* ([1988] Lexis Citation 2473).
21 *Ibid.*
22 Lynton Tucker, Nicholas Le Poidevin and James Brightwell, *Lewin on Trusts*, 19th edn (Sweet and Maxwell, 2014) at 35-055.

the settlor has entrusted the trustee specifically to manage the trust fund, therefore the trustee should not be permitted to shift this duty onto any other person. A trustee is permitted to delegate any power only if the trustee has the authority to do so, either pursuant to the trust instrument or by an order of the court. In accordance with the Trustees Law, the actual ability to delegate is limited. Actual delegation by the trustee is permitted according to Section 25 of the Trustee Law, which states that any trustee intending to remain out of Cyprus for more than 14 days may, notwithstanding any rule of law or equity to the contrary, by power of attorney, delegate to any person (including a trust corporation) the execution or exercise during their absence from Cyprus of all or any trusts, powers and discretion vested in him as such trustee, either alone or jointly with any other person or persons. This power of delegation would not be workable in relation to delegating the power of investment because it is for a specific period. However, pursuant to Section 23, instead of acting personally, a trustee may employ and pay an agent, whether an advocate, banker, stockbroker or other person, to transact any business or do any act required to be transacted or done in execution of the trust. This would essentially permit a trustee to delegate to power of investment to an investment manager by employing such investment manager as an agent. Certain principles must be followed when appointing an agent. A trustee has a duty of care in relation to the appointment and the supervisions of the agent. If they wish to appoint an agent, they should appoint an agent that is appropriate for the circumstances[23] and they should review the actions of the agents and the investments being made.[24] In the event that they fail to do so, they could be liable for a breach of duty.

In recent years trustees have been found liable for a breach of duty; for example, in *Appleby Corporate Services (BVI) Limited v Citco Trustees (BVI) Limited,*[25] where it was decided that the trustees did not have sufficient procedures in place whereby they could be satisfied that the delegated authority was being properly exercised. Additionally, in *Manita Khuller v FNB International Trustees Limited,*[26] it was decided that the trustees had failed to pay attention to the functions and the responsibilities that it was delegating and had therefore not correctly delegated its investment function and was responsible to review the advice provided by the investment advisers. The trustees were thus held liable for a breach of their duty. As with all the duties that trustees have, they should always ensure that they are exercised with caution, taking into consideration the duty of care that they owe to the beneficiaries.

---

23 *Fry v Tapson* ((1884) LR 28 Ch D 268).
24 *Speight v Gaunt* ((1883) LR 22 Ch D 727).
25 Claim No. BVIHC (Com) 156 of 2011.
26 (2020) GCA 051.

7. Conclusion

The trustees' investments powers should always be exercised in the best interest of the beneficiaries. First and foremost, they must always ensure that they are following the terms of the trust instrument. Trustees must take care when exercising their power and ensure that they are acting reasonably in the circumstances. If necessary, they should seek the appropriate advice and in the event that they decide to delegate any function they should choose wisely and make sure that they have the relevant checks and procedures in place to properly supervise any agents. Taking such steps would make it difficult to prove that a trustee has breached its duty to the beneficiaries.

Protectors

Emily Yiolitis
Anemi Trustees Limited

1. Introduction

A 'protector' is a person appointed by the settlor to supervise certain actions of the trustee with the aim of ensuring that the wishes of the settlor are adhered to. Usually, a protector will hold one or more powers affecting what the trustees are to do, or not to do, with the powers granted to them and with the property settled into the trust, providing direction and restraint to the trustees, as appropriate. Appointing a protector is optional and the role of protector is separate and distinct from the role of trustee.

There is no Cyprus statute or case law on the subject of protectors. Where there is no applicable Cyprus legislation or precedent, English common law and equity are applicable in Cyprus and English authorities have persuasive force in the Cyprus court rooms in interpreting Cyprus law.

There are various matters to consider when deciding whether to appoint a protector and, once that hurdle is crossed, who to appoint. There are no restrictions on who can be appointed, even a settlor or a beneficiary may occupy this position, although this is not recommended as settlors may be taken as not having relinquished power and beneficiaries may find themselves in a position of conflict of interest. Settlors sometimes opt to appoint a family member or trusted adviser as protector. They may, however, opt to appoint a professional protector who has a better understanding of the role and how that role complements the role of trustee. Professional protectors also have advantages:

- they generally possess a greater understanding of general trust law;
- they are better equipped to deal with complex and unforeseen trust matters that may arise;
- they impart objective and impartial advice and are not susceptible to family bias; and
- they are often regulated entities.

The parties that are (mandatorily) required to set up a valid trust are the settlor, the trustees and the beneficiaries. The Cyprus legislation makes no reference to protectors and this role is one that has crept into practice following international example. Settlors are understandably reluctant to relinquish all control and title over hard-earned property settled into the trust and therefore seek ways to continue to exercise some control, whether directly through settlor reserved powers (see the "Settlor reserved powers trusts" chapter by Emily Yiolitis) or indirectly by appointing a trusted person to direct or veto certain powers of the trustees.

A settlor may opt to appoint a protector for a number of reasons, including that protectors provide a certain degree of security that the wishes of the settlor will be adhered to and can act as objective third-party mediators between the trust parties when the relationship is tense or breaks down or an unforeseen hurdle arises.

2. Selection of a protector

The first protector is appointed by the settlor. Although unconstrained by statute or regulation in Cyprus, the settlor's choice ought to be limited to persons qualified to undertake the responsibilities of the position. The person selected must be able as well as willing to serve. Protectors may wield a great degree of influence over the administration of a trust and as a result great care must be exercised in their selection. The question of who is qualified to act as a protector depends largely on the nature of the powers delegated to the protector under the trust deed. Protector powers that relate to the administration of the trust require, among other things, that the protector understands:

- what a trust is;
- what the relationship between the trust parties is;
- the legal requirements; and
- the constraints that apply to trusts, applicable taxes and related matters.

Who is willing to serve depends on the powers and responsibilities allocated to the protector, the amount of time and effort that would be required on their behalf to undertake the role and the possible liability attached to the role, which will usually depend on whether the role is one of a fiduciary or not.

3. Protector powers

The scope of the protector's role is limited to the specific powers conferred by the terms of trust deed and as such the powers granted to the protector should be carefully considered and drafted into the trust deed. Some of the powers often granted to protectors in Cyprus trusts include, but are not limited to:

- replacing the trustee where the latter resigns or is unable or unwilling to act;
- permitting or vetoing the addition to or removal from the class of beneficiaries;
- permitting or vetoing a change in the governing law of the trust; and
- appointing a successor protector.

Some powers may be more complex or specific to a particular trust, such as the power to make, direct or veto investment decisions, to consent to or veto the sale of trust assets or to allocate sale proceeds between income and capital. Protectors may be given positive powers, such as the power to appoint or remove trustees, or negative powers, such as the power to veto an addition to the class of beneficiaries. Depending on the nature and extent of the powers that may be granted by a settlor to a protector, it is also important that the tax residence of the protector be considered to avoid a potential challenge by tax or other authorities that the 'management and control' of a trust is actually located not (only) in the tax residence of the trustees or of the proper law of the trust but also in the tax residence of the protector. There may be further considerations to be had such as whether the Common Reporting Standard applies to a protector or whether a protector should be included as a party in a trust register (see the "Trusts and ultimate beneficial ownership registers in Cyprus" chapter by Eleni Drakou). These considerations may prevent an individual from accepting office or indeed a settlor from appointing a protector altogether.

4. Is the protector a fiduciary and are the powers bestowed on a protector fiduciary powers?

Whether a protector is deemed to be a fiduciary will determine the possible liability that the protector is exposed to, and the likelihood that a person will accept an appointment as a protector.

A trustee is unequivocally a fiduciary, a person who owes a fiduciary duty to the beneficiaries of a trust. As pronounced in *Armitage v Nurse*,[1] "there is an irreducible core of obligations" owed by the trustees to the beneficiaries and enforceable by them, which is fundamental to the concept of a trust. If the beneficiaries have no rights enforceable against the trustees, there is no trust. Although optional and 'secondary' to the role of trustee, the role of the protector in a trust may also be important and may significantly affect the administration of the trust, depending on the powers bestowed on the protector. If the protector is subject to a fiduciary obligation, as many courts globally have opined, the protector will be held accountable to a standard of care and behaviour befitting of a fiduciary, involving an affirmative duty to seek out information and to take positive action. If not, the powers of the protector will be deemed to be personal powers, which the protector may exercise 'selfishly' or 'whimsically' without taking into account the intent of the settlor or without having to act in the best interests of the beneficiaries and without being held accountable for a decision. Even where a power is unequivocally a fiduciary one, the standard of care that a protector will be held accountable for may again vary, depending on whether such a protector is a professional

1 *Armitage v Nurse* ([1998] Ch 241 (CA)).

protector, is remunerated or is simply a friend or relative occupying the position as a favour to the settlor.

A protector may be expressly appointed in the trust deed to act in a fiduciary or a non-fiduciary capacity. Where there is no express mention, the nature of the powers bestowed on the protector must be considered. Some jurisdictions have made the distinction easier by legislation. In the British Virgin Islands, the relevant statute[2] provides that a protector "is not liable to the beneficiaries for the *bona fide* exercise of the power". Nevis, on the other hand, states in its relevant ordinance[3] that "a protector shall owe a fiduciary duty to the beneficiaries of the trust or to the purpose for which the trust is created". Such contrasting positions make the task of determining whether a protector is a fiduciary in jurisdictions that have not expressly legislated on the matter even more confusing.

In the Bermuda case of *Von Knieriem v Bermuda Trust Company*[4] the protector held the power to replace the trustee and decided to exercise this power. The trustee petitioned the court for instruction. The court considered whether the protector was a fiduciary, and specifically whether the power bestowed on the protector to remove or replace the trustee was held in a fiduciary capacity. The court held that the power to remove and replace trustees was a core power to be exercised in the best interests of the beneficiaries. The court referred to the English case of *Re Skeats Settlement*,[5] where it was held that the person who holds the power to appoint new trustees has "the duty of selecting honest and good persons who can be trusted with the very difficult duties which trustees have to perform. He is bound to select to the best of his ability the best people he can find for the purpose" and, in this regard, the power of a protector to remove and replace a trustee was held to be a fiduciary one.

As a rule of thumb, it can be said that in determining whether a protector is acting in a fiduciary capacity, the terms of the relevant trust deed must be considered carefully because the determining factor is the settlor's intention, which is most often derived from the construction of the trust deed. Unless otherwise stipulated or construed (in respect of a particular power), and unless the protector is clearly acting in a personal capacity (eg, is also a beneficiary), the protector will usually be construed to hold a fiduciary role. Even a protector with negative powers of consent (veto powers) has been held to occupy a fiduciary position[6] and does owe a duty of care to the beneficiaries to consider whether the proposed exercise of the negative power is in the best interests of the beneficiaries. In the *Representation of Jasmine Trustees Limited*,[7] the court considered whether the appointment of new trustees and protectors had been

---

2 The British Virgin Islands Trustee Act 1961, Section 86(3).
3 The Nevis International Exempt Trust Ordinance 1994, Section 9 (as amended in 1995).
4 *Von Knieriem v Bermuda Trust Co* ([1994] Bda LR 50) (Berm Sup Ct 1994).
5 *Re Skeats Settlement* ((1889) 42 Ch D 522 at 526).
6 *Sociedad Financiera Sofimeca v Kleinwort Benson (Jersey) Trustees Ltd* ([1992] JCR 125).
7 *Representation of Jasmine Trustees Limited* ([2015] JRC 196).

validly exercised. The court held that the power of the protector to appoint trustees is a fiduciary power and that the holder of a fiduciary power must not exercise that power in a whimsical manner. The court identified a list of duties that a protector as a fiduciary owes to the beneficiaries when exercising the power to appoint a new trustee including but not limited to the following:

- to act in good faith and in the interests of the beneficiaries as a whole;
- to reach a decision open to a reasonable donee of such a power;
- to take into account relevant matters and only those matters; and
- to not act with an ulterior purpose.

In the recent case of *In the Matter of the Piedmont and Riviera Trusts*[8] the Royal Court in Jersey considered the extent and nature of the duty of a protector with a veto over certain trustee decisions. More specifically, the court considered whether the protector enjoyed an independent and genuine discretion to exercise the veto as they see fit, or whether the exercise of their discretion was limited to ensuring that the decision of the trustees was a valid and rational one (and if so, could not exercise the veto).

Departing from the rationale of the Supreme Court of Bermuda in *Re X Trusts*[9], in which the Bermuda Court considered this same matter and took the narrow view, the Jersey Court held that the role of the protector is not limited to a 'rationality' test of the trustee's decision, but that the protector has a paramount duty to act in the best interests of the beneficiaries and exercise its own independent judgement.

5. Resignation, absence or removal of a protector

While the selection and appointment of a protector is an important matter, it is equally important not to overlook the procedure by which a protector may resign, be removed or be replaced. This may be a difficult exercise in practice, particularly if the reasons for removal involve a breakdown of the relationship between the protector and the beneficiaries and/or the protector is reluctant to resign. To avoid delays or even a deadlock in the trust administration, the trust deed should stipulate clearly the conditions and procedure for the removal of a protector from office, voluntarily or involuntarily. The trust deed should have an express power of resignation, a foreseen procedure to deal with the death, incapacity or unresponsiveness of an appointed protector and an express power to remove the protector.

The easiest way to resolve a trust paralysis caused by the breakdown in the relationship between protector and beneficiaries is for the protector to resign. Trust deeds will usually provide the procedure for the resignation of the

---

8 *In the Matter of the Piedmont and Riviera Trust* ([2021] JRC 248).
9 *Re X Trusts* ([2021] Sc (Bva) 72 Civ).

appointed protector as well as for their replacement. From case law we can surmise that it is wise for a protector, once they realise that their position has become untenable, to tender their resignation (a protector who clings to an untenable position for too long will be removed by the court – *In the Matter of the K Trust*).[10] A protector may be more willing to resign if they can secure their indemnification. When resigning, a protector can usually expect to be indemnified out of the trust fund with respect to a claim against them stemming from their role as protector, if a relevant indemnity provision exists or even if it can be implied into the trust deed. The right of trustees to be indemnified out of the trust funds for their role is well established, but third-party holders of powers in relation to trusts, and specifically protectors, are less protected unless specific provision is made from the outset. In *Re French*,[11] Mr French, who had acted in the role of protector of a Manx trust, sought an indemnity out of trust funds with respect to legal fees in defending criminal charges in the United States that he claimed arose out of actions he took while he was the protector of the trust. The trustees were reluctant to pay because neither the trust nor its trustees were parties to the criminal proceedings. According to the provisions of the trust deed, Mr French had a right to an indemnity, but this was dependent on no wrongdoing on his part as protector. The Manx court held that where a right to an indemnity is specifically subject to there being no wrongdoing on the part of the protector, the trustee is not obliged to make an immediate payout and may wait to see whether such wrongdoing has been established before deciding whether to grant the indemnity. Relying on *Rawcliffe v Steele*,[12] the court held that the functions of a protector will often extend beyond the specific powers set out in the trust deed and will encompass a general supervisory role, giving the power to the court to imply into the trust deed, where appropriate, a protector's right to an indemnity unless the trust deed contains an express indemnity provision to the contrary. The office of a protector, which is increasingly fiduciary in nature, should be protected by specific provision in the trust deed to minimise the possibility that a court being petitioned for an indemnity will be unsympathetic to the protector's plight.

The trust deed must also make provision for the contingency of a protector becoming unresponsive over a long period, incapacitated or in the event that they die. A procedure must be in place to fill the vacancy thus created and the trust deed should make express provision for how the trust is to be administered in the interim until the vacancy is filled. Likewise, it should be possible to remove and replace a 'burdensome' protector. In *Re Circle Trust*,[13] the trust deed

---

10 *In the Matter of the K Trust* (Royal Court 31/2015).
11 *Re French* ([2012] MLR 637).
12 *Rawcliffe v Steele* ([1993–1995] MLR 426).
13 *Re Circle Trust* ((2006) 9 ITELR 676).

contained a provision allowing a majority of the *sui juris* beneficiaries to appoint a protector in the event that an original protector had not been appointed. The two beneficiaries in the minority argued that the appointment of their father as protector by the majority beneficiaries was invalid as having been carried out irrationally and not in good faith. The court held that the majority of the *sui juris* beneficiaries did *prima facie* hold the power to appoint a protector and that being a fiduciary power the beneficiaries were obliged to exercise such power in good faith and that such exercise was subject to the review and scrutiny of the court.

Some trusts contain an express power of removal, but this raises the question of who should exercise this power – a settlor, a third party or a court. As a settlor reserved power it could be construed as endangering the very validity of the trust. The Bermudan case of *Re the AQ Revocable Trust*[14] demonstrates clearly that while a settlor can validly reserve certain powers, there comes a point where the extent of the powers can subsume the irreducible core needed for the existence of a valid trust. In this case, the settlor, who was also sole trustee, was given a power to remove and appoint trustees and to provide written approval for any transaction that would be "a complete release of the trustee (including the settlor) of any liability or responsibility of the trustee to any person in respect of this transaction". The court held that the concentration of powers in the settlor, in conjunction with the fact that he was the sole trustee, rendered illusory the trusts that he purported to create during his lifetime.

As the power to appoint a protector is a fiduciary power, likewise a power to remove a protector should be construed as fiduciary. The Jersey case of *In the Matter of the A Trust*[15] establishes that the test for the removal of a protector is the same as for the removal of trustees,[16] the test being that removal is warranted only if continuation would be "detrimental to the execution of the trusts". A decision to remove a protector is not one that should be undertaken lightly. The mere fact that some of the beneficiaries may disagree with the way in which the protector exercises their powers or a simple deterioration of relations should not alone justify removal. A removal can be justified if it can be proven that the continuation of the protector in office would harm the welfare of the beneficiaries or negatively impact on the administration of the trust.[17] It is 'safest' to leave the removal of a protector for a court to order rather than to a settlor or a third party (where the same questions of replacement may arise), as a court will be guided by informed considerations over the welfare of the beneficiaries and the effective administration of the trust.

---

14 *Re the AQ Revocable Trust* ([2010] 13 ITELR 260).
15 *In the Matter of the A Trust* ([2012] JCR 196A).
16 *Letterstedt v Broers* ((1884) 9 App Cas 371 (para 16 and 17)).
17 *In the Matter of the K Trust* (Royal Court 31/2015).

6. Conclusion

Deciding whether to appoint a protector and selecting a person to fulfil this role is an exercise that may be fraught with difficulties unless both appointor and appointee enter into the relationship fully cognisant of the possible eventualities. The protector is appointed to act as a supervisor to the trustee and mediator to the trust parties; their role is not to take over the duties of the trustee but rather to monitor the exercise by the trustees of their powers.

The option of appointing a protector should not be exercised by a settlor simply because it is an available option. Careful consideration must be undertaken to determine the necessity of a protector, whose powers may be broad and far-reaching and who may themself require monitoring and restraint. It is also important when deciding whether to appoint a protector to note that certain powers of the protector may be personal rather than fiduciary in nature, depending on the trust construction, and the trust parties may have no legal recourse against a protector who exercises such personal powers 'whimsically' (unlike as against a trustee, where by definition the role is a fiduciary one and the trust parties can initiate legal proceedings for wrongdoing or for a badly considered decision). On the other hand, a protector may be a useful go-between in awkward family disputes, providing an objective third eye and offering valuable insight regarding the initial desires of the settlor who may or may not still be in existence. Whether the benefits of appointing a protector as a guard against a trustee's potential malpractice or as a useful go-between outweigh the possible complications that may arise from deadlock, dubious legal recourse and connected expenses is an exercise that is particular to each specific trust and should be considered carefully from the outset by every settlor.

Non-charitable purpose trusts

Panayiota Kouzoupi
Christodoulos G Vassiliades & Co LLC

1. Introduction

Trusts can be classified in several categories and further separated into various other groups, depending on the type, the circumstances and the terms and conditions on which they are created. In essence, trusts provide individuals both profit-orientated and non-profit-orientated incentives to sort out their business and private affairs during their lifetime and after their death. Accordingly, trusts are used mainly as part of an investment or a commercial transaction, or even more frequently as a channel through which wealth management, asset protection, family inheritance and estate succession planning could be facilitated.

For the purposes of this chapter, we will focus on the non-charitable purpose trusts established in Cyprus in line with the provisions of the Cyprus International Trusts Law (Law 69(I)/1992), as amended by the International Trusts (Amending) Law 2012 (Law 20(I)/2012), and the International Trusts (Amending) Law 2013 (Law 98(I)/2013) (hereinafter collectively referred to as the 'International Trusts Law'). The ultimate aim is to discuss the statutory approval that such trusts have received within the jurisdiction of Cyprus, despite traditional English common law notions that tend to disapprove and hold them void.

To achieve these objectives, attention will be devoted to understanding what a non-charitable purpose trust is. We will elucidate, in this respect, which purposes are considered charitable and, moreover, illustrate some of the most common non-charitable purposes that have survived over time. With reference to some of the most remarkable cases and judicial arguments, we will further address English common law's opposing views regarding the validity of non-charitable purpose trusts. Following that, emphasis will be placed on the Cyprus International Trusts Law and in particular on the legal provisions by virtue of which international trusts for non-charitable purposes are statutorily approved, and therefore permitted to survive for years to come, uninterrupted in time, as compared to Cyprus local trusts for non-charitable purposes whose recognition depends on, among other things, sufficiently satisfying the English common law doctrines of the beneficiary principle and the rule against perpetuities. We will examine, in parallel, how conveniently the Cyprus International Trusts Law accommodates the English common law issue concerning the enforcement of such trusts by making it available for a trust enforcer to be appointed in an effort to ensure that Cyprus international trusts for non-charitable purposes could be properly enforced when it is deemed appropriate under the terms of the instrument creating them. In light of this, attention will be placed on offshore jurisdictions that have adopted a similar approach with the intention of achieving and securing an adequate enforcement mechanism for non-charitable purpose trusts governed under their laws.

Our discussion will begin with a synopsis of the legal framework regulating trusts established and operating under Cyprus laws.

2. Legal framework

Trusts originated from the principles of equity and have been developed through case law.[1] Legislators have progressively advanced Cyprus legislation in the field of trusts by creating a dynamic and modern legal environment. The enactment of the Cyprus International Trusts Law around 30 years ago, stands undeniably as a leading paradigm as it encourages the existence, recognition and operation of various types of trust, international trusts among them, as well the non-charitable purpose trusts.

The Cyprus International Trusts Law is regarded as a special law and, as such, is applicable exclusively to Cyprus international trusts. In the event of any inconsistency or conflict of law, its provisions are of superior power provided that Cyprus law is chosen as the governing law of the said international trust.

For the purposes of this chapter, it is sufficient to mention that the governing law of trusts established under the laws of Cyprus is the Trustees Law 1955 (Cap 193), which, to a great extent, is modelled on the Trustee Act 1925 (C 19) of England and Wales. The Cyprus legal system has been significantly influenced by the English legal system on account of Cyprus being a British colony for many years. Even following Cyprus' independence in 1960, English laws that were applicable in Cyprus before independence, as well as English common law and the principles of equity, are considered of persuasive authority. Hence, in the absence of a statutory provision in domestic law, legal practitioners and Cyprus courts by virtue of the provisions of Section 29 of the Courts of Justice Law (14 of 1960) consistently refer to and rely their legal argumentation and legal reasoning on them.

Finally, the Hague Convention on the Law Applicable to Trusts and their Recognition, is also applicable, following its ratification on a national level with the enactment of the Hague Convention on the Law Applicable on Trusts and their Recognition thereof (Ratifying) Law of 2017, (N 4(III)/2017).

---

1 David B Parker and Anthony R Mellows, *The Modern Law of Trusts*, 3rd edn (Sweet and Maxwell, 1975) at pp171–172.

3. Definitions

3.1 Purpose trusts

Express (private) trusts are trusts that are intentionally created by a person (ie, the settlor) who vests the trust property in the control of another person (ie, the trustee) to manage and administer the trust property for either the benefit of another person or group of persons, or for accomplishing a specified purpose. Express (private) trusts that are set up for an explicit purpose are called 'purpose trusts' and are widely employed to enable a cause or a bequest to be carried out.

In accordance with the definition stated in Section 2 of the Cyprus International Trusts Law, an international trust that is classified under the category of purpose trusts (or trusts for a purpose) refers to a trust, other than any of the following:

- trusts with beneficiaries being specific physical or legal persons, who are immediately ascertained or not; and
- trusts with beneficiaries being a group of specific physical or legal persons, capable of being ascertained by reference to a personal relationship or kinship.

It derives from the above definition that purpose trusts are trusts with no beneficiaries, which further concludes that such trusts are just a useful mechanism for advancing pure purposes of zero economic benefit to a physical person or a legal person. Apparently, as we will examine further below, the fact that purpose trusts are trusts with no beneficiaries has been the primary and most challenging issue in English common law, especially in the case of non-charitable purpose trusts.

Technically, purpose trusts are divided into two categories: charitable purpose trusts and non-charitable purpose trusts. To establish what construes a non-charitable purpose trust is essential to understanding in advance the exact arrangements that stand in law as charitable purposes.

3.2 Charitable purpose trusts

Charitable purpose trusts, as the name itself explicitly delivers, are extensively used as a vehicle for the advancement of charity objectives. Charitable purpose trusts can be established either as local trusts in line with the provisions of the Charities Law (Cap 41) or as international trusts, provided that the requirements and conditions stated in the International Trusts Law are completely fulfilled and satisfied. A noteworthy difference between the two types of charitable trust is that local trusts for charitable purposes are enforced

---

2 *Hadjinicolaou Theodora v Greek Schools Board of Nicosia* ((2011) 4 AAD 789) (Supreme Court of the Republic of Cyprus).

by the attorney general of Cyprus who acts as the *parens patriae*[2] of the trust, whereas international trusts for charitable purposes are enforced in accordance with the terms of the instrument establishing them.

Although there is no legal definition of what constitutes a 'charity' under the Charities Law, it could be reasonably suggested that it relates to philanthropy, as it inspires benevolent incentives and encourages actions of an advantageous character to happen or develop within the community.

In light of Section 7(1) of the Cyprus International Trusts Law, an international trust for charitable purposes will be regarded as such when its primary goal is the accomplishment of one or more of the following objects:

- the prevention or relief of poverty;
- the advancement of education;
- the advancement of religion;
- the advancement of health or saving lives;
- the advancement of citizenship or community development;
- the advancement of arts, culture, heritage or science;
- the advancement of amateur sports;
- the advancement of human rights, conflict resolutions or reconciliation, or the promotion of religious or racial harmony, or equality and diversity;
- the advancement of environmental protection or improvement;
- the relief of those in need, by reason of youth, age, ill-health, disability, financial hardship or some other disadvantage;
- the advancement of animal welfare; and
- any other reason beneficial to the public in general or which is connected with the aforementioned objectives.

Interested readers may refer to the "Charitable trusts and charitable organisations" chapter by Eleni Drakou for further analysis on the matter and a detailed examination of charitable purpose trusts established under Cyprus laws.

3.3 Non-charitable purpose trusts

Non-charitable purpose trusts, on the other hand, are associated with situations other than of a charitable nature as described above. Such trusts are widely employed to carry out the wishes of a person following their death, rather than in pursuit of profit. The most common arrangements that came into effect in English common law generally relate to the purposes for facilitating funeral expenses or providing for the pets and animals, or the estate of the deceased (ie, the settlor) after their demise.

Non-charitable purpose trusts are usually linked with specific arrangements for the caring of animals,[3] the building and maintenance of family graves and

3 *Pettingal v Pettingal* ((1842) 11 LJ Ch 176); *Re Dean* ((1889) 41 Ch D 552).

monuments,[4] or for the construction, care and preservation of tombs,[5] graves[6] and graveyards.[7] Such instances are indeed the objectives that have been sustained in English common law as the exception to the general rule that requires any purpose trust that is not a charitable trust within the intendment of the Preamble to the Charitable Uses Act 1601 (otherwise known as 'the Statute of Elizabeth') or does not fit into the traditional concept of 'charity' as communicated and further arranged in classes, or precisely speaking in "heads of charity" by Lord MacNaughten in the leading authority of the *Commissioner for Special Purposes of Income Tax v Pemsel*[8] to fail due to the uncertainty of identifying the person whom the power of enforcement has been accorded to as a result of having the beneficial interest over the property of the trust.[9] Non-charitable purposes may also include other reasonable arrangements or causes. For instance, such trusts could turn into a flexible mechanism for the protection of a person's (ie, the settlor's) valuable assets, artwork, collections, paintings, jewellery and memorabilia, or for the maintenance and preservation of a family property, among other things.

The main argument *per se*, is not what objective could be construed as a non-charitable purpose, but whether such trusts, by their very nature and substance, could successfully meet the three certainties and thus be accepted by courts as valid and enforceable trusts.

4. Non-charitable purpose trusts and the three certainties test

By way of principle,[10] express (private) trusts are considered valid as long as all of the following grounds (known as the three certainties) are present:

- certainty of intention;
- certainty of subject matter; and
- certainty of objects.

In consideration of this, the requisite intention of the settlor to create the trust must be made absolutely clear and the scope of the trust must be comprehensive and expressed in a precise and detailed manner. General, ill-defined and hypothetical terms must be avoided as they could cause a trust to fail due to uncertainty of its subject matter. Moreover, the object of the trust (ie, the beneficiary or beneficiaries of the trust) must be clearly ascertained. So, in the case of having persons bringing an action against the trustee in order to compel proper performance of the trust, the court should be in a position to

4 *Re Hooper* ([1932] 1 Ch 38).
5 *Lloyd v Lloyd* ((1852) 2 Sim NS 255; 61 ER 338).
6 *Trimmer v Danby* ((1856) 25 LJ Ch 424).
7 *Pirbright v Salwey* ([1896] WN 86 (Ch)).
8 [1891] AC 531 at 559.
9 *Re Endacott* ([1960] Ch 232).
10 *Knight v Knight* ((1840) 49 ER 58).

identify them with certainty as the persons who have a beneficial claim over the assets and hence the legal standing to proceed so. Likewise, where the trust is created for a purpose, such purpose should not be ambiguous or vague; but instead reasonable and communicated with precision, exactness and accuracy.[11]

When considering the validity and recognition of non-charitable purpose trusts in English common law, the main argument has always been in relation to the certainty of objects. This is due largely to the fact that non-charitable purpose trusts have no beneficiaries, and on that account a difficulty arises on identifying "somebody, in whose favour the court can decree performance",[12] as laid down by Sir William Grant MR in the leading case of *Morice v Bishop of Durham*[13] when establishing the beneficiary principle. Notable court decisions in the following years, such as *Re Astor's Settlement Trusts*[14] and *Re Endacott*[15], respected the notion and held that a trust is reasonably and effectively controlled as long as there exists a person, immediately ascertainable, on whose benefit performance is enforced should the circumstances warrant it. For instance, such circumstances may arise when the trustee fails to adhere to their obligations as imposed on them by the settlor through the trust deed or otherwise, or when misappropriating or misapplying the trust property.

In *Leahy v Attorney General for New South Wales,*[16] Viscount Simonds in his judgment remarkably delivered that:

> *a gift can be made to persons but it cannot be made to a purpose or to an object … unless the purpose or object be charitable. For a purpose or object cannot sue, but, if it be charitable, the Attorney General can sue to enforce it.*[17]

Of equal importance, is Goff J's argument in the landmark case of *Re Denley's Trust Deed,*[18] who stated that the "objection is not that the trust is for a purpose or an object *per se,* but that there is no beneficiary or *cestui que* trust",[19] signifying that the lack of persons with beneficial interest adequate enough to give them the legal standing and power of enforcement, may cause the trust to fail.

In other words, English common law notions have strongly supported – and continue to support up to the present moment – the fact that non-charitable purpose trusts may survive insofar as they fall within the exceptions of specified non-charitable purposes, while any arrangement to any other extent will cause the trust to fail.

---

11 *Brown v Burdett* ((1882) 21 Ch D 667).
12 *Morice v Bishop of Durham* ((1804) 9 Ves Jr 399 at 405).
13 (1804) 9 Ves Jr 399.
14 [1952] Ch 534 (HC).
15 [1959] EWCA Civ 5.
16 [1959] AC 457.
17 [1959] AC 457 (Privy Council) at 478-479.
18 [1969] 1 Ch 373.
19 [1969] 1 Ch 373 at 383.

5. Non-charitable purpose trusts and the English common law rule against perpetuities

In accordance with English common law, purpose trusts are also subject to the rule against perpetuities.[20] The rule against perpetuities, as introduced by Lord Nottingham in the historic *Duke of Norfolk's Case*,[21] basically prevents a person from remotely vesting an interest over the trust property for an indefinite period or for an excessive duration. The English common law perpetuity period applicable under the circumstances in Cyprus is set to cover a period lasting at "lives in being plus 21 years".[22]

The general rule is that purpose trusts, unless their objectives are of a charitable nature, are to be held void if their purposes are meant to be perpetual, even if they fall within the exceptions of the specified non-charitable purposes.[23] In view of the foregoing, any non-charitable purpose trust that is created with the intention to last beyond the perpetuity period, such as in the case of *Lloyd v Lloyd*,[24] is to be held void.

The English common law rule against perpetuities and related matters concerning the duration of the trusts are further developed elsewhere in this book.

6. Authorisation of non-charitable purpose trusts under Cyprus legislation

English common law tends to overrule purpose trusts except if they are for charitable purposes or unless they come within the exceptions of specified non-charitable purposes.[25] However, the Cyprus International Trusts Law draws attention as it provides otherwise. As compared to English common law, the Cyprus International Trusts Law recognises and generally allows for the existence of non-charitable purpose trusts. Pursuant to Section 7(3) of the Cyprus International Trusts Law, a Cyprus international trust is not void or voidable for the sole reason that it is created to carry out a non-charitable purpose, provided that in the cases where the trust is a non-perpetual trust, or where it could be terminated, the instrument establishing the trust specifies the circumstances whereupon it could be terminated, and further provides for the disposition of its net assets on its termination. Nevertheless, it should be considered that any such non-charitable purpose trust should be reasonable, certain as to what it is intended to achieve and, moreover, capable of being attained or accomplished.

Section 7(3) further states that Cyprus international trusts established in such a manner are enforceable by the settlor, the enforcer of the trust, their

---

20 *Musset v Bingle* ([1876] WN 170); *Pirbright v Salwey* ([1896] WN 86); *Re Hooper* ([1932] 1 Ch 38).
21 (1682) 3 Ch Cas 1; 22 ER 931.
22 *Re Kelly* ([1932] IR 255).
23 *Musset v Bingle* ([1876] WN 170).
24 (1852) 2 Sim NS 255, 61 ER 338.
25 *Re Endacott* ([1959] EWCA Civ 5).

personal representatives, or by the person or the persons mentioned by name in the instrument establishing the trust as the person or the persons who have been appointed for the purpose of enforcing the trust. The trust is enforceable by action of the aforementioned person or persons, even if such person or persons are not the beneficiaries of the trust.

It seems, therefore, that the enforceability obstacle that exists in English common law is significantly overcome in the case of Cyprus international trusts. The legislator's approach to introducing into Cyprus' legal system the role of the enforcer of the trust and subsequently according them the necessary legal standing has facilitated this important issue. Considering that purpose trusts are trusts with no ascertainable beneficiaries, they made it possible for legal or physical persons, and successors thereof, to exert the requisite control over the trustee and, if deemed necessary, to bring an action for the purposes of seeking proper and prudent performance of trustees' obligations.

In line with the legal definition stated in Section 2 of the Cyprus International Trusts Law, the enforcer of the trust is the person whose duty is to supervise the entire process by making certain that the objectives of the non-charitable purpose trust are achieved and its purposes are in fact duly fulfilled, while ensuring on the other hand that a proper enforcement will occur where the circumstances make it necessary or appropriate. Notwithstanding the fact that it is not mandatory under the Cyprus International Trusts Law to appoint an enforcer of a trust, non-charitable purpose trusts can be enforced by the settlor or the settlor's personal representatives.

A similar approach has been followed by other jurisdictions around the globe whose legislation authoritatively recognises the existence of non-charitable purpose trusts as valid arrangements.[26] Cook Islands have adopted a similar enforcement mechanism as the one in Cyprus for Cyprus international trusts. Correspondingly, non-charitable purpose trusts in Cook Islands are enforceable by the settlor or settlor's personal representatives or by the persons mentioned in the instrument establishing the trust as the persons appointed to enforce the trust even though such persons may not be the beneficiary or beneficiaries of such trust.[27]

The role of the enforcer of the trust is not a new concept, it has been used by other foreign jurisdictions as a central mechanism to secure proper enforcement. Specifically, in the Cayman Islands pursuant to the Special Trusts (Alternative Regime) Law 1997 (STAR), as incorporated into Part VIII of the Cayman Islands' Trust Law (2001 Revision), the legal standing of enforcing purpose trusts that are established under the STAR legislation is vested only on such persons who are in fact appointed as the enforcers of the said STAR trusts,

26 Paolo Panico, *International Trust Laws*, 2nd edn (Oxford University Press, 2017).
27 The International Trusts Act 1984 (14/1984), Section 12(2).

either in accordance with the instrument establishing them or by virtue of a court order in this regard, whether such persons are also being beneficiaries of the said STAR trusts or not.[28]

In the British Virgin Islands, the applicable law, the Trustee Act, Act 28 of 1961 as amended from time to time (Revised Edition 2020), stipulates a very interesting mechanism for securing the enforcement of such trusts. Accordingly, it is mandatory for every instrument creating a purpose trust to appoint an enforcer of the trust and, additionally, to provide for a successor in office.[29] The aforementioned law also requires for the appointment of at least one trustee who will be a designated person within the meaning of the applicable law,[30] whose responsibility will be to ensure that there is an appointed enforcer in office at all times. On occasions where the designated person has reasons to believe that there is no enforcer, or the appointed enforcer is not capable or willing of acting, and no other person is likely to be appointed in the near future, the designated person will refer the matter to the attorney general for support.[31] Subsequently, the attorney general will make an application to the court for the appointment of an enforcer of the trust.[32] The attorney general is not conferred with the power of enforcement of a non-charitable purpose trust; however, they are granted a supervisory role so that they can make certain that an enforcer who is duly capable, fit and willing to fulfil their duties under the instrument establishing the trust is at all times appointed. The court may also appoint or substitute an existing enforcer should it be deemed expedient under the circumstances.[33]

Likewise, the statute of the Isle of Man imposes a mandatory obligation of having an enforcer of trust appointed under the instrument establishing the trust for enforcement purposes. Moreover, it specifies that the instrument establishing the trust must further provide for the appointment of an enforcer in the event of a vacancy in their office, or in the event of an enforcer ceasing to be independent of the trustee or if for any reason the enforcer is incapable, unable or unwilling of acting.[34]

The same approach has been adopted in the Republic of Mauritius. By virtue of the Trusts Act 2001 (14/2001), as amended, there will be an enforcer who, on effectively accepting the role,[35] will have the duty to enforce the purpose trust in accordance with terms of the instrument establishing it and, of course, according to its purposes.[36]

---

28 Section 100(2).
29 Trustee Act, Act 28 of 1961, as amended, (Revised Edition 2020), Section 84A(3)(d).
30 Section 84A(1) as substituted by the amending Act 6 of 2013; Section 84A(3)(c).
31 Trustee Act, Act 28 of 1961, as amended, (Revised Edition of 2020), Section 84A(10).
32 *Ibid*, Section 84A(11).
33 *Ibid*, Section 84A(9).
34 Purpose Trusts Acts 1996 (AT 9/1996), as amended, Section 1(1)(d).
35 Section 21(3).
36 Section 21(1).

Of particular interest is the approach followed in Bermuda in light of the fact that the statutory obligation of having to actually appoint an enforcer of the trust in order to make such trusts enforceable, has been waived.[37] By virtue of the Trusts (Special Provisions) Amendment Act 1998, such trusts can today be enforced by any authorised person either being persons who are authorised to do so by reason of being appointed to act for that purpose, or by the settlor, trustee or any other person as the court may consider as having a sufficient interest to enforce the trust.[38] The attorney general is also given the power of enforcement when the court is satisfied that there is no other person capable and willing to enforce the trust.[39]

In a similar way, the laws of the Bahamas by virtue of the Purpose Trusts Act 2004 (17/2004) confer the legal standing on authorised applicants[40] who can seek enforcement of a purpose trust without stipulating any mandatory requirement for such person to be actually officially appointed as the enforcer of the trust.[41]

In Belize, according to the Belize Trusts Act, Chapter 202 (Revised Edition of 2000), the enforcement power is conferred on the protector of the trust. The attorney general is empowered to appoint a protector if they have reason to believe that no protector has been appointed or if the protector who is appointed is unwilling or incapable of acting.[42]

In essence, many countries (including Cyprus) have charged persons with the right of enforcement, so it can be secured that non-charitable purpose trusts are efficiently controlled by dutiful persons and thus, functioning in a satisfactory way for the purpose of achieving the reason of their very existence.

Yet, on a closer examination of Section 7(3) of the Cyprus International Trusts Law, it emerges that it is not only the beneficiary principle that has been conveniently waived in the case of Cyprus international trusts for non-charitable purposes, the English common law rule against perpetuities has also been abolished and entirely excluded from consideration. Non-charitable purpose trusts that are established under the International Trusts Law therefore remain valid and enforceable for an unlimited period.

Whereas Cyprus international trusts are beyond of the scope of the beneficiary principle and the rule against perpetuities, local trusts remain bound by these doctrines. This is because the Cyprus International Trusts Law is applicable exclusively to Cyprus international trusts and is therefore irrelevant in the case of local trusts. Instead, local trusts for non-charitable purposes are governed predominantly by English common law and the principles of equity.

---

37 Trusts (Special Provisions) Act 1989, Section 14.
38 Section 12B (1).
39 Trusts (Special Provisions) Amendment Act 1998, Section 12B(1).
40 Section 6(2).
41 Section 6(1).
42 Belize Trusts Act, Chapter 202 (Revised Edition of 2000), Sections 15(1)(c), 15(2).

Matters regarding their interpretation and validity are subject to satisfying the traditional English common law doctrines, which follows that local trusts for non-charitable purposes, in contrast to Cyprus international trusts, could eventually fail due to uncertainty, unless they fall within the exceptions sustained in English common law and, of course, provided that they comply with the English common law rule against perpetuities.

7. Conclusion

Cyprus is a trust-friendly country with a modern legal system in the field of international trusts that can arguably compete with any other leading jurisdiction in this area. Non-Cyprus residents, either physical persons or legal persons, who wish to set up an international trust, are given motivations to structure their affairs and implement their wishes in an economically stable country with an extensive network of double tax treaties that offers considerable tax advantages. By virtue of the Cyprus International Trusts Law, foreign investors are given the option to establish an indefinitely long continuing trust for accomplishing their purposes, which, given that Cyprus law is chosen as the proper law, could simultaneously serve as an asset protection vehicle against creditors, forced heirship or claims arising in tort, contract, bankruptcy or liquidation proceedings against the settlor.

With the enactment of the Cyprus International Trusts Law, Cyprus has progressively paved the way to approve non-charitable purpose trusts, despite the strong arguments of English common law. The Cyprus International Trusts Law, among other things, recognises and conditionally allows for the existence of non-charitable purpose trusts, which in effect can be enforced in accordance with the terms contained in the instrument establishing them. Taking this as a paradigm, it is worth considering that the time might have come for the legislators to examine and modernise existing laws and further implement reforms in the legal system with the aim of providing equivalent permissions for local non-charitable purpose trusts.

The trustee's ability to request directions from the court

Constantinos Constantinides
Stefanos Marangos
Christodoulos G Vassiliades & Co LLC

1. Introduction

The 2012 amendment of the Cyprus International Trusts Law 1992, namely Law 20(I)/2012, introduced new articles into the law, including Section 11A, which deals with the trustee's ability to request directions from the court on issues surrounding the trust. According to the minutes[1] of the House of Representatives, the rationale behind the amendment was the modernisation of the legislation to render Cyprus more competitive and attractive to investors compared to foreign jurisdictions. Section 11A, which has now been in force for more than a decade, deals with directions hearings and reads as follows:

> *11A (1) A trustee may apply to the court for directions concerning the manner in which the trustee may or should act in connection with any matter concerning an international trust and the court may make such order, if any, as it thinks fit.*
> *An application for directions must be made to a president of the District Court.*
> *(2) The court may, if it thinks fit*
> *a) make an order concerning*
> *i. The execution or the administration of any trust*
> *ii. The trustee or protector of any international trust, including an order relating to the exercise of any power, discretion or duty of the trustee or protector, the appointment or removal of a trustee or protector, the remuneration of a trustee or protector, the submission of accounts, the conduct of the trustee or protector and payments, whether payments into court or otherwise*
> *iii. A beneficiary or any person having a connection with the trust, or*
> *iv. The appointment or removal of an enforcer in relation to any non-charitable purposes of the trust*
> *b) make a declaration as to the validity or the enforceability of a trust*
> *c) rescind or vary any order or declaration made under this Law, or make any new or further order or declaration.*

1 Report of the Parliamentary Finance and Budget Committee on the proposed laws "The International Trusts (Amendment) Law of 2010" and "The International Trusts (Amendment) Law of 2011", accessed via www.parliament.cy.

(3) a) *An application to the court for an order or declaration under paragraph (2) may be made by the trustee, a beneficiary, a protector and with leave of the court, by any other person.*

3) b) *In the case of a purpose trust, an application to the court for an order or declaration under paragraph 2 may be made by the trustee, the settlor or his personal representatives or by the enforcer of the trust and with leave of the court, by any other person.*

4) Where the Court makes an order for the appointment of a trustee it may impose such conditions as it thinks fit, including conditions as to the vesting of trust property.

5) Subject to any order of the Court, a trustee, protector or enforcer appointed under this section shall have the same powers, discretions and duties and may act as if the trustee.

Section 11A has been constructed on the basis of the well-developed and extensively used Article 51 of Jersey's Trust Law 1984, as amended. Therefore, legal practitioners may seek guidance from common law and the principles of equity as applied in the jurisdiction of Jersey, which are also applicable in Cyprus by virtue of Article 29(1)(c) of the Courts of Justice Law 14/60 and the relevant case law. A comparative analysis of cases in both jurisdictions will follow.

2. The application of Section 11A in Cyprus

Based on paragraph 1 of Section 11A, a trustee is given a great opportunity by being enabled to apply to the court for almost any matter related to the administration of a trust.

Even though this chapter focuses on the ability of the trustee to proceed with an application, based on subparagraph 2 of Section 11A for the matters specified therein, the persons that may apply to the court to receive orders or declarations, extend beyond the trustee to the protector and the beneficiaries, as well as any other person who obtains the leave of the court. In Cyprus, when compared to the jurisdiction of Jersey, more applications have been brought forward through persons rather than trustees.

Section 11A provides a court with wide powers to assist with the administration of an international trust and resolves disputes that may arise as discussed in the relevant case law. However, there are certain limitations to these powers.

Trust proceedings can take various forms, ranging from the almost consensual application for directions to cases involving hostile claims. As the cases show, it is not easy to formulate principles that can be safely applied to different types of case in all their diversity.[2]

2 *In the Matter of JP Morgan 1998 Employee Trust* ([2013] JCA 146).

In *Re Buckton*[3] it was held that there are three principal categories of proceeding:

- applications by trustees for directions or guidance on a question of construction;
- a similar kind of application brought by someone other than the trustee (ie, as per subparagraph 2 of Section 11A); and
- hostile claims by a beneficiary.

In case of so-called 'hostile claims', a distinction may be drawn where a hostile claim is initiated by a beneficiary alleging a breach of the terms of the trust by the trustee or any fiduciary duty and those claims where an allegation of fraud or embezzlement exists against the trustee, thus giving rise to an alleged commitment of a civil wrong. The proper course of action in case of the latter would be that of a civil legal action, instead of an application under Section 11A.

This is because in cases where a civil wrong is allegedly committed, the court will not be able to award damages within the framework of an application based on Section 11A. The case law suggests that the short character of the application under Section 11A discourages hostile proceedings of this kind being raised.

In general, the types of application raised under the provisions of section 11A in Cyprus are:

- applications in relation to the removal or appointment of trustees;
- applications concerning the disclosure of documents and information by trustees to the beneficiaries; and
- applications in relation to the administration or execution of a trust.

2.1 Applications in relation to the removal or appointment of trustees

General Applications 1036/13 and 1037/13[4] before President Ioannides, as he then was, is an example where such an issue arose. Specifically, within the ambit of the said applications, among others, orders of the court were sought in relation to:

- the execution and administration of the trust;
- the removal of the original trustee and their replacement by a new trustee;
- the removal and replacement of the protector of the trustee;
- an order in relation to the execution of the duty by the original trustee to provide accounts of the administration of the trust;
- an order whereby the original trustee would be instructed to present a detailed account of the expenses of the trust; and

---

3 *Buckton v Buckton* (1906 B 1879).

4 In regard to the HPH Settlement international trust. Accessed via www.cylaw.org/cgi-bin/open.pl?file=apofaseised/pol/2017/1120170410.htm&qstring=1036%20w%2F1%2013.

- an order whether the trustee sought to be removed is entitled to any remuneration and, if so, for the court to determine such a remuneration among others.

Those applications were accompanied by affidavits, and the court proceeded a step further as it concluded that it was necessary to hear oral testimonies including the cross examination of the witnesses and decide the issues raised in the said applications on their merits. The court dismissed the applications because it considered that the testimony was not trustworthy. Even though those applications were initiated by the settlor of the trusts, not the trustee, it is important to note how the court procedurally treated the applications. The court argued that Section 11A is an article of substantive law standing on its own without any reference to Order 55 of the Civil Procedure Rules being necessary and proceeded with the trial of the applications after joining them despite the fact that the matters raised therein concerned complex issues and were also related to other legal proceedings.

2.2 Applications concerning the disclosure of documents and information by trustees to beneficiaries

General Application 62/2018[5] before President E Efrem includes a thorough analysis of this issue. The application was filed by the beneficiaries of the trust who sought an order for the removal and replacement of the trustee of the discretionary trust due to an alleged breach of a legal duty on behalf of the trustee to provide necessary information to the applicants. The applications also sought a declaration of the court, recognising the right of the beneficiaries of the trust to request the removal and replacement of the trustee due to his denial to provide them with requested information while he was allegedly under a legal obligation to do so. Despite the allegations made by the trustee in the affidavit accompanying the objection to the application that the trust under review was an international trust, the court concluded that the trust was not international but domestic as the settlors obtained Cyprus residency one year before its formation.

After analysing the matter in relation to the duty of the trustee to provide information, while clarifying that the trust under consideration did not fall within the ambit of the law but in the ambit of Cyprus Domestic Trust Law (Cap 193), the court concluded that the trustee, being a trustee of a discretionary trust the terms of which gave her wide powers in the exercise of her duties, was not legally obliged under that legislation to provide such information. The court added that in any case, once the request by the beneficiaries was made for

5 In regard to the Goaliva Trust. Accessed via www.cylaw.org/cgi-bin/open.pl?file=apofaseised/pol/2019/2120190313.htm&qstring=62%20w%2F1%202018.

the provision of relevant information, she responded to the request by providing information in a manner within her rights, which in no way breached the terms of the trust. The court decided that the obligation of the trustee to provide information was not a legal obligation but an obligation arising under the trustee's general obligations due to the nature of her capacity and her position.

In conclusion, under the specific circumstances of the case the court decided that the trustee was not under a legal obligation to provide information to the beneficiaries. It also concluded that the beneficiaries did not prove any reason for the removal of the trustee and dismissed the said application.

2.3 Applications in relation to the administration or execution of a trust

Within the context of the General Applications 1036/13 and 1037/13, one of the orders sought was in relation to the administration or execution of the trust. The main assertions were that the trustee company did not properly administer the trusts *inter alia* by fulfilling its duty of providing financial statements to the beneficiaries along with allegations of discrepancies and he should therefore have been replaced. The court accepted the testimony of the director of the original trustee company, who provided proof that the beneficiaries were in fact properly informed in relation to the matters of the trusts, and rejected those allegations as unreliable therefore dismissing the applications.

3. Nature of the application in Cyprus

3.1 General application to the court or originating summons

In General Application 103/2016,[6] where an order was sought for the removal of the trustee, an issue arose as to whether the case was properly brought forward through the form of an originating summons instead of a legal action.

The court analysed the distinction between a legal action and an originating summons through Order 55 Rule 1 of the Civil Procedure Rules. It explained that an originating summons is another method through which a legal procedure may begin. Besides the instances specifically mentioned in the said order, there are also other instances where an originating summons is specifically mentioned in a legislation as the proper method of bringing a matter in court requesting a remedy (ie, Cap 189, Articles 53 and 54).

The court discussed the Supreme Court case *Junport International Ltd* Appeal 115/17 and mentioned that it follows from the said judgment that even in the cases where an originating summons is in fact contemplated by the law, the court retains discretion to set aside such a summons. This discretion is used if

---

6 In regard to the Goaliva Trust. Accessed via www.cylaw.org/cgi-bin/open.pl?file=apofaseised/pol/2017/2120170388.htm&qstring=103%20w%2F1%202016.

the court concludes that the matter brought forward through it is complex and it is necessary to hear a testimony. In that case, a claim through a civil action is preferred.

The court analysed Section 11A(2)(a)(ii) and its reference to the word 'application' by stating that the law does not clarify whether the reference in the law included an originating summons. The court then decided to set aside the application because the application under review was so complex with serious allegations that it could not be settled without the provision of an oral testimony, hence stating that the procedure was not properly initiated. The complexity of that application was due to the economic differences under the trust as well as the fact that the applicants disputed the manner in which the trustee arrived at an estimate of $20 million for the sale of the disputed share package, with allegation of an illegal sale, embezzlement and violation of basic terms of the trust due to conflict of interest.

The applicants later brought General Application 62/2018 before President E Efrem, who further analysed this issue on the basis of different facts. Efrem concluded that, based on the facts under review), an originating summons based on Order 55 was the appropriate legal means to initiate the proceedings, which may be initiated without leave of the court. This was due to the role held by the applicants as beneficiaries of the trust, which gave them the right to apply to the court for the removal and/or dismissal of the trustee based on Article 55 of Cap 193.

3.2 Nature of the application of Article 51 in Jersey

As to the nature of applications for directions by trustees at paragraph 13 of the judgment in the case of *M and other Trusts*[7] the following were stated:

> *It is common for trustees in Jersey to seek the directions of the Court in relation to matters concerning the administration of trusts. These are brought under Article 51 of the 1984 Law. Usually the trustee will have reached a decision itself but will seek the Court's blessing on the grounds that the decision is of a 'momentous' nature (see Re S Settlement [2001] JLR N 37, Jersey Unreported 2001/154). In other cases the trustee will surrender its discretion to the Court. Some applications are Beddoe applications properly so called, in the sense that they seek directions as to whether the trustee should institute or defend legal proceedings. Others concern decisions in relation to a variety of matters relating to the administration of the trust, eg, whether to sell a major trust asset.*

In *Bedell Cristin Trustees Limited*[8] the matter of the jurisdiction of the court under Article 51 was raised within the context of an application for an interim payment from a trust fund. The court considered that the trustee had not

7 [2012] JRC 127.
8 [2005] JRC 109.

surrendered its discretion to the court, thus it did not leave it to the court to reach a decision on the matter at stake in its essence but merely asked whether the trustee's decision to refuse to make an interim distribution was a reasonable one under the circumstances.

The court did not exploit its power under the article to reach a decision and mentioned that its role was not to substitute its own view for that of the trustee's, unless the trustee surrendered its discretion to the court. The court stated that whether the trustee wished to surrender his discretion was entirely a matter for the trustee and that the court should apply its jurisdiction on a sensible and principled basis and not constitute itself as it were in the position of a trustee.

In the English case of *Public Trustee v Cooper*,[9] the High Court identified a non-exhaustive list of categories of case where it would be proper for a trustee to invoke the jurisdiction of the court, namely:

- where the court is asked to consider whether the proposed conduct is within the trustee's powers;
- where the court considers whether the proposed course of action is a proper exercise of the trustees' powers;
- consideration of a surrender of discretion by the trustee to the court; and
- where the trustees have actually acted and that action is being attacked as being outside of the trustee's powers or an improper exercise of the trustee's duty.

3.3 Where the court is asked to consider whether the proposed conduct is within the trustee's powers

A recent case in which an application was made was *In the Matter of the P Trust*[10] in which the trustee – Fenlight Trustees Limited – applied under the mechanism of Article 51 to ask the court whether a restriction with regard to the disclosure of specific documents to the settlor was within his powers.

The settlor (representor) had two trusts – P and N – of which Fenlight Trustees Limited was the trustee of Trust P, which was for the benefit of D, one of the settlor's sons. The settlor had another trust for the benefit of his other son (F), whose trustee was Company 2. The two trusts had equal shares and co-owned a successful trading company (Company 1). The application was made by the trustee following a breakdown of the relationships between D and the settlor as well as F. This breakdown inevitably affected the working relationship between the trustees of the two trusts – Fenlight Trustees Limited and Company 2.

Therefore, Fenlight Trustees Limited was concerned that access to this information should not be given to the representor, which could risk ending up

9 [2001] WTLR 901.
10 [2021] JRC 205.

in the hands of Company 2 and F, hence providing them with an insight to confidential advice and generally to legal dealings of Fenlight Trustees Limited as part of the P trust, which could give them an illegitimate commercial advantage in their dealing with Fenlight Trustees Limited.

Following Fenlight's application under Article 51, the court accepted the proposed conduct by the trustee, and held that even though in this case the trustee was obliged to disclose to the settlor in light of his duty to act in the best interests of the beneficiaries as a whole and the trust, under these circumstances, the proposal to refuse the extension of this obligation to the personal and financial affairs of D in order to avoid the aforementioned advantage, fell within the powers of the trustee.

3.4 Where the court considers whether the proposed course of action is a proper exercise of the trustees' powers

The most common use of this mechanism is the trustee's right to ask for the blessing of the court for momentous decisions defined as "a decision of real importance for the trust",[11] which are set to have substantial influence on the trust. The trustees tend to use this mechanism to protect the trustee from a possible claim by a disappointed beneficiary.

In *Re S Settlement,*[12] the court set out the test to be applied where the approval of a momentous decision made by the trustee is requested by the court – whether:

- the trustee's decision has been formed in good faith;
- the decision is one that a reasonable trustee properly instructed could have reached; and
- the decision has not been vitiated by any actual or potential conflict of interest.

The court in *Representation of Hawksford (Jersey) Limited*[13] and the *Representation of Maram Trust*[14] stressed that the application of the test is strict as in no way can the court deviate from it before it grants a blessing.[15]

In the matter of the *Wigwam Trust*[16] for the test of approving a momentous decision, the court was assisted by the Court of Appeal in *Kan v HSBC International Trustee Limited,*[17] where a momentous decision was defined as a decision of real importance for the trust, and where the trustee seeks the court's

11 *Kahn v HSBC International Trustee Limited, O Poon, K Poon and Franckel* (2015).
12 [2001] JLR 37.
13 [2018] JRC 171.
14 [2020] JRC 062.
15 Stephen Alexander, Katie Hooper, "When is a trustee's decision momentous and is momentousness sufficient?", *Trusts & Trustees*, 26(8–9) (November 2020), 775–782.
16 [2020] JRC 228.
17 [2015] JCA 109.

approval for the decision, the legal test to be applied would be the one developed in *Re S Settlement*.[18] The court said at paragraph 18 that:

When the court is to give approval for a momentous decision the court needs to be satisfied as to the rationality of the decision; the lengths to which the court must go in examining the process by which the trustee arrived at the decision must depend upon the particular decision. In some cases the decision may be a difficult and doubtful one, requiring fine judgment in the face of competing considerations; in others the decision may be obvious. In the former cases the quality of the decision-making process will be more important than the latter.

It then went on to state that the result of the court giving its approval should be that the beneficiaries will be unable thereafter to complain that the exercise constitutes a breach of trust or can be set aside as flawed. It also stated the benefits the beneficiaries may have under such an application to cross examine the trustee or request the disclosure of documents otherwise not available to them without the context of such proceedings. Specifically, at paragraph 19:

Furthermore, when trustees are seeking approval for a decision they have already reached, the beneficiaries are unlikely to have the same advantages of cross-examination or disclosure of the trustees' deliberations as they would have in proceedings to challenge the exercise of the power once made. For that reason, the trustees should put before the court all relevant considerations (supported by evidence) and they should explain their reasons for reaching the decision, even though they are not otherwise obliged to make such disclosure to the beneficiaries. But the process by which the trustees satisfy the court that the legal test has been met should not be confused with the substance of the test itself. Furthermore, each case will need to be decided on its own facts, and the degree of detail that is required from a trustee cannot be uniform in all circumstances. In some cases, a trustee's decision may come out of the blue, and if so it may require both the beneficiaries and the court to be given the background and the context in considerable detail: in other cases, such as this, a trustee's decision may emerge from a situation that is well known to the interested parties, and that is likely to have an impact on the degree of detail required from the trustee by the court.

In the recent case of *Re Arpetaz Settlement*,[19] the trustee applied to the court and asked for approval of:

- the trustee's decision to enter into a settlement agreement;
- the prospective actions of the trustee in performing its obligations under the settlement agreement; and
- the decision of the trustee to write-off various loans made for the principal beneficiary and thereafter terminate the trust.[20]

18 [2001] JLR N 37.
19 [2020] JRC 161.
20 *In the Matter of the Re Arpetaz Settlement* [2020] JRC 161.

The court approved the trustee's decision. This was one of the very rare cases in which the Jersey Royal Court blessed a trustee's decision to submit to the jurisdiction of the English High Court raising questions on issues surrounding the administration of a Jersey trust.[21]

3.5 Consideration of a surrender of discretion by the trustee to the court

Under certain circumstances the trustee has the discretion to surrender their powers to the court. In such case the court is asked to make the decision based on the evidence provided, even though it should be emphasised that, as conveyed by the case law, in taking a decision after the surrender the court has no greater power than the trustee.[22]

One of the rare cases in which the trustee felt the need to surrender its discretion to the court was in *In the Matter of the AE Settlement.*[23] The trustee managed three trusts – the AE Settlement, the CE Settlement and the IE Settlement – settled by three brothers who sought to separate their joint interests in the trusts.

The main issue was that the trusts owned shares in three Irish companies for which an independent chartered accountant was appointed to analyse their internal management and his reports identified significant issues such as excessive remuneration for directors and unpaid taxes. The trustee's attempt to further investigate the companies was met with significant opposition by the directors of one of the companies who had links with the CE family. Given the conflict of interest involved, the trustee made an application under Article 51 for surrendering his jurisdiction and asked directions from the court regarding how to handle the matter.

The court's decision was that the directors of the Irish companies were obliged to disclose any information that could assist the trustee in his duties as well as to accept cross-examination, and that the only way to achieve a fair separation of the trusts was to use this information and see to what extent the CE directors had already benefited through the companies.[24]

This case is an indication of the broad powers of the court in relation to the administration of a trust.

It should be noted, as stated in *Public Trustee v Cooper*, that the court will only accept a surrender of discretion for a good reason. The most obvious good reason being either that the trustees are deadlocked or disabled as a result of a conflict of interest. The Jersey Court of Appeal in *Re B Settlement*[25] at paragraph 27 made the point that a trustee who had accepted office in the terms of a trust

21 *Ibid.*
22 *In the Matter of the CE Settlement* [2010] JRC 085.
23 [2010] JRC 085.
24 *In the Matter of the AE Settlement* [2010] JRC085.
25 [2010] JLR 653.

instrument was not entitled to hand over performance of the trusteeship to the court and that a surrender of discretion should be regarded as a last resort that would normally be accepted by the court only in relation to a specific exercise of discretion where no sensible alternative exists.

3.6 Where an action taken by a trustee is attacked as being outside of the trustee's powers or an improper exercise of the trustee's duty

A case in which the trustees' actions were attacked was in *MM v SG Hambros Trust Company (Channel Islands) Limited,*[26] in which the settlor challenged the trustee's decision to sell the only asset of the company.

The trustee decided that the asset could not be rented to generate income as it would require extensive refurbishment to be profitably utilised, but there were no available funds for the necessary renovation.

The settlor challenged this decision and instead argued that the trustee should have borrowed funds for the refurbishment and repaid the loan from future rental income, a proposal that was duly rejected by the trustee as this would reduce the life tenant's income.

The court upheld the decision of the trustee finding it to be reasonable as the sale offer was an "exceptionally good offer".

4. Conclusion

It remains to be seen how trustees will use and take advantage of the provisions of Section 11A of the International Trusts Law for their benefit in Cyprus, as well as how the case law will develop and whether it will clarify the matter of the definition of the word 'application' as already discussed in the proceedings in first-instance cases without the matter being clarified.

Contrary to Jersey's jurisdiction, applications for directions by trustees have not yet been brought forward in Cyprus to receive the approval of the court for trustees' decisions. This is an area that in Jersey has been greatly developed and the principles of equity as applied therein may be taken under consideration when similar issues and cases arise in Cyprus. Such principles were developed under the framework of the English decision in *Public Trustee v Cooper,* which may be applied by the Cypriot courts in the absence of a local precedent or statute.

As a result, it would be interesting in the near future to monitor the case law to view whether the application and use of Section 11A will develop to mirror Jersey's Article 51, as jurisdictional differences and characteristics of the Cyprus international trust may affect the applications which may be brought forward under Section 11A.

---

26 [2010] JRC 037.

Perpetuity and duration

Paolo Panico
Private Trustees SA; Chair – STEP Europe

Cyprus is a land of contrasts. A less conspicuous area where this is particularly true is the perpetuity periods applicable to trusts. While the Cyprus International Trusts Law has abolished any rule against perpetuities and currently allows international trusts to last for an indefinite duration, domestic trusts governed by the Trustee Law 1955 (Cap 193) are still subject to the English rule against perpetuities in the form pre-dating the Perpetuities and Accumulations Act 1964, which was enacted in the United Kingdom after Cyprus became independent of the British Empire on 16 August 1960.

1. Domestic trusts – the rule against perpetuities under the *Duke of Norfolk's Case*

Domestic trusts governed under the Trustee Law 1955 must respect the traditional rule against perpetuities in the version dating back to the *Duke of Norfolk's Case*.[1]

A classic definition of the rule can be taken from John Chipman Gray's handbook: "No interest is good unless it must vest, if at all, not later than twenty-one years after some life in being at the creation of the interest."[2] The notion of perpetuities originated in England under a statute of 1285 by Kind Edward I, *De Donis Conditionalibus*,[3] which created entails in such a form that the rights of successive owners of an estate would not be impaired. In other words, after a gift of land the donee could not dispose of it and on the donee's death the estate would pass to his heirs. This device was attractive to the aristocracy who could thus preserve their estates within their families indefinitely, with no risk of forfeiture for treason or felony or because of creditors as a result of an improvident disposition.

A side effect of entails was a restriction on the royal privilege over the land, which triggered a judicial reaction under the *Taltarum Case*.[4] Legislation was then introduced, mainly under the reigns of Henry VII and Henry VIII, to

1 3 Ch Cas 1, 22 Eng Rep 931 (1682).
2 J Gray, *The Rule Against Perpetuities*, 4th edition (Little, Brown, 1942), Section 201.
3 13 Edw I, c 1 (1285).
4 2 Edw IV, Michaelmas Term 25.

undermine the creation of perpetual title to land. A doctrine was thus affirmed that land cannot be held in perpetuity as this would effectively withdraw it from commerce and free circulation in the economy.

The doctrine of the rule against perpetuities and the details of its application were reviewed by Lord Nottingham, the Lord Chancellor sometimes referred to as 'the Father of Equity', in the *Duke of Norfolk's Case*, where the relevant arrangement was in fact upheld as not being a perpetuity.

The defendant in the *Duke of Norfolk's Case* was Henry Howard, Duke of Norfolk and premier peer of England, who in such capacity took precedence over all non-royal nobles except the Archbishop of Canterbury and the Lord Chancellor. The claimant was his younger brother Charles. The controversy arose as to which of the two was entitled to a particular estate, the barony of Grostock, which had been settled on trust by their father.

The main features of the trust are best described in a classical academic account of the case by Herbert Barry:

> *Without attempting technical accuracy, it may be said that the substance and effect of the transactions, expressed in modern terms, were as follows: The property was to be held for the use of the Earl during his own lifetime, and then for his widow. Then during the life of the eldest son, Thomas Howard, later Duke of Norfolk, and of his issue male, if any; it was to be in trust for the benefit of the second son, Henry Howard, and the heirs male of his body; but with the proviso – and this was the essential feature involved – that in case the eldest son, Thomas, should die without issue during the life of Henry and thereby the Earldom with the estates accompanying it should descend to Henry, then the trust as to this Grostock barony was to be for the benefit of the brother Charles and the heirs male of his body.*[5]

The fifth Duke of Norfolk and Earl of Arundel, who had settled the trust, died in 1652 and his widow died in 1673. Their eldest son Thomas was mentally disabled but succeeded his father as Duke of Norfolk until his death in 1677. His younger brother Henry had arranged for him to be detained in Padua (Italy) and prevented from marrying until he recovered from his mental disease. As a result, Thomas died without leaving any heirs and Henry became the sixth Duke of Norfolk, inheriting all related estates, including the Grostock barony. His younger brother Charles sued, claiming that such estate had vested in him under the terms of their father's trust.

The case came before the Lord Chancellor in January 1681 but a decree in favour of the claimant was not issued until one year later, in January 1682. The reason for this long delay was the complex political situation in which the Lord Chancellor was involved, which ultimately led him to dissolve Parliament on King Charles II's command.

---

5 H Barry, "The Duke of Norfolk's Case", *23 Virginia Law Review* 5, 538 (1937), 546–547.

The Lord Chancellor was assisted in his judgment by three very senior judges, Lord Chief Justice North, Lord Chief Justice Pemberton and Lord Chief Baron Montague. They all unanimously agreed that the Grostock barony inured to Henry, the sixth Duke of Norfolk, because the device that his father had attempted to create under the trust was in fact void for perpetuity.

Lord Nottingham found for Charles and ruled that the disposition was not void for perpetuity.

The fifth Duke of Norfolk's intention is very clearly summarised by Herbert Barry:

The documents in this case are complex, but the purpose of the Earl of Arundel was simple and laudable. His eldest son, Thomas, who as such would inherit the titles and the estates, was mentally defective; he would inevitably inherit if he outlived his father, but he would leave no descendants. The second son, Henry, if he survived this older brother, would succeed to the inheritance, but until that event he might be in strained circumstances. The father desired to make a provision that certain property should be enjoyed by his second son, Henry, until he succeeded to the inheritance, and then that it should pass to the younger son, Charles.[6]

The question was whether a contingent future estate in remainder such as that one could take effect. Lord Nottingham, in his capacity as Lord Chancellor, replied: "Yes – provided the contingency will wear out in a short time." He did not elaborate what a 'short time' should be, but he mentioned that it should be "a contingency to happen in a life".[7]

The subsequent history of the case is also interesting. Lord Nottingham died in December 1682, a few months after his decree on this case. He was succeeded by Lord North, one of the three judges who had expressed dissenting opinions in the *Duke of Norfolk's Case*. Unsurprisingly, on an appeal by Henry, Duke of Norfolk, Lord North reversed his predecessor's decree on 15 May 1683[8] and stated that:

A perpetuity is a thing odious in law and destructive to the commonwealth; it would put a stop to commerce and prevent the circulation of the riches of the Kingdom, and therefore it is not to be countenanced in equity. If in equity you should come nearer to a perpetuity than the rules of common law would admit, all men being desirous to continue their estates in their families would settle their estates by way of trust, which might indeed make well for the jurisdiction of the court, but would be destructive to the commonwealth.

No further appeal was possible at the time: the jurisdiction to review belonged to the House of Lords but Parliament had been dissolved in 1681 by the Lord Nottingham in his capacity as Lord Chancellor.

---

6 *Ibid*, at 552.
7 *Ibid*, at 553.
8 1 Vernon's R 163.

However, King James II summoned Parliament again in May 1685 and on 19 June of the same year a full house almost unanimously accepted Charles's motion to reverse. In fact, Charles Howard had in the meantime become the seventh Duke of Norfolk after his brother Henry's death, but had decided to bring the matter before the House of Lords for reversal even though he had inherited all the estates accompanying the title.

It is ironic to notice that the case, which is usually quoted as the authority establishing the rule against perpetuities in the form corresponding to a rule against remoteness, was in fact a decision that upheld a disposition as it found that it was not a perpetuity.

The standard term for perpetuity, corresponding to life in being plus 21 years, was established in the 100 years following the case. The principle was spelt out in the following terms in *Thellusson v Woodford*: "The established length of time during which the vesting may be suspended is during a life or lives in being, the period of gestation and the infancy of such posthumous child."[9]

A consequence of this rule is that successive estates of unborn children are void for perpetuity. This principle was first expressed in *Hay v Earl of Coventry*: "The law is now clearly settled that an estate for life may be limited to unborn issue, provided the devisor does not go farther and give an estate in succession to the children of such unborn issue."[10]

Similarly, in *Moneypenny v Dering*,[11] Lord St Leonards said: "Then the rule of law forbids the raising of successive estates by purchase to unborn children, that is, to an unborn child of an unborn child. With this rule I have never meant to interfere, for it is too well settled to be broken in upon." This rule is also known as 'the rule in *Whitby v Michell*' after a nineteenth-century case.[12] The facts in this case concerned land that was settled on a husband and a wife for life, with remainder to their eldest unborn daughter and further in remainder for that daughter's children born during her parents' lifetime. The destination to the grandchildren (ie, the children of an unborn child at the time of the settlement) was held to be void for remoteness or perpetuity.

These rules are still in force in Cyprus in relation to domestic trusts governed by the Trustee Law 1955. The Perpetuities and Accumulations Act 1964,[13] which came into force in England on 16 July 1964, relaxed the rule by introducing a 'wait and see' approach that would not determine a trust to be void from the outset if there was a chance that the interests under it would vest within the perpetuity period. Further, the rather complex and unpredictable 'life in being

---

9 (1792) 4 Ves 227.
10 (1789) 3 T 83 at 86.
11 (1852) 2 DM & G 145, at 170.
12 *Whitby v Mitchell* ((1889) 42 Ch D 494).
13 13 Eliz 2, c 55.

plus 21 years' rule could be replaced by an easier 80-year perpetuity period. The Perpetuities and Accumulations Act 2009[14] further relaxed the rule by introducing a fixed perpetuity period of 125 years. None of these statutes applies in Cyprus as they were enacted in the United Kingdom after the Republic became independent on 16 August 1960.

2. International trusts – perpetual duration

The opposite approach applies under the Cyprus International Trusts Law, where the rule against perpetuities was expressly repealed and international trusts can therefore last for an unlimited period.

The original Section 5 of the Cyprus International Trusts Law 1992 established, as a general rule, that international trusts could last for a maximum duration of 100 years. International trusts for a purpose, whether charitable or not, could last indefinitely.[15]

The distinction between an international trust for beneficiaries and an international purpose trust was repealed under the 2012 International Trust Amending Law (Law 20(I)/2012), which introduced a new Section 5:

(1) In respect of an international trust created on or after the commencement of this Law and subject to the terms of the trust:

(a) there shall be no limit on the period for which a trust continues to be valid and enforceable, and

(b) no rule against perpetuities or remoteness of vesting or any analogous rule applies to a trust or to any advancement, appointment, payment or application of property from a trust.

(2) Except where the terms of the trust expressly provide to the contrary, no advancement, distribution, appointment, payment or application of income or capital from the trust to another trust shall be invalidated solely because the other trust continued to be valid and enforceable beyond the date on which the first trust must terminate.

Paragraph 5(1)(b) expressly repeals the rule against perpetuities or remoteness of vesting in relation to a Cyprus international trust that may last indefinitely. Further, subsection 5(2) provides that a distribution from one trust to another cannot be invalidated simply because the recipient trust lasts beyond the perpetuity period of the distributing trust. This appears to suggest that a distribution from a Cyprus domestic trust to a Cyprus international trust is valid

---

14 2009, c 18.

15 The Cyprus International Trusts Law (1992 version), Section 5. Duration of international trust: (1) For the purposes of this law and notwithstanding any legal provision to the contrary, or of a rule of law of the Republic of Cyprus or of any other country the duration period of an international trust may continue until the 100th anniversary of the date on which it came into existence when it will terminate, unless terminated sooner due to a relevant direction in the instrument creating it or for any other reason; (2) Subsection 1 will not apply to charitable trusts or trusts for a purpose referred to in this law, which may continue in force without any time limitation.

even though the second trust can last indefinitely while the first one must abide by its perpetuity period.

Section 2 of the Cyprus International Trusts Law sets the conditions for a trust to be international and governed by that law: the settlor and the beneficiaries were not Cyprus residents in the year before the creation of the trust and at least one trustee must be resident in Cyprus.

To the extent that the Cyprus International Trusts Law is an example of state-of-the-art, flexible and effective trust statute, it is to be hoped that in a not-so-distant future its provisions will be made available to Cyprus resident families as well. For now, Cyprus resident settlors must choose either a foreign governing law for their trusts or cope with the antiquated and sometimes obscure provisions of the Trustee Law 1955.

Forced heirship: the 'firewall legislation'

Stella Kammitsi
Raza Corporate Services Ltd; Chair – STEP Cyprus

Trusts, especially discretionary ones, are an essential and popular tool for post-death inheritance planning. They are an alternative to wills, which can expressly provide for how one wishes one's assets to be administered and distributed after death to the heirs. In most jurisdictions trusts are used to minimise inheritance tax burdens and considerable asset transfer fees. In some other jurisdictions though, where strict heirship rules are in place, trusts are used, particularly the *inter vivos* ones, for the settlor/testator to have freedom and absolute discretion on the distribution of the estate's assets.

In Cyprus, inheritance tax has never been substantial, and in recent years it has been completely abolished under the Estate Duty (Amending) Law 2000 for any person who is domiciled in Cyprus and dies after the 1 January 2020. However, if the death occurred before 1 January 2020, inheritance tax on properties applies.

Regarding inheritance tax rates, for transfers from parents to children nothing is paid and for transfers between spouses and third-degree relatives 0.1% on the value of the property as of 1 January 2013 is paid. In case of transfer of the immovable property to a trust the transfer fees are a flat amount of €50 irrespective of the property value.

Considering the above it could be concluded that trusts in Cyprus are effective for succession and inheritance planning and are useful to bypass the complicated system of forced heirship imposed by Cyprus law.

1. Cyprus law on wills and succession

Succession in Cyprus is regulated mainly by two pieces of national law: the Wills and Succession Law[1] (Cap 195), which governs the law in relation to wills and succession in Cyprus; and the Administration of Estates Law[2] (Cap 189), which provides for the procedure to be followed in executing a will and the administration of the estate of a deceased person. These two laws supplement one another and both date back to when Cyprus was a British colony before 1960,

1 Wills and Succession Law, Cap 195 as amended by 75/1970, 100/1989, 96(I)/2015.
2 The Administration of Estates Law (Cap 189) as amended by 157/1985, 45/1990 and 2(I)/1994.

which explains why their provisions are old-fashioned and brief. They apply only to a deceased individual who was domiciled in Cyprus at the time of death.

Relevant laws include the Probates (Re-Sealing) Law (Cap 192) and the EU Succession Regulation 650/2012,[3] also known as Brussels IV, which governs cross-border issues of succession within the European Union.

The Probates (Re-sealing law) Law (Cap 192) applies to individuals who have passed away in the United Kingdom or another Commonwealth country and who, on death, had immovable property in Cyprus. It provides for the procedure that must be followed to reseal before the Cyprus courts the grant of probate or letters of administration from another Commonwealth country.

Brussels IV came into force on 17 August 2015 and its principal aim has been to unify laws across EU member states. It applies to any residents and citizens of any of the members states or to individuals who own assets in any of the EU member states. It provides that the laws of the member state where an individual 'habitually resides' when they make a will or when they die should govern the succession of their assets as a whole (both movable and immovable). This applies unless it can be proved that the deceased was more closely connected with another country on death, or the deceased had expressly chosen the laws of their own nationality to apply.

Brussels IV does not apply to the United Kingdom (which is also no longer an EU member), or to Ireland and Denmark, as they have opted out.

2. Forced heirship regime

Cyprus is a jurisdiction that historically relies on strong family bonds and protecting the preservation of family assets within the circle of close relatives, and its law imposes considerable restrictions on the testator's freedom as to whom to dispose their estate to on death. Immediate family members (eg, a spouse, children, grandchildren and parents of the deceased) are protected as they are entitled by law to a substantial part of the deceased's estate under the regime of forced heirship.

Cap 195 provides that succession to the deceased's estate may be either by will or by the operation of law, or by will and the operation of law. However, the testator cannot freely dispose of all their property by will, such right is limited to the 'disposable portion'. The rest of the property – which is referred to as the 'statutory portion' – must be distributed to the closest relatives of the deceased and is thus 'reserved' for them. These are the closest relatives surviving the spouse, the children or grandchildren (when the children have died during the deceased's lifetime).

---

3 Regulation (EU) 650/2012 of the European Parliament and of the Council of 4 July 2012 on jurisdiction, applicable law, recognition and enforcement of decisions and acceptance and enforcement of authentic instruments in matters of succession and on the creation of a European Certificate of Succession.

The calculation of what is the 'disposable portion' and what the 'statutory portion' depends on who the surviving relatives of the deceased are at the time of death, as well as their family relationship with the deceased.

According to Section 41 of Cap 195, as subsequently amended by Law 100/1989, the disposable portion is calculated as follows if, at the time of death the deceased:

- had a spouse and a child, or a spouse and descendants of a child, or no spouse but a child or descendant of a child, the disposable portion cannot exceed a quarter of the net value of the deceased's estate;
- had a spouse or father or mother but no child or descendants of a child, the disposable portion cannot exceed half of the net value of the estate of the deceased; or
- had no spouse, no child, no descendant of a child and no father or mother, the deceased is free to dispose of their whole estate as they wish.

This means that the un-disposable statutory portion is:

- half of the estate if the deceased leaves a spouse or parent but no children; or
- three-quarters of the estate if the deceased leaves children; or
- not applicable if the deceased has no spouse, no child and no parent alive.

If the deceased left a will naming a specific individual as their executor, the executor will be able to act in accordance with the will only on probate being granted by the court.[4] Where in the will the testator disposes of more than the disposable portion, the will is not rendered void but the disposition will be reduced to the disposable portion as indicated by law.

The testator may, through their will, dispose of property that is acquired after the execution of the will and the disposable portion is ascertained at the time of the testator's death.

The Cypriot rules of inheritance apply to any person who is domiciled in Cyprus and/or who holds immovable property in Cyprus irrespective of domicile.

Before July 2015, pursuant to Section 42 of Cap 195, any person whose father was born in the United Kingdom or in any other member country of the Commonwealth was exempt from the forced heirship provisions. Law 96(1) of 2015[5] withdrew this exemption and the forced heirship provisions now apply to anyone who dies after the 17 August 2015 while domiciled in Cyprus and to the succession to any real estate located in Cyprus, regardless of the domicile of the deceased.

The forced heirship regime applies to anyone who dies domiciled in Cyprus

4 Section 14 of Cap 189.

5 Bylaw 96(1), 2015, Article 42 of Cap 195, was removed altogether.

irrespective of nationality. Further, if pursuant to the provisions of Brussels IV, Cyprus is considered as the deceased's country of 'habitual residency', then the Cyprus succession laws will be applicable to the estate (Article 4). This applies unless it can be shown that the deceased was 'manifestly more closely connected' with another state, in which case the laws of this state will apply instead those of Cyprus.

This can be overridden, by virtue of Article 22 (Choice of Law) of Brussels IV, which provides that any EU citizen may choose expressly in their will that the law of their country of nationality be the applicable law to the succession of their estate. Further, if the deceased was not habitually resident in Cyprus at the time of their death, the court of a member state in which assets of the deceased are located will have jurisdiction on the succession matters of the deceased.

For example, if a British citizen lives in Cyprus and retains a house in England, the provisions of Brussel IV apply and Cyprus will be considered as the country of 'habitual residence'. If, however, a Frenchman dies in France and has a holiday home in Cyprus, French succession laws apply except for the holiday home in Cyprus, where the Cyprus law is applicable.

3. Absence of a will

If the testator dies intestate, the Cyprus courts will authorise a person to administer the deceased's estate, granting 'letters of administration' to the 'administrator' of the estate.

The estate will, through an administration process, be distributed to the deceased's relatives based on the degree of their relationship under the rules of intestacy. Any of the deceased's debts, taxes and liabilities (including funeral expenses) will have priority and must be paid first. The administration procedure is supervised by the Cyprus courts exercising their probate jurisdiction.

Pursuant to Section 44 of Cap 195, for the estate to be disposed of to the relatives, the surviving spouse's portion must be calculated, since a prior share must be set aside for them. The spouse is entitled to both part of the statutory portion and the disposable portion that may or may not remain undisposed of. The surviving spouse's share is determined based on the existence of other surviving heirs and their degree of kinship to the deceased. It is calculated as follows:

- If, in addition to the spouse, the deceased has any children or descendants of children who died before the deceased, they are all notionally allocated equal portions. If a child of the deceased died during the deceased's lifetime, then their children (ie, the grandchildren) will receive the share that their parent should have received if they were alive.
- If at the time of their death the deceased leaves a surviving spouse but

no children or a descendant of a child, but at least one relative of third-degree kinship to the deceased (not necessary in the direct line and thus it can be parents, grandparents, aunts, uncles or nephews and nieces) or closer, the surviving spouse is entitled to half of the statutory portion and undisposed portion. The number of ancestors or descendants within the third degree of kinship that the deceased leaves on death is immaterial when calculating the spouse's share. Even if the deceased leaves one such ancestor or descendant, the surviving spouse's share will still be limited to half.
- If besides the surviving spouse the deceased leaves only relatives of fourth-degree kinship (ie, cousins or siblings of grandparents or grandchildren of a sibling), the surviving spouse is entitled to the three-quarters of the statutory and undisposed portions.
- In case of no relatives within the fourth-degree of kinship at the time of the deceased's death, the surviving spouse is entitled to the whole statutory and undisposed portions.
- If the deceased leaves two lawful surviving spouses, the share is equal. This is quite a strange provision, as bigamy in Cyprus is, by virtue of law, an offence.

After the calculation of the spouse's share, the remaining portion is distributed to the relatives of the deceased according to the degree of kinship and in equal shares (except half-brothers or half-sisters who will receive half of the share that the siblings receive). Descendants of brothers and sisters who died during the lifetime of the deceased are also entitled to the share of the corresponding brother or sister, *per stirpes*.

Where there is neither a surviving spouse nor a relative within the sixth degree of kinship, all the deceased's estate is transferred to the government.

The relatives of one class exclude relatives of a subsequent class. For example, if the deceased leaves a child and a brother, only the child is entitled to the statutory portion.

4. Domicile – main criterion for Cyprus succession law

For the Cyprus succession law to be applied, the deceased must be domiciled in Cyprus at the time of their death.[6]

'Domicile' is a common law concept used to determine which legal system applies to an individual and it is distinct from nationality or residency. An individual cannot have two domiciles at the same time, and it can often be complex to determine which domicile applies. Pursuant to Section 6 of Cap 195, an individual is domiciled or deemed domiciled in Cyprus if they have a Cyprus

6 Section 5 of Cap 195.

domicile of origin (given at birth) or they have acquired a domicile of choice in Cyprus.

The law is quite gender prejudiced regarding its provisions on domicile of origin, as the domicile of a legitimate child will be considered the same as the father's domicile at the time of the child's birth. If the child is illegitimate or posthumous, the child's domicile of origin will be that of its mother at the time of the child's birth.

The domicile of choice is acquired by establishing a residence in Cyprus with the intention to reside there permanently or indefinitely. The domicile of origin is lost when a domicile of choice is acquired.

Irrespective of the domicile of origin or choice, individuals who have been tax residents in Cyprus for at least 17 out of the past 20 years prior to the tax year in question, will be deemed domiciled in Cyprus for the purposes of the Special Defence Contribution Law.[7]

5. Distinction between movable and immovable property and Cyprus law

The Cypriot domicile is not the only criterion for the Cyprus succession laws to be applied as the Cyprus law makes a further distinction between movable and immovable property and assets – it is a 'scissionary system'.

The distinction between movable and immovable property is set out in the Immovable Property Law (Cap 224).[8] The law of the domicile of the testator at the time of their death governs the disposal of movable property, even where the testator was Cypriot.

Where the testator was domiciled in Cyprus at the time of their death, Section 5 of Cap 195 regulates the succession in relation to the movable property, whether in Cyprus or abroad, as well as the succession in immovable property located in Cyprus. Therefore, in this instance, the restrictions imposed by Cyprus law on the statutory portion apply. This has been also re-enforced in common law in the case of *Kochino v Irfan*.[9]

In *Irfan*, the deceased, who at the time of his death was domiciled in Cyprus, died intestate in 1969. He possessed movable and immovable assets in Cyprus, two houses in London and had money deposited at an English bank. He had a spouse, brothers and sisters. The widow filed proceedings against the administrators of her husband's estate and the brothers and sisters of the deceased for the division of the estate. The Nicosia District Court held that the immovable property in London, which consisted of the two houses, was exempt from being brought into account in relation to the division of the estate that

7 Special Contribution for the Defence of the Republic Law (Law 117(I)/2002, as amended).
8 The Immovable Property (Tenure, Registration and Valuation), Cap 224 (as amended).
9 *Siddika Mehmet Kochino v Derviche Irfan* ((1976) 1 CLR 240).

was in Cyprus. The widow filed an appeal to the Supreme Court, which held that "that the notion of 'estate' in Section 5(a) of Cap 195 cannot be treated as including immovable property outside Cyprus".

This case reinforced the application of the provisions of Section 5 of Cap 195 regarding the disposal of immovable property in Cyprus, but that do not extend to immovable property located abroad.

It can be argued that Cap 195 conflicts with Brussels IV where the provisions of the latter may apply. Section 5(b) provides that the said law regulates the succession to immovable property even if the deceased was not domiciled in Cyprus. However, under Brussels IV there is no distinction between movable and immovable property, and it applies to both. It specifically provides that the law of the country where the deceased is habitually resident on death or when they make their will shall govern the succession of their assets as a whole (both movable and immovable property). By way of example, if a French national who lived in Paris dies intestate leaving, among other assets, a holiday home in Paphos, then Brussels IV should apply and the Paphos property should be subject to French laws of inheritance and succession and the heirs should not have to deal with the Cyprus forced heirship regime.

If the deceased left a will, under Brussels IV, the law of the country where the deceased was habitually resident will govern the will. However, this can be overridden if the nationality or the laws of the country where the deceased was 'manifestly more closely connected' is chosen as the will's governing law. The latter is rarely used and only in exceptional cases. For example, if a Cypriot national residing in Greece dies leaving immovable and movable assets in Cyprus and immovable property in England, pursuant to Brussels IV, Greek succession law will apply, as at the time of death the deceased was habitually resident in Greece. Of course, Greek law will determine how to deal with the immovable property in England. If, however, the deceased left a will governed by Cyprus law, the whole of their assets will be subject to the Cyprus forced heirship regime except their immovable property in England, which will be governed by UK law in light of Brexit and as the United Kingdom has opted out of the provisions of Brussels IV.

6. Further issues arising from a will

Besides the forced heirship provisions of the Cyprus law, further complications may arise in case of a will. Even though leaving a will is the most common approach for setting out *inter vivos* how assets are to be disposed of on death, it still triggers various risks as confusion may be caused by having more than one will made at various times and thereby finding it difficult to discover which is the valid will and which has been revoked, or in cases where the will has been destroyed (eg, burned or torn) or lost.

Further, the testator may marry and have children or further children after the will has been drafted and the will, when executed, carried no provisions covering the prospects of a new marriage and any children born after the will's date.

Testamentary wills do not operate automatically on death in the same way as a deed of trust for transferring assets to the next class of beneficiary. It is necessary to go through probate and obtain a grant of probate[10] and a tax clearance certificate.

7. How to avoid forced heirship restrictions

This can occur in three different ways:

- the deceased making gifts of their estate during their lifetime;
- the heirs of the deceased making a declaration of renunciation; or
- the deceased setting up a trust.

The first option of making *inter vivos* gifts of the estate may not be favourable since, prior to their death, the deceased may have wished to keep full ownership and control over their assets. Further, any disposal of assets *inter vivos* may cause family discrepancies and disputes that one may wish to avoid while alive.

Cyprus has no claw-back restrictions regarding lifetime gifts and thus any gifts made *inter vivos* by the deceased (of any value and amount and at any time) are excluded from the estate unless it can be proved that at the relevant time of making the gift the deceased was mentally incapable of understanding what they were signing, or it is proved to be a fraudulent transfer made in bad faith for defrauding creditors and objections are raised within certain timeframes from the date the gift was made.

The second option of the renunciation of rights to the deceased's estate is subject to the full discretion and decision of each heir and can be made only after the death of the testator and within a three-month period from the date that the heir found out about the deceased's death and provided the said individual is an heir of the deceased.[11]

The third option of setting up a trust is examined in detail below.

7.1 Setting up a trust and avoidance of forced heirship provisions: *inter vivos* trusts and testamentary trusts

(a) *Testamentary trusts*

Testamentary trusts are created under a will of the deceased and take effect on the death of the testator. They are also sometimes referred to as 'will trusts' or 'trusts under will'. The trust established under a person's will does not come

---

10 Section 14 of Cap 189.
11 Section 51 of Cap 189 and the Administration of the Estates Rules 1955.

into force until after their death.[12] In effect, once it is created it remains dormant until the death of the testator who created the trust and, during that time, the settlor may introduce changes to the trust.

In addition, after the death of the testator a testamentary trust becomes irrevocable and questions regarding the validity of the trust that could arise must be resolved applying not only the law of trusts but also the law of succession, because of the interrelation between both laws.

If the testamentary trust is not in line with the forced heirship provisions and the deceased was domiciled in Cyprus at the time of their death this will give rise to the need to have a strict interpretation of the law. On death the assets form part of the estate, so it is not possible to transfer any of them at that time into a trust beyond the 'statutory portion' that the heirs are entitled to pursuant to Cap 195. What will be possible is to specify which assets of the estate will be inherited by specific heirs at the portion to which they are entitled. Regarding the 'disposable portion', the testamentary trust will not be subject to these restrictions.

Thus, even if a testamentary trust is considered as valid, it must abide by the forced heirship provisions regarding the 'statutory portion' and does not operate automatically in the same way as *inter vivos* trusts for transferring assets to the next class of beneficiaries. Further, since it forms part of a will, it is necessary to go through probate and obtain a grant of probate and a tax clearance certificate for Cyprus assets.

(b) Inter vivos *trusts*

Inter vivos trusts are created during the settlor's lifetime and on their creation the assets cease to belong to the settlor and are placed under the control of the trustee, although they do not belong to the trustee's own estate. On the settlor's death these assets do not constitute part of their estate and the forced heirship regime cannot be applied to them. If the settlor and beneficiaries fall within the classifications set out in the Cyprus International Trusts Law and the chosen law of the Cyprus international trust (CIT) is the law of Cyprus, then all questions relating to CITs will be determined in accordance with the laws of Cyprus without reference to the law of any other jurisdiction. This protects against the application of foreign laws such as forced heirship laws and CITs are considered immune from forced heirship claims.

Section 3(1) of the Cyprus International Trusts Law provides explicitly that it does not recognise heirship claims against trust assets nor does the Cyprus law on inheritance and succession or those of any other jurisdiction in any way affect the transfer or disposition of assets to a CIT, nor do these rights affect the validity of a CIT.

---

12 *Vanderplank v King* (1843) 3 Hare 1; *Lord Duncannon v Smith* (1845–1846) 12 Cl and Fin 546, HL.

These provisions are further strengthened by Section 3(4) of the law, which provides that:

No international trust and no disposition of property to or under such a trust, shall be void, voidable, or liable to be set aside or subject to any implied term, nor shall the capacity of any settlor, trustee, enforcer, protector or beneficiary be questioned, and no settlor, trustee, enforcer, protector, beneficiary or third party shall be subject to any obligation or liability or be deprived of any right, claim or interest, by way of right to inheritance.

This is not limited to rights of inheritance under Cyprus law, but is left open to apply to the inheritance laws of any other country and any such transfer to the trust cannot be successfully challenged.

In effect, the terms of the Cyprus International Trusts Law prevail over any legal provisions as to the inheritance of property in case of the settlor's death. The validity of any transfer or disposition of property into a CIT cannot be challenged by any succession laws of either Cyprus or any other jurisdiction.

All questions relating to CITs are to be determined in accordance with the laws of Cyprus without reference to the law of any other jurisdiction. This subsequently offers protection against the application of any forced heirship rules of any foreign law.

Further, the Cyprus International Trusts Law, as amended, provides specifically that the CIT or the disposition of trust assets will not be void or voidable or capable of being set aside or be subject to any implied terms and in no circumstances will the capability of the settlor, the trustee, the protector or the beneficiary be subjected to any obligations or be questioned.

The protection and security over the assets of a CIT are enhanced when the CIT expressly indicates Cyprus law as its governing law. Section 12A(3) of the Cyprus International Trusts Law provides that the CITs are governed by the law that the settlor has chosen as indicated in the terms of the trust deed. This precludes the application of any other foreign or local law irrespective of any other conflict of law provisions in force in Cyprus. This is considered a fundamental rule that, as a matter of public policy, must be abided.

Where no governing law has been chosen, the trust is governed by the law to which the trust is more closely related, and the Cyprus International Trusts Law sets out certain guidelines enabling the court to identify the law to which the trust is more closely related. The choice though has the limitation that the validity and other matters, as these are identified in Section 3(1A) of the law, are governed exclusively by Cyprus law, irrespective of the provisions of the foreign law chosen.

Regarding Cyprus local trusts, Cyprus forced heirship rights do not apply on the same basis as for the CITs as Cap 193 does not have similar provisions to those of the Cyprus International Trusts Law. However, as the assets are transferred to a trust *inter vivos*, upon death those assets do not belong to the deceased for the forced heirship provisions to apply to them.

8. Cyprus law versus EU law and the Hague Convention

The forced heirship provisions of the Cyprus legislation may be challenged by virtue of specific EU regulations or under the Hague Convention.

EU Regulation 650/2012 (Brussels IV) of 4 July 2012 entered into force on 17 August 2015, making cross-border successions easier. It applies to all EU countries except Ireland and Denmark. It aims to ensure that only one law determines how an estate is dealt with. It applies to all assets in the member states that have implemented the regulation regardless of the place of death or the citizenship of the settlor or even if the deceased has no connection to those EU member states.

The law of the EU member state where the deceased was habitually resident at the time of their death will apply to their succession. However, if the deceased was 'manifestly more closely connected' with another state, then the law of that other state will apply. EU citizens have the right to choose the law of their country of nationality to apply to their estate, whether it is an EU or non-EU member state.[13]

A European Certificate of Successions is issued that allows proof in other EU countries of who are the heirs, legatees, executors of the will or administrators of the estate. Judgment of inheritance issued in one member state will be automatically recognised in all the other member states.

It could be argued that the laws of the last habitual residence of a deceased EU national on succession and inheritance may take precedence over the provisions of the Cyprus International Trusts Law. Despite this EU regulation, the national laws of inheritance still apply for the following matters:

- who is to inherit;
- the percentage of the share that goes to the children and spouse;
- property and family law; and
- tax issues related to succession assets.

Further, reliance on the provisions of Section 12C of the Cyprus International Trusts Law may be sought and it could be argued that any decision or judgment in relation to heirship rights is contrary to this specific provision of the law and further extends the argument by relying on the provisions of Article 40 of EU Regulation 650/2012, which permits a member state to refuse recognition of a decision that is manifestly contrary to its public policy (*ordre public*) in the state in which recognition is sought (provided any of the grounds prescribed in the provisions of the said regulation exist).

However, in Cyprus there is no legislation providing a definition of what is meant by the concept of 'public policy'. This matter was considered in the case of *Pilavachi & Co Ltd v International Chemical Co Ltd*,[14] where the Supreme Court defined it "as the totality of values, perceptions and ideas on which the ethical,

13 Article 22 ('Choice of Law') of EU Regulation 650/2012.
14 *Pilavachi & Co Ltd v International Chemical Co Ltd* ((1965) 1 CLR 97).

financial and political order which regulates Cypriot society is based from time to time".[15]

It appears to be the duty of the judge to verify that all their decisions on the specific matter follow the Cyprus fundamental principles of public order, which must include the essential principles of justice, public morality and ethics.

In *Pilavachi* the Supreme Court referenced the following probable classification of cases indicated by Professor Cheshire,[16] in which an English court will refuse to enforce a foreign acquired right on the ground that its enforcement would conflict with overriding principles of English public policy (which most likely also apply to Cyprus as it is a common law jurisdiction):

- where the fundamental conceptions of English justice are disregarded;
- where the English conceptions of morality are infringed;
- where a transaction prejudices the interests of the United Kingdom or its good relations with foreign powers; and
- where a foreign law or statute offends UK conceptions of human liberty and freedom of action.

In the same case the Supreme Court also referred to what Sir William Holdsworth specifically indicated in his *History of English Law*,[17] where he stated:

In fact, a body of law like the common law, which has grown up gradually with the growth of the nation, necessarily acquires some fixed principles, and if it is to maintain these principles, it must be able, on the ground of public policy or some other like ground, to suppress practices which, under ever new disguises, seek to weaken or negative them.

The Supreme Court further noted that for the enforcement of a judgment to be contrary to public policy in Cyprus, it should be against the principles of the established law.

8.1 Recognition and enforcement of foreign judgments

A further concern is the recognition and enforcement in Cyprus of civil and commercial judgments issued in another EU member state pursuant to the laws of another jurisdiction regarding forced heirship claims over a CIT following the provisions of Regulation (EC) 44/2001 of the Council 2002[18] on international jurisdiction.

It appears that Section 12B of the Cyprus International Trusts Law overcomes this concern by specifically providing that:

15 *Isaia, Diomedes v Ktimatiki Eteria Kleanthis Englezos Ltd* ((1974) 11 JSC 1114).

16 See Professor GC Cheshire, *Private International Law*, 5th edn (Clarendon Press, 1957), p154 and following.

17 Sir William Searle Holdsworth, *A History of English Law*, volume VIII, book IV, part II (Sweet & Maxwell Ltd, 1937), p55.

18 Regulation (EC) 44/2001 of the Council of 22 December 2000 on international jurisdiction was superseded on 10 January 2015 by Regulation (EC) 1215/2012.

Without prejudice to the provisions of Council Regulation (EC) No. 44/2001 of 22 December 2000 on jurisdiction and the recognition and enforcement of judgments in civil and commercial matters, the Court shall have jurisdiction where:

(a) the governing law of a trust or a particular aspect of a trust is the law of the Republic;

(b) the trustee of any trust is resident in the Republic;

(c) in the case of a company acting as a trustee company offering administrative services, provided that it is incorporated in the Republic;

(d) any trust property is situated in the Republic;

(e) the administration of any trust is carried out in the Republic;

(f) the parties submit to the jurisdiction of the Court;

(g) the instrument creating or evidencing the trust contains provision for the referral of any dispute to the jurisdiction of the courts of the Republic:

Provided that such jurisdiction will be exclusive unless the instrument creating or evidencing the trust provides otherwise.

However, this in effect prohibits the enforcement of foreign judgments as provided in EU Regulation 1215/2012 and in order to be in compliance with the said regulation any court judgment issued by another EU member state should be recognised and enforced in Cyprus even where it conflicts with provisions of the Cyprus International Trusts Law (eg, forced heirship provisions).

In the 2018 Cypriot case *Arip xxx v xxx Trustee Services Ltd*, the Larnaca District Court[19] examined the issue of enforcement of a UK judgment in relation to immovable property situated in England owned by a CIT.

More specifically, the court was asked to examine whether a CIT based on the provisions of Sections 3(1A), 3(4), 12A, 12B and 12C of the Cyprus International Trusts Law and/or based on the Hague Convention on trusts and its ratification by Law 4(III)/2017,[20] the Cyprus courts have exclusive jurisdiction on all matters related directly or indirectly to the trust, including any assets that directly or indirectly belong to it. The applicant was seeking restriction on the enforcement of a judgment issued by UK courts against the CIT, with a special focus on immovable property located in the United Kingdom over which the UK courts had exclusive jurisdiction.

One important part of the decision that the judge concluded was that the specific trust could not be classified as a CIT since there was no Cyprus trustee appointed. Therefore, the provisions of the Cyprus International Trusts Law did not apply. Further, the court stressed that the requested prohibition of the enforcement of the UK court judgment on immovable property in England is beyond the jurisdiction of the Cyprus courts, irrespective of the fact that the

---

19 *Arip xxx v xxx Trustee Services Ltd* (5/18, 24 October 2018, Larnaca District Court).

20 The Hague Convention on the Law Applicable to Trusts and the Recognition of these (Sanctions) Law of 2017 (Law 4(III)/2017).

owner is a Cyprus trust. This decision was based on the provisions of Article 24 of Regulation (EC)1215/2012[21] (known as the 'Brussels Recast Regulation') and it also indicated that these provisions prevail over the provisions of the Cyprus International Trusts Law.

An argument that could be raised to overcome this prohibition is that the foreign judgment is contrary to the public policy and order of Cyprus, and to seek to rely on the provisions of Section 12C of the Cyprus International Trusts Law, which provides that:

The provisions of this Law shall apply to international trusts containing a clause electing the law of the Republic as the governing law, irrespective of any other provisions relating to the rules on conflict of laws applicable in the Republic and shall constitute a fundamental rule of law, whose observance is a matter of public order.

This argument could be further supported and reinforced by reference to the provisions of Article 45(1)(a) of the Brussels Recast Regulation, which allows EU member states to refuse recognition of a judgment that is manifestly contrary to its public policy (*ordre public*), although it further provides that it does not apply to wills and succession matters.

One could conclude that a foreign judgment issued on matters pertaining to a CIT, to which the Cyprus courts are considered to have exclusive jurisdiction (pursuant to Section 12B of the Cyprus International Trusts Law), will not be enforceable in Cyprus on the basis of it being contrary to public policy and on the exclusion indicated by the Brussels Recast Regulation.

8.2 Ratification of the Hague Convention and the forced heirship rules

A further challenge for the forced heirship rules is raised by the Hague Convention of 1 July 2005 and the Law Applicable to Trusts and their Recognition, which was ratified by Cyprus by virtue of Law 11/1976.[22]

Particular attention is placed on the following two articles of the Hague Convention:

- Article 2 provides that a trust is "a legal relationship created – *inter vivos* or on death – of a person, the settlor, when assets have been placed under the control of a trustee for the benefit of a beneficiary or for a specific purpose".
- Article 15 provides that "the Convention does not prevent the application of provisions of the law designated by the conflicts' rules of the forum, in so far as those provisions cannot be derogated from by

21 Brussels Recast Regulation is the EU Regulation 1215/2012 of the European Parliament and of the Council on jurisdiction and the recognition and enforcement of judgments in civil and commercial matter.

22 On 15 March 2017 the Republic of Cyprus ratified the Hague Convention of 1 July 1985 with the Law Applicable to Trusts and on their Recognition, 4(III)/2017.

> voluntary act, relating in particular to the following matters ... (c) succession rights, testate and intestate, especially the indefeasible shares of spouses and relatives".

Article 15 further provides that "if recognition of a trust is prevented by the application of the preceding paragraph, the court shall try to give effect to the objects of the trust by other means".

A very valid argument raised regularly by Cypriot legal professionals is that, considering the above provisions, Cyprus should not have ratified the Hague Convention, being a common law country that recognises the notion of trusts, as these two provisions conflict with its local laws and are not in line with the favourable provisions of the Cyprus International Trusts Law. Section 12B of the Cyprus International Trusts Law provides for exclusive jurisdiction of the Cypriot courts to the exclusion of foreign judgments on issues pertaining to CITs.

It could be further argued that the specific provisions of Article 15 of the convention do not apply to common law countries that recognise the concept of trusts in their local laws and that these provisions are strictly applicable to civil law jurisdictions in the absence of specific trust laws in their national laws.

In examining the background that led to the introduction of the convention, it can be established that its initial intention and aim was mainly to introduce the concept of trusts in the legislation of civil law jurisdictions where trusts as a concept do not exist and to set out the general procedure for all signatory countries in the application and recognition of trusts regardless of their own legislation. On this basis, it can be concluded that the Hague Convention did not intend to harmonise the rules regulating national trust legislation in the contracting states and thus, despite the accession to the convention, each contracting state whose legislation deals with the concept of trusts should continue to keep their specific provisions of the law.

Regarding the forced heirship provisions, particular attention must be paid to the provisions of Article 15 of the Hague Convention, which indicates that it does not apply to 'succession rights' and thus not to the forced heirship provisions of each national law. Based on the above examination of the Hague Convention in relation to Cyprus, it can be safely concluded that Article 15 is not applicable to Cyprus because is a common law country and due to grounds of *ordre public*. However, this will not be the case in a civil law jurisdiction where the trusts are recognised pursuant to the Hague Convention and thus any forced heirship rules will prevail.

8.3 Extent to which Cyprus International Trusts Law prevails over other local and foreign laws

Where a CIT is governed by Cyprus law, the provisions of the Cyprus

International Trusts Law will prevail and apply despite any conflicting provisions in other Cyprus laws. On consideration of public policy and order, the provisions of the law in relation to CITs will prevail – and this is a defence to any forced heirship provision. Further, Article 1 of the 1971 Convention on the Recognition and Enforcement of Foreign Judgments in Civil and Commercial Matters, provides that the provisions of the convention do not apply to decisions concerning the capacity of persons or questions of family law, including personal or financial rights and obligations between parents and children or between spouses and questions of succession. The said convention was ratified by Cyprus by virtue of Law 11/1976.[23]

Section 21 of the convention also provides that judgments rendered in a contracting state will not be recognised or enforced in another contracting state unless the two states who are parties to the convention have signed a supplementary agreement to this effect.

EC Regulation 44/2001 on Jurisdiction and the Recognition and Enforcement of Judgments in Civil and Commercial Matters (known as 'Brussels I' (repealed by Regulation 1215/2012)) should also be examined. Brussels I facilitates the recognition process as its Article 36 provides that a judgment given in a member state, which is enforceable in that member state, will be automatically recognised in the other member state without any special procedure required. Further, Article 39 provides that a judgment given in a member state, which is enforceable in that member state, will be enforceable in the other member state without any declaration of enforceability being required. However, Brussels I and Regulation 1215/2012 do not apply to matrimonial matters, wills and succession, bankruptcy, social security, as well as arbitral succession awards.

Another concern may be the Hague Convention on Choice of Court Agreements 2005,[24] which applies to judgments on the merits in civil and commercial matters where there is an exclusive choice of court agreement in place (unless one party is a natural person who is acting for primarily personal, family or household purposes). Such an agreement must be in writing or another form that renders it accessible for subsequent reference.

However, the Hague Convention 2005 specifically excludes, among other things, any family law matters, as well as wills and succession.[25] One reason for this exclusion is that these matters do not normally arise from a contractual relationship and thus do no fall within the scope of the convention. Another reason is the more specific international and national laws that should take precedence.

---

23 The Law on the Convention on the Recognition and Enforcement of Foreign Judgements in Civil and Commercial Matters and Supplementary Protocol (Ratification) Law of 1976 (Law 11/76).

24 The European Union has signed and ratified the Hague Convention 2005 in 2015 on behalf of all EU member states and it entered into force from 1 October 2015. It has the status of EU law within the European Union and thus is directly applicable to Cyprus.

25 Article 2 'Exclusions from scope' of the Hague Convention on Choice of Court Agreement 2005.

It appears that as forced heirship is regarded as strictly a succession and family matter which EU Regulations and Conventions try to limit within the ambit of national law and public policy, the provisions of the Cyprus laws regarding local trusts and CITs will take precedence over any forced heirship claims in Cyprus, especially regarding movable assets and immovable property located in Cyprus.

Asset protection trusts

Peter G Economides
Totalserve Management Limited

An asset protection trust is a trust created with the aim to protect, preserve and insulate the assets of a settlor against potential creditors or third persons who may have a claim against a settlor's estate. In essence, there is no need to designate a trust as an asset protection trust since every trust that is properly set up is an asset protection trust because the assets settled into a trust are by definition segregated from the rest of a settlor's estate and can no longer be absorbed to satisfy the settlor's debts or liabilities. It is vital for a trust to be 'properly' set up for the asset protection features to kick in. 'Properly' encompasses a number of considerations, one of the most important is that the trust be set up well before financial difficulties arise or a lawsuit is filed against the settlor. Asset protection is a precautionary measure and not a remedy. Action to insulate assets must be undertaken preventively to build a firewall against potential claims.

While we have established that in essence every trust set up is an asset protection trust, it would be wrong to suggest that asset protection is either quickly or easily achieved once a trust is set up. When contemplating the set-up of a trust, it is vital to protect one's assets so as not to be lured by potentially damaging facilitative provisions 'advertised' by a number of trust jurisdictions that are each competing to get a slice of the global-trust-industry pie. Although trusts today come with an array of attractive features – settlor reserved powers, revocation, firewall provisions, protectors with significant powers – they should be used with caution to ensure that they do not result in the downfall of the very protection that the settlor is seeking to achieve.

1. Cyprus and asset protection

Cyprus has specific asset protection provisions embedded in its legislation, the International Trusts Law of 1992 (Law 69(I)/1992), as amended by Law 20(I)/2012 and Law 98(I)/2013.

Section 3(2) of the law, specifically provides that, notwithstanding any laws of Cyprus or any other country, a Cyprus international trust (CIT) will not be void or voidable and no claim may be made in respect of the transferred assets in the event of the settlor's bankruptcy or liquidation or in any actions or proceedings against the settlor unless and to the extent that it is proven to the satisfaction of the court that the international trust was made with the intent to defraud the creditors of the settlor at the time of the transfer of their assets to the trust, setting a statutory time limit of two years for the duration of which such action can be brought against a trustee of the CIT. Specifically, Section 3(3) of the law provides that there is a two-year limitation period from the date of the transfer or disposal of the assets into the trust for a creditor to challenge the trust, with the burden of proof on the creditor who must prove to the satisfaction of the Cyprus courts that the trust was created by the settlor with the intent to defraud the creditor.

Further, under Section 3(4) of the law, no disposition of property to such trust will be void, voidable or liable to be set aside by reasons such as that the applicable laws of any jurisdiction may not recognise the concept of a trust, prohibit, make it contrary, or by way of any jurisdictional judicial or other judgment.

2. Potential pitfalls

Despite the specific asset protection features of the International Trusts Law, asset protection will not be secured if the basics of trust law are not adhered to; that is, if the settlor does not effectively relinquish control of the trust assets in favour of the trustees who will become the legal owners of the transferred assets. A trust arrangement that is successfully challenged and found by a relevant court to be a 'sham', 'illusory' or 'bare' trust, would not offer protection from third-party creditors. This is not specifically a Cyprus law matter but rather a common consideration for trusts in any jurisdiction based on the facts of each case, where, for example, the settlor's true intention is proven not to effectively divest beneficial ownership of the trust assets from themself and/or through certain actions that make it clear that the settlor continues to keep effective control of the assets.

Based on the 2017 English landmark High Court case of *Pugachev*[1] involving New Zealand trusts, these considerations become more relevant than ever. This case also adds that trustees may contribute to a common intention, together with the settlor, to 'defraud' creditors, even by simply showing 'reckless indifference' to the true facts of the case.

As such, regardless of how strong or solid the CIT domestic provision may be for asset protection and even though there are no Cyprus court-case precedents that successfully render a CIT void, increased due care is needed and should be exercised by professional trustees so that a trust is properly established and run, taking into account various elements, including but not limited to the extent that various powers are vested in any persons other than

1 *JSC Mezhdunarodniy Promyshlenniy Bank v Pugachev* ([2017] EWHC 2426 (Ch)).

the trustees themselves, including the settlor or even the protector. Relinquishing effective control to the trustees and not reserving an undue amount of settlor reserved powers are a central part of these considerations. Settlor reserved powers are considered separately in this book (see the "Settlor reserved powers trusts" chapter by Emily Yiolitis) but a short summary here will serve to demonstrate how they can compromise the asset protection features of a CIT, or in fact any trust.

3. Powers reserved by a settlor

Asset protection is one of the main reasons settlors want to establish a trust; however, at the same time, many settlors want to keep control of their assets. Section 4A in the 2012 amendment to the law lists the following powers that can now be reserved by the settlor:

- powers of revocation, amendment of the terms of a trust or powers that arise wholly or in part from the trust;
- powers in relation to the allocation, distribution, payment or disposition through other means of income or capital from the assets of the trust or the issuing of directions in relation to such granting, distribution payment or disposal;
- powers of the corporate director or officer or the issuing of binding directions in relation to the appointment or removal of any corporate director or officer of any company belonging in whole or in part to the trust;
- the issuing of binding directions to the trustee in relation to the acquisition, holding, disposal, administration, lending, pledging or charging of the assets of the trust or the exercise of any powers or rights resulting from the ownership of such assets;
- the appointment or removal of any trustee, protector, beneficiary or supervisor on the application of the trust;
- the appointment or removal of an investment manager or investment adviser;
- the power to change the applicable law of the trust or the forum of management of the trust; and
- the restriction on the exercise of any powers or the discretion of the trustee with the ability of the settlor to demand that such powers be exercised only with the prior approval of the settlor or any other person specifically mentioned in the trust deed.

The law further provides that in instances of powers being reserved by the settlor, the trustee will not be considered as acting in breach of the trust nor can any intention to defraud be attributed to the settlor for the purposes of Section 3(2) of the law.

Also, Article 2 of the Hague Trusts Convention[2] provides that "the reservation by the settlor or certain rights and powers is not necessarily inconsistent with the existence of a trust". However, there is insufficient guidance on which 'certain rights and powers' are acceptable for a settlor to reserve and at what point the reservation becomes equivalent to a settlor not relinquishing a proprietary interest to the trustees at all.

There are no Cyprus cases on settlor reserved powers, but Cyprus courts are required to apply common law and equity doctrines unless otherwise provided by any laws of Cyprus – and in this case, Cyprus case law is silent. Cyprus courts will rely on English case law, which is not binding but is of persuasive authority. Several court cases seeking to set aside a trust on the basis of settlor reserved powers have been successful, preventing the trust from properly conserving and protecting the assets settled into it.

In the Cayman Islands case of *Tasarruf*[3] the settlor's power to revoke the trust was scrutinised. A judgment for damages had been awarded against the settlor in Turkey and a receiver sought to enforce the judgment by access to the trust funds. The Privy Council held that the power of revocation reserved to the settlor was a personal rather than a fiduciary power and as such formed the property of the holder of that power. As a result, when a receiver was appointed, the receiver was deemed to have stepped into the settlor's shoes with the right to exercise the power of revocation, which he forthwith proceeded to exercise, revoking the trust and returning the trust funds to the settlor so that they could be absorbed to satisfy the damages judgment.

In *Whaley v Whaley*[4] the Court of Appeal demonstrated the willingness of the family courts to look at the actual context hidden behind trust structures. Mr and Mrs Whaley were married for 20 years and had four children. Mr Whaley estimated the overall assets for division to be around £3 million, whereas Mrs Whaley estimated the total assets to be around £12 million, because she believed that the trust assets should be included. The court considered that the creation of the trust by the husband, had the objective of alienating assets from himself at a time when he knew that his marriage was breaking down. Even though, the validity of the trust was not questioned, the Court of Appeal, by taking into consideration the timing, the structure and operation of the trust up until then, held that the assets would likely be made available to the husband if he asked the trustees to make a distribution in his favour. The court ruled in Mrs Whaley's favour.

The case of *Akhemedova*[5] concerned the divorce of Tatyana Akhmedova from

2 The Convention of 1 July 1985 on the Law Applicable to Trusts and on their Recognition (HCCH 1985 Trusts Convention).

3 *Tasarruf Mevduati Sigorta Fonu v Merrill Lynch Bank and Trust Company* ([2012] 1 WLR 1721, [2011] UKPC 17).

4 *Whaley v Whaley* ([2011] EWCA Civ 617).

5 *Akhmedova v Akhmedov* ([2021] EWHC 545).

the Russian oligarch, Farkhad Akhemedov. In December 2016 Mr Akhemedov was ordered to transfer to his wife assets worth £435 million. Proceedings by Mrs Akhemedova in various jurisdictions ensued to secure these funds, culminating in a judgment by the English High Court in which she successfully obtained orders under Section 423 of the Insolvency Act 1986 and Section 37 of the Matrimonial Causes Act 1973 against her husband and trustees of a number of Liechtenstein trusts holding assets worth $650 million. The judge held that Mr Akhemedov used complex ciphers as "a series of schemes designed to put every penny of [his] wealth beyond her reach" and was unconvinced that orders to set the trust aside would be unenforceable in Liechtenstein. An undisclosed settlement was reached between the former spouses. This judgment also clarifies that Section 423 of the Insolvency Act 1986 has extraterritorial reach – the court dismissed arguments that there was insufficient connection to England to justify the court exercising its Section 423 jurisdiction, notwithstanding that the respondents and the assets in question were located in Liechtenstein. This is a clear warning bell for provisions such as Section 3(2) of the Cyprus Law, which provides that "notwithstanding any laws of Cyprus or any other country, the CIT shall not be void or voidable and no claim may be made whatsoever in respect of the transferred assets in the event of the settlor's bankruptcy or liquidation or in any actions or proceedings against the settlor". As we see in the cases of Rubylovlev and Akhmedova, the court's reach may be long and extraterritorial. It is worth noting that Cyprus has fallback legislation post-Brexit, the Foreign Judgments (Reciprocal Enforcement) Law, Cap 10, a law enacted when Cyprus was still a British colony, which provides for the registration of "judgments obtained in the Courts of the United Kingdom". This law remains in force and provides for registration of English judgments, despite Brexit.

4. Risk of a sham

A sham will be found if the settlor and trustee have a common intention, from which can be inferred that the true status is different from that stated in the trust deed that both parties signed. Sham is frequently used in divorce cases to show that while a settlor purports to transfer legal title of assets to a trustee for the benefit of stipulated beneficiaries, the true intention of the settlor, which the trustees may confirm through their action or inaction, is always to retain ownership of, and associated rights and interests in, the settled assets.

If a court finds a trust to be a sham, the trust's creation will be annulled, and the trustees will be considered to have been mere nominees holding the settled property on a resulting trust for the settlor, who will remain the legal and beneficial owner for all intents and purposes. In the Jersey case of *Abdel Rahman*[6]

6 *Abdel Rahman v Chase Bank* ([1991] JLR 103).

where a settlor, despite purportedly relinquishing control in favour of the trustees, continued in practice to exercise full control of the trust and its assets, often withdrawing substantial funds from the trust without the knowledge or reaction of the trustee, it was held that the trust was a sham since both the settlor and the trustee treated the trust fund as the property of the settlor. A sham can be inferred where there is a common intention between settlor and trustee that the relationship they enter into does not create the legal rights and obligations that they give the appearance of creating. This common intention is not easy to infer, particularly if the trustee is a professional trustee, but may be established where there is a common intention of a settlor and trustee to give a false impression to third parties.

5. Firewall provisions

A number of jurisdictions, Cyprus being no exception, have introduced firewall provisions in an effort to convince potential clients or jurisdiction shopping settlors that their jurisdiction is best suited to cater to the settlor's asset-protection needs. In a world where assets, heirs and spouses may be spread over several countries and business and property ownership is increasingly cross-border, there are justifiable concerns of prospective settlors or their advisers over questions of applicable law, forum and international conflict of laws principles. These will often require in-depth analysis of the domicile of the parties, situs of the assets (particularly if they comprise immovable property), review of bilateral and multilateral treaties and international conventions, as well governing law clauses and so forth. Firewall provisions are provisions included in legislation to appease settlors that these considerations are irrelevant because the law and forum of the jurisdiction where the trust is set up will apply. Cyprus for example has Section 12C of the law (as defined below), which provides that where a trust instrument is governed by Cyprus Law, then the provisions of the law apply thereto notwithstanding any other conflicts of law rules that are effective in Cyprus. It buttresses this position by stating that this is a fundamental rule, the observance of which is a matter of Cypriot public order. Cyprus of course is not alone in having enacted firewall provisions – similar sections are found in various other trust jurisdictions including Guernsey, Bermuda, Cayman and Jersey. Firewall provisions that purport to protect the trust assets from jurisdictional hearings that may not recognise trusts, or where unfavourable or conflicting provisions may apply (eg, as to matrimonial property), have however come under scrutiny in recent years and it would be wise not to rely unduly on them for protection.

In *Rybolovlev*,[7] the Swiss Federal Supreme Court considered Cyprus held trust assets in the context of the Swiss matrimonial regime in one of the first cases

7 *Rybolovlev v Rybolovleva* (5A_259/2010), 26 April 2012.

since Switzerland's ratification of the Hague Trusts Convention. The case concerned the provisional attachment of various assets of the husband, Mr Rybolovlev, including assets held in two discretionary, irrevocable CITs, after the wife filed for divorce. The marriage was governed by the Swiss matrimonial regime of partnership of jointly acquired property. In 2009 the Geneva first-instance court rejected the wife's application for provisional attachment. In 2010 the Geneva Court of Appeal decreed the provisional attachment over the husband's personal worldwide assets by prohibiting him to dispose of them, as well as over the foreign trust assets (extending the restriction to the trustees), pending the liquidation of the couple's matrimonial regime. The decision of the Court of Appeal was confirmed by the Swiss Supreme Court in 2012.

Similarly, in *Geneva Trust Company (GTC) SA v IDF*,[8] which examines the robustness of the Cayman firewall provisions, Justice Kawaley held that the purpose of a firewall provision is to ensure that certain matters in respect of Cayman Islands trusts be determined as a matter of Cayman law (meaning that a foreign court applying Cayman Islands law may be permissible), rendering the firewall provision a governing law provision rather than an exclusive jurisdiction provision.

6. Conclusion

Asset protection continues to be an important feature of trusts and can protect assets settled into a trust from third-party creditors. However, the protection afforded is not automatic and care must be taken to ensure that the core principles in relation to trusts, being that a settlor relinquishes control to trustees who properly manage the trust fund in favour of the beneficiaries, are adhered to. Tools that enable settlors to retain control should be used with caution, as should overly complex structures that may be decreed ciphers or undue reliance on firewall provisions. A regular review of the particular circumstances of each trust and its assets and parties will assist trustees to identify potential risks and adapt to changing circumstances.

8 *Geneva Trust Company (GTC) SA v IDF and MF*, Grand Court of the Cayman Islands, FSD 248 of 2017, Kawaley J, 21 December 2020.

The trustee's liability to third parties and mistake

Nicky Xenofontos
N Xenofontos LLC

1. Introduction

Trusts are not corporate entities – they have no legal personality and therefore cannot own property in their own right, sue or be sued. Title to the trust property vests in the trustee, who in turn have standing to sue or to be sued in their capacity as trustee. Of course, this is a basic notion in trust law, yet it entails some intractable consequences for trustees contracting with third parties.

On undertaking professional trusteeship, trustees may assume the management of a trust, handling trusts with the ultimate objective of safeguarding assets for the beneficiaries.

2. Duties of trustees generally[1]

To avoid liability, trustees must have a comprehensive understanding of their duties, as well as where these duties come from. If trustees are aware of their responsibilities, they will be able to adopt procedures giving them the highest possible extent of protection against any future liabilities. Trustees' duties and responsibilities come from three main separate sources.

The first source is the actual trust documents (ie, the instrument establishing the trust (eg, the deed of settlement or the trust deed)) and other ancillary documents pertaining to the general management of the trust such as a statement of investment policies and procedures, as well as custodial, administration and investment management agreements, as is the case. The principles of the common law fiduciary duties, applicable in Cyprus, are the second source, and the final source is the legal framework.[2] The legal framework applies to all types of trust. Trustees are personally liable for breaches of their duties that result in loss or damage suffered by the beneficiaries. Trustees can also be liable for improperly obtained benefits. However, liability will not be imposed for the purpose of punishing a trustee. The most common duties of a trustee are:

- the duty to comply with the terms of the trust;

1 The "Trustee investment powers and delegation" chapter by Savvas Georgiou elaborates on general trustee investment powers and delegation.
2 The Trustees Law (Cap 193) and the Cyprus International Trusts Law, 69(I)/1992.

- the duty to act personally;
- the duty of loyalty;
- the duty of care;
- the duty to act impartially towards the beneficiaries; and
- the duty to safeguard the trust's assets.

It may seem that these duties are quite intimidating, but they are generally common-sense duties that would be expected from an ordinary person when entrusted with holding assets for the benefit of another.

2.1 The main duties

(a) Duty to terms and effectively managing a trust

Perhaps the first and most obvious duty of a trustee is to know, understand and adhere to the terms of the trust deed as prescribed. This may seem obvious, but sometimes trustees do not pay much attention to the specific terms of the trust deed and fail to properly apply them, resulting in a breach of trust. A breach of trust occurs when a trustee contravenes the terms of the trust or the duties of a trustee. Trustees are jointly and severally liable for breach of trust to their beneficiaries where the breach has given rise to a loss. Holding the legal title to the assets, trustees are responsible for administering and operating the trust in accordance with its terms, so that the beneficiaries who are entitled to the assets are fairly treated.

Where trustees are in any doubt about how any power conferred on them is exercised or whether the description of a particular power is ambiguous, they should, as a matter of prudence, apply to the competent court for directions regarding an interpretation of how that power should be exercised and retain legal counsel for advice relating to the powers and how they should best be exercised. The power to apply to the competent court for directions when trustees are doubtful about how to exercise or apply a power during the term of their trusteeship is afforded to them by Section 11A of the Cyprus International Trusts Law.[3]

Ancillary to the duty to manage a trust efficiently – apart from familiarity with the terms of the trust, the trust's assets and liabilities, the circumstances of the beneficiaries and the purpose of the trust – trustees should put effective systems in place to ensure that appropriate decisions are made in a timely manner, considering the interests of the beneficiaries at all times. Such systems, apart from prudent decision-making, essentially include retaining proper record-keeping and preparing books of account for the trust so that trustees have an accurate picture of the trust's investments, assets and liabilities.

---

3 "The Cyprus International Trusts Law 1992–2012: new dynamics" chapter by Chrysthia Papacleovoulou-Vassiliou analyses the provisions of the Cyprus International Trusts Law in more detail.

(b) *Duty of loyalty*

The basic principle and cornerstone of a fiduciary relationship, such as the role of trustees, is that trustees owe fiduciary duties towards beneficiaries. Trustees must administer the trust solely in the interest of the trust beneficiaries and cannot place their interest in conflict with that of the beneficiaries', nor should they profit personally from their role that they have been appointed to undertake other than by charging a fee for their professional services. In particular, trustees, by reason of their status, will be held in breach of this duty if they secure a benefit, even if the benefit was not obtained at the expense of the trust. Under common law, trustees have an affirmative duty not to delegate acts that they could be reasonably required to perform personally. A trustee could, however, employ agents and attorneys where reasonable under the circumstances, and any delegation of powers or duties must be conducted in such a manner that a prudent individual undertaking delegation of powers or duties should, at a minimum, have analogous skills. The duty of a power holder, just as that of a trustee, is held and exercised with the same standard of reasonable care, skill and caution, and trustees are further bound to exercise the same care when selecting an agent. Where there are multiple trustees, all trustees carry dual accountability for their own actions, inactions and decisions, as well as those of their co-trustees. Under common law, when there are multiple trustees, each has an obligation to participate in trust administration unless otherwise specified by the trust deed. When one trustee breaches their fiduciary duty, the other trustees are required to compel them to redress this breach.

(c) *Duty of care and skill*

During the management of a trust, professional trustees are expected to ensure that their responsibilities and duties are carried out with due care and skill. In a chain of Victorian case law, a principle was established whereby when a trustee makes an investment decision, they must act as "a prudent man of business" would act in the management of their own affairs. As a general rule, trustees are satisfactorily discharged of their duties if they take all precautions that an "ordinary prudent man" would take.[4] Professional trustees who profess particular levels of expertise are held to a higher standard of care, which is also expected from corporate trustees.[5] This objective test, where the level of expertise has a direct effect on the standard of care required, is likely to be applied by the courts when faced with a question relating to the exercise (or not) of this duty of care and skill and apart from resulting from statutory duties

---

4 Per Lord Blackburn in *Speight v Gaunt* ((1883) LR 9 App Cas 1). The test is an objective one weighed against the standard of an "ordinary prudent man of business", where they are making an investment for the benefit of other people for whom they felt morally bound to provide, *Learoyd v Whiteley* ((1887) 12 AC 727).

5 *Re Waterman's Will Trust* ([1952] 2 All ER 1054).

in most countries, professional corporate trustees are liable for "liability for breach of trust if loss is caused to the trust fund because they neglect to exercise the special care and skill which they profess to have".[6] In *Bartlett* it was decided that there is undoubtedly an enhanced higher standard over professional trustees and such standards, abilities and expertise that corporate trustees should exercise. In *Bartlett*, a claim was made against a trustee for compensation for losses incurred during the administration of the trust. The court held that for it to order an account by the trustee on the basis of wilful default, and thereafter hold the defendant liable not only for assets that have come into their hands but also in respect of assets that ought to have come into their hands, the claimant must plead and prove at least one act of wilful default.

Brightman J considered the nature of the remedy of restitution: "the so-called restitution which the [trustee] must now make to the plaintiffs ... is in reality compensation for loss suffered by the plaintiffs ... not readily distinguishable from damages except with the aid of a powerful legal microscope." The trustee's obligation is to restore to the trust estate the assets of which they have deprived it. The trustee in this case was Barclays Bank, which was obliged to act in relation to shares, and to the controlling position that they were bestowed with, in the same manner as a 'prudent man of business'. This prudent man of business must act in such manner as is necessary to safeguard the investment. One way of doing this was that if facts come to the prudent man of business's knowledge that tell him that the company's affairs are not being conducted as they should be, or that result in an enquiry, the prudent man of business should take suitable action. Such action will unquestionably consist of making necessary enquiries and consulting with the directors on the points and knowledge that have come to the trustee, as well as convening a general meeting to replace one or more directors. A prudent man of business should not be content with mere knowledge of the company's affairs such as shareholders receive during annual general meetings, but since a trustee has the power to do so, they should go further and check that they have enough information to enable them to take responsible decisions and actions either to let matters proceed as they are proceeding, or to intervene if they are unhappy. A trustee could take action to mitigate this outcome, limiting a trustee's duties to those that are set out in the trust documents. The legacy of *Bartlett* was the creation by professionals in the trust industry of so-called 'anti-*Bartlett*' clauses in trust deeds. Such clauses are drafted to exclude the duty of a trustee to supervise or intervene in the business affairs of companies in which the trust holds shares. The first-instance decision and 2017 judgment of the Hong Kong Court of Appeal[7] concerning a Jersey law governed trust, initially cast doubt on

6 *Bartlett v Barclays Bank Trust Co Limited* ([1980] 1 All ER 139).
7 *Zhang Hong Li v DBS Bank (Hong Kong) Limited.*

the efficacy of such clauses. However, on further appeal, in a 22 November 2019 judgment, the Hong Kong Court of Final Appeal[8] basically restored the *status quo* and confirmed that anti-*Bartlett* clauses effectively exempt trustees from any liability for losses incurred in transactions by a trust's underlying investment companies, unless they become aware of actual dishonesty. This decision is of wider importance to the common law trust jurisdictions as the relevant principles are likely to be the same. Following these two precedents, most, if not all, trust deeds contain such clauses.

(d) Duty of impartiality

Most trustees are accountable to two types of beneficiary – present and future. Present beneficiaries rely on the income from the trust. Typically, future beneficiaries are paid the principal remaining in the trust after the present beneficiaries pass away. According to the duty of impartiality, trustees have a duty to deal with both the income beneficiary and the remainderman objectively. Consequently, trustees must ensure that the trust property produces a reasonable income while being preserved for the remaindermen. That said, trustees are saddled with a duty of impartiality and must treat future and income beneficiaries fairly and equitably. Because of the duty of impartiality to balance competing interests, trustees cannot invest solely or primarily in assets that have no potential for capital appreciation but produce a high stream of income unless the trust agreement specifically provides for it, and trustees cannot invest solely or primarily in aggressive growth stocks that produce little or no income.

Trustees cannot prefer one beneficiary or one group of beneficiaries over another without a proper reason. There must be procedural fairness in the trustees' decision making, therefore trustees cannot be advocates or judges and should not differentiate between beneficiaries. In numerous precedents it has been well established that trustees "must act in the best interest of their beneficiaries".[9]

Despite the general principle that trustees must treat all beneficiaries equally, the terms of the trust deed must be taken into consideration for any limitations on distributions. This comes to the importance of having a well written and clear trust deed, allowing trustees to have clear, simple language and flexibility so that they can adjust to changing circumstances to reach a settlor's goal, something that is usually provided in letters of wishes. Time spent drafting careful language can save considerable anguish and even help avoid years of expensive bickering in court.

---

8 *Ibid*, [2019] HKCFA 45.

9 *F & C Alternative Investments (Holdings) Ltd v Barthelemy* (No 2) [2011] EWHC 1731 (Ch), [2012] Ch 613 at (227), *Foo Jee Seng v Foo Jhee Tuang* [2012] SGCA 41, [2012] 4 SLR 339, Sing CA.

3. Trustees' liabilities

The role of a trustee (including an executor administering an estate) is a potentially complex and onerous one. There are numerous considerations, potential risks and liabilities. Responsibilities arise out of the duties that trustees take on once appointed.

3.1 Liability to third parties

One of the most important areas that trustees should always bear in mind is when they enter into agreements and contracts with third parties, as not only can their liability arise for not exercising due care and skill under the law, but it may also arise under contract law.

3.2 Contractual liability of trustees

When trustees purport to enter a contract in the proper course during the administration of a trust, it is imperative that before doing so they perform a due diligence exercise and a risk assessment for the proposed transaction, weighing the pros and cons. Any loss to the trust assets arising out of non-performance on the part of the trustees are recoverable from the assets and perhaps even personally from the trustees if it can be proved that the trustees acted without diligence. Contractual liability may arise where trustees enter contracts either directly or indirectly via their agents and are liable as principals for trust obligations entered into by agents acting on their behalf. Thus, it is assumed that the contract is free from any defect of consent such as a party's mental incapacity, force and worry or error that would make the contract void or voidable and breach the principle of *auctor in rem suam* ('one who acts in their own interest') and are voidable at the instance of the beneficiaries. The legal outcomes for trustees when any contract is entered into during management depends mostly on whether they had the actual power to enter into such a contract and under what capacity they did so. The conventional justification for imposing personal liability on trustees is that third parties do not know the extent of the trust estate. In entering into a contract, they therefore rely on the personal credit of the trustees and their assurances about the value of the trust estate, as the contractual parties do not know whether the actual value of the trust assets is sufficient to cover any claim that may arise during the performance (or not) of the contract should any breach occur.

Regarding *ultra vires* contracts, the first issue that third parties (and even beneficiaries) should consider is whether such contracts can be challenged on the lack of *vires* ('powers') under both common law principles and contract law. It has already been discussed that under common law trustees' powers are limited to those expressed in the trust deed and may also be implied under specific circumstances. If trustees are of the opinion that entering a contract is indeed to the benefit of the trust but does not have actual power to do so, it would be prudent to vary the trust or seek directions from the court where a power of variation is not contained in the trust deed. As the legal owners of the trust property, trustees can give a good title to any third party with whom they transact. One view that an *ultra vires* transaction can be reducible is where third parties know that the title to the property in question was held by the trustees.[10] If we consider that this is good faith, then it may mean that third parties ought to have made enquiries as to whether the transaction was within the powers of the trustees and that they would have been in good faith only if they honestly believed that to be the case. But if third parties have acted in good faith, unless they have actual knowledge of the lack of *vires* then the title of most onerous third parties will be unchallengeable as few will be in bad faith.[11]

3.3 Liability for debts and losses

The liabilities of trustees, and of the directors of corporate trustees, is a misunderstood topic. Under trust law, as applied in most countries, trustees, either as a legal person (corporate trustee) or an individually appointed person, incur the legal obligations to pay debts and other liabilities arising from their administration of the affairs and activities of the trust. In the course of the administration of a trust, liabilities in contract or in tort or otherwise, to other involved parties to the trust other than the *cestui que trust* (the person who has an equitable interest in the trust (ie, the beneficiary)), may similarly arise. In the absence of an express stipulation relieving trustees from liability, trustees are personally liable to contracts made by them for the benefit of the trust as a whole, and by extension the beneficiaries, and may be sued.

Trustees are personally liable for the debts of the trust, including tax debts attributed to them on behalf of the trust. To be able to meet the debts of the trust, trustees are usually entitled to be indemnified out of the trust's assets. However, such an indemnity may not cover all expenses, especially where the trustee acts in bad faith or incurs debts in breach of the trust. Given the overlap between trust law, company law and contract law, it is not always straightforward to determine whether a trustee is liable to trust creditors or the trust assets, or even whether the beneficiaries can be accessed to pay for the trustees' debts and whether the directors of a corporate trustee will be personally liable. On this basis, understanding the liability of trustees and their rights of indemnity is extremely important. Failure to properly review and tackle these issues can expose the trustees to personal liability. In general, trustees are personally liable for any debts or liabilities incurred in their role as trustee of a

---

10 JM Halliday, *Conveyancing Law and Practice in Scotland*, 2nd edn, ed by IJS Talman (W Green, 1997), paras 1-25; WM Gordon, *Scottish Land Law*, 2nd edn (W Green, 1999), paras 16.30–16.31).

11 DA Brand, AJM Steven and S Wortley, *Professor McDonald's Conveyancing Manual*, 7th edn (Tottel Publishing, 2004), para 3.8.

trust, whether in contract or tort.[12] This is the case irrespective of whether trustees have a right to be indemnified from the assets of the trust.

Likewise, as in the case of debts, trustees can be held liable for any debt incurred when acting as a trustee, regardless of whether the trustee can benefit personally from the trust. Most modern deeds contain a clause limiting trustees' liabilities; however, what many trustees fail to appreciate is that this limitation of liability applies between the trustee and the beneficiaries, not between the trustee and the world at large. This means that if a trustee contracts with a third party (eg, a bank), the trustee must ensure that the terms of that contract limit the trustee's liability and is binding on third parties (eg, the trust's bankers).

Any limitation of liability must be stated expressly. Simply entering into a contract or agreement as a trustee is generally insufficient to ensure limitation of liability. This suggestion was confirmed in *Williamson v Bennet*,[13] where a trustee who failed to complete a property purchase entered into on behalf of a trust was found to be personally liable for the subsequent loss on sale. While accepting that the trustee had entered the agreement on behalf of the trust, the judge hearing the matter re-stated the fact that a trustee is personally liable unless liability is excluded by the terms of the agreement.

Using corporate trustees could perhaps be a safety net regarding the issue of liability. As such, trustees could act as directors of a trustee company, rather than in a personal capacity. However, the unconsidered interpolation of a trustee company can leave its directors liable for failure to meet corporate obligations.

In the New Zealand High Court case *Vance & Levin v Lamb & Simpson*,[14] the director of the corporate trustee was held liable for failing to act in the best interests of the company by not testing the market before selling trust property in a non-arms-length transaction. This case emphasises that there are ways for a third party to attack a corporate trustee even when it undertakes a transaction that is permissible under the terms of the trust.

The decision to appoint the corporate trustee in this case, which was essentially to reduce the trustees' liability to the trust's bankers and the Inland Revenue Department, failed to consider that there may have been risks that could fall on the corporate trustee itself. When considering acting as a director of a corporate trustee, certain matters should be kept in mind, especially when it seems that losses may occur during a transaction, as the director's actions could consequently amount to a failure to act in the company's best interests, breach of duty or even fraudulent trading. In this case, it was proved that the director failed to act in the best interests of the company by failing to ensure that the corporate trustee obtained the best possible price for the sale of the

---

12 *Vacuum Oil Co Pty Ltd v Wiltshire* ((1945) 72 CLR 319 at 324–325, 335).
13 *North Carolina Supreme Court case* (112 S.E.2d 48 (1960)).
14 Civ 2007-485-343.

trust assets, not only due to the eventual sale of the assets at a loss but also failure to test the current market conditions. Consequently, the director was personally liable to any third-party creditors, having left the corporate trustee unable to meet liabilities, irrespective of whether such liabilities were incurred as a trustee. It is well established practice that directors are responsible for any harm done to a company, and care must be taken when appointing a corporate trustee to ensure compliance with both trust and corporate obligations – the responsibility is dual.

3.4 Liability for delict and other wrongs

One of the main areas where trustees might become liable to third parties is delict.[15] In Scotland, there is only one reported private delict case,[16] where a decree was granted against the trustees as trustees but expenses were awarded against them as individuals. Lord Moncrieff held that since the action had been brought against the trustees as trustees, a decree had to be granted in that form. But he went on to say:

> *had it not been for the form of the crave of the initial writ I should have felt that there was great force in the pursuer's contention [for decree to be granted against trustees as individuals]. The sum sued for is claimed as due in respect of the action of the trustees themselves in the conduct of the business as carried on by them after the settlor's death. To make payment of such a claim trustee are* prima facie *liable as individuals.*

It was quoted by Mackenzie Stuart[17] that:

> *Where the trustees, in administering the trust, have been found liable in damages to third parties, either through their own acts in good faith and for the intended benefit of the trust, or through the fault of persons employed by them, the damages which the trustees have paid, or for which they have become liable, are chargeable against the trust estate.*

3.5 The law of mistake

There have been several cases in the United Kingdom where courts have found in favour of trustees seeking to rectify their mistakes. Even the most diligent of trustees can make mistakes, and in the event of a breach, they can seek to have transactions set aside. When deciding whether a trustee is in breach, the court will apply an objective test – they will ask what a reasonably prudent trustee would have done in the circumstances. The rule in the well-known case of *Hastings-Bass*,[18] concisely surmised in *Sieff v Fox*:[19]

---

15 'Delict' is the Scottish word for 'tort' as most widely used to define civil wrongs.

16 *Mulholland v MacFarlane's Trustees* (1928 SLT 251).

17 A Mackenzie Stuart, *The Law of Trusts with Special Reference to the Trusts (Scotland) Act 1921 and Recent Decisions* (W Green & Son, 1932), p335.

18 [1975] Ch 25.

19 ChD 23 Jun 2005.

> *Where trustees act under a discretion given to them by the terms of the trust, but the effect of the exercise is different from that which they intended, the court will interfere with their action if it is clear that they would not have acted as they did had they not failed to take into account considerations which they ought to have taken into account, or taken into account considerations which they ought not to have taken into account.*

The conclusion of this case was criticised in 2013 in the Court of Appeal cases of *Pitt v Holt*[20] and *Futter v Futter*.[21] Subsequently, the Supreme Court held that the *Hastings-Bass* rule had been misapplied, as the intention of the rule was initially designed to protect beneficiaries against the improper conduct of trustees, but over time it had become a way of getting out of trouble for trustees. In *Pitt*, the Supreme Court allowed the trust to be relieved from the unforeseen tax liability on the grounds of mistake.

In further analysis, the court held that the test for mistake in the context of a voluntary settlement requires a connective mistake of sufficient magnitude that it must be unjust to leave the mistake uncorrected.

Such magnitude requires a mistake as to the legal nature of the transaction or as to a matter of fact or law that is basic to the transaction. The mistake could relate to the transaction's effect (object) or consequences. The above two cases of *Pitt* and *Futter* confirm that the *Hastings-Bass* rule can no longer be relied on to resolve mistakes by trustees; nonetheless, there have been rulings where trustees have successfully pleaded mistake.[22] More recent cases have shown that the courts appear to be taking a softer approach on trustee mistake and have even intervened to correct trustees' mistakes,[23] allowing the correction of a trust deed for failing to include provisions enabling trustees to provide for other beneficiaries.[24]

Relying on mistake will, however, not be available in every case. In *Price v Saundry*,[25] the Court of Appeal had to consider the circumstances in which trustees are entitled to be indemnified from the trust fund for the costs that they incur in court proceedings and reversed the judgment on the costs relating to the indemnity. It decided that if a breach of trust or misconduct is established, causing loss to the trust fund, then the trustee can be deprived of their

---

20 [2011] STC 809.

21 [2010] EWHC 449 (Ch).

22 *Kennedy v Kennedy* [2014] EWHC 4129 (Ch) (8 December 2014): the court set aside part of a transaction on the basis of a mistake; *Freedman v Freedman* [2015] EWHC 1457 (Ch) (21 May 2015): an inheritance tax charge, was successful in having it set aside on the basis of mistake; *Der Merwe v Goldman* [2016] EWHC 790 (Ch) (11 April 2016): the claimant's transfer of property into an interest in possession trust triggered an IHT entry charge which he had not anticipated. He successfully argued mistake to have it rescinded; *Bainbridge v Bainbridge* [2016] EWHC 898 (Ch): the claimants, a father and son farming partnership, transferred land into a discretionary trust, without realising a capital gains tax liability would arise. The transfer was set aside on the grounds of mistake.

23 *Smith v Stanley* [2019] 2 WLUK 174.

24 *ABC v JKL* [2019] EWHC 2416 (Ch).

25 [2019] EWCA Civ 2261.

indemnity from the trust. The court stated that misconduct should be "construed widely to include not only misconduct in the sense of dishonesty but also misconduct which is unreasonable in the circumstances". It made clear that misconduct does not extend to a mistake on the part of a trustee, and not only did it consider that the account in this case demonstrated that there had been serious misconduct, but also breaches of trust. The trustee was ordered to pay her own costs personally and those of the claimant.

Looking at these recent 2019 case law developments, the courts appear willing to sanction the reversing of genuine mistakes and can help only when a mistake is indeed rectifiable. Trustees could genuinely have made a mistake. The position in Cyprus is regulated by Contracts Law,[26] where 'mistake' is defined as:

where both the parties to an agreement are under a mistake as to a matter of fact essential to the agreement, the agreement is void. An erroneous opinion as to the value of the thing which forms the subject-matter of the agreement is not to be deemed a mistake as to a matter of fact. A contract is not voidable because it was caused by a mistake as to any law in force in Cyprus; but a mistake as to a law not in force in Cyprus has the same effect as a mistake of fact (section 21). In section 22, a contract is not voidable merely because it was caused by one of the parties to it being under a mistake as to a matter of fact.

These provisions constitute a codification of English case law.

In an interesting Jersey case,[27] the settlor had established a deed of settlement and in the following years he exercised his power to add more people as beneficiaries, including his girlfriend. On the settlor's death, the new trustees that took over sought the court's directions as the deed of declaration that added his girlfriend as a beneficiary was not witnessed and so failed to follow the procedure as described in the settlement. The question faced by the court was whether the equitable doctrine that equity can facilitate the defective execution of a power could be applied. It was argued by one of the beneficiaries that the doctrine could not include the girlfriend since she did not fall into the categories recognised in the doctrine and confirmed by the courts and could not be expanded to include a girlfriend. On the other side, the trustees claimed that the doctrine would need to be examined under the lens of the modern society in which we live and to contemplate modern family relationships that are recognised in today', relationships that are not restricted merely to wives and children but also to girlfriends, stepchildren and same-sex partners. In conclusion, the court held that the doctrine could be applied under the circumstances of this case, based on its evidential findings that the settlor had the moral intention, inferred from his actions, to provide for his girlfriend after

26 Sections 21 and 22, Cap 149.

27 *In the Matter of the Shirnovic Trust* ([2012] JRC081).

his passing. It was stated that "the general principle is an entirely beneficial one and prevents errors in formality leading to real hardship for those to whom the donee of the power owes a moral or natural obligation and resulting in the clear intention of the donee being defeated for no good reason".

This decision is noteworthy by the fact that it shows that the courts will not hesitate to go beyond formalities and interfere in a trust deed when necessary. The court also noted that a different argument could as well be used in this case; that of alleged intention to overcome the defective deed. In certain circumstances where there is an intention to obtain a particular result that could be concluded only by the exercise of a certain power, the courts may hold that the exercise of such a power may be inferred from the facts of the case.

The main ingredients of an international trust law – some proposals for reform

Paolo Panico
Private Trustees SA; Chair – STEP Europe
Nicky Xenofontos
N Xenofontos LLC

1. Introduction

Three options are currently available for the creation of a trust in Cyprus, depending on the personal situation of the settlor. This broad freedom of choice corresponds to some important restrictions for domestic settlors that are not faced by their foreign counterparts. A reform of this area of Cyprus law may be envisaged in two respects. On the one hand, some aspects of the Cyprus International Trusts Law may need to be updated in order to keep up with the evolution of the international practice. On the other hand, in light of the mobility of affluent families worldwide, the existing distinction between 'international' and 'domestic' trusts appears to be outdated and does not correspond to any real economic or social needs.

This chapter will first set out the current situation, with the three options available to an aspiring settlor of a Cyprus trust, then suggest some lines of reform, concentrating mainly on the Cyprus International Trusts Law. We have no ambition to recommend a comprehensive set of reforms, but we believe that some of the areas covered in this chapter should be considered by Cypriot lawmakers to maintain the international attractiveness of the island as a fiduciary centre of choice.

2. Trusts in Cyprus: the three options

The Cyprus International Trusts Law, as originally enacted in 1992 (Law 69/1992), was an up-to-date statute that positioned Cyprus as an international leading trust jurisdiction. Its amendments in 2012 reflected some notable developments in international practice, including in particular:

- the repeal of the rule against perpetuities for all types of trust;
- the ability for settlors to retain certain powers ('reserved powers trusts');
- a robust set of creditor protection provisions ('asset protection trusts');
- a set of private international law provisions offering protection against foreign forced heirship claims ('firewall legislation');

- a flexible regulation of the trustees' duty to provide information to the beneficiaries;
- a provision empowering the court to issue directions at a trustee's request; and
- a broadened provision on the taxation status of a Cyprus international trust, its income from sources abroad and locally.

These aspects are discussed in detail in the corresponding chapters of this book.

All these provisions have addressed the requirements of many foreign settlors who considered Cyprus a suitable trust jurisdiction before they decided to move their residence to the island. International trusts cannot be created by Cypriot resident settlors since one of the requirements for the application of the Cyprus International Trusts Law is that the settlor and the beneficiaries were not resident in Cyprus in the year preceding the creation of the trust.[1]

Domestic trusts can be created by Cypriot resident families relying on the Trustee Law 1955 (Cap 193), which was heavily influenced by the English Trustee Act 1925. A telling difference in the names of the two statutes must not be overlooked. The Cyprus International Trusts Law refers to 'trusts' and attempts to be a comprehensive regulation of Cyprus trusts with an international component (non-resident settlors and beneficiaries). The Trustee Law 1955 regulates 'trustees' or more precisely contains a number of provisions relating to the powers and duties of trustees in the same way as its original English model.

Based on the application of English common law and the doctrine of equity pursuant to the Courts of Justice Law 14/1960, the principles of English (and more generally Commonwealth) case law can be followed for all the matters where the Trustee Law 1955 is silent.

Cypriot families may also rely on a foreign law to create their trusts, which are enforceable in the island pursuant to the Hague Convention on the Law Applicable to Trusts and on their Recognition of 1 July 1985 (the Hague Trusts Convention), which was ratified under Law 4(III)/2017.

The applicable framework for the creation of trusts in Cyprus consists as a result of three options:

- the Cyprus International Trusts Law for foreign settlors;
- the Trustee Law 1955 for resident settlors; and
- any foreign law provided that the conditions of the Hague Trusts Convention are met.

1 Section 2 of the Cyprus International Trusts Law.

Despite the breadth of options available, some elements of incongruity exist between a state-of-the-art international trust law that was carefully crafted to take advantage of the main developments in the industry, and a domestic legislation dating back to the 1920s and in some cases still relying on antiquated case law.[2]

Ten years after the last update of the Cyprus International Trusts Law (and 30 years after its original enactment), some additional amendments may be required to keep pace with developments that had not been covered in the 1992 and the 2012 versions of the law. These are minor improvements to an already excellent piece of legislation.

At the same time, it would be desirable to harmonise the international and the domestic trust laws, possibly by repealing the Trustee Law 1955 altogether and making the Cyprus International Trusts Law available to domestic as well as foreign settlors. Alternatively, the two statutes may be amalgamated into a single, consolidated one, giving rise to a 'Cyprus Uniform Trust Code', equally available to domestic and foreign settlors.

The existence of an 'offshore' statute that is only available to foreign settlors appears to be an outdated approach that is not practised in any other EU member state.[3] The first option of repealing the domestic law is probably more easily achievable, while the second option of enacting a consolidated 'Uniform Trust Code' is likely to be more demanding and potentially time consuming.

On this basis, it appears that the most expedient way to achieve a comprehensive reform of the Cyprus trust law would require three concurrent steps:

- a reform of the Cyprus International Trusts Law;
- the repeal of the Trustee Law 1955; and
- the extension of the reformed Cyprus International Trusts Law to both foreign and domestic settlors.

It must be emphasised that these measures would have no impact for tax purposes, to the extent that the taxation of trusts depends on the residence of their beneficiaries, as discussed in the "Taxation" chapter by George Economides.

In the remaining part of this chapter, we will review the areas that we believe require some reform in the Cyprus International Trusts Law, at least for its continued application to foreign settlors as a state-of-the-art piece of trust legislation. We hope that a reform project will also encompass the extension of this law to Cypriot resident settlors, but we will not discuss the ways to achieve this result here.

---

2 An example is the rule against perpetuities, as is discussed in the "Perpetuity and duration" chapter by Paolo Panico.

3 A comparable example was the Offshore Trusts Act 1988 of Malta, which was repealed when the country entered the European Union and at the same time the institution of the trust was grafted onto the domestic legal system by way of several amendments to the Civil Code and the enactment of a Trusts and Trustees Act of general application.

3. The Cyprus International Trusts Law: some proposals for reform

In an ever-changing and challenging environment, geographically, socially and family-wise, modernising laws should be a priority for lawmakers. The modernisation of the Cypriot trust law is one aspect that needs addressing. Trusts are widely used by people and businesses, they are a significant way of managing assets and are occasionally used in complex situations, especially when beneficiaries are scattered around various jurisdictions. The Cyprus International Trusts Law was enacted in 1992 and partially amended in 2012. In the meantime, competing financial centres such as Singapore, New Zealand, the British Virgin Islands, Jersey, Guernsey and even the United States have updated their laws and been innovative in supporting a vibrant trust and estate-planning industry.

Some areas of the Cyprus International Trusts Law require modernisation either because some developments have taken place internationally since its original enactment in 1992 and its reform in 2012 or because they relate to aspects that were not considered in either version of the law. These proposed lines of reform are recommended even if the Cyprus International Trusts Law was to remain reserved for foreign resident settlors. It is hoped that a further-reaching approach may be considered by Cypriot lawmakers with a view to extending this legislation to Cypriot resident settlors, and in that case the proposed reforms would be even more relevant.

We have identified the following areas where reform is recommended:

- the trustee's liability to third parties;
- the beneficiaries' ability to terminate the trust;
- the ability for the trustees and beneficiaries to unanimously vary the trust;
- the court's powers to remedy a mistake by the trustee;
- the trustee's duty to disclose information to the beneficiaries;
- the trustee's powers and duties;
- the court's powers in relation to trusts; and
- the role and powers of protectors.

Most of these aspects correspond to some notable development in international practice and were matched by case law or statute law in some other leading trust jurisdiction. It is therefore appropriate for Cyprus practitioners and lawmakers to consider these developments carefully to ensure that the island does not lag behind competing international financial centres for the attractiveness of their trust laws.

3.1 Trustees' liability to third parties

Trustees' liability to third parties was not addressed in either the 1992 version of the Cyprus International Trusts Law or in the 2012 amendments.

Accordingly, the traditional English approach is still applicable in Cyprus. In other words, the Cyprus trustees of international or domestic trusts are personally liable for the obligations that they properly incur in the exercise of their functions.[4] The rationale for this approach is that trusts are not legal persons: the only persons in a trust arrangement are the trustees and as such they have personal and unlimited liability for any deals they enter into, in the same way as if they were entering into such deals in a personal capacity in their own right. Of course, trustees have a right of recourse to the trust fund for any properly incurred obligations in the performance of their office. It is also possible for trustees to directly make payments out of the trust fund rather than personally advance the expenses and be reimbursed.[5]

However, some hurdles may exist in this mechanism. If the trust fund is insufficient to cover the obligations properly incurred by the trustees, the latter will ultimately be personally liable for the difference. Some recent English case law illustrates this situation – for example, where the trustees of a sports club took a loan in their capacity and were requested by the bank to repay the amount that the club was unable to settle.[6] In some other cases, if the trustees are liable for a breach of trust their ability to access the trust fund may be impaired. The Australian practice of 'trading trusts', where the trustee is often an *ad hoc* company with a nominal paid-up capital, demonstrates that this situation may lead to a significant risk to the trust creditors.[7]

The US practice, followed by some leading international trust jurisdictions, has introduced a notion of limited liability, where trustees contracting with a third party in their express capacity are liable for properly incurred obligations only within the limit of the trust fund.

The Uniform Trust Code, which is a model of uniform legislation adopted in two-thirds of the United States and the Code of the District of Columbia, contains an express provision to this effect at Section 1010(a):

Except as otherwise provided in the contract, a trustee is not personally liable on a contract properly entered into in the trustee's fiduciary capacity in the course of administering the trust if the trustee in the contract disclosed the fiduciary capacity.

Article 32(1) of the Trusts (Jersey) Law 1984 provides that:

Where a trustee is a party to any transaction or matter affecting the trust –

(a) if the other party knows that the trustee is acting as trustee, any claim by the other party shall be against the trustee as trustee and shall extend only to the trust property;

(b) if the other party does not know that the trustee is acting as trustee, any claim

---

4 The authority to this effect is still *Muir v City of Glasgow Bank* ((1879)) 4 App Cas 337).

5 *Re Blundell* ((1888) 40 Ch D 370).

6 *Marston Thompson & Evershed plc v Bend* (1997) *Law Society Gazette* 94(39) (15 October 1997).

7 *Octavo Investments Pty Ltd v Knight* ((1979) 144 CLR 360).

by the other party may be made against the trustee personally (though, without prejudice to his or her personal liability, the trustee shall have a right of recourse to the trust property by way of indemnity).

The Privy Council provided an ultimate confirmation of the validity of these provisions in *Investec (Trust) Guernsey Ltd v Glenalla Properties Ltd*[8] on appeal from Guernsey. The case concerned one of the most prominent clients of the Icelandic bank Kaupthing, which led to its eventual bankruptcy. The matter before the Judicial Committee of the Privy Council was whether the Guernsey trustees of a Jersey trust could rely on the statutory provision above and have their liability limited to the trust fund or should be held personally liable for the loans they had contracted with the bank, which would ultimately lead to a call on their professional insurers. The Privy Council confirmed that the trustees of a Jersey or a Guernsey trust enjoy the limitation of liability that is provided under the corresponding statutes:[9]

In the Board's opinion, the time has come to recognise that as a general rule the common law will recognise and give effect to limitations of liability which arise under an entity's constitutive law by reason of the particular status or capacity in which its members or officers assume an obligation.

It is recommended that a provision similar to the one under Jersey or Guernsey law should be introduced into the Cyprus International Trusts Law to remove an antiquated approach that dates back to the Victorian times, when it was seen as an incentive for prudent behaviour on the part of trustees.

It is worth emphasising that this provision limits a trustee's liability for properly incurred liabilities in the exercise of its office. It does not limit a trustee's personal and unlimited liability to the beneficiaries to make good any losses resulting from a breach of trust. Article 32(2) of the Trusts (Jersey) Law 1984 contains an express provision to this effect: "Paragraph (1) shall not affect any liability the trustee may have for breach of trust."

3.2 Beneficiaries' ability to terminate the trust

Many international financial centres have included in their trust statutes a provision enacting the 'rule in *Saunders v Vautier*'.[10] An example is Section 53(3) of the Trusts (Guernsey) Law 2007:

Without prejudice to the powers of the Royal Court under subsection (4), and notwithstanding the terms of the trust, where all the beneficiaries are in existence and have been ascertained, and none is a minor or a person under legal disability, they may require the trustees to terminate the trust and distribute the trust property among them.

---

8 [2018] UKPC 7.
9 *Ibid*, para 88.
10 (1841) 4 Beav 115.

This provision was extensively reviewed by the Guernsey Court of Appeal in *Molard International (PTC) Limited v Rusnano Capital AG (in liquidation)*,[11] a case brought by the sole beneficiary of a trust who requested the trustee bring the trust to an end and transfer out the entire trust fund. The facts of the case were peculiar but in no way unheard of. The sole named beneficiary was in fact a default beneficiary and the trustee had wide power to add beneficiaries that would eventually allow for the appointment of the persons intended by the settlor. Unfortunately, no beneficiaries had been added in the meantime. On this basis the court relied on a provision under Section 53(4) of the Trusts (Guernsey) Law 2007 that allowed an order to be issued with a view to obtaining a fairer result.

Apart from the specific facts of that case, the rule in *Saunders v Vautier* allows the beneficiaries of a trust to unanimously terminate it in advance of any trust period specified by the settlor. They must all be in agreement, all adults and capable of acting, and they must represent 100% of the trust fund. The rule also applies in the case of a discretionary trust, provided that all these conditions are met.[12]

This approach is adopted by all the trust jurisdictions that follow the English model. It applies 'notwithstanding the terms of the trust', which means that no voluntary derogation is admitted. This circumstance may cause some settlors an understandable concern. There are ways to mitigate this risk, mainly with a careful drafting of the terms of the trust so that the beneficiaries are an open class at any given point in time ("the children and remoter issue of the settlor") or they have contingent interests ("A will become a beneficiary when he graduates, B when she starts her independent professional practice") and as a result they are not 'beneficiaries' until a certain condition is met.

The US approach is more reassuring for settlors. It is based on the notion of the 'material purpose' for which the settlor decided to create the trust. This doctrine relies on a 19th century Massachusetts decision, *Claflin v Claflin*.[13] The facts of the case were similar to those in *Saunders v Vautier*, where a sole beneficiary was allowed to terminate a trust on attaining a majority without complying with the additional conditions imposed by the settlor. In Claflin the court did not allow an early termination of the trust because that would breach a material purpose that the settlor had intended to pursue.

A modern enactment of the 'material purpose' approach can be read at Section 87 of the Trustee Act 1998 of the Bahamas:

(1) Notwithstanding any rule of equity or practice of the Court to the contrary, neither a beneficiary who is solely interested in the trust property nor all the beneficiaries

---

11 (2019) GCA 077.
12 *Sir Moses Montefiore Jewish Home v Howell and Co (No z) Pty Ltd* ([1984] 2 NSWLR 406).
13 149 Mass 19, 20 NE 454 (1889).

who together are all the persons interested in it, shall be entitled, though in existence and ascertained and of full capacity, to terminate or modify the trusts affecting the property, if this would defat a material purpose of the settlor or testator in creating the trust, unless the settlor is living and also consents.

(2) The material purposes of the settlor or testator for the purpose of subsection (1) may be ascertained from the trust instrument (directly or by inference) or by collateral evidence.

To the extent that trusts are increasingly used by affluent settlors with a view to arranging their estate-planning objectives, a rule that preserves the 'material purpose' pursued by the settlor against the beneficiaries' impatience to take control of the trust property deserves to be considered with attention. After all, some recent research expressed serious doubts about the validity and the desirability of the rule in *Saunders v Vautier*.[14]

On this basis, it appears desirable to include a provision similar to that under Bahamian law into the Cyprus International Trusts Law. It would provide certainty that the settlor's intention would be carried out without risk that some impatient beneficiaries could derail it. A clear, statutory rule to that effect would also avoid complex drafting techniques to mitigate the risk of an undue early termination of a trust by its beneficiaries.

3.3 The ability for the trustees and beneficiaries to unanimously vary the trust

If among the beneficiaries there are minors, incompetent or unborn people, the rule in *Saunders v Vautier* does not apply unless the court is joined in representation of such beneficiaries who are unable to express valid consent. The court does not approve of the proposed arrangement; it takes part in it on behalf of the minor, incompetent or unborn beneficiaries. This is an extension of the rule in *Saunders v Vautier*, which was enacted under the English Variation of Trusts Act 1958. Equivalent offshore enactments exist in most leading trust jurisdictions. An example is Article 47 of the Trusts (Jersey) Law 1984:

(1) Subject to paragraph (2), the court may, if it thinks fit, by order approve on behalf of –

(a) a minor or interdict having, directly or indirectly, an interest, whether vested or contingent, under the trust;

(b) any person, whether ascertained or not, who may become entitled, directly or indirectly, to an interest under the trust as being at a future date or on the happening of a future event a person of any specified description or a member of any specified class of persons;

(ba) any person, if the court is satisfied that despite reasonable effort to find such person, the person cannot be found;

14 J Langbein, "Why the Rule in *Saunders v Vautier* Is Wrong", in PG Turner (ed), *Equity and Administration* (Cambridge University Press, 2016).

(bb) any person, if the court is satisfied that the person falls within a class of beneficiary and that because of the number of persons falling within that class it is unreasonable for the person to be contacted;

(c) any person unborn; or

(d) any person in respect of any interest of his or hers that may arise by reason of any discretionary power given to anyone on the failure or determination of any existing interest that has not failed or determined, any arrangement, by whomsoever proposed and whether or not there is any other person beneficially interested who is capable of assenting thereto, varying or revoking all or any of the terms of the trust or enlarging the powers of the trustee of managing or administering any of the trust property.

(2) The court shall not approve an arrangement on behalf of any person coming within paragraph (1)(a), (b), (ba), (bb) or (c) unless the carrying out thereof appears to be for the benefit of that person.

An equivalent provision exists under Section 10 of the Cyprus International Trusts Law.

The presence of beneficiaries who are unable to validly express their consent may be another effective way to avert the risk of an early termination of the trust under the rule in *Saunders v Vautier*. However, to the extent that the potentially detrimental consequences of the rule in *Saunders v Vautier* are prevented by a codification of the 'material purpose' approach, as is recommended in paragraph 3.2 (above), a more flexible approach may be followed in relation to the variation of trusts, which does not require the involvement of the court.

Some US states and some offshore jurisdictions have recently enacted statutory provisions allowing for a private representation of minor, incompetent or unborn beneficiaries that avoid the involvement of the court in the variation of a trust. An example is Section 58A of the British Virgin Islands Trustee Ordinance, which was enacted under the Trustee (Amendment) Act 2003 and provides for the appointment of an officer to approve an out-of-court variation of trust on behalf of beneficiaries who cannot give a valid consent. A more recent example is Section 3338 of the Delaware Code, which provides for non-judicial settlement agreements.

Codifying this aspect in the Cyprus International Trusts Law would allow such a modern approach to be adopted in Cyprus. Provided that the required protections are in place for the interests of those beneficiaries who cannot consent for themselves, this would save time and expense for the beneficiaries and the trustees who wish to vary a trust instrument when no other provisions allow it under the terms of the trust.

3.4 The court's power to remedy a mistake by the trustee

The rule in *Hastings-Bass*, dating back to a precedent of the mid-1970s on perpetuities,[15] was developed in the offshore trust industry at the beginning of the 21st century. Its formulation can be summarised with the words of Lloyd LJ in *Sieff v Fox*:[16]

> *The best formulation of the principle seems to me to be this. Where a trustee acts under a discretion given to him by the terms of the trust, but the effects of the exercise is different from that which he intended, the court will interfere with his action if it is clear that he would not have acted as he did had he not failed to take into account considerations which he ought to have taken into account, or taken into account considerations which he ought not to have taken into account.*

In many cases this rule was relied on by trustees when a distribution to the beneficiaries triggered some unexpected tax consequences. In most circumstances the rule concerned offshore trustees who had not properly planned in relation to UK tax.

The extent of the rule was significantly reformed in the United Kingdom under the Supreme Court decision in the joint cases *Futter v HMRC* and *Pitt v HMRC*.[17] As a result, the rule can now be applied in an English context if the trustees' failure to consider relevant circumstances in the exercise of their powers is of such a serious nature as to be a breach of trust. For this reason, the rule is now also known as a rule of 'inadequate deliberation'.[18] At the same time, the Supreme Court modernised the doctrine of mistake, which can still be relied on by trustees when the consequences of their acts are different from their forecasts.

A different path was followed in several offshore jurisdictions, where the original and more generous version of the rule in *Hastings-Bass*, predating the Supreme Court decision, was enacted in specific legislative instruments.

Some examples are Jersey, where Articles 47B–47J were added under the Trusts (Amendment No 6) (Jersey) Law 2013, Bermuda, where a new Section 47A was inserted into the Trustee Act 1975 under the Trustee Amendment Act 2014, and the Cayman Islands, where Section 64A of the Trusts Law (2020 Revision) codified the rule in *Hastings-Bass*.

It may be useful to codify a version of the rule in *Hastings-Bass* in the Cyprus International Trusts Law. This would provide a clear statutory framework for relief where the trustee (or any other power holder) has made a mistake in the exercise of their powers. In such an event, where trustees or other fiduciaries make a mistake in the exercise of their powers, it stands to reason that the innocent beneficiaries should have relief from the unwanted effects of that mistake.

---

15 *Re Hastings-Bass* ([1975] Ch 25).

16 [2005] 1 WLR 3811, 3836.

17 [2013] UKSC 26.

18 A discussion of the case law before and after the UK Supreme Court decision and the application of the rule in *Hastings-Bass* can be read in P Panico, *International Trust Laws*, 2nd edition (Oxford University Press, 2017), chapter 5.

Incorporating such a statutory provision would easily assist the courts to remedy certain cases of mistake by way of a statutory provision thus making the process more efficient. Moreover, it would provide for a *de facto* statutory power for courts to set aside the exercise of any power by trustees on the grounds of inadequate deliberation and ultimately treat the mistake as never having occurred, either in whole or in part and either unconditionally or on such terms and subject to such conditions as the court may think fit under the circumstances.

It remains to be debated whether the appropriate version of the 'rule' should be the more lenient one applied in some offshore jurisdictions or the one resulting from the UK Supreme Court decision in *Pitt* and *Futter*. In both cases the Cypriot courts would be able to rely on a statutory framework to exercise their discretion. To the extent that the court has ultimate discretion whether to exercise such power, it appears to be desirable to adopt a more generous version of the rule (ie, its 'offshore' version) because the imposition of too stringent conditions and the concrete risk that a trustee invoking the rule could be exposed to personal liability for breach of trust might stifle its application in practice.

3.5 Trustees' duty to disclose information to the beneficiaries

Section 11(1) of the Cyprus International Trusts Law represents a modern approach to a trustee's duty to disclose accounting information to the beneficiaries to the extent that it allows a trustee to grant disclosure only when "in his opinion such disclosure is necessary and secures the lawful interests of the trust".

This approach is consistent with the leading authority in this field, *Schmidt v Rosewood Trust Ltd*,[19] where the Privy Council concluded that a beneficiary's right to information is not a consequence of that beneficiary's entitlement to the trust property but is a condition for the beneficiary to be satisfied that the trust fund is being properly managed in the best interests of all the beneficiaries.

Subsequent case law has further refined the principle spelt out in *Schmidt v Rosewood*. For example, in *Erceg v Erceg*[20] the Supreme Court of New Zealand discussed a list of criteria that trustees should consider before they decide whether to disclose information to the beneficiaries and how much to disclose. The same criteria must be applied by the court dealing with a beneficiary's application in case of disagreement. The list of relevant criteria includes:

- the documents sought, which may need to be evaluated separately;
- the context for the request and the objective of the beneficiary in making the request;

19 [2003] 2 AC 709.
20 [2017] NZSC 28.

- the nature of the interests held by the beneficiary seeking access;
- whether there are issues of personal or commercial confidentiality;
- whether the documents sought disclose the trustees' reasons for decisions; and
- the likely impact on the trustee and the other beneficiaries if disclosure is made.

An amendment to Section 11 of the Cyprus International Trusts Law regarding disclosure and confidentiality along these lines should happen in two ways. On the one hand, disclosure of information to the beneficiaries should be expressly permitted in addition to the current provision that limits it to trust accounts and incomings and outgoings of the trust fund. On the other hand, if some of the criteria that trustees are expected to follow in their decision-making process were codified along the lines specified by the New Zealand Supreme Court in *Erceg*, the entire process would be more reliable and transparent and any controversy in front of a Cypriot court could find some objective statutory terms of reference.

Due to the relative scarcity of Cypriot case law, a reliable statutory regulation of this aspect of trust law would spare the requirement to consider a number of foreign precedents in court proceedings and would allow settlors, trustees and beneficiaries to rely on a single, comprehensive and modern statutory reference that could be considered as a model by other jurisdictions.

3.6 Trustees' powers and duties

Some proposed reforms to the Cyprus International Trusts Law may not necessarily reflect certain new international developments in the practice of trusts but could streamline the activity of trustees and the exercise of their powers. Again, a more extensive statutory regulation of the trustee's powers and duties may simplify the exercise of the function and provide a clear reference in case of doubt or controversy.

Of course, the right balance must be carefully maintained to avoid an over-regulation of the office of trustee. The following are some areas where we believe that additional codification could be beneficial to the profession:

- Introducing a statutory duty for trustees to maintain and keep trust accounts, not necessarily audited financial statements but management accounts as a minimum so that if any disgruntled beneficiary claims any wrongdoing by trustees, there are records of incomings and outgoings from the trust fund. This would also work to the benefit of trustees as it would codify the duty of care owed to beneficiaries and the trust as a whole.
- Although provision is made for trustees to comply with all anti-money laundering legislation and regulations, it would perhaps be more

significant to amend the current section of the Cyprus International Trusts Law[21] and specifically refer to the new rules on the UBO Trusts Registry for the sake of clarity and not having to refer to separate laws, regulations and directives.

- Inclusion of statutory provisions regarding trustee decisions where there is more than one trustee to be taken by majority. The issue of unanimous decisions is important where trustees come into a situation of deadlock and if this issue is not resolved, it may usually lead to applications for the courts to decide. This is costly and time consuming. The problem may be solved by a statutory provision specifying by way of default that when there is more than one trustee they will decide by majority.
- Inclusion of a new section on liabilities of trustees for breach of trust. Currently, there is no statutory reference or provision as to a trustee's general liabilities (only to liability as to investments) and such remedies for breach can only be inferred from case law and looking into the experience of other common law jurisdictions for guidance.
- Inclusion of statutory provisions as to trustee indemnification and release of powers. Such provisions are, as current practice, only contained in the trust instrument. The topic of trustee indemnity is a relevant one and it would be beneficial to rely on some statutory provisions clarifying, among others, a trustee's right of retention of the trust property until a satisfactory indemnity for future liabilities has been provided.
- Provisions setting out how trustees should conduct themselves and what should be taken into account regarding insolvent trusts.

3.7 The court's powers in relation to trusts

The express powers conferred on the court in the Cyprus International Trusts Law are in Section 11A, which was added under the 2012 amendments.

A court of equity has a supervisory role over all fiduciary offices, including that of trustees. No statutory provisions are required to that effect and the case law applicable to domestic trusts is also applicable to international trusts. However, in the context of the Cyprus International Trusts Law, it would be useful if some statutory provisions clarified the powers of the court in a comprehensive way. An example could be Article 51 of the Trusts (Jersey) Law 1984.

A similar statutory provision could be useful both for the functioning of the Cyprus International Trusts Law in relation to foreign settlors and in the event that it became the only trust statute in Cyprus.

A statutory expansion of the court's powers would be welcome, for example, orders as to contingent rights or unborn persons, vesting orders in place of

21 Section 12E of the Cyprus International Trusts Law.

conveyance by an infant mortgagee, vesting orders consequential an order for sale or mortgage of land, vesting orders as to stocks and choses in action, vesting orders in relation to an infant's beneficial interests, power to relieve trustee from personal liability, power to make beneficiary indemnify for breach of trust. Most of these powers already impliedly vest in the Cypriot courts but some statutory guidance grouping them in a dedicated section could contribute to clarity and effectiveness.

A development that Cyprus could follow in this area is represented by Section 58B of the British Virgin Islands Trustee Ordinance, which was enacted under the Trustee (Amendment) Act 2021 and allows the court to order a variation of trust without the consent of the beneficiaries if it is "expedient in the circumstances then existing".

It also remains to be discussed whether a specialised court or division should be put in place to deal with trust matters. An example to this effect is the Chancery Court that was created in the state of Wyoming in 2019 and was influenced by the 18th-century model of the Delaware Court of Chancery, which equally specialises in trust and corporate matters.

The Cyprus court system underwent some significant modifications in 2022, some of which are summarised in the chapter "The Cypriot legal system: an overview" by Eleni Louca, and perhaps the newly established Commercial Court could deal also with trust matters.

3.8 Protectors' role and powers

Detailed provisions relating to trust protectors are not included in the Cyprus International Trusts Law apart from a definition of the office that was inserted under the 2012 amendments. Incorporating specific provisions regarding protectors, their role, powers, duties and obligations would greatly enhance any issues and conflicts that may arise during the administration of a trust. Such duties, powers and obligations could be clearly set out to state by virtue of which prorectors exercise their powers and discretions conferred to them under the trust instrument.

In particular, some default provisions comparable to those under Article 24A(2) of the Maltese Trusts and Trustees Act or Section 86(2) of the British Virgin Islands Trustee Ordinance could provide guidance as to the powers that may be conferred on the office of protector. These provisions should have a default nature and their application should be subject to the terms of the trust in order not to hinder the settlor's full freedom to determine the limits and the function of the trust protector.

A new statutory codification of the role of protector could also allow the Cyprus lawmakers to make a choice between the 'narrower view' and the 'wider view' of the protector's powers following the two decisions of the Bermuda

22 [2021] SC (Bda) 72 Civ.

Supreme Court in *Re the X Trusts*,[22] which upheld the narrower view, and the Jersey Royal Court in *Re Piedmont and Riviera Trust*,[23] which opted for the wider view. The two approaches concern a protector's consent powers. The narrower view maintains that protectors are bound to express their consent when the trustee's proposed decision is one that any rational and duly informed trustee would make. The 'wider view' on the other hand provides that protectors must exercise their own discretion and are at liberty to withhold their consent to a proposed trustee decision, even though it is rational and within the remit of the trustee's powers, if they as protectors are not happy to permit it. The resulting dialectics between the trustee and the protector with a view to agreeing on the best decision may be the settlor's intended result.

4. Conclusion

Accepting trusteeship and managing a trust is not something to be taken lightly. Anyone considering taking up the role will need to know what legal duties, responsibilities and potential liabilities are involved. While most people in the industry would find it difficult to name a single situation in which a trustee has actually suffered personal loss and liability, anyone wishing to become a trustee should know what the potential risks could be. Ultimately, being a trustee is all about trust!

Statutory laws of trust management need to be expanded and a default trust regime established to provide trustees the tools they need to establish and manage trusts and estate-planning vehicles for the modern family. Another reason why codifying the current local legal framework may be useful is that practitioners find it easier to do their job when they have a comprehensive statute law in front of them. With the greater use of trusts, statutory guides are necessary to help answer questions that frequently arise, eliminating the need to refer to the courts, saving precious time and money, as practitioners would find the answers to simple matters in statutes that would conveniently deal with practical problems that surface in ordinary trust dealings, as opposed to theory-heavy tools and rules that may not provide much guidance.

The suggested reforms would introduce improvements to the Cypriot trust law framework, providing more concise and clear language for professionals undertaking trusteeship and ensure that Cyprus remains a leading jurisdiction for the establishment, administration and maintenance of Cyprus international trusts. A distinction between a state-of-the-art international trust law and a partially antiquated domestic law is no longer useful and is to some extent unfair.

If any of the reforms that we have suggested in this chapter were to take place in relation to the Cyprus International Trusts Law, we respectfully

23 [2021] JRC 248.

recommend that the two laws should be harmonised. This may happen either by repealing the Trustee Law 1955 altogether and extending the International Trusts Law to Cypriot resident beneficiaries or by amalgamating the two statutes into a consolidated 'Cyprus Uniform Trust Code'.

We hope that at a next anniversary of the Cyprus International Trusts Law we will be able to review a single, consolidated Cyprus Trusts Law that will govern all types of trust in the island.

Analysis of Cyprus case law involving Cyprus international trusts

Chrysthia Papacleovoulou-Vassiliou
Open University of Cyprus

1. Introduction

The Cyprus courts have reviewed numerous civil actions and originating summons applications involving Cyprus international trusts (CITs). CITs are often challenged in civil actions for being used as sham trusts or instruments for fraud. Most cases remain pending with no final decision on the merits, except the determination of interim order applications or procedural aspects. It is expected that over the next few years Cyprus case law on CITs will evolve and provide some concrete guidance. The Cyprus courts are keen to uphold the validity of the CIT and to follow dutifully the provisions of the Cyprus International Trusts Law 1992 as amended.

A review of the case law on CITs reveals that most cases relate to the same facts, parties and issues. Moreover, most cases that have been decided on involve interlocutory injunctions and interim order applications, applications for the service of judicial documents out of jurisdiction, applications for substitute service, applications for the filing of supplemental affidavits and other technical civil procedure issues, without a final determination of the merits.

2. Form of legal filing

There is no Supreme Court guidance on legal filing, whether by way of application or civil action.[1] Section 11A(1) of the Cyprus International Trusts Law 1992 as amended, provides that "a trustee may file an application to the Court for directions regarding the manner in which he may or should act with regard to any matter concerning an international trust and the Court may issue

1 See Civil Procedure Rules, Order 55, declaration on originating summons: i) Any person claiming to be interested under a deed, will or other written instrument, may apply to the court by originating summons (Forms 50 and 51) for the determination of any question of construction arising under the instrument, and for a declaration of the rights of the persons interested. ii) The court or judge may direct such persons to be served with the summons as they think fit. iii) The application should be supported by such evidence as the court or judge may require. iv) The court or judge will not be bound to determine any such question of construction if in their opinion it ought not be determined on originating summons.

any order as provided for in subsection (2)".[2] Based on Section 11A(1), cases involving CITs could be filed by an application under Order 55 of the Civil Procedure Rules; namely, an originating summons application. Nevertheless, the circumstances of the case may require that a civil action be filed instead of an originating summons application. Recent district court judgments shed light on the matter.

In *Re Junport International Ltd and others*,[3] Judge Nathanael explained that Order 55 is used where there is no dispute as to the facts, and therefore it is incorrect to use Order 55 when the facts of the case are or may be disputed.[4] Order 55, Rule 1 states that:

> *Any person claiming to be interested under a deed, will, or other written instrument, may apply to the Court by originating summons (Forms 50 and 51) for the determination of any question of construction arising under the instrument, and for a declaration of the rights of the persons interested.*

Form 50 relates to the use of an originating summons in matters that result from wills, while Form 51 relates to matters of the trusts in the will of a deceased testator. Judge Nathanael has clarified that an originating summons application may be used in other appropriate cases, since it means any summons other than a summons in an ongoing procedure or matter, and that unless it is specified by law that a procedure must commence by writ of summons, then the procedure may commence by writ of summons or by originating summons, as determined by the plaintiff/applicant.

In in *Re Wycombe Settlement and Arip v Trustee Services Ltd*,[5] the court considered that under the circumstances of the case and the nature of the claim, the filing of an originating summons under Rule 55 of the Civil Procedure Rules was the incorrect legal procedural step. An originating summons application has the sole purpose of determining the interpretation of documents or deeds and the rights of interested parties. An originating summons application ought to be used for the determination of the rights of the signatories of the trust instrument, because, under Order 55, a court may issue only 'declarations', not 'orders'.[6]

---

2 Under Section 11A(1), the Greek text uses the word 'αίτηση'. Legislature does not clarify whether this was an originating summons application, an interim application or other procedure, which is the source of the ambiguity.

3 *In re Junport International Ltd and others* (115/2017, 15 September 2017), per Judge Nathanael – the scope of Order 55 of the Civil Procedure Rules has been expanded to include the execution of wills and trusts, and that the originating summons is used when the matter relates to the interpretation of a deed or law or a question of purely legal matter. The use of an originating summons application is suggested because of the simple procedure and speed of adjudication, and there are no witnesses and no writ of summons or defence statements, among other things.

4 The term in Greek is 'Δικόγραφα'.

5 *In Re Wycombe Settlement and Arip v Trustee Services Ltd* (5/18, 24 October 2018), Larnaca District Court, President of the District Court M Papamichael. "Declaration On Originating Summons – Any person claiming to be interested under a deed, will, or other written instrument, may apply to the Court by originating summons (Forms 50 and 51) for the determination of any question of construction arising under the instrument, and for a declaration of the rights of the persons interested."

Therefore, an originating summons application should be used for issues relating to determination of, *inter alia*:

- the interpretation of deeds and the rights of interested parties;[7]
- where facts are undisputed or not complicated and therefore no oral testimony must be provided;[8] and
- where the matter relates to the interpretation of the trust settlement for the determination of rights or obligations.[9]

An application to remove a trustee may be filed by way of an originating summons application where there are undisputed facts or there are no claims of fraud or demand for damages.[10]

A writ of summons is required for matters that relate to:

- the determination of the jurisdiction of the court for the execution of a judgment of a foreign court;
- the validity of a trust;
- the transfer of property to a trust;
- the determination of the ownership of the proprietary assets in a trust;
- whether the trust is a CIT;[11]
- allegations or claims of fraud or claims for damages; and[12]
- disputed questions of fact as to whether the trustee acted honestly and reasonably or in breach of trust.[13]

A different position was taken in *Re the application of HPH Cayman Limited in the matter of the International Trust, The HPH Settlement v Daventree Trustees Ltd,* where the court considered that an application filed to determine matters under Section 11A of the Cyprus International Trusts Law, that the legal basis of such application is Section 11A itself, as it is a provision of substantive law.[14] The

6 See *Terzis Iosif v Maria Karia Kekkou Petoufa* ((2011) 1 AAD 336), where the Supreme Court on the matter of the interpretation of a will, held that the executors, administrators or interested parties may, under Civil Procedure Rule 55, apply to the court to determine certain ambiguous or disputed matters in relation to the administration of the estate of a deceased, and the court has jurisdiction to hear and resolve such matters by giving directions, though not direct orders. The court may give directions and guidance to the administrators or executors of a will as to the way administrators or executors ought to act, in order to comply with the court judgment.

7 *In Re Wycombe Settlement and Arip v Trustee Services Ltd.*

8 *Gorbachev v First Link Management Services Ltd, as Trustee for the Goaliva Trust,* originating summons application 62/2018, 5 March 2018, for the removal of the trustee and the appointment of a new trustee (judgment 8 April 2019).

9 *Gorbachev v First Link Management Services Ltd, as Trustee for the Goaliva Trust.*

10 *Gorbachev v First Link Management Services Ltd, as Trustee for the Goaliva Trust.*

11 *In Re Wycombe Settlement and Arip Trustee Services Ltd.*

12 The court clarified that if the beneficiaries applying to remove the current trustee make claims of fraud or deceit, that the facts are complicated and oral testimony must be provided, or they claim monetary damages against the current trustee, then a writ of summons must be filed. *Gorbachev v First Link Management Services Ltd, as Trustee for the Goaliva Trust.*

13 Generally endorsed under Rule 1, Order 2, or specially endorsed under Rule 1, Order 6.

14 *Re the application of HPH Cayman Limited, in the matter of the International Trust The HPH Settlement v Daventree Trustees Ltd,* Originating Summons applications 1036/2013 and 1037/2013, final judgment 15 July 2017, per Judge Ioannides.

court noted that the inclusion of Order 55 of the Civil Procedure Rules in the legal basis of the application, wrongly so, would not lead to the rejection of the application merely on this ground.[15]

3. Interpretation of Section 11A: matters pertaining to a trust[16]

In *Re the application of HPH Cayman Limited in the matter of the International Trust, The HPH Settlement v Daventree Trustees Ltd,*[17] the court held that a settlor may by application ask the court to remove the trustee or protector of a CIT. In accordance with the new Section 11A(3)(b), an application to the court to issue an order that relates to the execution or management of any trust, the trustee or protector in relation to the appointment, termination or the exercise of power, among other things, could be filed by the trustee, the settlor, their personal representatives or any person so authorised by the court.

On the facts of the case, the court observed that in the civil action *Frabran Holdings Co Limited v Daventree Trustees Limited* (13792/2003), a receiver had been appointed with extended powers that effectively replaced the powers of the trustee of the trust settlements. The court rejected the application to remove and replace the trustee and protector of the trust settlements on a number of grounds:

- eight years had lapsed without any action taken by the plaintiff;
- the applicant had never contacted the receiver to ask for the accounts that had been prepared; and
- an application to remove the receiver was pending before the court in relation to 13792/2003.

The plaintiffs sought an order through their application, ordering Daventree Trustees Ltd to deliver to the new trustee possession of all the proprietary assets of the trust settlements. These proprietary assets had already been transferred to the receiver on 5 May 2005. The court therefore refused to issue contradictory orders. The court, *obiter*, stated that if the trustees had been replaced by other trustees and not the receiver, then the applications would succeed.[18]

---

15 See *Kontou v Global Capital Ltd* ((2003)1 AAD 192) where the appellants invoked Order 55, in excess, since the matter was the set aside or cancellation of the order was governed by Order 40, Rules 16–17, and the Supreme Court held that there was no confusion, or detriment or unjust influence of the case by reason of the form used in the application or the legal basis of the application.

16 These are analysed in detail in "*The trustee's ability to request directions from the court*" chapter by Constantinos Constantinides and Stefanos Marangos, and are therefore only briefly referred to herein.

17 *Re the application of HPH Cayman Limited, in the matter of the International Trust The HPH Settlement v Daventree Trustees Ltd.* HPH Cayman Ltd, as settlors of the HPH Settlement and the HPH Distribution Settlement 2, sought directions from the court as to the management of the trust and duties of the trustees, as well as orders to cease the protector and the original trustees, Daventree Trustees Ltd, and orders for the trustees to provide accounts for the management of the trust assets and expenses. The trustees objected on the grounds that this was an attempt by the liquidator to gain control of the assets of the trusts. HPH Cayman Ltd was under liquidation and the liquidator had filed lawsuit 4414/2012 disputing the validity of the trust settlements, and ostensibly controlled HPH Cayman Ltd through its directors.

4. Courts would consider whether the trust in question is a CIT

In *Re Wycombe Settlement and Arip v Trustee Services Ltd*, although the court had issued *ex parte* the *quia timet* injunctions, it cancelled the orders on the basis that it had no authority or jurisdiction to issue the injunctions since the trust had failed to satisfy the three cumulative conditions for the establishment of the CIT.[19] The trustee of the CIT at the time of the creation, and at all times, was not a Cyprus resident, but a resident of Switzerland. When the conditions for the establishment of a CIT are not satisfied, the trust will be treated as a local trust and governed by the Trustees Law (Cap 193).[20]

5. Cyprus courts have jurisdiction to issue interlocutory relief to preserve assets

In the high-profile case of *Elena Rybolovleva v Dmitry Rybolovlev*,[21] the wife filed for divorce in Switzerland and claimed that she was entitled to 50% of the assets acquired during her marriage, in the region of $6 billion to $12 billion, including shares in the largest producer of fertilisers in Russia, Uralkali, which were held through nominee shareholders in Cyprus and assets held through CITs. While Rybolovleva succeeded in obtaining interlocutory relief, including worldwide Mareva injuctions (freezing orders), on appeal the Supreme Court quashed the orders because the applicant failed to disclose all facts and misled the court as to matters of foreign law.[22] The parties are under a duty to disclose in good faith when they apply *ex parte* to the court to obtain a remedy and this duty extends not only to facts but also to legal issues.

In another case, the applicants' failure to disclose that the trust did not meet the conditions for the establishment of a CIT, and the fact that it misinformed the court as to the law, could be grounds to cancel interim orders or security measures that have been granted.[23]

6. Territorial jurisdiction of courts: determined by the trustee's residency

In *Al Assam v Latimer (Management Services) Limited*,[24] the beneficiaries of a discretionary CIT filed a civil action against the trustees and an investment

18 The court also stated that if the plaintiff HPH Cayman Ltd asserts the invalidity of the HPH Settlement and the HPH Distribution Settlement 2 by reason that the trust property had been stolen from HPH Cayman Ltd, then the proper claimant is not HPH Cayman Ltd but its liquidator.

19 *In Re Wycombe Settlement and Arip Trustee Services Ltd.*

20 *Gorbachev v First Link Management Services Ltd*, for the removal of the trustee and appointment of new trustee, 8 April 2019, where Judge Efraim noted that the settlors of the trust were residents in Cyprus in the calendar year prior to the creation of the trust and that the trust settlement expressly stipulated that the trust was governed under Cyprus law and subject to the jurisdiction of the Cyprus courts.

21 *Dmitry Rybolovlev v Elena Rybolovleva* ((2010) 1 AAD 82).

22 No final judgment on the merits has been issued to date.

23 *Dmitry Rybolovlev v Elena Rybolovleva*; and *Memory Corporation Plc v Sidhu* ([2000] 1 WLR 1443).

24 *Al Assam v Latimer (Management Services) Limited*, Civil Action 376/2019, 31 May 2019, district court level.

adviser claiming, among other things, breach of fiduciary duties, fraud, negligence and other tortuous acts with respect of the investments made by the trustees. Accordingly, the district court issued *ex parte* interim orders to disclose information and to preserve documents. The claimants/beneficiaries, however, filed the application before the Larnaca District Court. Following an objection by the trustees for lack of territorial jurisdiction of the district court, the court confirmed that the Nicosia District Court had territorial jurisdiction to hear the dispute, as this was the place of residency of the trustees, and dismissed application and quashed the interim orders issued *ex parte*. The saga continued with an application before the Nicosia District Court, whereby the beneficiaries/ plaintiffs filed a new summons application seeking the issuance of the interim orders, which was dismissed by the court.[25]

7. Exclusive jurisdiction service of judicial documents

In *EMD Trust Ltd as trustee for the EMD Trust v Edrina Aashika Sharma*,[26] an application to serve the case documents against the defendant by way of an email was upheld by the district court. In *Saunders v Hewitt*,[27] the district court considered the question of service of judicial documents. The court affirmed that EU Regulation 1393/2007[28] supersedes provisions of national law on the matter of the service of judicial documents,[29] which must be done in accordance

25 *Al Assam v Latimer (Management Services) Limited*, Civil Action 13/2019, 16 July 2019.

26 *EMD Trust Limited, of Larnaca in its capacity as trustee of the CIT (the EMD Trust) v Edrina Aaskika Sharma*, Originating Summons application 68/2017, 17 April 2018.

27 *Saunders v Hewitt*, Civil Action 4202/2019, 23 March 2021, Nicosia District Court. According to the facts of the case, AJH was the settlor of a CIT established in 2015 and the trust property consisted of 50% shares in the share capital of a Cyprus holding company, which in turn held the entire share capital of another company. The plaintiffs were the two children of AJH from her first marriage, who sued, among other defendants, the trustees of the CIT and the third husband of the deceased (with whom AJH was married at the time of her death) who was the beneficial owner of the CIT, as well as the ultimate beneficial owner of the remaining 50% shareholding in the Cyprus holding company. AJH left a will for her estate in Gibraltar, which consisted of a bank account, where the dividends issued by the Cyprus holding company were transferred. According to AJH's will, the plaintiffs were nominated as the heirs and beneficiaries of her estate, at 45% share each with the residuary 10% was left to her granddaughter. According to the facts, there were monthly dividends of approximately £18,000. The plaintiff's children claimed that the trustees were under a duty in accordance with the instructions of the settlor to pay the dividends to them through the Gibraltar account, and that even after the death of AJH these payments would continue to be made to the bank account in Gibraltar and then the heirs would receive their share in accordance with the last will and testament of AJH in Gibraltar. The plaintiffs filed a law suit in Cyprus and sought, *inter alia*, the issuance of a number of interim orders including the determination of the terms of the instrument creating the CIT that relate to the beneficiaries of the CIT and the obligations of the trustee to pay the dividends through the Cyprus company to the Gibraltar account, an order to protect the trust assets from any future actions of the trustee, as well as a tracing order to trace the dividends and any other assets that relate to the shares of the Cyprus holding company.

28 Regulation (EC) No 1393/2007 of the European Parliament and of the Council of 13 November 2007 on the service in the member states of judicial and extrajudicial documents in civil or commercial matters (service of documents), and repealing Council Regulation (EC) No 1348/2000.

29 See *VKC Qualitity Investments Ltd v Shammusi*, Denn Alabi, Shitta Bey, Supreme Court, 4 March 2014; also *Alpha Bank Cyprus Ltd v Si Senh Dau κ.ά.*, (2013) Supreme Court judgment p1935; also *HE.NI.PA. Estates Co Ltd v Club Dido Gesmbh* ((1995) 1 CLR 371), where the Supreme Court affirmed that the EU regulation intends to remove the hurdles to service of judicial documents and that it intends to expedite and improve the service within the member states to ensure the benefits of the internal market. It considered that the Cyprus civil procedure rules must be modernised and that, until this is done, the courts are obliged to interpret the civil procedure rules in such a way as to facilitate the procedure.

with Article 4(2) "in any appropriate means", so long as the content of the documents coincides with the documents sent. The court found that that the Service Regulation is not applicable where the address of the recipient is unknown,[30] as in this case, and that the plaintiffs can fall back on civil procedure rules and apply for permission of the court for substitute service, where service to the known email address was allowed.[31]

8. Courts will uphold right of beneficiaries to receive distribution from a trust

In a judgment on the merits relating to the CHC saga,[32] *Frabran Holdings Co Limited v Daventree Trustees Ltd*, the court upheld the right of a beneficiary to receive distribution from the trust settlement.[33] Clause 1.3(a) of the HPH Settlement identified as a beneficiary any natural or legal person, who at the time of creation of the HPH Settlement was registered as a shareholder of the Czech company Havardsky Prumyslovy Holding SA (HPH).[34] The plaintiffs were a number of companies that were registered shareholders in HPH, where Chvatik was the beneficial owner. Chvatik satisfied the court as to the source of wealth and assets and that she was the real beneficial owner of the plaintiffs. The court held that the trustees were under a duty to proceed with the distribution in the case of the HPH Settlement and that the plaintiffs were allowed to receive dividend distribution from the settlement.

9. Courts will not uphold claims of beneficiaries to be included in a trust

The most controversial saga of cases involves the estate of the late Oleg Zakharov and Providencia Holding Ltd.[35] The Cyprus courts protected the CIT

30 Article 1(2) of Regulation (EC) 1393/2007.

31 Civil Procedure Rules, Rule 48, part 13.

32 A number of applications and civil actions were filed under these facts.

33 *Frabran Holdings Co Limited v Daventree Trustees Limited*, 13792/2003, joined with *Husky Trading Co Ltd v Daventree Trustees Limited*, 13842/2003, 25 April 2017, Judge Efraim. The plaintiffs – companies beneficially owned by Jitka Chvatik – filed a civil action against the trustees of the HPH Settlement and the HPH Distribution Settlement as beneficiaries of the CITs, claiming their right to receive distribution. The defendant trustee, claimed that the plaintiffs were not beneficially owned by Chvatik, but in reality controlled by her son Victor Kozeny who was convicted on charges of major fraud against HPH and misappropriation of assets belonging to HPH, thus being an attempt to usurp more assets from the trusts, that no valid distribution application was filed by the plaintiffs in relation to the HPH Settlement, whereas in relation to the HPH Distribution Settlement, no distribution date or value of distribution were determined. The provisions of the two trust instruments in question were identical.

34 The liquidator of the Czech company Havardsky Prumyslovy Holding AS filed a civil action disputing the validity of the two trust settlements, Civil Action 11217/04 before the Nicosia District Court, where a court settlement was reached so that the shares of the defendant Daventree Trustees Limited would be transferred to a company jointly owned by the lawyers of the parties. Subsequently, the liquidator disputed the legality of the settlement, claiming that he had not authorised this, and filed numerous civil actions and applications. He also filed an application to join the civil action as a party in the 13792/2003 case, but this was rejected by the court.

35 The late Oleg Zakharov had two sons, Vladimir and Alexander Zakharov, who were the named beneficiaries of two CITs, the 'Spring CIT' and the 'Milto CIT', and a minor daughter Anastasia Zakharova, who was not included in the trust settlements. Providencia was the trustee for the Spring

from claims of heirs of the deceased because the heirs were not named beneficiaries of the trust. The courts will protect and uphold the rights of the named beneficiaries of the CITs.

10. Duties of trustees

The general duties of trustees that apply to CITs are:

> *manifold [including ... the duty to obey the terms of the trust unless directed to do otherwise by the court; the duty to safeguard the trust assets, including duties to maintain the trust property, as well as to ensure that it is applied in accordance with the directions set out in the trust instrument; the duty to act even-handedly between beneficiaries ...; the duty to act with reasonable care, meaning generally a duty to act as though a prudent person of business acting on behalf of someone for whom one feels morally bound to provide; duties in relation to trust expenses; ... the duty to distribute the trust property.*[36]

Further, that the:

> *trustee is bound by all of the obligations in the trust instrument. The trustee may not consider that she is imbued with powers which are more extensive than those set out in the trust instrument, except to the extent that the trust instrument is silent about some power which is granted to the trustee by ... statute or by case law.*[37]

Particularly, that:

> *each trustee is bound by all of the obligations in the trust instrument. Failure to obey the terms of the trust will constitute a breach of trust. In general terms, a trustee does not have powers which are more extensive than those set out in the trust instrument. One clear exception to this principle arises in circumstances in*

Trust and through Providencia, 85% of the shareholding in Rosinka Joint Stock Company, a Russian company that held substantial immovable property. Providencia was managed by nominee shareholders controlled by the law firm Andreas Neocleous LLC. Igor Zhigachov, a Russian lawyer, was appointed protector of the Spring Trust. After the death of Zakharov, there was a break in the relationship between the protector, Zhigachov and Neocleous. Apparently, there were letters of wishes by the late Zakharov expressing the wish to divide the assets to the three children equally; however, these were never signed or executed. Zhigachov attempted to remove Neocleous from Providencia and appoint other fiduciaries as trustees. Anastasia Zakharova, through her mother Elena, filed a lawsuit against the CITs, Providencia as the trustee and a number of companies through which the assets of the CITs were held. Neocleous, who controlled Providencia, filed a memorandum of appearance in the proceedings and a statement of defence confirming the claims of Anastasia Zakharova and accepted the issuance of a judgment, including a declaratory judgment that Anastasia was also a beneficiary of the Spring Trust. The protector and the two beneficiaries, Vladimir and Alexander, successfully applied for *certiorari* to quash the judgment on the grounds that it determined their rights without giving them an opportunity to present their case before the court and therefore was against the principles of natural justice to hear both parties. Neocleous, through Montrago Trustees Ltd, attempted to maintain control in Providencia, and was even found to have colluded with the assistant attorney general of Cyprus to commence criminal proceedings against persons in relation to the change of ownership and management of Providencia. In the criminal case, the assistant attorney general Rikkos Erotokritou, Panayiotis Neocleous and Neocleous LLC were found guilty of bribing a public official. See *Rikkos Erotokriou v the Republic of Cyprus*, Criminal Appeals 53/2017, 64/2017, 66/2017 and 68/2017, Supreme Court, 15 December 2017.

36 Alastair Hudson, *Equity & Trusts*, 7th edn, Routledge, 2021, p353, para 8.3, referred to in *Frabran Holdings Co Limited v Daventree Trustees Ltd*; the Trustees Law (Cap 193).

37 *Ibid*, p354, para 8.3.1.

which there is no trust instrument, or in circumstances in which the trust instrument is silent on a particular point... A failure to carry out any action required by the trust or the performance of an unauthorised action will constitute a breach of trust.[38]

In *Frabran Holdings Co Limited v Daventree Trustees Ltd*, the court determined that the trust settlements provided for a duty to distribute as the preamble affirmed that the purpose of the trusts was the distribution of moneys to the beneficiaries from the trust property as soon as possible in an orderly and fair manner; and clause 7 stipulated a duty to distribute the subject to a valid distribution application.[39] Once the trustees determined the distribution term, and the quotient in trust value in accordance with the trust instrument, they were bound by the duty to distribute.[40] The court further determined that the trust instrument made no express reference to a particular form for the distribution application, nor to the website where such form could be found, and therefore the distribution application could take the form of a deed, subject to the adherence of the required provisions.[41] What is important is the content of the deed containing the application, not the form. The court found that the trustees were under a duty to consider the beneficiaries' application and to notify them. Moreover, that trustees must exercise their discretion to determine the validity of a distribution application reasonably, in accordance with the provisions and intent of the trust settlement, not capriciously.[42]

The trustee's obligation to provide information to beneficiaries may be determined in the trust settlement. In *Gorbachev v First Link Management Services Ltd, as Trustee for the Goaliva Trust*,[43] the court considered that generally, "trustees bear only a limited obligation to provide information to beneficiaries in relation to the administration and management of the trust fund and in relation only to the part of the trust fund in which they have a proprietary interest".[44] The court has the inherent power to take over the trust and review the actions of the trustee, including ordering access to information where it

---

38 *Ibid*, p356, para 8.3.2.

39 Clause 7 of the trust settlements provided that "The Trustee shall pay monies in an amount equivalent to the Distribution Value to a Beneficiary on the next Distribution Day following the determination by the Trustee that the Distribution Application from that Beneficiary was valid".

40 The trustees had not determined a distribution period for the HPH Distribution Settlement and therefore had no duty to distribute. The civil action was determined as premature and dismissed.

41 The court considered that "equity looks to the intent rather than the form". *Snell's Equity*, 27th edn (Sweet & Maxwell, 1973), p39: "Courts of Equity make a distinction in all cases between that which is matter of substance and that which is a matter of form; and if it finds that by insisting on the form, the substance will be defeated, it holds it to be inequitable to allow a person to insist on such form, and thereby defeat the substance." *World Tide v Vasiliko Cement* ((1989) 1 AAD 273); and *Chrysostomou Chalkousi Sons v Chaklousi Sons* ((1978) 1 CLR 10).

42 The court considered, *obiter*, that any involvement in criminal and illegal activities would constitute grounds to dismiss the application for distribution, even where this was not expressly provided in the trust instrument. The purpose of the creation of a trust cannot be the promotion and providing a benefit to a person that engages in illegal activities.

43 *Gorbachev v First Link Management Services*.

44 Alastair Hudson, *Equity & Trusts*, 7th edn, Routledge, 2021, pp35–370, para 8.4.1–8.4.9.

deems necessary.[45] Where the trust settlement makes no provision, there is a right to access to information based on the ownership of property.[46]

> *A beneficiary is entitled to see all documents as to the management or condition of the trust, but not documents relating to the exercise of the trustees' decisions in relation to the management of the trust...*[47] *The trustees may be required to disclose the material on which they based their decision, but they are not obliged to divulge their reasoning in reaching the decision that they did: this may have the effect that the trustees are not obliged to disclose any material on which they based their decision if that would reveal the reasoning behind their decision.*[48]

In *Gorbachev v First Link Management Services Ltd*, Judge Efraim concluded that based on the aforementioned analysis and Cap 193, there is no legal duty on the trustee to provide information, but it results from their obligations and the nature of the position of trusteeship. The court thus dismissed the application, which invoked the existence of such a legal duty and the alleged violation, as groundless. Therefore, in the case of a discretionary trust, including a CIT, a beneficiary of any class has the right to information as to the value of the property and income of the trust as well as to the manner of the management of the trust,[49] but there is no general duty on trustees to provide information or access to information.[50]

11. Power of the court to remove a trustee and appoint a new trustee

The power of the court to remove a trustee and appoint a new trustee is inherent in Section 40(1) of the Trustees Law (Cap 193).[51] In exercising its discretionary power to allow an application for the removal of the current trustee, the court should bear in mind that the broad principle is that "trustees exist for the benefit of those to whom the creator of the trust has given the trust estate" and that the main guide for the court "must be the welfare of the beneficiaries" having looked carefully into the circumstances of the case.[52] The courts may exercise the power to remove the current trustee where there is

---

45 *Schmidt v Rosewood Trust Ltd* ([2003] 2 WLR 1442).

46 *O' Rourke v Darbishire* ([1920] AC 581) held that: "This has nothing to do with discovery. The right to discovery is a right to see someone else's document. A proprietary right is a right to access to documents which are your own."

47 Alastair Hudson, *Equity & Trusts*, 7th edn, Routledge, 2021, p360, para 8.4.4.

48 *Ibid*, pp362–363, para 8.4.6.

49 *Murphy v Murphy* ([1999] 1 WLR 282); and *Re Ralli's WT* ([1964] 2 WLR 144).

50 *Gorbachev v First Link Management Services Ltd.*

51 *Gorbachev v First Link Management Services Ltd*, where Judge Efraim interpreted Section 40(1) of the Trustees Law (Cap 193) in relation to local trusts, stating Section 40(1) gives the power to the court to appoint new trustee in replacement of existing trustees, which includes the inherent power to remove trustees. Section 55 of Cap 193 stipulates who has *locus standi* to apply to the court for the appointment of a new trustee. Such application ought to be filed by a writ of summons under Order 1, Rule 2 of the Civil Procedure Rules or by originating summons application under Rule 55 of the Civil Procedure Rules. The court reserves the discretion to decide whether, on the facts of the case, the matters ought not to be resolved by way of an originating summons application (Rule 55, Order 4).

52 *Letterstedt v Broers* ((1884) 9 App Cas 371).

evidence of wrongdoing, fraud, even where the relations between the trustees and the beneficiaries have broken down to the extent that:

it has become impossible or difficult for the administration to be completed.[53] *The direct intervention by the Court in the administration of a trust by the removal of the trustee must be justified by evidence that their continuation in office is likely to prove detrimental to the interests of the beneficiaries. A lack of confidence or mistrust are therefore not sufficient in themselves to justify removal unless the breakdown in relations is likely to jeopardize the proper administration of the trust.*[54]

This is objectively determined, having regard to the circumstances on a case-by-case basis.

An application to remove the current trustee must:

- contain the grounds for the removal;
- name the proposed new trustee; and
- include evidence as to the capacity of the new trustee and their consent to the appointment.[55]

As a rule, the appointment as trustee of a person that is also the advocate of a beneficiary of a trust, should be avoided.[56] A beneficiary or a beneficiary's solicitor or spouse should not be placed in a position where their duty and interest, or two inconsistent duties, conflict. Courts may allow such an appointment "where there are advantages to be gained from such an appointment, and no disadvantages ... though it would be slow to do so".[57]

Where the removal of the current trustee and replacement is sought by way of interlocutory relief, the courts ought not, at the stage of the adjudication of an interim order application, grant this relief. The purpose of interlocutory relief should be to preserve the *status quo ante*, pending the adjudication of the case and not to prejudice the result on the merits.[58]

12. Breach of duty to provide information or access to information

In *Gorbachev v First Link Management Services Ltd*, the court confirmed that in the case of a discretionary trust where the trustee retains the absolute discretion to exercise powers as they deem fit for the benefit of the persons that have or may

---

53 See *Williams, Mortimer & Sunnucks: Executors, Administrators and Probate*, 20th edn (Sweet & Maxwell, 2013), para 62-15, referred to in *Angus v Emmott* ([2010] WTLR 531).

54 *Letterstedt v Broers* ((1884) 9 App Cas 371); *John Arthur Williams James and Stephen Neil Mountford v Kathleen Louise Williams et al* ([2015] EWHC 1166 (Ch)); *Michaelide v Paraskevaidou-Mavronikola*, Civil Appeal E34/16, 7 July 2017.

55 *Gorbachev v First Link Management Services Ltd*; *Michaelide v Paraskevaidou-Mavronikola*, Civil Appeal E34/16, 7 July 2017.

56 See Lynton Tucker, Nicholas Le Poidevin and James Brightwell, *Lewin on Trusts*, 19th edn (Sweet & Maxwell, 2014), para 14-052: "the donee of a power of appointing new trustees should not appoint the solicitor of a beneficiary or of a trustee; but such an appointment though not one which the court would make or sanction, is not invalid."

57 *Snell's Equity*, 33rd edn (Sweet & Maxwell, 2018), para 27-019.

58 *In re the Yiasemi Trust, Polosmak v Fellaco Services Ltd*, Originating Summons application 90/2015, District Court of Larnaca, 25 October 2018.

in the future have an interest in the trust, and further has the power to add or remove classes of beneficiaries, the duty to provide information is limited. In fact, the duty is satisfied if the trustee provides answers or explanations to the beneficiaries, including reasoned explanation for not providing all or some information. The trustee is under no duty to provide information as to the manner of the exercise of the trustee's discretion in the decision-making. Therefore, the court will not remove a trustee solely on the ground of refusal to provide information or grant access to such information to beneficiaries.

12.1 Bankrupt trustee

It is the duty of the court to remove a bankrupt trustee,[59] a trustee convicted of dishonesty or a trustee that is shown unfit to be in charge of other people's property, except where the trustee's "bankruptcy was due to misfortune and who was entirely free of moral blame".[60]

12.2 Financial state of trustee

The beneficiaries seeking to remove the current trustee must demonstrate the trustee's bad financial state, which puts the capacity of the trustee to manage the trust in doubt; or that the trust property or the welfare of the beneficiaries is at risk.[61]

13. Power of the court to appoint a receiver to preserve assets

In *Frabran Holdings Co Limited v Daventree Trustees Ltd*, the court, following an interim order application on behalf of the plaintiffs/beneficiaries of the trust, appointed a receiver for the two trust settlements, to enter and obtain, and protect all the assets of the trusts as well as all income and interest and to transfer these and safeguard these in Cyprus, as well as all powers as they deem fit to protect the trust assets.[62]

14. Exclusive jurisdiction clauses and Brussels I Regulation (Recast) 1215/12

In *EMD Trust Ltd as trustee for the EMD Trust v Edrina Aashika Sharma*,[63] the district court considered the Brussels I Regulation (Recast) 1215/12, on choice-of-court provisions in trust instruments,[64] in particular:

---

59 *Re Banker's Trust* ((1875) 1 ChD) 43–44. "A necessitous man is more likely to be tempted to misappropriate trust funds than one who is wealthy; and besides, a man who has not shewn prudence in managing his own affairs is not likely to be successful in managing those of other people."

60 AJ Oakley, *Parker and Mellows: The Modern Law of Trusts*, 8th edn, p566, pp568–569.

61 *Gorbachev v TU Reflections Ltd as Trustee for the Gamini Trust*, Originating Summons application 274/2018, judgment 10 January 2020.

62 *Frabran Holdings Co Limited v Daventree Trustees Limited*, 13792/2003, joined with *Husky Trading Co Ltd v Daventree Trustees Limited*, 13842/2003, interim order 5 May 2005.

63 *EMD Trust Limited, of Larnaca in its capacity as Trustee of the Cyprus International Trust 'The EMD Trust' Edrina Aaskika Sharma*, Originating Summons application 68/2017, 17 April 2018.

64 Article 25(3) of the Brussels I Regulation (Recast).

> *Article 25(3) deals with choice-of-court provisions in trust instruments. This provision was introduced by the 1978 Brussels Convention. It extends the regime of choice-of-court 'agreements' to unilateral instruments creating a trust. The settlor of the trust may include a choice-of-court clause among the terms and conditions governing that trust. Art 25(3) establishes the validity and effectiveness of that clause, resulting in the exclusive jurisdiction of the designated court or courts to rule on any controversy deriving from the 'internal relationships' in the trust.* ***Art 25 is limited to proceedings brought against a settlor, trustee, or beneficiary, when relations between these persons or their rights and obligations under the trust are involved.***[65]

The court held that Section 25(3) does not extend to third parties that do not relate with the CIT[66] and have not consented to the instrument creating the trust and the jurisdiction clause therein. Accordingly, the court granted a stay of proceedings in accordance with the provisions of Sections 29 and 30 of EC Regulation 1215/12 pending the adjudication of the litigation in the United Kingdom.

Similarly, in *Re Wycombe Settlement and Arip v Trustee Services Ltd,*[67] a judgment was issued in England against Maksat, the husband of the applicant Mrs Arip, to pay to the judgment debtors approximately $300 million on accounts of fraud and deceit. Mrs Arip sought to obtain preventive and *quia timet* injunctions, as well as numerous interlocutory orders including:

- a declaratory order that the trust in question is a CIT and the trust property in England belongs to the CIT and is not available for execution of the English judgment;
- injunctions to protect the trust property located in England; and
- orders restricting or preventing the judgment creditors from executing the judgment or taking any measures against the assets of the trust located in England.

---

65 My emphasis.

66 See *Crociani v Crociani* ([2014] UKPC 40 at 20: "Accordingly, while it was right to confirm that a trustee is *prima facie* entitled to insist on and enforce an exclusive jurisdiction clause in a trust deed, the weight to be given to the existence of the clause is less (or the strength of the arguments needed to outweigh the effect of the clause is less) than where one contracting party is seeking to enforce a contractual exclusive jurisdiction clause against another contracting party." The court determined the issue on jurisdiction interpreting the trust clause, which provided that: "thereafter the rights of all persons and the construction and effect of each and every provision hereof shall be subject to the exclusive jurisdiction of and construed only according to the law of the said country which shall become the *forum for the administration* of the trusts hereunder." Drummond and Shah comment that the term 'forum' may sometimes have a meaning associated with a court, it may simply refer to the place where trusts are administered. If the intention is to confer exclusive jurisdiction over all trust disputes on the courts of a particular country, *Crociani* underscores the need for clear and simple drafting. Though, even where an exclusive jurisdiction clause is successfully created, the weight to be given to it is less than the weight to be given to such a clause in a commercial contract. Privy Council rules on trust jurisdiction clauses: *Crociani v Crociani* ([2014] UKPC 40) (bedellcristin.com).

67 *In Re Wycombe Settlement and Arip Trustee Services Ltd.* A judgment was issued in England against Arip's husband for fraud and deceit. Arip sought to obtain interim orders declaring that the trust was a CIT, that the assets in the trust would be declared as assets of the trust and therefore unavailable for the judgment creditors of the English judgment, and to prevent the execution of the judgment and taking of steps against the assets of the trust that were located in England.

The court considered the scope of the exclusive jurisdiction of the Cyprus courts under Section 12(B)[68] of the Cyprus International Trusts Law 1992 as amended. The court confirmed that the exclusive jurisdiction of the Cyprus courts is limited by the provisions of EU Regulation 44/2001, as replaced by the Brussels I Regulation (Recast) 1215/12, which supersedes Cyprus law.[69] The court clarified that the exclusive jurisdiction under Section 12(B) does not extend to third parties, such as judgment creditors that are not related to the trust, but binds only the parties that sign it or are at least bound by a deed that introduces this clause. For a party to be bound by the exclusive jurisdiction clause, such party must provide express consent. Likewise, exclusive jurisdiction clauses in the trust settlements are binding only in civil actions against the settlor, the trustee or the beneficiary of a trust, not against third parties.

Moreover, Section 12B does not guard the trust against a judgment creditor who has successfully obtained a judgment in one member state and seeks to enforce such judgment in Cyprus under the recast regulation. Article 24(5) of the recast regulation provides that in proceedings concerned with the enforcement of judgments, the courts of the member state in which the judgment has been or is to be enforced have exclusive jurisdiction. Therefore, Cyprus courts have no authority to refuse to execute a judgment issued by the courts of another member state under Article 24(1) of the recast regulation and Article 22 of the Lugano Convention in relation to rights *in rem* over immovable property. The rationale of Article 24(5) is linked to the state's monopoly to use force in its own jurisdiction and have exclusive jurisdiction over matters that relate to enforcement of a judgment in their territory.[70] The judgment confirmed that Cyprus courts do not have the authority to deprive the right of a judgment creditor in another member state to seek enforcement and execution of that judgment in other member states. Cyprus courts cannot usurp the authority of the courts of the other member state to determine whether such court has jurisdiction, or not, to adjudicate the matter.[71]

---

68 Section 12(B) of the Cyprus International Trusts Law 1992 as amended.

69 EU law has supremacy over Cyprus law and the Cyprus Constitution following the Fifth Amendment of the Cyprus Constitution – Article 1A: "No provision of the Constitution shall be deemed to annul laws enacted, acts done or measures taken by the Republic which become necessary by reason of its obligations as a member state of the European Union, nor does it prevent Regulations, Directives or other acts or binding measures of a legislative character, adopted by the European Union or the European Communities or by their institutions or competent bodies thereof on the basis of the Treaties establishing the European Communities or the Treaty of the European Union, from having legal effect in the Republic."

70 Andrew Dickinson and Eva Lein (eds), *The Brussels I Regulation Recast* (Oxford University Press, 2015); *Komu v Komu* (Case C-605/14); *Magiera v Magiera* ([2016] EWCA Civ 1292) – English courts had jurisdiction to adjudicate the dispute as the subject matter of the civil action was the sale of immovable property in England and related to the external and not internal relationships of the trust. The court set aside and dismissed the originating summons application on these grounds *In Re Wycombe Settlement*, Larnaca District Court, President of the District Court Paraskevaidou Karakanna.

71 Judgment issued in relation to an application by the judgment debtor to set aside the civil action filed by Arip – identical to the Originating Summons application 5/18 *supra* in *Arip v Cooperton Management Ltd*, Civil Action 969/2018, Larnaca District Court, judgment 1 September 2020, President of the District Court Paraskevaidou Karakanna.

15. CITs and Article 35 of the Brussels I Regulation (Recast) 1215/12

Pursuant to Article 35 of the Brussels I Regulation (Recast), the Cyprus courts may order interlocutory, provisional or protective measures, even though a court of another member state has been given – or has accepted – jurisdiction to rule on the merits of the case, in particular under the terms of a jurisdiction clause. In *Kravitz as trustee for the Aegean Litigation Trust v Grady Properties Corporation SA*, the court upheld an application for the granting of interlocutory relief, including orders to preserve assets, disclosure information as to proprietary assets Norwich Pharmacal[72] and Chabra[73] orders against persons who are not parties in the proceedings under Article 35 in aid of proceedings in Luxemburg.[74] In the same case, the court cancelled the interim orders when the Luxembourg proceedings were concluded.[75]

16. Norwich Pharmacal orders in aid of execution of judgment

In *Kazakhstan Kagazy JSC, Prime Estate Activities Kazakhstan LLP v Geoglobal Ltd*,[76] the court confirmed that Norwich Pharmacal orders may be issued as post-judgment orders in aid of execution provided that the responded is "involved in defeating execution, a 'wrong' in addition to the fact of the judgment".[77] Norwich Pharmacal relief is available only where there is an additional wrong

72 A Norwich Pharmacal order was first granted in *Norwich Pharmacal Co v Customs and Excise Commissioners* ([1974] AC 133) and takes its name from this case. A Norwich Pharmacal order is a disclosure order, usually granted following an application by the plaintiff when other methods of obtaining information or documents from a third party are not available, to allow a prospective plaintiff to obtain necessary information and documents from a third party that will enable the plaintiff to plead its case against the wrongdoer, trace assets or bring proprietary claims. The third party may have been innocently involved in the wrongdoing but may have documents or information that would lead the plaintiffs to identify a proper defendant to an action or to obtain information to plead a claim. This information is usually sought to facilitate the commencement of proceedings against that wrongdoer. Cyprus courts are guided by English case law in relation to Norwich Pharmacal orders.

73 A Chabra order is a freezing order against a third party that is not a party to the substantive legal proceedings and against whom the plaintiff or claimant has no cause of action. It was first granted in *TSB Private Bank International SA v Chabra* ([1992] 1 WLR 231). It is addressed against the defendant and encompasses any assets that may be held by the third party in their capacity as trustee or nominee of defendant, intending to protect assets by prohibiting the third party from dissipating or parting with the assets. Courts would issue Chabra orders provided: (a) there is a 'good reason to suppose' that assets held by a third party could later be available in the proceedings at hand to satisfy a judgment against the defendant, demonstrating that the defendant has 'substantive control' (*Dadourian Group International v Azuri* ([2005] EWHC 1768)); (b) it is 'just and convenient' for the court to grant such an injunction (*Yukos Capital Sarl v OJSC Rosneft Oil Co* ([2010] EWHC 784)); and (c) a Chabra order may be granted where: (i) the third party holds, is using, has exercised or is exercising a power of disposition over or is otherwise in possession of assets, including claims and expectancies of the judgment creditor or potential judgment creditor; or (ii) some process, ultimately enforceable by the courts, is or may be available to the judgment creditor as a consequence of a judgment against that actual or potential judgment creditor, the third party may be obliged to reveal property or otherwise contribute to the funds or property of the judgment creditor to help satisfy the judgment against them.

74 *Kravitz as trustee for the Aegean Litigation Trust v Grady Properties Corporation SA*, 309/2019, Nicosia District Court, 9 July 2020, Judge Charalambous.

75 *Kravitz as trustee for the Aegean Litigation Trust v Grady Properties Corporation SA*, 309/2019, Nicosia District Court, 14 December 2020, Judge Christodoulidou Messiou.

76 The Wycombe and Jailau Settlements saga continued in numerous other judgments. In *Kazakhstan Kagazy JSC, Prime Estate Activities Kazakhstan LLP v Geoglobal Ltd*, Civil Action 913/2019, Nicosia District Court, 16 February 2021, the plaintiffs sought to obtain Norwich Pharmacal orders against defendants who were not party to the English proceedings in order to obtain documents that would reveal whether the Wycombe and Jailau Settlements were sham trusts used by Maksat to hide embezzled funds.

of seeking to avoid judgment and the respondent is involved in this wrong.[78] The court will not permit the jurisdiction to be used for wide-ranging disclosure or gathering of evidence, as opposed to focused disclosure of necessary information.[79] The jurisdiction of the court is confined to the statutory regime of the Foreign Courts (Evidence) Law (Cap 12).

17. Reserved powers of protectors

In *Andreas Koukounis & Co LLC v Lieferzeit Limited*, the district court considered the matter of the reserved powers of the protector.[80] Judge Malachtos considered that in accordance with the trust instrument, the CIT in question was an irrevocable trust, but that in accordance with Section 5(a) of Annex 4, the powers to appoint new or additional trustees were vested in the protector. The court held that even through the provision did not provide the power to terminate the trust, it is evident that with the appointment of additional trustees, the protector could limit or remove the control of the plaintiff on the matters of the CIT and the shares of the four companies. The court held that the powers of the protector in Article 2 of the Cyprus International Trusts Law 1992 as amended include the power to appoint or remove a trustee and further that

---

77 See *Mercantile Group (Europe) AG v Aiyela* ([1994] QB 366): The respondent must be "mixed up at the very least in dishonest attempts to defeat execution". In *Alliance Bank JSC v Zhunus* ([2015] EWHC 714 (Comm)): "if a party comes to court inviting that interference, it is necessary to put forward evidence to support it. If falls well short of the necessary threshold simply to say that, because the settlor is alleged on the basis of the evidence to have been someone who has dishonestly obtained money, that provides some footing for inferring that the trustees have been a party to a dishonest arrangement ... there must be 'common intention' on the part of both settlor and trustee, albeit 'reckless indifference' as to the genuineness of the trust documents on the part of the trustee will suffice to constitute intention. The task is made more difficult still because the 'shamming intent' must be proved at the time that the trust was created and trust documents entered to."

78 "[W]rong of willful evasion, not merely involvement in trade with the judgment debtor." *NML Capital v Chapman Freeborn* ([2013] EWCA Civ 589), 30 January 2015.

79 *Ramilos Trading Ltd v Buyanovsky* ([2016] EWHC 3175 (Comm)).

80 *Andreas Koukounis & Co LLC v Lieferzeit Limited*, Civil Action 780/2014, Larnaca District Court, 11 June 2014 by President of the District Court Malachtos (currently a Supreme Court judge). Interestingly, the facts of this case are notable, as this is a lawsuit filed by the lawyers who were also fiduciary service providers of a CIT, against, *inter alia*, the CIT, 'the JB Discretionary Trust', the settlor and the protector, as well as four companies that the plaintiffs offered nominee services, for a claim of approximately €144,000 for fiduciary and legal services rendered between 2012 and 2014. While the provision of the services was undisputed, the amount for such services was challenged by the settlor as exorbitant, unjustified and arbitrary. The plaintiffs sought the issuance of freezing orders over the assets and bank accounts of the CIT, as well as a declaratory order that the plaintiffs were the sole trustees of the CIT and to stop any discharge or dismissal save by its own written consent. The settlor was also the ultimate beneficial owner (UBO) of four companies that the plaintiffs offered nominee shareholding, nominee directorship and secretary services. The plaintiffs sought to obtain an interlocutory prohibition order, prohibiting any changes in the board of directors, shareholding or secretary. The settlor, who was also one of the two beneficiaries of the CIT, as well as the UBO of the four companies, claimed that he had terminated the services of the plaintiffs in November 2013 and had appointed another person to act as trustee for the CIT. The protector of the trust, the son of the settlor and the other beneficiary of the CIT, by a deed of appointment and removal of trustee removed the plaintiff and appointed another person to act as trustee, invoking Article 5(a) of Annex 4 of the JB Discretionary Trust. The plaintiffs objected that the protector had the power to remove them from the position of the trustee under Cyprus International Trusts Law 1992 as amended, as well as under the trust instrument. In March 2014, the settlor, as authorised signatory of the bank account of one of the companies, transferred £55,000 to the new fiduciary firm by Mavrokordatos. Also in March 2014, the new fiduciary firm filed applications to the Registrar of Companies of Cyprus to change the directors and secretary of the four companies.

"section 2A states that the powers that are conferred to the protector are additional to any powers conferred by virtue of the provisions of the CIT instrument".

18. Reserved powers of settlors

In *Saunders v Hewitt*,[81] the district court considered the issues of the reserved powers of the settlor as well as substitute service. The court affirmed that Regulation (EC) 1393/2007[82] supersedes provisions of national law on the matter of service of judicial documents,[83] which must be done in accordance with Article 4(2) "in any appropriate means" so long as the content of the documents coincides with the documents sent. The court found that that the service regulation is not applicable where the address of the recipient is unknown,[84] as in this case, and that the plaintiffs can fall back on civil procedure rules and apply for permission of the court for substitute service, where service to the known email address was allowed.[85] The court determined that the case involved a CIT, and considered Section 2A[86] affirming that the reserved powers of the settlor are in addition to the powers expressly vested by

---

81 *Saunders v Hewitt*, Civil Action 4202/2019, 23 March 2021, the Nicosia District Court. According to the facts of the case, AJH was the settlor of a CIT established in 2015 and the trust property consisted of 50% shares in the share capital of a Cyprus holding company, which in turn held the entire share capital of another company. The plaintiffs were the two children of AJH from her first marriage who sued, among other defendants, the trustees of the CIT and the third husband of the deceased (with whom AJH was married at the time of her death) who was the beneficial owner of the CIT, as well as the UBO of the remainder 50% shareholding in the Cyprus holding company. AJH left a will for her estate in Gibraltar that consisted of a bank account, where the dividends issued by the Cyprus holding company were transferred. According to AJH's will, the plaintiffs were nominated as the heirs and beneficiaries of her estate, of 45% share each and the residuary 10% was left to her granddaughter. According to the facts, there were monthly dividends of approximately £18,000. The plaintiff children claimed that the trustees were under a duty in accordance with the instructions of the settlor to pay the dividends to them through the Gibraltar account, and that even after the death of AJH these payments would continue to be made to the bank account in Gibraltar and then the heirs would receive their share in accordance with the last will and testament of AJH in Gibraltar. The plaintiffs filed a law suit in Cyprus and sought, *inter alia*, the issuance of a number of interim orders including the determination of the terms of the instrument creating the CIT that relate to the beneficiaries of the CIT and the obligations of the trustee to pay the dividends through the Cyprus company to the Gibraltar account, an order to protect the trust assets from any future actions of the trustee, as well as tracing order to trace the dividends and any other assets that relate to the shares of the Cyprus holding company.

82 Regulation (EC) 1393/2007 of the European Parliament and of the Council of 13 November 2007 on the service in the member states of judicial and extrajudicial documents in civil or commercial matters (service of documents), and repealing Council Regulation (EC) 1348/2000.

83 See *VKC Qualitity Investments Ltd v Shammusi-Denn Alabi*, Shitta Bey, Supreme Court, 4 March 2014; also *Alpha Bank Cyprus Ltd v Si Senh Dau κά*, (2013) Supreme Court, p1935; also *HE.NI.PA. Estates Co Ltd v Club Dido Gesmbh* ((1995) 1 CLR 371)), where the Supreme Court affirmed that the EU Regulation intends to lift the hurdles to service of judicial documents and that it intends to expedite and improve the service within the member states to ensure the benefits of the internal market, it considered that the Cyprus civil procedure rules need to be modernised and that until this is done, the courts are obliged to interpret the civil procedure rules in such a way as to facilitate the procedure.

84 Article 1(2) of Regulation (EC) 1393/2007.

85 Civil Procedure Rules, Rule 48, part 13.

86 Section 2A of the Cyprus International Trusts Law 1992 as amended: "2 . The powers and authorities conferred on the trustee, protector, settlor and enforcer by the provisions of this Law, respectively, shall be supplemental to the powers and authorities which may be conferred on them in accordance with the terms of an international trust and the powers and authorities of this Law apply if and so far only as a contrary intention is not expressed in the terms of the trust and shall have effect subject to the terms of the trust and shall be subject to the terms of the same."

the trust instrument, provided that they are not contrary to the provisions of the trust instrument[87] and that reserved powers may be vested in the settlor under Article 4A.[88] According to the facts of the case, that the settlor had, at the time prior to her death reserved powers and had properly exercised them.

19. Nominee shareholders must follow wishes of UBOs

In *Andreas Koukounis & Co LLC v Lieferzeit Limited,*[89] the court dismissed the application submitted by the lawyers who were acting as fiduciaries and nominee shareholders and officers of four companies, seeking the issuance of interlocutory relief prohibiting any changes in the shareholding and directorship in the companies following a fall out over their unpaid legal and fiduciary fees. The court held that after a breakdown of the relationship between the UBO and the nominee, it is not just and fair to issue a court order, so that the management and administration of the company can be held to ransom in

---

87 The court referred to and followed *Andreas Koukounis & Co LLC v Lieferzeit Limited.*

88 The court dismissed the application for set aside of the service, despite the fact that one of the grounds of the application was that the service was not properly concluded because the documents served were not translated by a sworn translator of Cyprus under Law 45(I)/2019 – a law to provide for the registration and regulation of the Sworn Translator Services in Cyprus. Section 2 of the law provides that "'certified translation' means a valid and accurate translation of a written text or document under the provisions of this Law from a foreign language into the Greek or Turkish language and *vice versa*, as well as from the Greek into the Turkish language and *vice versa*, on which the official seal of the Republic and the appropriate stamp duty are affixed". Section 15 provides that "Translations of written texts or documents made by a sworn translator under the provisions of this Law shall be considered as certified translations and shall be admitted as such by the courts and the authorities of the Republic". This is complemented by Section 14, which allows for translations by persons other than sworn translators only in "exceptional circumstances and if deemed necessary due to the specialised content of the written text or document or/and due to urgent circumstances". Documents translated by advocates "may exceptionally be admitted as certified translations by the courts and the authorities of the Republic if accompanied by an affidavit stating in each case the exceptional ground for which the translation is made". Considering that this law is a specific law, and supersedes the application of the general law, it is highly advisable where documents in a language other than the official languages of Cyprus (namely Greek and Turkish) are used, to be translated by a sworn translator of Cyprus.

89 *Andreas Koukounis & Co LLC v Lieferzeit Limited*, civil action 780/2014, Larnaca District Court, 11 June 2014, President of the Malachtos District Court (currently a Supreme Court judge). Interestingly, the facts of this case are notable, as this is a lawsuit filed by the lawyers who were also fiduciary service providers of a CIT, against, *inter alia*, the CIT 'the JB Discretionary Trust', the settlor and the protector, as well as four companies that the plaintiffs offered nominee services, for a claim of approximately €144,000 for fiduciary and legal services rendered between 2012 and 2014. While the provision of the services was undisputed, the amount for such services was challenged by the settlor as exorbitant, unjustified and arbitrary. The plaintiffs sought the issuance of freezing orders over the assets and bank accounts of the CIT, as well as a declaratory order that the plaintiffs were the sole trustees of the CIT and to stop any discharge or dismissal save by its own written consent. The settlor was also the UBO of four companies that the plaintiffs offered nominee shareholding, nominee directorship and secretary services. The plaintiffs sought to obtain an interlocutory prohibition order, prohibiting any changes in the board of directors, shareholding or secretary. The settlor, who was also one of the two beneficiaries of the CIT, and the UBO of the four companies, claimed that he had terminated the services of the plaintiffs since November 2013 and to appoint another person to act as trustee for the CIT. The protector of the trust, the son of the settlor and the other beneficiary of the CIT, by a deed of appointment and removal of trustee removed the plaintiff and appointed another person to act as trustee, invoking Article 5(a) of Annex 4 of 'the JB Discretionary Trust'. The plaintiffs objected that the protector had the power to remove them from the position of the trustee under Cyprus International Trusts Law 1992 as amended, as well as under the trust instrument. In March 2014, the settlor, as authorised signatory of the bank account of one of the companies, transferred £55,000 to the new fiduciary firm by Mavrokordatos. Also in March 2014, the new fiduciary firm filed applications to the Registrar of Companies of Cyprus to change the directors and secretary of the four companies.

the hands of the nominee lawyers, out of the control of the real businessmen who own it, with all the risks that this may have on their business activities and transactions. Further, that the legislative provisions giving the right to shareholders to remove and in this way control directors, make it clear that the final and absolute control of the company is in the hands of its owners.[90] When shares are held under a nominee set up for and on behalf of UBOs, the nominee shareholders must follow their wishes.

90 *Re Duomatic Ltd* ([1969] 1 Ch 365, [1969] 1 All ER 161).

Taxation

George Economides
E & G Economides LLC

1. International trusts

1.1 Introduction

This chapter explains how Cyprus international trusts (CITs) are taxed in Cyprus and how to ensure the obtaining of Cyprus Double Tax Treaty and applicable EU directive benefits in cases where this trust receives foreign income that is subject to foreign withholding taxes (eg, dividends, interest or royalties).

The development of Cyprus as a favourable jurisdiction for the establishment of international trusts has evolved over the years offering added dynamic benefits. Cyprus has a most attractive tax regime with respect to trusts and has equally concluded a wide network of favourable double tax treaties (DTTs). Non-tax-related benefits include that Cyprus does not impose any exchange control limitations, enables the relocation of a trust.

CITs may be used efficiently for asset protection and wealth management, for estate planning, as a will substitute and also as the means to preserve confidentiality on the anonymity of the owner of assets, securities and other property that may be vested in the trust.

Notwithstanding the above, CITs are also used regularly for international tax planning purposes. Indicatively, the use of a trust can affect the accumulation of profits in another tax efficient and effective jurisdiction.

Finally, the Cyprus International Trusts Law offers the settlor and beneficiaries the opportunity to relocate to Cyprus and become tax residents there, on the condition that neither were residents of Cyprus during the calendar year preceding the year of the trust's establishment. Such relocation, if it takes place, does not affect the validity of the CIT.

1.2 Cyprus taxability of CITs

As per Section 12(1)(a) of the Cyprus International Trusts Law (Law 98/2013), it is stated that:

The income and profits of an international trust which are earned or deemed to have been earned from sources within and outside the Republic shall be subject to every form of taxation imposed in the Republic in the case of a beneficiary who is resident in the Republic.

Moreover, in Section 12(1)(b), it is stated that:

In the case of a beneficiary who is not a resident in the Republic, the income and profits of an international trust which are earned or deemed to have been earned from sources within the Republic shall be subject to every form of taxation imposed in the Republic.

What this means in practice is that all incomes of qualifying CITs are tax neutral in Cyprus, provided the beneficiaries remain non-Cyprus residents and the CIT does not have Cyprus-sourced income or immovable property situated in Cyprus.

Non-residents taxable on Cyprus sourced income can be based on a number of instances, namely:

- income from a permanent establishment in Cyprus (exemptions apply);
- income from an office or salaried services exercised in Cyprus;
- pensions deriving from past employment exercised in Cyprus and annuities borne by a Cyprus resident, except pensions paid by, or out of funds created by, the Government of Cyprus or a local authority;
- rentals in Cyprus;
- royalties in Cyprus; and
- trading goodwill in Cyprus.

1.3 Application of DTT and EU directive benefits

Cyprus has a wide network of favourable DTTs and has access to applicable EU directives, the benefits of which can be utilised by tax residents of either of the contracting states. However, trusts are not expressly included within the definition of a tax resident pursuant to the DTT provisions and equally do not qualify as persons or bodies of persons. As such, trusts do not generally qualify for such DTT benefits.

On the other hand, Cyprus tax resident trustees, whether physical or legal persons, qualify as 'persons' for DTT purposes and would also be considered as taxable persons.

Further, international case law generally supports the extension of DTT benefits to trustees conditional on the satisfaction that the place of effective management of the trust is essentially the place of tax residency of the trustee. Respectively, preservation of the effective management and control of the trust in Cyprus is crucial. Care should be taken to avoid any direct or implied control of the trust by the beneficiaries and/or settlor.

Given this, CITs should generally be able to obtain DTT and applicable EU directive benefits on the basis of the Cyprus resident trustees who own the trust property and are effectively managing the trust.

Notwithstanding the aforementioned, and as there are non-Cyprus resident beneficiaries to the trust, some jurisdictions may still not consider the trustees as qualifying persons for obtaining the DTT and EU directive benefits.

1.4 How to secure DTT and EU directive benefits

To ensure that DTT and EU directive benefits are obtained and inherent risks are mitigated, a carefully planned and implemented structure should be considered.

Provided that the use of a trust cannot guarantee treaty protection in all cases, the use of an underlying Cyprus resident company could be considered for activities that could benefit from DTT and EU directive provisions. Such activities could be transferred to this underlying Cyprus company that will carry out these activities. In line with this, a company is considered to be tax resident of Cyprus, and respectively eligible for DTT and EU directive benefits, provided the effective management and control of the company is exercised in Cyprus (eg, by Cyprus resident directors) (see Figure 1 for ease of reference).

Figure 1. Outline diagram

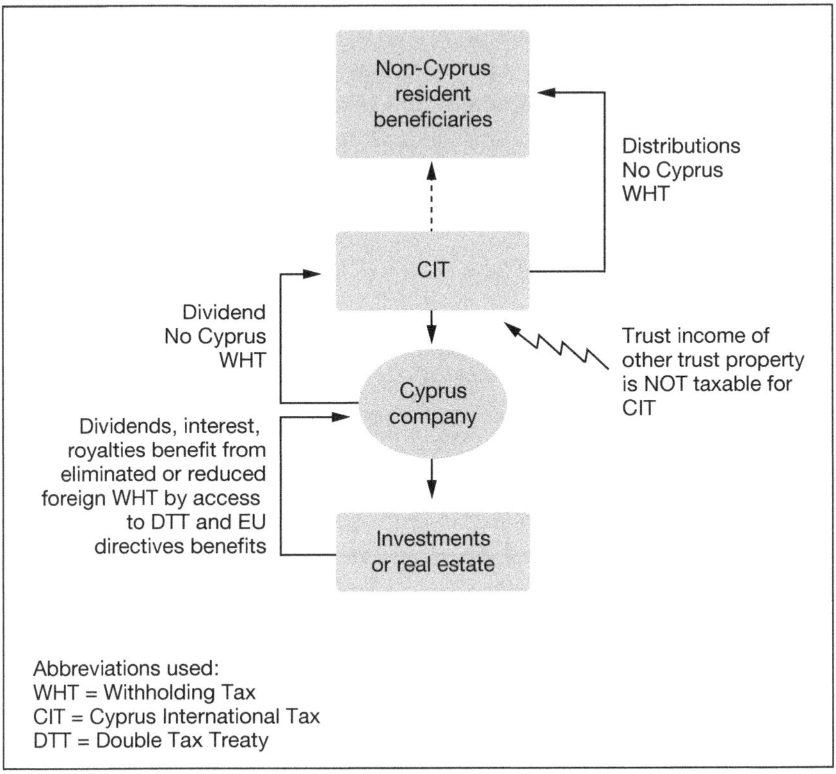

Provided that the correct professional advice is sought and obtained, trusts can maximise the tax benefit of prudent investors and organise their business matters in a way that best suits their particular circumstances and needs. Once the question of choice of the place of residence of the trust for the purposes of taxation and the governing law are settled in a satisfactory manner, accounting for the 'relatedness' of the chosen domicile, then a CIT can prove a most efficient means of organising and protecting the business and assets of settlors worldwide.

2. Domestic trusts

2.1 Introduction

A Cyprus domestic trust is considered a trust of which either the settlor or one of the beneficiaries are residents of Cyprus, whereas a CIT is a trust established under the provisions of the Cyprus International Trusts Law.

In brief, Cyprus tax residency for individuals is determined solely by the number of days of actual stay in Cyprus.

As per the tax law, a person physically residing in Cyprus for more than 183 days in any calendar year is, from a Cyprus perspective, automatically considered to be tax resident in Cyprus for that given year (without any other conditions). Individuals who are considered Cyprus tax residents are subject to tax in Cyprus on their worldwide income, both from sources in Cyprus and abroad.

The Cyprus tax legislation has been amended so that, as from 1 January 2017, it is possible for an individual to also become a Cyprus tax resident by being physically present in Cyprus for at least 60 days in any calendar year, subject to certain conditions being cumulatively met.

2.2 Taxability of Cyprus trusts

The Cyprus taxation of trusts is governed by Article 31 of the Income Tax Law, which provides that:

> *trustees ... entrusted with the management, control or administration of any property or business on behalf of any person, shall be chargeable to tax in respect of income derived from such property or business in like manner and to the like amount as such person would be chargeable if he had received such income personally, and every such trustee ... shall be answerable for doing all matters and things required to be done under this Law for the purpose of assessment and payment of tax.*

The term 'person' is defined and refers to Cyprus tax resident persons.

What this means in practice is that trusts are transparent for Cyprus tax purposes. As such, the income of the trust is assessable on each Cyprus tax resident beneficiary at the time the income is earned at the level of the trust and irrespective of any actual distribution to the beneficiary. Such income should then be taxed to the extent (ie, proportion) that there are Cypriot tax resident beneficiaries, in accordance with the nature of the income and on each such Cyprus resident beneficiary's personal tax circumstances.

The term 'trustees' is not defined and it is understood to apply to any trustee of any jurisdictional trust that has Cyprus tax resident beneficiaries and/or Cyprus-sourced income (eg, rent from Cyprus-based properties).

Thus, the trustees are responsible for arranging relevant tax compliance, payments and related administrative tax issues on behalf of any Cyprus tax resident beneficiaries and/or for Cyprus-sourced income earned at the level of the trust.

Therefore, the trustees need only consider Cyprus tax issues arising as a result of the beneficiaries from the year that they will become Cypriot tax residents.

2.3 Income generated at the level of the trust

The most common types of income expected to be earned by the trust can be in the form of dividends, interest and capital gains (ie, in case of disposals of assets). The taxability of these is examined in turn below.

(a) Dividends and interest

Since trusts are tax transparent for Cyprus tax purposes, any dividends and/or interest paid to the trust by its asset portfolio is deemed as having been earned by the beneficiaries. As such, dividends/interest would be assessable to the extent and proportion that they are deemed to relate to the Cypriot tax resident beneficiaries.

Dividends and passive interest (eg, from bank deposits) received by Cypriot tax residents are specifically exempt from personal income tax. However, they are generally subject to special defence contribution (SDC) at the rates of 17% and 30%, respectively. SDC does not apply to Cyprus residents who are non-domiciled for tax purposes.

Any foreign tax withheld at source prior to receipt of the dividends/interest, may be claimed as credit against Cyprus tax, only to the extent that such incomes result in Cyprus tax. As such, where dividends and interest do not generate Cyprus taxation, the related foreign tax suffered cannot be claimed as credit against other taxable elements nor would it be possible to claim a refund in Cyprus.

(b) Capital gains from disposal of assets

Gains from disposals of investments included in the portfolio of assets will be assessable to the extent and proportion that they are deemed to relate to the Cypriot tax resident beneficiaries of the trust. Having said that, the Cyprus tax legislation explicitly provides that gains from disposal of shares is exempt from tax in Cyprus, provided that the unlisted companies whose shares are disposed do not hold immovable property in Cyprus.

Moreover, according to Circular 2008/13 issued by the Cyprus Tax Department, the definition of 'shares' includes other qualifying 'titles' such as any type/class of shares (ordinary, preference, founders), options on titles, debentures, bonds, futures/forwards/swaps on titles, repos on titles, as well as undertakings for collective investment in transferable securities.

As such, any capital gains corresponding to the beneficiaries from disposal of assets by the trust would be specifically exempt from tax in Cyprus without any relevant conditions.

(c) ***Income of a revenue nature***

In cases where a Cyprus trust earns revenue nature income (including gains from trading in cryptocurrencies, forex, commodities, interest that is considered to be active), then such income/gain would need to be assessed to the extent/proportion of the Cyprus resident beneficiaries.

The personal income tax rates to date are:

Income	Tax rate (%)
0–€19,500	0
€19,501–€28,000	20
€28,001–€36,300	25
€36,301–€60,000	30
Above €60,000	35

2.4 Distributions made by the trust to the beneficiaries

Future distributions towards the Cyprus tax resident beneficiaries:

- if made out of tax-exempt trust income (eg, dividends, passive interest, capital gains) will have no additional Cyprus tax issues for the beneficiaries; and
- if made out of revenue nature trust income, will have no additional Cyprus tax issues for the beneficiaries, to the extent that the relevant amounts have been taxed in the year that the trust earned that income.

2.5 Taxability of income when interposing a Cypriot company

In cases where an underlying Cypriot subsidiary company is incorporated and interposed between the trust and some (or all) of the assets of the trust, the various types of income generated by the assets held under the company would accrue at the level of the company and would be taxed according to the relevant provisions of the corporate income tax legislation.

The Cyprus corporate income tax rate is 12.5% on the revenue-nature taxable profits of the company (ie, after deduction of tax allowable expenses incurred wholly and exclusively for the generation of taxable income). Certain types of income are tax exempt (eg, gain from sale of shares and other qualifying titles).

Other types of passive nature income are exempt from corporate income tax, but subject to SDC. For example, dividend may be subject to SDC at 17% with the most likely scenario of being tax exempt based on easy to meet participation conditions – and passive interest subject to SDC at 30%.

Subsequently, the Cyprus company could pay dividends towards the trust. Such dividends would not be subject to any Cyprus withholding tax, provided that the beneficiaries are either non-Cypriot tax residents or Cypriot non-domiciled tax residents.

Notwithstanding this, in cases where the trust has Cypriot tax resident beneficiaries, then any dividends corresponding to such beneficiaries would be subject to SDC at 30%.

2.6 Mixture of resident and non-resident beneficiaries

Any income earned by the trust, irrespective of whether it is sourced from Cyprus or from abroad, remains under the ambit of the Cyprus tax law, provided that the beneficiaries are Cypriot tax residents. In such cases, the income is assessable on the beneficiaries at the time when it is earned, irrespective of any actual distributions to the beneficiaries.

On the other hand, in case of non-Cypriot tax resident beneficiaries, they are taxed only on the basis of income from sources in Cyprus (if any).

Complications may arise where there is a mixture of Cypriot and non-Cypriot tax resident beneficiaries. In such cases, it will be necessary to apportion the various sources of income between the beneficiaries. If there is no actual distribution of income, the trustee would need to decide on what would be a correct or fair way of apportioning the income between the resident and non-resident beneficiaries, and between each non-resident beneficiary.

Another potential complication arises in case of discretionary beneficiaries who are not entitled to any income until a distribution is made to them. In cases of Cypriot tax resident discretionary beneficiaries, the trustee would need to account for and to pay the relevant tax on receipt of the income. However, there is no guarantee that the Cypriot beneficiaries will ever receive any distributions of income from the trust or they may only receive capital.

The Cyprus Tax Department has yet to issue any guidance on the matter. Notwithstanding, STEP Cyprus has carried out a number of meetings with the commissioner of taxation and has set out various suggestions, the main one being that income should be taxed only on distribution to the beneficiaries, instead of on receipt.

Trusts and ultimate beneficial ownership registers in Cyprus

Eleni Drakou
Michael Kyprianou & Co LLC

1. Introduction

The registration of beneficial ownership information on trusts and similar legal arrangements has been implemented to enhance the transparency of financial transactions, corporate and other legal entities, as well as trusts and similar legal arrangements, aiming to improve the existing preventive framework and to more effectively counter terrorist financing.

To enable the effectiveness of the prevention of money laundering and terrorist financing, and to enhance the integrity of the financial system, non-transparent structures should be eliminated. Enhancing transparency and access to beneficial ownership information can contribute to combating the misuse of trusts and similar legal arrangements, as well as to enhancing the integrity of, and confidence in, the financial system.

The interconnection of EU member states' registries of beneficial owners of trusts and similar legal arrangements is deemed essential for accessibility to information and the avoidance of multiple registration of the same trust and similar legal arrangements within the European Union. Cooperation between member states is vital for the effective monitoring and registration of information on the beneficial ownership of trusts and similar legal arrangements.[1]

2. The Cyprus Register of Beneficial Owners of Express Trusts and Similar Legal Arrangements

Aiming to implement the provisions of the Fifth Anti-Money Laundering EU Directive 2018/843 into its domestic legislation, Cyprus amended the Prevention and Suppression of Money Laundering and Terrorist Financing Law 188(I)/2007 (the AML/CFT Law) on 23 February 2021[2] by establishing the registers of ultimate beneficial owners, including the Register of Beneficial Owners of Express Trusts and Similar Legal Arrangements (CyTBOR).

1 Directive (EU) 2018/843 of the European Parliament and of the Council of 30 May 2018 amending Directive (EU) 2015/849 on the prevention of the use of the financial system for the purposes of money laundering or terrorist financing, and amending Directives 2009/138/EC and 2013/36/EU.

2 13(I)/2021.

As per the amended law, the Cyprus Securities and Exchange Commission (CySEC) establishes and maintains CyTBOR, in which information is submitted with regard to express trusts, similar legal arrangements, the beneficial owners of express trusts and the beneficial owners of similar legal arrangements.[3]

CySEC has issued the Directive on the Prevention and Suppression of Money Laundering and Terrorist Financing (Register of Beneficial Owners of Express Trusts and Similar Legal Arrangements).[4] The directive entered into force on its publication in the *Official Gazette of the Republic of Cyprus* on 18 June 2021. The directive was issued by virtue of Section 61C(4)(a)(d) to clarify definitions of the AML/CFT Law and to provide guidance in relation to the register's operation, management, maintenance and update.

In line with the register's provisions, CySEC has developed an online platform for CyTBOR. CyTBOR was established based on Section 61C(4)(a) of the AML/CFT Law. Through CyTBOR, information on beneficial owners of express trusts and similar legal arrangements is registered, disclosed, managed, kept and updated, while access to the register is carried out through CyTBOR's system. CyTBOR's online platform has been operational as of 17 May 2022.

CyTBOR records the beneficial ownership of express trusts and similar legal arrangements. Through CyTBOR's platform, trustees can submit information on beneficial ownership regarding express trusts and similar legal arrangements in compliance with their registration obligations in accordance with Sections 61C(5)(a) and 61C(5)(b) of the AML/CFT Law. At the same time, authorities, as well as natural or legal persons demonstrating a legitimate interest, or a person requesting access in respect of an express trust or similar legal arrangement which it owns or controls, can conduct a search and identify the settlors, trustees, protectors (if any), beneficiaries or any other natural person exercising final control over an express trust or similar legal arrangement, through direct or indirect ownership or by other means.

The purpose of CyTBOR is to enhance transparency in relation to the ownership and control of express trusts and similar legal arrangements, which is expected to act as an impetus in the fight against the use of the financial system for money laundering and terrorist financing purposes.

CyTBOR is an independent register, distinct from other registries. Every express trust and similar legal arrangement that is registered with CyTBOR is allotted an individual registration number. Trusts that have been registered with CySEC, the Cyprus Bar Association or the Institute of Certified Public Accountants, in compliance to the provisions of Section 25A of the Law Regulating Companies Providing Administrative Services and Related Matters (196(I)/2012), are not transferred to CyTBOR automatically, and as such the

3 The AML/CFT Law 188(I)/2007, Section 61C(4)(a).
4 RAA 257/2021.

registration process to CyTBOR is still required as per Section 61C of the AML/CFT Law and the directive, irrespective of any other registration of the same trust in accordance with the registration obligations as per Section 25A of the Law 196(I)/2012.

As per Section 2 of the AML/CFT Law, 'beneficial owner' means the natural person or persons who ultimately own or control the customer or the natural person on whose behalf a transaction or activity is being conducted and includes at least the following:

a) In the case of corporate entities:

(i) the natural person who ultimately owns or controls a legal entity through direct or indirect ownership of a sufficient percentage of the shares or voting rights or ownership interest in that entity, including through bearer shareholdings, or through control via other means, other than a company listed on a regulated market that is subject to disclosure requirements consistent with EU law or subject to equivalent international standards that ensure adequate transparency of ownership information. A shareholding of 25% plus one share or an ownership interest of more than 25% in the customer held by a natural person is an indication of direct ownership.

A shareholding of 25% plus one share or an ownership interest of more than 25% in the customer held by a corporate entity, which is under the control of a natural person, or by multiple corporate entities, which are under the control of the same natural person, is an indication of indirect ownership. This applies without prejudice to the right of member states to decide that a lower percentage may be an indication of ownership or control.

(ii) The natural person holding a higher managerial position, if, after having exhausted all possible means and provided there are no grounds for suspicion, no person has been identified under point (i) or if there is any doubt that the person identified, is the beneficial owner.

The obliged entities should keep records of the action taken to identify beneficial ownership under points (i) and (ii).

b) In the case of trusts:

(i) the settlor;

(ii) the trustee(s);

(iii) the protector, if any;

(iv) the beneficiaries, or where the individuals benefiting from the legal arrangement or entity have yet to be determined, the class of persons in whose main interest the legal arrangement or entity is set up or operates; and

(v) any other natural person exercising ultimate control over the trust by means of direct or indirect ownership or by other means.

c) In the case of legal entities such as foundations and legal arrangements similar to trusts, the natural person holding equivalent or similar positions to those referred to in point b).

Obliged entities are defined in Section 2A of the AML/CFT Law and include:

- credit and financial institutions;
- natural or legal persons exercising professional activities undertaking to provide material assistance or advice on tax matters and independent legal professionals participating on behalf of a client in a financial or real estate transaction;
- natural or legal persons incorporating companies or other legal persons, acting as a director or secretary of a company, a partner of a partnership, providing registered office, acting as trustee or trustee of express trusts or a similar legal arrangement, holding the shareholding capital of corporate entities and registering such a shareholder in the respective registers of registered shareholders on behalf of third parties;
- estate agents, in certain cases;
- providers of gambling services;
- persons trading in goods for which the payment is made in cash for amounts equal to or greater than €10,000;
- Crypto asset service providers;
- persons supervised by CySEC under the provisions of the Cyprus Securities and Exchange Commission or any other law; and
- persons trading or acting as intermediaries in the trade of works of art where the value of the transaction amounts to €10,000 or more.

According to section 61C(5)(b) of the AML/CFT Law, subject to the provisions of paragraph (c), express trusts and similar legal arrangements will be registered in CyTBOR if:

- the trustee of an express trust or the person holding an equivalent position in a similar legal arrangement is established or residing in Cyprus; or
- the trustee of an express trust or the person holding an equivalent position in a similar legal position, who is established or resides outside the European Union, enters into a business relationship or acquires immovable property in the name of the express trust or similar legal arrangement in Cyprus.[5]

---

5 The AML/CFT Law, Section 61C(5)(b).

The above definitions are applicable to trustees of both existing and new express trusts or persons holding an equivalent position in similar legal arrangements that could be existing or new. Therefore, the trustee's place of establishment or residence is crucial to define whether there is an obligation for registration.

Section 2 of the AML/CFT Law defines a 'business relationship' as a business, professional or commercial relationship between the client and the obliged entity, related to the business activities of the obliged entity. Such a relationship is expected at the time of the establishment to have a particular duration. The trustee of an express trust or the person holding an equivalent position in a similar legal arrangement, whose place of establishment or residence is outside the European Union, is required to assess and determine whether it is entering into a business relationship in Cyprus, as defined under Section 2 of the AML/CFT Law. If that is the case, there is an obligation to register the express trust and similar legal arrangement in CyTBOR.

Registration with CyTBOR is compulsory, except for express trusts and similar legal arrangements that have a certificate of registration from the register of another member state that is established as per Section 31(31) of the EU Directive, provided that:

- the trustee of such express trust or the person holding an equivalent position in such similar legal arrangement is established or residing in a member state other than Cyprus;
- where there is more than one trustee or person holding an equivalent position, one of them is established or residing in Cyprus; or
- if the trustee of an express trust or the person holding an equivalent position in a similar legal arrangement has multiple business relationships in different member states including Cyprus.[6]

Therefore, provided that a certificate is granted from another member state, the express trust may be exempt from the registration obligation, even if one of the trustees is established or residing in Cyprus. Express trusts or similar legal arrangements that are active or valid on CyTBOR's starting date must be registered, even if they are terminated later on. An express trust will be deemed to be a trust established expressly by a settlor at their own will, voluntarily, and will not include trusts arising by operation of law or trusts for which the settlor shows no express intention or decision for the establishment of a trust or a similar legal arrangement, such as an implied trust[7] or a constructive trust. The trustees should assess whether a trust is considered an express trust.

---

6 *Ibid*, Section 61C(5)(c).
7 Directive, Section 3(2).

The trustee in an express trust or other equivalent person established or residing in Cyprus must submit to CySEC an application for registration in CyTBOR within 15 days of appointment.[8] The same obligation stands for the trustee of an express trust or other equivalent person established or residing outside the European Union that establishes a business relationship or acquires immovable property in the name of the express trust or similar legal arrangement in Cyprus. Such an application must be submitted within 15 days of the day of forming the business relationship or acquiring the immovable property.[9]

In case the express trust or similar legal arrangement has multiple trustees or persons holding an equivalent position, one of them should be appointed for the completion of the registration, as well as for the submission of any future changes in the registered information.

The information provided for registration in CyTBOR must include the following with regard to the express trust or similar legal arrangement:

- name;
- country and date of incorporation and/or establishment;
- applicable law;
- termination date (if any);
- with regard to a similar legal arrangement, the type of such arrangement;
- information on the country of establishment or residence of the trustee or other equivalent person, as well as their residential address;
- where a trustee or other equivalent person is established or resides outside the European Union and establishes a business relationship in the name of the express trust or similar legal arrangement in Cyprus, the date of commencement of the business relationship, the name of the person with whom the business relationship is established together with the letter of agreement that governs the business relationship;
- where a trustee or other equivalent person is established or resides outside the European Union and acquires immovable property in the name of the express trust or similar legal arrangement in Cyprus, the registration number and address of the immovable property together with title deeds of the immovable property; and
- any other information and/or supporting documents that are deemed necessary by CySEC for identification purposes.[10]

The trustee of an express trust or the person holding an equivalent position in a similar legal arrangement must ensure that the information communicated

---

8 Directive, Section 5(1).
9 *Ibid*, Section 5(2).
10 *Ibid*, Section 5(3).

to CySEC is adequate, accurate and up to date.[11] In case any change is made to the information submitted to CyTBOR, there is an obligation to notify CySEC within 15 days of the date on which such change became known to the trustee of an express trust or the person holding an equivalent position in a similar legal arrangement,[12] ensuring that the information communicated to CySEC is adequate, accurate and up to date.[13] The changes may refer to changes to the identification details of the beneficiaries (eg, change in name and surname of the settlor, the trustee or person holding an equivalent position or the beneficiary, change in passport details, country of residence, etc), or changes with regard to the appointment or removal of beneficiaries.

CySEC has the right to accept or reject an application for registration in CyTBOR, to impose penalties in case that information for registration has not been provided, to suspend the registration, as well as to take measures in case the information provided is inaccurate.

Relevant information necessary for identification purposes must be provided to CySEC for registration in CyTBOR in the case of:

a) trusts:
- settlor;
- trustee;
- protector;
- beneficiary or, in case the person being beneficiary of the express trust or similar legal arrangement has not yet been determined, the category of persons for the benefit of which the express trust or similar legal arrangement has been mainly established or operates; or
- any other natural person exercising ultimate control over the trust through direct or indirect ownership or with other means; and

b) as to legal entities, such as the foundations and legal arrangements similar to trusts, the natural person holding a similar position as per point a).[14]

Such identification information should include the person's full name and father's name, date and place of birth, nationality or nationalities, residential address, number, type and country of issuance of identification document, year of death where applicable, date on which the natural person became a beneficial owner, the nature and extent of the rights that are directly or indirectly held by each beneficial owner, the person's role in the express trust or similar legal arrangement, and any other information or supporting documents that are deemed necessary by CySEC for identification purposes of the beneficial owner.[15]

---

11 The AML/CFT Law 188(I)/2007, Section 61C(6)(b).
12 Directive, Section 7.
13 The AML/CFT Law 188(I)/2007, Section 61C(7)(a).
14 The AML/CFT Law, Section 61C(1)(a).
15 Directive, Section 5(4).

In the case of the beneficiary, or if the beneficiary of the express trust or similar legal arrangement has not yet been determined, the category of persons for the benefit of which the express trust or similar legal arrangement has been mainly established or operates, the information required for each category of beneficiaries includes a description of the class of beneficiaries and its members, and the nature and extent of the interest of each class of beneficiaries.[16]

In case a legal person holds such positions, the identification information must include the legal person's name and type, registration number, country and date of incorporation, the address of its registered office, its role in the express trust or similar legal arrangement, the information referred to above with regard to the beneficial owners of the legal person (Section 5(4)), and any other information or supporting documents that are deemed necessary by CySEC for identification purposes of the beneficial owners.[17]

CySEC may decide to approve, or not, an application for registration in the CyTBOR when the application for registration in CyTBOR is duly completed and complies with the law and the directive.[18]

Following the registration of an express trust or similar legal arrangement with CyTBOR, proof of its registration becomes available through CyTBOR and can be issued by the trustee of the express trust or the person holding an equivalent position in a similar legal arrangement.

In cases where the information or documentation provided are incorrect, incomplete or false, CySEC may suspend the registration of an express trust or similar legal arrangement in CyTBOR for a period deemed necessary.[19] If the registration is suspended, CySEC will serve notice to the trustee of an express trust or the person holding an equivalent position in a similar legal arrangement with a 15-day deadline to correct the relevant information and provide, if necessary, explanations to CySEC. On their compliance with this notice, the trustees of an express trust or the persons holding an equivalent position in a similar legal arrangement should inform CySEC, and CySEC will decide whether to continue or to lift the suspension of the registration. CySEC's decision whether to suspend the registration and to continue or lift the suspension of registration, does not prejudice CySEC's right to take further action according to Section 61C(9) of the AML/CFT Law (eg, to impose penalties or delete the registration).

In case a person does not comply with or infringes the provisions of Section 61C of the AML/CFT Law or the directive, CySEC may take all or any of the following measures:

- impose a penalty not exceeding €500,000, and in the event of a

---

16 Directive, Section 5(5).
17 *Ibid*, Section 5(6).
18 *Ibid*, Section 8.
19 *Ibid*, Section 9(1).

recurrence of the infringement €1 million, depending on the importance of the infringement; and
- suspend the registration of or delete an express trust or similar legal arrangement from CyTBOR.[20]

In case of non-submission of the information for registration in CyTBOR as per the directive, CySEC may impose a €200 penalty and a further €100 penalty for each day of omission, with a maximum total penalty of €20,000.[21]

The directive provides for the payment of annual fees and subscriptions to CySEC by the trustee or other equivalent person for the purposes of registration and renewal of registration of an express trust or similar legal arrangement in CyTBOR.[22]

Access to the competent supervising authority, the Unit for Combating Money Laundering (MOKAS), the customs department, the tax department and the police is provided free of charge.

On submission by obliged entities or natural or legal persons demonstrating a legitimate interest or a controlling interest, of a request for access to CyTBOR, a subscription will be paid to CySEC for the total number of the express trusts or similar legal arrangements to which the request pertains, which will grant one-month access to CyTBOR.[23]

The information registered with CyTBOR is not publicly available. CySEC can provide access to the register to:

- the competent supervising authority, MOKAS, the customs department, the tax department and the police, with no restrictions;
- the obliged entities as defined in Section 2A of the AML/CFT Law, within the context of conducting due diligence and undertaking identification measures for their clients;
- any natural or legal person demonstrating a legitimate interest – subject to acceptance by the Cyprus Securities and Exchange Commission; and
- any natural or legal person who submits a written request to CySEC in respect of an express trust or similar legal arrangement that it owns or controls, or has controlling participation in a company or other legal entity, including through direct or indirect ownership, or through bearer shares or control by other means, excluding participation in a company or other legal entity referred to in Sections 61A(1)[24] and 61B(1)[25] of the AML/CFT Law or established in a member state other than Cyprus.

---

20 The AML/CFT Law, Section 61C(9)(v).

21 *Ibid*, Section 61C(9)(a)(iv).

22 Directive, Section 10 and the AML/CFT Law, Section 11.

23 Directive, Section 10.

24 Section 61A(1) refers to companies and any other legal entities incorporated in Cyprus.

25 Section 61B(1) refers to societies, a foundations, federations, associations, within the meaning given to them in accordance with the provisions of the Law on Societies and Institutions and other Related Matters, and institutions within the meaning ascribed to the term under the provisions of the Charities Law.

If access is granted, any natural or legal person with a legitimate interest or a controlling interest, will have access to the beneficial owners' name, month and year of birth, country of residence and nationality, and the type and extent of the rights they hold in the trust or similar legal arrangement.[26]

The element of the legitimate interest will be decided by CySEC on a case-by-case basis. CySEC will take into account whether the person requesting access to the information has satisfactorily proven, through supporting evidence, that the person's interest is exclusively related and contributes to the combating of money laundering and the financing of terrorism, including evidence and information from previous actions and activities taken to that direction.[27] Access to CyTBOR by a natural or legal person demonstrating a legitimate interest may be granted on the submission of a duly justified request by the person to CySEC. If CySEC judges that the existence of a legitimate interest can be *prima facie* demonstrated, CySEC will inform the trustee or other equivalent person of the request for access and of its conclusions regarding the existence of the legitimate interest, giving a deadline of 10 days for the submission, if they wish, of written representations. After taking into account any written representations that may be submitted, CySEC will communicate its final decision to the applicant and the trustee or other equivalent person.[28]

CySEC may grant access to CyTBOR to obliged entities, provided that CySEC receives a statement by the obliged entity that the access relates exclusively to the taking of measures relating to customer due diligence and identification, along with consent by the trustee or other equivalent person to the proposed access, and any other information or document considered necessary by CySEC. Any refusal to provide consent on the part of the trustee or other equivalent person will not prejudice the right of the obliged entity to take any other measures, including the termination of its business relationship with the express trust or similar legal arrangement. The obliged entity will have access to the full name, month and year of birth, country of residence and nationality, nature and extent of the rights held directly or indirectly on the beneficial owner of an express trust or similar legal arrangement.[29]

Section 61C(16)(a) of the AML/CFT Law provides for exceptions from access to the information, in exceptional cases and after a detailed assessment of the exceptional nature of the circumstances. The access may be excluded by CySEC, on a case-by-case basis, to all or part of the information in relation to the beneficial owner of a registered express trust or similar legal arrangement in case granting access to the obliged entities, persons that demonstrate legitimate interest or having controlling interest, would result in exposing the beneficial

---

26 The AML/CFT Law, Section 61C(12).
27 *Ibid*, Section 61C(12)(c).
28 Directive, Section 13.
29 *Ibid*, Section 12.

owner to a disproportionate risk of fraud, kidnapping, blackmail, extortion, harassment, violence or intimidation, or the beneficial owner is a minor or otherwise legally incompetent. The trustee of an express trust or the person holding an equivalent position in a similar legal arrangement may submit to CySEC an access exemption request through CyTBOR. The reasons justifying the request must be clearly stated. CySEC may ask that further information be provided. From the date the request is submitted through CyTBOR, access to the particular information that is the subject matter of the request is suspended until CySEC issues a decision, unless the access is provided to obliged entities. In case CySEC's decision is positive, access to the relevant information will be exempt, except for the credit and financial institutions and the competent supervising authority, MOKAS, the customs department, the tax department and the police. In case the decision is negative, the applicant may appeal as per the provisions of Article 146 of the Constitution.[30]

CySEC has full access to the data and information submitted to and maintained in CyTBOR. At the same time, CySEC keeps an audit trail of who accessed information for an express trust or similar legal arrangement. A trustee of an express trust or a person holding an equivalent position in a similar legal arrangement will not have access to an audit trail with regard to access granted to such information.

If differences or discrepancies are identified between the information kept in CyTBOR and the information at the disposal of the supervising authority, the customs department, the tax department and the police, or the obliged entities, the relevant body may submit a report describing and justifying each difference or discrepancy. CySEC will inform the trustee or other equivalent person of the report, requesting its positions.

In case CySEC concludes that the information kept in CyTBOR on the beneficial owners of an express trust or similar legal arrangement is false, inaccurate or incomplete, it will request the trustee or other equivalent person proceed with corrections or amendments within a period to be determined by CySEC and will inform the person that submitted the report.[31]

If a registered express trust or registered similar legal arrangement has been deleted from the register, CySEC will maintain the information of the said trust or similar legal arrangement and of their beneficiaries in the register for a 10-year period from deletion; however, after a lapse of five years from deletion, access is permitted only for the conduct of administrative and criminal investigation by the supervising authorities, as well as MOKAS, the tax department, the customs department and the police.[32]

---

30 *Ibid*, Section 15.
31 *Ibid*, Section 16.
32 The AML/CFT Law, Section 61C(10).

CyTBOR is interconnected with the European central platform[33] and, as such, the financial intelligence units of other member states have access to CyTBOR. The competent supervising authority, MOKAS, the customs department, the tax department and the police should freely provide timely information to the respective authorities of other member states.[34]

33 The AML/CFT Law, Section 61C(17)(a).
34 *Ibid*, Section 61C(19).

Appendix

Below is a list of key legislation relating to trust law in Cyprus, along with weblinks to the full text.

Cap 193 The Trustee Law 1955
www.cylaw.org/nomoi/arith/CAP193.pdf

Cap 337 Evcaf and *Vakfs* Law 1955
www.cylaw.org/nomoi/arith/CAP337.pdf

Cyprus International Trusts Law 1992 to 2012
www.olc.gov.cy/olc/olc.nsf/All/7ED54938E4890175C225860D002DAF63?OpenDocument&highlight=International%20Trusts%20Laws

About the authors

Constantinos Constantinides
Senior associate, Christodoulos G Vassiliades & Co LLC
c.constantinides@vasslaw.com

Constantinos Constantinides is an advocate in Nicosia. He holds a law degree from the University of Essex and a master's in corporate and commercial law from University College London.

He has practised law for more than 14 years, during which time he has been involved in a number of corporate and commercial litigation cases, both at a domestic and international level. His areas of expertise include shareholder dispute resolution, asset recovery, employment law, property law, corporate and commercial litigation.

Eleni Drakou
Partner, Michael Kyprianou & Co LLC
eleni.drakou@kyprianou.com

Eleni Drakou is a partner in the private client, real estate and corporate department of Michael Kyprianou & Co LLC in Cyprus. She holds degrees in law and management, and has specialised in private client matters and real estate transactions while based at the firm's offices in Cyprus and Greece.

Eleni is a member of the Cyprus Bar Association, the Investment Migration Council and a board member of STEP Cyprus.

She regularly represents investors in their business and real estate transactions in Cyprus and advises clients on tax, corporate matters, estate planning, immigration matters and succession planning. She has assisted a number of local and international clients to execute their wills with regard to their Cyprus assets, while representing families on probate issues. She also advises charitable institutions operating in Cyprus or wishing to be established under the Cyprus law.

Eleni has participated in panels and international conferences where she has presented on Cyprus tax and investment regimes. She has contributed to international legal and tax guides analysing the Cyprus regulations on private client matters.

George Economides
Partner, E & G Economides LLC
george.economides@economideslegal.com

George Economides is a partner at E & G Economides LLC, a full-service, highly ranked and proficient law firm based in Limassol, Cyprus. He is also the vice chair of Totalserve Management Limited.

His areas of focus are tax, real estate, immigration and technology with intellectual property and the General Data Protection Regulation. George is a member of the Cyprus Bar Association, the Individual Tax and Private Client Committee of the International Bar Association, the International Tax Planning Conference and STEP.

He frequently works with high-net-worth individuals and international law firms and associates providing advice on restructurings, investments, acquisitions and disposals of either assets, intangible assets or real estate. He also represents and generally advises international companies and groups of companies that have relocated and headquartered to Cyprus in such sectors as ship owning, ship management, e-commerce, investment, financial services and real estate.

George has also been recognised by the *Legal 500* and has co-authored various publications on consecutive occasions on topics such as mergers and acquisitions, tax, lending and finance and technology/digital business.

Peter G Economides
Founder and honorary chair, Totalserve Management Limited
peter.economides@totalserve.eu

Peter G Economides is a fellow member of the Association of Chartered Certified Accountants, a member of the Institute of Certified Public Accountants of Cyprus and is active in various other international professional associations.

One of the first STEP members, Peter founded the Cyprus branch in 2003 and served as chair for eight years. He also served as a council member of STEP for five years. Moreover, Peter is the founder and honorary chairman of Totalserve Management Limited (trust and corporate services), as well as the founder and chairman of PG Economides & Co Limited (audit firm) and Cloudlayer8 Limited (cloud and IT services).

With 50 years of experience in the wider professional services industry, Peter has been instrumental in the landscaping of various related legislations, including Cyprus trust law. He regularly contributes articles to the international professional press and lectures at various conferences around the globe. Peter is the honorary consul of Cape Verde in Cyprus.

Savvas Georgiou
Head of Limassol office, Christodoulos G Vassiliades and Co LLC
savvasg@vasslaw.net

Savvas Georgiou graduated from the University of Warwick in 2005 with an LLB. He then completed the bar practice course and was called to the bar as a barrister of the Honourable Society of the Middle Temple in 2006. On his return to Cyprus, he qualified as a Cyprus advocate in 2007.

Savvas joined Christodoulos G Vassiliades and Co LLC in 2007 and is currently the head of the Limassol office. As a corporate and contractual drafting lawyer he has been involved in a wide range of corporate, shipping and corporate finance transactions, including joint ventures, private equity transactions, securities offerings and other financings.

He also specialises in Cyprus trust law assisting clients to establish Cyprus international trusts and Cyprus trusts, which includes advising clients on the appropriate way to draft the relevant trust documents to accurately reflect clients' intentions. In addition, he has assisted certain trustees in relation to the administration of a trust.

Stella Kammitsi
Lawyer and managing director, Raza Corporate Services Ltd; Chair – STEP Cyprus
stella@kammitsi.com

Stella Kammitsi is a qualified lawyer and has been a member of the Cyprus Bar Association since 1992. She runs her own law firm and her fiduciary company, Raza Corporate Services Ltd, which is regulated by the Cyprus Bar Association. She specialises in corporate, banking, trust and estate succession planning and commercial law. She obtained her LLB (Hons) from the University of Leicester in 1990 and her LLM in international banking law from Boston University, School of Law in 1991.

Stella is a regular speaker at various international conferences and has an extensive network of international lawyers, accountants and auditors. She is a member of the boards of various companies and associations including, among others, chair of STEP Cyprus, board member of BPW Cyprus and president of its Committee for Legal Affairs, as well as chair of the BPW International Standing Committee for Legislation. She has previously served as chair and vice chair at the Housing Finance Corporation (appointed by the Council of Ministers) and president of the Cyprus Women's Lobby.

Panayiota Kouzoupi
Senior associate and advocate, Christodoulos G Vassiliades & Co LLC
panayiotak@vasslaw.net

Panayiota Kouzoupi is a senior associate and advocate in the corporate department and the shipping department of Christodoulos G Vassiliades & Co LLC, a leading law firm in Cyprus, recommended by *Legal 500* as a top-tier firm with Tier 1 recognition in commercial, corporate, mergers and acquisitions, and maritime and admiralty.

Panayiota is a licensed advocate registered with the Cyprus Bar Association and has practised law in Cyprus since 2015. She holds an LLB (Hons) and an LLM (awarded with distinction), both obtained from the University of Surrey.

Panayiota is heavily involved in various corporate, commercial and shipping transactions providing in-depth and specialised expertise of the highest professional standard. In addition, since the beginning of her legal career she has handled diverse legal and business matters, both domestic and international, related to a wide range of areas including company law; contract law; employment law; mergers and acquisitions; maritime and admiralty; and trusts and estates, as well as corporate governance, compliance and insolvency procedures.

Eleni Louca
Manager, Christodoulos G Vassiliades & Co LLC
elenilo@vasslaw.net

Eleni Louca holds an LLM awarded by the National and Kapodistrian University of Athens. She also holds an LLB in European Union law (commercial) awarded by the University of Leicester. Eleni has been a member of the Nicosia and the Cyprus Bar Association since 2011, and is registered with the Athens Bar Association under the status 'European Lawyer'.

Her main field of practice is corporate law. She has experience in trust law matters and other areas of law of compliance and regulatory nature.

Stefanos Marangos
Associate, Christodoulos G Vassiliades & Co LLC
stefanos.marangos@vasslaw.com

Stefanos Marangos is a graduate of political economy (BSc) from King's College London. He has also completed the graduate LLB (GDL conversion) at the University of Law, London. He subsequently joined Christodoulos G Vassiliades & Co LLC to complete his legal training and in September 2022 joined the firm as a litigation associate.

Stefanos has served for five years at the European Youth Parliament – the biggest youth platform in Europe, with offices in 40 European countries – holding different positions including that of project manager and head of fundraising. In 2019 he served as president of the Executive Committee of the European Youth Parliament in Cyprus. He is fluent in Greek and English and conversational in Spanish and French.

Paolo Panico
Chair – Private Trustees SA; Chair – STEP Europe
paolo.panico@privatetrustees.net;
paolo@panico-chambers.eu

Paolo Panico is a Scottish solicitor, chair of Private Trustees SA, an independent trust company in Luxembourg, and a director of Teton Trust Company LLC, a regulated Wyoming trust company. He has an academic interest in the law of trusts and foundations and teaches courses at the University of Luxembourg and the University of Liechtenstein. He has published, among other works, *Private Foundations, Law and Practice* (Oxford University Press, 2014) and *International Trust Laws* (2nd edition, Oxford University Press, 2017). Paolo is a board and council member and chair of the Europe Region of STEP, deputy chair of the International Tax Planning Association, a member of the executive committee of the Italian Trust Society and an academician of the International Academy of Estate and Trust Law.

Chrysthia Papacleovoulou-Vassiliou
Lecturer of commercial law,
Open University of Cyprus
chrysthia.papacleovoulou@ouc.ac.cy

Chrysthia Papacleovoulou-Vassiliou is a lecturer of commercial law at the Open University of Cyprus. She is a qualified lawyer and has been a member of the Cyprus Bar Association since 2004. Chrysthia holds an LLB from King's College, London and an LLM in Anglo-American law (with commendation) from City University, London. She completed, with a scholarship, her PhD thesis "The Emerging Global Corporation" at Birkbeck, University of London.

Chrysthia is an honorary fellow of the Association of Fellows and Legal Scholars of the Centre of International Legal Studies, and was recently appointed as examiner on company law by the Cyprus Bar Council. Chrysthia has extensive experience and expertise in corporate and commercial law, civil and cross-border commercial litigation, and also as an expert witness on Cyprus law in international commercial arbitration and High Court of Justice proceedings. Her academic research interests focus on company law, cross-border commercial judicial disputes, corporate and tax planning, trust law and international commercial and investment arbitration. She has taught numerous modules at private and state universities in Cyprus, as well as at Birkbeck, and has presented papers at local and international conferences. Chrysthia is the author of several book chapters and articles in international legal journals on commercial and company law matters.

Evi Papacleovoulou
Barrister, advocate at law, mediator and arbitrator,
Law Chambers Nicos Papacleovoulou LLC
evi@papacleovoulou.com

Evi Papacleovoulou obtained her LLB (Hons) and LLM in EU law and taxation with merit from King's College, London, as well as the international postgraduate tax law diploma from Zurich. Evi is a practising lawyer and barrister, a member of the Cyprus Bar Association (CBA) and has served on the CBA's various committees. She is the managing partner at Law Chambers Nicos Papacleovoulou LLC, founded in 1978, with extensive experience in company and commercial law, M&A, contract law, conflict of laws, trust law, trust management and administration, wills, probate, administration of estates and estate planning, private law, conveyancing and property law, immigration, AMLD and litigation, advising both private and business clients in Cyprus and internationally.

Evi is a member of STEP and a board member of STEP Cyprus, of which she acts as secretary. Evi is a qualified mediator and arbitrator and has chaired panels in international and domestic commercial and civil matters. She is a member of the Chartered Institute of Arbitrators and Mediators; a documentary credit specialist of the Chartered Institute of Financial Services of the School of Finance and the International Financial Services Association, UK; certified in international trade and finance from IFS School of Finance, UK; a member and chartered director of the Institute of Directors, UK; a member of the International Association of Risk and Compliance Professionals; an associate member of the Chartered Institute of Tax Advisors, UK; and a member of the Chartered Institute of Legal Executives of the UK.

Evi is a scientific collaborator at the University of Cyprus teaching business and commercial law. She is a PhD candidate and regularly lectures on commercial matters.

Richard FG Pease
Solicitor (England and Wales); Consultant (Geneva, Switzerland)
richard.pease@bluewin.ch

Richard Pease qualified as a solicitor in England before joining a leading firm in the City of London. In 1976 he moved to Geneva and joined Switzerland's largest law firm, Lenz & Staehelin, becoming a partner in 1985 and heading the firm's private client group. In 1990 he was engaged by the Central Bank of Cyprus to draft a modern law of trusts (the Cyprus International Trusts Law 1992). Richard advised the government of Mauritius on revisions to its trust law and was co-draftsman of the St Kitts Foundation Law 2005. He was co-founder of the Geneva branch of STEP in 1992 and was worldwide chair of STEP in 2006–2007. Richard now acts as a consultant in international tax and estate planning. He enjoys reading historical novels and sailing on Lake Geneva, or the warmer waters of the Mediterranean and the Caribbean.

Nicky Xenofontos
Founder and managing partner,
N Xenofontos LLC
nicky@xenofontosllc.com

Nicky Xenofontos was born and raised in Johannesburg, South Africa. She obtained her LLB and LLM (EU law) from the University of Leicester.

Nicky is a licenced insolvency practitioner, a certified trusts and estates practitioner (TEP – STEP UK), a member of the board of directors of STEP Cyprus and a certified anti-money laundering compliance officer from the Cyprus Securities and Exchange Commission. She is an active member of the Cyprus Bar Association Companies Committee, where she heads the Trusts and International Business Companies sub-committee and the IP committee.

She is the founder/managing partner of the law firm N Xenofontos LLC. The firm established NextStep Legal Training Centre, accredited by the Cyprus Bar Association for continuing professional development.

Major areas of expertise and practice include trusts, estate and inheritance planning, corporate insolvency/restructuring, IP law, general corporate and commercial law, advising on compliance and regulatory matters and providing general legal advice and legal opinions. Nicky's main area of expertise is trust law, acting as trustee/protector and counsel for corporate and individual clients.

Emily Yiolitis
CEO, Anemi Trustees Limited
emily.yiolitis@anemitrustees.com

Emily Yiolitis studied jurisprudence at the University of Oxford, Trinity College, obtaining her law degree in 1997. She received her postgraduate degree in legal studies in comparative European law from the European University Institute in Florence and was awarded her postgraduate degree in jurisprudence from Oxford University in 2000. Emily was a *stagiaire* at the European Commission in 1998 and a Robert Schuman Scholar in the Legal Service of the European Parliament in Luxembourg, in the Department of Internal Regulations in 2000.

In Cyprus, Emily founded her own law firm, Aristodemou Loizides Yiolitis in 2005. Her firm merged with Harneys LLC in 2010, where she continued as partner until her appointment to the position of Minister of Justice and Public Order of the Republic of Cyprus on 29 June 2020. She served as minister for one year, until her resignation in June 2021. Today, she heads Anemi Trustees Limited as CEO and has founded a new law firm, Emily Yiolitis LLC. Emily specialises in tax, corporate and trust law.

About Globe Law and Business

Globe Law and Business was established in 2005. From the very beginning, we set out to create law books that are sufficiently high level to be of real use to the experienced professional, yet still accessible and easy to navigate. Most of our authors are drawn from Magic Circle and other top commercial firms, both in the United Kingdom and internationally.

Our titles are carefully produced, with the utmost attention paid to editorial, design and production processes. We hope this results in high-quality publications that are easy to read and a pleasure to own. Our titles are also available as ebooks, which are compatible with most desktop, laptop and tablet devices. In 2018 we expanded our portfolio to include journals and Special Reports, available both digitally and in hard copy format, and produced to the same high standards as our books.

In 2021, we were very pleased to announce the start of a new chapter for Globe Law and Business following the acquisition of law books under the imprint Ark Publishing. Our law firm management list is now significantly expanded with many well known and loved Ark Publishing titles.

We are also pleased to announce the launch of our online content platform, Globe Law Online. This allows for easy search and networked access across firms. Key collections include the Law Firm Management Collection, Private Client and Energy and the Energy Transition. Email me at sian@globelawandbusiness.com for further details or to arrange a free trial for you or your firm.

Sian O'Neill
Managing director
Globe Law and Business
www.globelawandbusiness.com